Ritual and Spontaneity

in the

Psychoanalytic Process

Ritual and Spontaneity
in the
Psychoanalytic Process

A Dialectical-Constructivist View

Irwin Z. Hoffman

THE ANALYTIC PRESS
1998   Hillsdale, NJ   London

Published by The Analytic Press, Inc.
101 West Street, Hillsdale, NJ 07642
www.analyticpress.com

Cover image: Paul Klee, *Open Book (Offenes Buch)*, 1930.
               Photography by David Heald © The SRGF, New York
Cover design by Andrea Schettino

Typeset by CompuDesign, Charlottesville, VA

Library of Congress Cataloguing-in-Publication Data

Hoffman, Irwin Z.
Ritual and spontaneity in the psychoanalytic process :
A dlialectical-constructivist view / Irwin Z. Hoffman
        p. cm.
   Includes bibliographical references and index.
   ISBN 0-88163-362-3
   1. Psychoanalytic therapy. 2. Psychoanalysis. I. Title.
BF 175.4.C68H64 1998
616..89'17--dc21

for Library of Congress   98-29422
                                                 CIP

Contents

Acknowledgments

Since this book was written over a period of almost 20 years, it is virtually impossible for me to identify and acknowledge all the people who offered helpful commentary on one or another chapter as they appeared in their earlier versions. Contributions have come from formal discussants, from the anonymous readers of papers submitted for publication, and from students, patients, friends, colleagues, and family members.

I will restrict myself to naming just a few people whose critical commentary and support have been invaluable since the time that the idea of the book itself began to take shape. First, the late Merton Gill, with whom I worked closely for many years, especially in the late 1970s and early 1980s, gave his own trademark kind of close reading to many of the chapters, along with thought-provoking extensive discussions. Merton conveyed a sense of conviction regarding the value of this work that helped overcome my own doubts. Stephen Mitchell's personal and intellectual companionship and critical readings have contributed immeasurably to my formulating and thinking through ideas. Paul Stepansky, as Editor-in-Chief of The Analytic Press, helped greatly to get the book launched when, in 1991, he sent me a detailed yet concise critique of my work up to that time and invited me to submit a manuscript. Since then, his suggestions regarding readings as well as clinical and philosophical issues have been extremely valuable. I am also grateful to him for his patience since I believe one or two "deadlines" may have passed since 1991. David Feinsilver has read and commented on many of the chapters. His reflections, informed by a wide range of clinical experience, including his many years working with schizophrenic patients at Chestnut Lodge, have been theoretically challenging and illuminating. The entire book is informed by a longstanding dialogue with Louis Fourcher. His multidisciplinary expertise, along with his integrative, creative thinking, has enriched and contextualized my own understanding of the psychoanalytic process throughout.

My wife Ann read every word of the manuscript several times in the most painstaking way, commenting on everything from style to substance, a labor of love if ever there was one since her time was already taken up with her own work. I am indebted to Ann also for creating the book's comprehensive index.

Among many others who have read chapters or sections and offered constructive critiques as well as support I want especially to thank (in alphabetical order) Neil Altman, Barbara Artson, Jessica Benjamin, Susan Burland, Jody Davies, Darlene Ehrenberg, Emmanuel Ghent, Joan Leska, Elizabeth Perl, Pauline Pinto, Owen Renik, Suzanne Rosenfeld, Donnel Stern, and Patrick Zimmerman. I would also like to mention the postdoctoral fellows in the psychoanalytic psychotherapy program at Northwestern University between 1985 and 1992 and those psychiatric residents and fellows at the University of Illinois whom I have supervised over the years. These people included some extraordinary talented therapists who would sometimes imaginatively "apply" my point of view in ways that were quite illuminating to me.

I am indebted also to my children. In the end, I managed to take long enough to get the book done so that my son Mark, now off to college, could contribute his own reflections on issues of mutual interest and even his own critical commentary on various parts of chapters that he found time to read. As for Daniel, about to enter high school, his sense of humor and his own form of wisdom have added perspective to the work. Seeing the development of both children has contributed to my sense of the poignancy of the human appetite for change and growth against a background of inescapable loss.

＊   ＊   ＊   ＊   ＊

I am grateful to the periodicals cited below for permission to republish these articles, with revisions: Chapter 2, "Death Anxiety and Adaptation to Mortality in Psychoanalytic Theory," *The Annual of Psychoanalysis*, 7:233–267, 1979; Chapter 3, "The Intimate and Ironic Authority of the Psychoanalyst's Presence," *The Psychoanalytic Quarterly*, 65:102–136, 1996; Chapter 4, "The Patient as Interpreter of the Analyst's Experience," *Contemporary Psychoanalysis*,

19:389–422, 1983; Chapter 5, "[Discussion:] Toward a Social-Constructivist View of the Psychoanalytic Situation," *Psychoanalytic Dialogues*, 1:74–105, 1991; Chapter 6, "Conviction and Uncertainty in Psychoanalytic Interactions" (originally titled "Some Practical Implications of a Social-Constructivist View of the Psychoanalytic Situation"), *Psychoanalytic Dialogues*, 2:287–304, 1992; Chapter 7, "Expressive Participation and Psychoanalytic Discipline," *Contemporary Psychoanalysis*, 28:1–15, 1992; Chapter 8, "Dialectical Thinking and Therapeutic Action [in the Psychoanalytic Process]," *The Psychoanalytic Quarterly*, 63:187–218, 1994.

Introduction

STARTING POINTS

The general perspective on the psychoanalytic process advanced in this book was born primarily out of the microcosm of my clinical experience. I'm not sure whether it was from the very beginning or not, but it seems as though in certain respects, almost as far back as I can remember in my career as a therapist, I found myself working in a certain way with my patients. To that extent, the writing project became a matter of conceptualizing that way of being a therapist, a matter of explicating the implicit principles and assumptions that were at work in the process as I experienced it. Of course, in reality it was not that simple or that linear. In the first place, the external influences—personal, professional, theoretical, and cultural—that shaped my clinical experience were myriad. In the second place, just as unformulated (Stern, 1983, 1997) or implicit (Gendlin, 1973) experience generated the construction of principles, so too did the principles, once formulated, shape my way of working and my way of construing what I was doing. For the most part, as with the chicken and the egg, there is little sense trying to determine which came first. Moreover, in both directions the linkage is not simply a matter of cause and effect. There is a "space" between the source of influence and its impact, a gap in which I am present as an agent, as a choosing subject. The unformulated aspects of clinical experience are ambiguous; there is more than one good way to organize a set of principles that fit them, and consciously or unconsciously I am "choosing" among them. Conversely, the principles, once crystallized, are not prescriptive in a singular way. There is wide latitude for how they may be implemented, and the path taken, in turn, generates a new current of unformulated or implicit experiencing.

The movement of my own thinking within this dialectical-constructivist circle was partly catalyzed by my exposure to points of view that seemed decidedly incompatible with my way of working and with my experience of the process. This sense of contrast provided the background for defining my own position. While I was absorbing ideas drawn from multiple perspectives, including, early in my graduate training, client-centered theory, and progressing later to various psychoanalytic points of view, I began at a relatively early stage to react against an attitude that these varied perspectives seemed to have in common: the idea that either all clients or patients, or those with certain psychological conditions, required very specific, rather narrowly defined approaches or treatments as a route to amelioration or cure of symptoms or to further psychological development. This common feature amounts to an objectivist, technically rational stance (Schön, 1983). Granted the value of bringing a scientific impulse to bear in searching for factors that promote desirable change in the patient (see Gill and Hoffman, 1982b; Hoffman and Gill, 1988a,b), what seemed to be given insufficient attention within the framework of technical rationality was a place for the analyst's personal, subjective involvement, for partially blinding emotional entanglement, for the uniqueness of each interaction, for uncertainty and ambiguity, for cultural bias, for chance, for the analyst's creativity, for the moral dimensions of choice, and for existential anxiety in the face of freedom and mortality. All of these factors seemed alive and prominent in my clinical work but denied or underemphasized in what seemed to be the prevailing paradigm for doing exploratory psychotherapy and psychoanalysis.

At the same time, early on I found support and inspiration for my own thinking in Eugene Gendlin's (1962) conceptualization of the movement of experience from the level of "implicit experiencing" to that of verbalization, a movement that entails the creation, not merely the discovery, of meaning; in Merton Gill's (1982a) passionate commitment to taking account of the analyst's involvement as a person in the analytic process and to recognizing the inevitability of mutual influence in the shaping of the participants' experience from moment to moment; in Samuel Lipton's (1977a) emphasis on what he viewed as a discarded legacy of Freud: the importance of the personal relationship and of the analyst's spontaneity in tandem with his or her technique; and in Heinrich Racker's (1968) pioneering contribution to our understanding of "the meanings and uses of countertransference," a contribution that integrates the realms of the intrapsychic (the world of internal object relations) and the interpersonal in the context of the everyday nitty-gritty details of analytic work. Over time, I came upon many other theorists whose ideas seemed compatible with and helped shape my own, as will become apparent in the pages that follow.

Collectively, a broad movement seemed to be emerging in psychoanalysis with contributions from various schools under various headings: intersubjectivity, relational-conflict theory, constructivism, feminist critical theory. This overarching movement, which undoubtedly affected my own thinking, seemed to be running parallel to related developments in other fields under the broad banner of "postmodern thought." I want to emphasize, however, that postmodernism itself is heterogeneous (Elliott and Spezzano, 1996), and that certain versions of it, particularly radical relativism, are no more in harmony with my own thinking than extreme forms of objectivism. Indeed, I have recently found much of value in the writings of philosophers and literary theorists, for example, Nagel (1986), Taylor (1989), Nussbaum (1990, 1994), McGowen (1991), and Norris (1990), who are critical of certain aspects of postmodernism and who may be associated with, or may actually identify themselves with, some form of critical realism. As is true of many viewpoints when examined closely, my own may cut across widely recognized categories such as realism and constructivism, objectivism and relativism, and modernism and postmodernism, especially when these terms are defined in narrow, dichotomous, and overly exclusionary ways.

Before going further, I should point out that throughout this book the terms conventionally associated with psychoanalysis proper (e.g., psychoanalyst, analyst, psychoanalysis, analysand) are used interchangeably with those conventionally associated with psychoanalytic psychotherapy (e.g., psychoanalytic therapist, therapist, analytic therapy). For the kind of analytic-therapeutic process that I am interested in, the distinction between psychoanalysis and psychoanalytic psychotherapy is irrelevant (cf. Fosshage, 1997). My views in this respect follow the direction in which Merton Gill had moved in the last two decades of his life, although differences between Gill's emphasis and my own, as discussed in the next section, also emerged in this period.

I am proposing a single psychoanalytic modality in which there is a dialectic between noninterpretive and interpretive interactions.

Each has its place and each provides fertile ground for the emergence of the other. Therapeutic interpersonal interactions can be informed by critical reflection and understanding, just as the moment of reflection and interpretation, itself an interpersonal experience, can be enriched by the background of other kinds of interactions, therapeutic and nontherapeutic. The analyst bears the responsibility to contribute, through all aspects of his or her participation, to the creative development of the relationship. Also, taking into account the irreducible element of moral authority with which he or she is invested, the analyst is required to fulfill his or her role as a mentor with appropriate wisdom and humility. The orientation is not considered one that "compromises" a rationalist ideal of pure insight as the source of therapeutic action, even if the insight is into the nature of the transference or into transference-countertransference configurations. It is surely not a matter of being compelled, because of unfavorable conditions, "to alloy the pure gold of analysis freely with the copper of direct suggestion" (Freud, 1919, p. 168). On the contrary, the "gold" itself inheres in making optimal, creative use of the dialectic between interpersonal influence and critical, interpretive exploration.

COMPARISON WITH GILL'S VIEWPOINT

By the late 1970s and early 1980s, a period during which I worked closely with him (see Gill and Hoffman, 1982a,b), Gill had discarded his own earlier (1954) definition of psychoanalysis, namely, "Psychoanalysis is that technique which, employed by a neutral analyst, results in the development of a regressive transference neurosis and the ultimate resolution of this neurosis by techniques of interpretation alone" (p. 775). Having already dismissed, in his 1954 paper, the "extrinsic" criteria of frequency of visits and the use of the couch as irrelevant to the definition, Gill proceeded to take issue with the "intrinsic" criteria he had formerly identified as essential: the neutrality of the analyst, the systematic induction of a regressive transference neurosis, and its resolution through techniques of interpretation alone (Gill, 1979, 1982a, 1984a; and see Hoffman, 1996, for my own account of Gill's intellectual history). Instead, he regarded the analyst as inevitably biased and personally involved rather than neutral; he opposed any manipulation to induce regression; and he saw suggestive influence as ubiquitous even in the act of interpretation. Nevertheless, he tried to draw a sharp line between psychoanalytic psychotherapy on the one hand, and both psycho-analysis and "psychoanalytic therapy" on the other. "Psychoanalytic therapy" was the term reserved for the modality utilizing psychoan-alytic technique but with less than the conventional frequency of vis-its, or with the patient sitting up (Gill, 1991, 1994). The central issue for Gill was whether a systematic attempt was made to analyze the transference. If that attempt was made, the approach was essentially that of psychoanalysis or psychoanalytic therapy; if not, the approach was that of psychoanalytic or other forms of exploratory psychotherapy. The line seemed to blur insofar as Gill recognized that patients differed in the degree to which they would be receptive to the analysis of the transference. Practically speaking, the most that could be expected of the analyst was that he or she analyze the trans-ference "as far as possible" (1994, p. 97). The spirit of the work, however, in psychoanalysis and psychoanalytic therapy alike, was to try to minimize the influence of unanalyzed suggestive interaction and to maximize the new experience that coincided with the analy-sis of the transference, whereas in psychoanalytic psychotherapy the emphasis fell more on suggestive influence, sometimes analyzed, sometimes not, as a source of change.

My difference with Gill centers on the role of interactions that do not involve transference interpretations, as compared with those that do. Gill took a position like that of Strachey (1934) in elevating the moment of transference interpretation to special status in terms of its mutative potential. While I agree that such moments can be very powerful, to put so much weight on them, in my view, is to overesti-mate their transcendent potential relative to simultaneous, unwitting interpersonal influence. Conversely, I believe that Gill's emphasis underrates the power of noninterpretive interactions, especially when they are informed by an ongoing thread of critical reflection on the transference and the countertransference. Again, it is the overall rich dialectic of the two that I see as distinguishing psychoanalysis from other therapeutic modalities.

Gill's trust in the power of explicit interpretation of transference has various consequences. For example, as I wrote in a revision of my account of Gill's intellectual history:

> In my view, Gill, in his enthusiasm for the analysis of the transference may have been excessively impatient regarding the time it might take for certain transference-countertransference patterns to unfold and for the participants to work their way out of them. In the same vein, I do not believe he gave sufficient weight to the dialectical and paradoxi-cal relationships between analyzed and unanalyzed interactions and

between repetition and new experience (Hoffman, chapters 7 and 8; Ghent, 1992; Pizer, 1992). To have given them greater weight might have promoted a sense that larger units of time were necessary to assess the quality of analytic work. I believe the impatience might also reflect an underestimation of the analyst's personal involvement and an ironically "classical" expectation regarding the ease with which the analyst could transcend it. In a relatively late paper (Hoffman and Gill, 1988b), Gill and I reflected critically on signs of this attitude in our own coding scheme [Hoffman, 1996, fn. p. 48].

Another correlate of Gill's belief in the power of the analysis of the transference was his faith in systematic, empirical research as a source of knowledge about the process and as a way to settle disputes arising from differing theories of technique. Emphasis on a single technical variable lends itself to such empirical study and to hypothesizing that more of this particular kind of intervention will have significant, desirable effects on process and outcome. A greater emphasis on factors such as the uniqueness of each analytic dyad, the complexity of the interplay of interpretation and other kinds of interaction, the importance of spontaneous personal engagement, and the ambiguity of the clinically relevant data, lends itself to less optimism about systematic empirical research and greater regard for the individual reports of individual analysts, understood, to be sure, in relation to their theoretical and personal biases. Such case reports, accumulated, collated, and critically reviewed, deserve to be regarded as the harvest of a very suitable, clinically relevant research method in our field (Hoffman, 1987).

OVERVIEW OF THE BOOK

Turning to the substance of the book itself, it was written over a period of years, with versions of many of the chapters published as articles along the way. The order of the chapters corresponds roughly with the order in which the previously published papers appeared, with two exceptions. Chapter 1, "The Dialectic of Meaning and Mortality in the Psychoanalytic Process," was written recently, with the intention of expanding upon a wide range of issues that are addressed in the book. Chapter 3, "The Intimate and Ironic Authority of the Psychoanalyst's Presence," belongs, chronologically speaking, immediately before or after chapter 8 (according to when it was written versus when it was first published). Its location here reflects a desire to demonstrate immediately the relevance of the preceding chapter on death anxiety to dialectical constructivism, particularly its moral implications in a psychoanalytic context. With these two exceptions, the chapters appear in the order in which they were written.

The literature cited in each chapter is, for the most part, literature that was cited in the corresponding paper as it was originally published. Occasionally, a more recent reference has been added, but no systematic attempt has been made to bring each chapter up to date in that regard. The citations, therefore, reflect the influence of literature on my thinking at the time of the original writing.

Chapters 1, 9, and 10 are published here for the first time. The book is named after chapter 9, a choice that reflects my interest in highlighting the importance of the central thesis of that piece. In a dialectical way, the final two chapters may be said to "introduce" the ones written earlier, since they articulate principles that are implicit and less developed in some of the the earlier chapters, but which nevertheless could be said in large measure to underlie them.

The first chapter of the book, "The Dialectic of Meaning and Mortality in the Psychoanalytic Process," ranges over many issues taken up in more detail throughout. It can be read as a more substantive introduction than the general overview presented here. One objective of this chapter is to bring into focus the way in which the dialectic of meaning and mortality has always been in the background of my conceptualization of a "social-constructivist" and later a "dialectical-constructivist" point of view, even though the issue of mortality is not addressed explicitly in some of the chapters. The dialectic entails an appreciation of the interdependence of one's sense of one's own being and one's sense of one's mortality. Ironically, therefore, a human being's sense of self, threatened as it may be by awareness of mortality, is also profoundly jeopardized by a "promise" of immortality.

Some other key features of dialectical constructivism are introduced here, including the interplay of the givens of reality and latitude for interpretive choices.[1] The ambiguous aspects of experience

---

1. The word "choice" is used throughout this book in a manner that encompasses both the experience of self-conscious, active choosing and the passive, unconscious organizing of experience in a manner that can be reflected upon and understood only *in retrospect* as a kind of choosing. Only at that later point, with that reflection, does the person have the opportunity to participate more actively as a self-conscious agent in reaffirming or altering the original way of being. When referring to the more

leave room for such choices at the same time that they limit the range of reasonable possibilities. The element of choice leaves analysts with a prospect of personal influence from which they may wish to retreat, preferring to formulate what they are doing as merely following the patient's lead, whether conscious or unconscious. Freud's "tragic objectivism," which finds conflict at the core of the patient's internal reality, is contrasted with the "romantic objectivism" of Kohut, Winnicott, and Loewald, which finds a unified self at the core. Tragic objectivism renders self-fulfillment virtually impossible because of the multiplicity of the patient's aims, whereas romantic objectivism leaves the door open to that possibility, given the right environmental conditions. Critical or dialectical constuctivism, with its emphasis on ambiguity and construction of meaning, confronts the analyst and the patient with the element of freedom that remains, despite the constraints of given realities, to shape the patient's life story, both as it has been lived and as it moves into the future. It has in common with tragic objectivism a sense of sacrifice and loss regarding the paths not taken, although those paths, in the constructivist view, are largely unspecified and indeterminate.

The psychoanalytic situation is a particular instance of the effort to construct meaning and affirm worth in a highly skeptical, unstable, and uncertain world. For many people in western society, particularly those belonging to the educated, middle and upper socioeconomic classes, the universal need for authority, having lost a secure mooring in religion and even, in our postmodern era, in science, finds a surrogate in the psychoanalyst or analytic therapist (cf. Rieff, 1966).[2] He or she acts as a kind of secular clergy (a "secular

---

passive, unconscious process, the word is actually being used *metaphorically* to capture a dimension of experience that is neither simply a given that the person as an agent is not implicated in at all, nor an alternative that the person has actively decided upon. In his advocacy of "action language," Schafer (1976) is critical of the literal application, in psychoanalytic theory, of mechanistic language to human experience and behavior, where he feels the language of human agency is warranted. In my view, however, action language is no less metaphoric than mechanistic language for that intermediate realm in which neither mechanistic terms nor the terms of self-conscious, intentional choice apply in a literal sense.

2. See Altman (1995) for discussion of the historical elitism of psychoanalytic therapy and psychoanalysis. Altman argues that contemporary developments in relational perspectives on the psychoanalytic process (including the contributions of this author) lend themselves to clinical application with lower socioeconomic groups.

pastoral worker" as Freud, 1926b, put it), helping people navigate their way through life on the basis of subjective, often conflictual feelings and attitudes, resting upon nebulous and precariously grounded value systems.

To the extent that the analyst conceives of himself or herself merely as offering a service based upon technical expertise, doing analysis can be a relatively comfortable way to make a living. To the extent, however, that the analyst conceives of his or her role, correctly in my view, as combining technical expertise with a special quality of love and affirmation, one that derives part of its power from the inheritance of the mantle of clerical authority, the occupation can be a source of some unspoken and usually disclaimed embarrassment. The exchange of a presumptively transformative form of love for money can be painfully awkward, particularly in light of the analyst's awareness of his or her personal limitations and self-serving motives. Ultimately, these aspects of the analyst's identity must not only be overcome but also transformed into a wellspring of therapeutic action. Such a transformation is made possible by attention to the dialectic (i.e., the interdependence and interweaving) of, on the one hand, psychoanalytic ritual, which raises the analyst to a special level of power and authority, and, on the other hand, the analyst's spontaneous personal participation, which reveals him or her to be a person like the patient: merely mortal, potentially caring, creative, generous, and wise, but also, just as surely, narcissistic, vulnerable, affirmation-seeking, and partially blind. The transformation is made possible, too, by the understanding that coming to terms with the way in which the analyst is a "poor substitute" for all-powerful, loving parents, for the benevolent gods, holds the key to maximizing potentials for committed living, since there is no love object or object of interest that can ever be more than a "poor substitute" for that impossible ideal. Even more generally, the peculiarities and absurdities of the psychoanalytic situation (e.g., the exchange of money for love) are seen as analogous to the peculiarities and absurdities of life itself (paying with one's mortality for the privilege of living at all) so that in coming to terms with the one there is leverage for coming to terms with the other.

The second chapter, "Death Anxiety and Adaptation to Mortality in Psychoanalytic Theory," offers a detailed examination of Freudian and certain post-Freudian perspectives (in particular, those of Hartmann, Erikson, and Kohut) on death anxiety, perspectives that are generally characterized by avoidance and denial. The chapter also includes a review of one part of a research project that I carried out years ago on the adaptation of parents to fatal illness in children. This is the one chapter in the book that is not focused on the psychoanalytic process as such. As shown in the preceding chapter, "The Dialectic of Meaning and Mortality," however, the dialectical constructivism that I am espousing is intimately tied to death anxiety and adaptation to mortality since all socially constructed reality goes on "in the face of chaos" (Berger and Luckmann, 1967, p. 103), in the face of the prospect of nonbeing and meaninglessness. The perspective here is like that of Heidegger as portrayed by Jones (1975): "[living authentically] means doing, during all the days of one's life, whatever it is one is doing in the moody understanding that one is going to die" (p. 315). The way in which the parents in the study reviewed here come to terms with the deaths of their children, especially their determination to frame the child's abbreviated life in order to give it a sense of meaning, integrity, and completeness, illustrates the courageous construction of reality by human agents over and against the threat of meaninglessness.

Because this chapter was written originally in 1979, its constructivist implications are not yet fully developed or even explicit except where footnotes have been added in this republished version. A point that appears here that is particularly relevant to a dialectical-constructivist perspective is that death anxiety is linked to anxiety about time extending endlessly, to infinity. Freud's claim that the unconscious can grasp only a sense of one's immortality because death cannot be "pictured" denies the fact that a sense of time going on "forever," with or without one's own presence, is unimaginable and yet anxiety provoking. As discussed in chapter 1, the prospect of death, terrifying as it may be, is also integral to the individual's sense of self.

Chapter 3, "The Intimate and Ironic Authority of the Psychoanalyst's Presence," conceptualizes the nature and implications of the analyst's moral authority in a secular world bereft of divine authority and of any serious conviction regarding an afterlife. The psychoanalytic situation is not a sanctuary from the inexorable flow of time. Choices are being made at every moment, choices that "count" in the patient's life against the background of the absolute certainty of death. The analytic therapist is implicated in those choices, passively or actively. Therapists are involved in what patients "make" of the past, of moments in the "here and now," of their lives as they move into the future. The analyst cannot be merely a neutral investigator of the patient's internal life or an empathic servant of the patient's true self. Because the patient's experience is multifaceted,

intrinsically ambiguous in many ways, and partially opaque, it docs
not serve up "data" that can simply be followed as guides to understanding and action. It cannot preempt the analyst's involvement as
a moral authority and coconstructor of the reality of the patient's
experience. The analyst functions not only as a source of general
affirmation but also as a moral influence in relation to the patient's
specific choices. Because the power of the analyst's authority is so
under question in the culture and so critically examined within the
psychoanalytic situation itself, what remains of it, which is likely
to be substantial and perhaps essential, can only be described as
ironic. Clinical vignettes are presented to illustrate these and
related issues.

The fourth chapter, "The Patient as Interpreter of the Analyst's
Experience," explores the symmetrical side of the dialectical interplay of the asymmetrical and symmetrical aspects of the process.
Written in its original form about a decade before chapter 3, it is
somewhat retrogressive in that it does not adequately attend to a
number of key dialectics governing the psychoanalytic process. In my
zeal to debunk the fallacy of the blank screen, I failed to give due
respect to the importance of the dialectic between the analyst's personal visibility and relative invisibility, a dialectic that is actually
given more attention in the preceding chapter and that is explored in
various contexts throughout the book. What is being fleshed out
here, with perhaps something of the quality of an overcorrection to
the myth of the blank screen, are the symmetrical or mutual aspects
of the process. In emphasizing them, short shrift is given to the element of wisdom associated with the idea of the analyst as more hidden than the patient, modified as that conception must become when
we make the transition from dichotomous to dialectical thinking.
Another dialectic that is obscured in this chapter is that between
interpretive reflection on transference-countertransference enactments and the fact of those enactments per se. Instead, there is an
implication of a dichotomous relationship between the two. It was
only later that I began to appreciate more fully the dialectical relationships between enactment and interpretation and between repetition and new experience. Reflective interpretations are partly
expressive of countertransference rather than fully transcending of
it. And enactments may be paradoxically integral to the emergence
of new understanding and of new ways of being in the analytic relationship and in the world. On the one hand, by not giving sufficient
weight to the dialectic of the symmetrical and asymmetrical aspects
of the relationship, in particular, by undervaluing the asymmetrical

aspects, this chapter probably ends up moving too far from the traditional paradigm.[3] On the other hand, because of its relative inattention to the dialectic of enactment and new experience, in particular because of its undervaluing of the paradoxically therapeutic potentials of enactments, it probably doesn't deviate from the traditional paradigm enough. Again, as in the case of chapter 2, reflections that are more in keeping with my current views can be found in the footnotes to this chapter.

An important distinction is made here between what I termed conservative and radical critics of the blank screen conception of the role of the analyst. The conservative critics want to emphasize the real interpersonal influence of the analyst, usually thinking of it as benign and separating it from the development of the transference. Transference is identifiable as distorting of the reality of the analyst's participation and of some aspect of the relationship. The analyst is viewed as equipped to recognize and interpret such distortions when they come up. In contrast to the conservative critics, the radical critics see the analyst as implicated in the emergence of transference and also as unable definitively to state the truth regarding his or her participation, which includes the complementary countertransference (Racker, 1968). What is going on in each person's experience is ambiguous and open to a range of plausible interpretations. The analyst is not the neutral arbiter of reality, but is challenged to struggle collaboratively with the patient to arrive at a sense of what is taking place both interpersonally and intrapsychically. Ambiguity and uncertainty do not, however, connote the disappearance of an objective reality and the rule of unqualified relativism. On the contrary, it is objectively the case that experience is intrinsically ambiguous. Racker's view of countertransference, particularly his notion of complementary identification, which bridges the interpersonal and intrapsychic domains, heavily influenced the perspective advanced in this chapter.

Chapter 5, "Toward a Social-Constructivist View of the Psychoanalytic Situation," returns to a more fully developed constructivist

---

3. A possible misunderstanding here is that an increased appreciation of the value of the asymmetry is associated with a more conservative attitude toward self-expression and self-disclosure, which is not actually correct. Within certain limits, if anything, my own sense of freedom in my analytic work has grown in that regard. But the operative phrase here is "within certain limits." The sense of freedom has developed along with increased conviction about establishing the limits of such accessibility and a deeper understanding of the importance of not exceeding them.

viewpoint, formally announcing the perspective of "social constructivism." This chapter was written as a discussion of papers by Aron (1991), Greenberg (1991), and Modell (1991), in the inaugural issue of the journal *Psychoanalytic Dialogues*. Nevertheless, I believe the paper stands on its own. Although the reader would surely benefit from reading the three papers as background, I hope enough is said in my discussion about the points that I am addressing to convey the gist of them accurately.

No term can capture every aspect of one's point of view or be so free of ambiguity as to preclude misunderstanding. The term "social" in "social constructivism" was chosen to highlight, among other things, the fact that the patient's experience in the analytic situation does not emerge in a vacuum but is rather heavily influenced by the analyst's contribution. The term "constructivism" points to the element of choice that the participants have in interpreting the ambiguous aspects of the recent and distant past, and, further, in shaping the immediate and future course of the analytic relationship. But the term leaves the door open to "guilt by association" with radical relativism, with the impression that reality is a function merely of social consensus rather than being anchored (1) in some kind of independent, preexisting world, whether shaped by human activity or not, and (2) in the quality of a person's experience (a part of that preexisting world), which, even with its ambiguity, constrains what can legitimately be said about it or what can be authentically born out of it in terms of action.[4] In addition to the link with unrestrained "epistemological relativism," social constructivism conjures up, for some, the specter of unrestrained "moral relativism" (Arrington, 1989), the sense that anything goes as to what can qualify as a good way to live as long as it is sanctioned by a particular culture or subculture. These connotations were never what I intended in using the term. Partly in order to discourage such misunderstanding I have recently eschewed the term "social" and turned to other modifiers of "constructivism" such as "critical" and "dialectical," terms that are intended to convey a belief in an objective framework within which constructive activity takes place. That objective framework is made up, in part, of the characteristics of human action and experience, which dialectical constructivism, itself, regards as universal.

---

4. Although I cite Kenneth Gergen uncritically in this chapter (chapter 5), I differ with him as I do with pragmatists such as Rorty to the extent that these theorists and philosophers view reality as a function merely of social consensus.

Although the notion of dialectics had not yet been elevated to the status of a title or subtitle at this stage, at the heart of chapter 5 is an emphasis on multiple figure-ground, dialectical relationships in the analytic process, including, for example, the dialectic of objectivity and subjectivity, of interpersonal and intrapsychic, of initiative and responsiveness, of transference and countertransference, and of authority and mutuality. Indeed, although in many respects I am sympathetic to the views advanced by the theorists I am discussing here, my criticisms of the positions put forward by Aron and Greenberg in these particular papers have to do partly with their tendency (like my own in chapter 4) to overcorrect the excesses of a one-person paradigm by substituting a two-person model with various technical implications. In the process, they sometimes lose the advantages of thinking in terms of the dialectic of one-person and two-person perspectives. Thus, for example, the emphasis falls on the emergence of the analyst's subjectivity and on the value of its "visibility" in the analytic process, at the expense of giving sufficient theoretical weight to the simultaneous value of the analyst's "invisibility," and more encompassingly, to the value of the tension between the two. It is not just the child's healthy interest in the subjectivity of the mother that is the relevant precursor of the intersubjective dynamics of the analytic situation (Aron, 1991), but also the primal scene, understood literally and figuratively as pointing to the developmental value to the child of the parents' maintenance of privacy in certain aspects of their lives. That privacy and that exclusion probably promote the child's idealizing attitude toward the parents, just as encountering their subjectivity promotes identification with them. Against that background, the analyst's self-concealment has value in concert with self-expressive and revealing behavior. Either pole can, of course, be overdone at the expense of the other.

One contribution of this chapter is the distinction between the drive-relational axis and the objectivist-constructivist axis. The independence of those axes was anticipated in 1983 in "The Patient as Interpreter" (chapter 4), where it was shown that the conservative and radical critiques of the blank screen cut across all the major theoretical schools. In chapter 5, I argue that much of relational theory, including interpersonal and self-psychological theory, is objectivist, corresponding often to what is referred to in chapter 4 as the conservative critique, whereas drive theory contains the seeds of a constructivist point of view and hence of the radical critique as well. Again, the hallmark of the objectivist view is the claim that the analyst can effectively remove himself or herself from the interpersonal field, whether to make confident judgments about the reality of the transference and the countertransference, or to offer an empathic responsiveness that is free of personal bias, or to plan interventions that a particular patient "needs," given an assessment of his or her condition, state of mind, or "pathogenic beliefs." Examples are given of theorists cited by Aron and Greenberg who, I suggest, are "incompatible bedfellows" for the constructivist viewpoint. It is argued that Freudian thought, which is often cast as the objectivist foil for the allegedly more constructivist leanings of relational theory, contains within it a tension between the environmentalism of the trauma theory and the endogenous excesses of drive theory, a tension that virtually "begs" for a dialectical-constructivist resolution. Freud begins to move in that direction in his later theory of anxiety, a movement that Greenberg (1991) explores in his own way.

Chapter 6, "Conviction and Uncertainty in Psychoanalytic Interactions," was written in part to demonstrate the place of the analyst's "conviction" in a constructivist orientation in which so much emphasis is placed on the value of uncertainty. Conviction and uncertainty in this model both have more of a personal, subjective, countertransferential underpinning than they do in a model in which the analyst is seen as a neutral investigator. Also, the center of the analyst's attention and concern shifts slightly from the health of the patient, viewed in isolation, to the health of the whole therapeutic relationship, which must, of course, include the analyst's health. That perspective encourages the analyst, for example, to "speak his or her mind," particularly when the patient seems to be impinging on him or her in a destructive way.

Differences are articulated with other theorists with whom there is the appearance of some common ground, most notably Pine (1990) and Schafer (1983, 1992). Pine's model illustrates what I call "open-minded positivism," an approach that is implicitly diagnostic and prescriptive. The openness that is encouraged allows the therapist to try various kinds of interventions, coming out of one or another theoretical viewpoint, with the understanding that if one approach doesn't "work" in terms of furthering understanding or other aspects of the process, another can be tried. From a constructivist perspective, what is missing from the open-minded positivist (or objectivist) viewpoint is recognition of the analyst's countertransferential involvement. That involvement leaves the question open as to the meaning of the analyst's participation and as to the kind of enactment or corrective experience that is being played out. What is also missing is recognition of the extent to which the analyst's choices, even his or her theoretical choices, are underdetermined by "the data," that is, by whatever the analyst gathers to be the case regarding the patient's experience. Other more or less conscious factors—personal, moral, aesthetic—influence what the analyst says and does.

Schafer is viewed as an advocate of what I call the "limited constructivist view," one that is also devoid of recognition of the implications of the analyst's personal involvement, focusing instead on his or her theoretical biases. Nevertheless, the atmosphere that the more thoroughgoing constructivist view encourages in the analytic situation has an interesting forerunner in Schafer's "Talking to Patients" (1974), in which he advocates a more natural, spontaneous responsiveness on the part of the therapist (at least for therapists doing time-limited psychotherapy, with the implications for psychoanalysis left ambiguous). It is my view that the more dramatic examples that are sometimes offered of the analyst's self-expression or self-disclosure obscure the more general principle that it is important for the analyst, within the constraints of the analytic role, "to be himself or herself," acting and speaking with a certain quality of personal authenticity. Schafer fails to ground his own advocacy of a more "natural" manner for the analyst in a revised theory of countertransference and a constructivist view of the interaction. Instead, the foundation remains the "limited constructivist view" that, ironically, promotes the very scientistic, "impersonal" diction to which Schafer was objecting in this relatively early paper.

Chapter 7, "Expressive Participation and Psychoanalytic Discipline," elaborates specifically on the dialectic of the analyst's personally expressive and responsive participation and his or her more standard analytic discipline. One point of emphasis in this chapter is the continuity of the flow of the analyst's and patient's experiences in the session. At every moment the analyst is acting in one way or another that has not yet been reflected upon and cannot be fully determined by "rational" considerations. Thus noninterpretive and interpretive interactions form a kind of dialectic in which something "expressive" is always going on that escapes explicit understanding. An approach to the use of countertransference is articulated which stands midway between those of Racker (1968) and Lipton (1977a). In keeping with the view advanced by Lipton, it acknowledges and encourages the analyst's personal spontaneity, followed by attention to the possibility of allusions to it in the patient's subsequent associations as the basis for interpretation. In keeping with Racker's view, and unlike Lipton, it also encourages the emergence of at least tentative understanding, even at the moment of "spontaneous" action, based directly on the analyst's experience of the counter-transference. Several dimensions relevant to describing the analyst's personal participation are identified: the affective content or tone, the degree of anticipation and preestablished understanding, the extent to which the analyst feels he or she is responding to pressure from the patient as opposed to something arising from within himself or herself, and the extent to which the analyst feels that the expressive activity is part of a repetition or part of a new experience for the patient. Clinical vignettes are presented to illustrate these factors, but are focused especially on the dialectic of repetition and new experience in the process.

Chapter 8, "Dialectical Thinking and Therapeutic Action," develops the notion of dialectical thinking more fully, including, for the first time, a relatively elaborate clinical example and offering bridging concepts to developmental theory. Principles introduced in chapter 3, "Intimate and Ironic Authority," are further elaborated and illustrated here. In fact, although the paper that corresponds with chapter 3 was originally published two years *after* the one that corresponds with chapter 8, they were written in the reverse order, so that this chapter *does* represent an emphasis that jelled somewhat later.

Beginning with the observation that many contemporary psychoanalytic writers have reported that the process often takes a leap forward when they have deviated from their more customary ways of working, when they have "thrown away the book," I build an argument for maintaining a sense of the dialectic between, on the one hand, the core of analytic discipline, which entails the analyst's consistent self-subordination in the interest of the patient's long-term well-being, and, on the other hand, the analyst's personal subjective participation.

The therapeutic action of the psychoanalytic process, as discussed in chapter 3, depends on a special kind of power with which the analyst is invested by the patient and by society, a power that is enhanced by adherence to psychoanalytic rituals, including the asymmetrical aspects of the arrangement. At the same time, it is important that the analyst engage with the patient in a way that is sufficiently self-expressive and spontaneous so that a bond of mutual identification can develop between the participants. At the core of the generic "good object" is an element of uncertainty as the analyst struggles to find an optimal position relative to this dialectic between formal psychoanalytic authority and personal responsiveness and self-expression. At the core of the generic "bad object" is an uncritical commitment to one side of the dialectic at the expense of the other.

A detailed clinical example is used to illustrate the way in which dialectical thinking is woven into the therapeutic action of the process. An important aspect of the illustration is that it entails a triangle that consists, superficially, of a female analysand, a male candidate analyst (the author), and an "overseeing" psychoanalytic institute. But that triangle is taken to another level of abstraction that offers a bridge to developmental theory. At this second level, the relevant tensions are among the patient's immediate conscious desire, the analyst's inclination to respond as he might outside the analytic situation, and the analyst's "marriage" to analytic principles, to the "book" of abstinence. Although the patient has a wish to capitalize on points of weakness in that marriage that she detects, she also has an investment in its being maintained for her long-term benefit. The analyst and the patient both thrive on the synergy of the analyst's personal involvement and his or her relatively detached, theoretically informed analytic attitude. The participants' "survival" is jeopardized by a deterioration of the dialectic of personal responsiveness and psychoanalytic restraint, a complete collapse resulting in either suffocating incestuous involvement or deadening isolation.

Chapter 9, "Ritual and Spontaneity in the Psychoanalytic Process," brings together many themes developed in the preceding chapters and integrates them with a view of the analyst's affirmation of the patient as pitted against the dark side of the analytic frame and, at the same time, the dark side of the human condition. With respect to the former, the analyst could be viewed as exploitative, playing upon the patient's neediness from a position of power. With respect to the latter, life itself can be viewed as a seduction that is followed by disillusionment, abandonment, and death—in other words, as a cruel deception. The love of parental figures in critical periods of childhood helps to buffer the impact of reflective human consciousness, particularly as it comes up against the terror of mortality. When the injuries of childhood are sufficiently traumatizing, the added insults of the human condition can be unbearable. The analyst is in a position to counter these assaults on the patient's sense of worth through a powerful kind of affirmation, one that is born out of the dialectic of psychoanalytic ritual and personal spontaneity. The interplay of the two can triumph over cynicism and despair and cultivate the patient's capacity for expansive and committed living.

Among the new concepts introduced here is the notion of liminal space, a transitional zone, identified by the anthropologist Victor Turner (1969), between structured, hierarchical, role-related ways of being and spontaneous, relatively unstructured, egalitarian ways of being. Many experiences occur in that liminal zone, which is "neither here nor there." An example within the analytic situation is the time period between the moment the analyst says it's time to stop and the moment the patient leaves the office. In this period the sense of analytic ritual is suspended, and the analyst and the patient are together more simply as fellow human beings. Nevertheless, even then the sense of the power of the ritual is in the background, so that the liminal interaction has a special kind of charge.

This chapter includes the most detailed and extended clinical illustration in the book. A key liminal moment demonstrates the cocreation by analyst and analysand of a quality of relatedness that is new and generative, even as the specter of potentially destructive forms of enactment is evoked. The case affords an especially poignant look at the interplay of neurotic and existential anxiety. The patient's primary symptom, a kind of vertigo, could be viewed as rational, whereas the usual sense of balance and confidence that people maintain in their everyday lives could be viewed as illusory, grounded essentially in denial. The case also offers the opportunity to explore the relationship between "drive" and "deficit," with particular attention to the issues highlighted by classical theory and self psychology. The two perspectives in this case play themselves out in a special manner, in that the patient had an interest in self psychology, which he seemed, at times, to use defensively. The chapter closes with a series of dreams bearing on the termination of the analysis, including one that synthesizes multiple themes, ending finally with an account of the last hour in which analyst and analysand try to coconstruct a "good-enough ending" for that hour and for the analysis.

"Constructing Good-Enough Endings in Psychoanalysis," the final chapter, explores various facets of termination, including its relation to the analyst's and the patient's mortality. In some instances, continuing the analysis indefinitely, expecting that only the death of the analyst or of the patient will bring it to an end, may be the wisest course. In most cases, however, deliberately constructing an ending is viewed as facilitating certain aspects of development. In particular, the patient and the analyst are confronted with the limitations of the analysis and, conversely, with the enormous role of chance in affecting the course of the process and the long-term "outcome." The healing potentials of the analysis are seen as partially offset by the traumatizing impact of the passage of time, of aging, of the anticipation of death. Work with an elderly patient is described to illustrate these and other issues.

Epilogues to the analyses of Diane (chapter 8) and Ken (chapter 9) are presented here. The "good outcome" is shown, again, to be significantly influenced by luck. Diane wrote to me five years after the termination to say that she was happy to announce that she had met and married a man with whom she was happier than she ever imagined she could be. The implications of that happy development in Diane's life are discussed in terms of the interplay of analytic influence, the patient's strengths, and sheer luck. The termination process in the case of Ken is revisited. In chapter 9 we looked at the evolution of internal object relations, enactments, and new experience as we approached the ending. Here we look at another aspect of the story, the practical factors that enter into the patient's decision to terminate, including considerations external to the analytic process per se, such as finding an excellent career opportunity in another city. Those considerations, too, however, are folded back into the analytic process and shown to have meaning and impact at both intrapsychic and interpersonal levels. Coconstructing a good-enough ending of an analysis, like coconstructing a good-enough ending of each analytic hour, is a value-laden process that exposes the myth of analytic neutrality in a dramatic way. The ending affords particularly rich opportunities for forging new experience out of apparent repetitions of old patterns.

After reviewing the termination with Ken, I turn to a series of postanalytic contacts that I had with this patient. The focus is on contacts that involved seeking Ken's permission to present and publish the paper and soliciting his responses to it. These "postanalytic" contacts are discussed as a special instance of "liminal" experience, the concept introduced in chapter 9. In this instance, what comes into the foreground is the analyst's vulnerability: his anxiety and guilt about "using" the patient for his own partially selfish motives. The patient's response creates, in effect, a figure-ground reversal, in that the analysand becomes a source of forgiveness, thereby overcoming the analyst's drift toward a sense of himself as the bad object. This reversal, which is usually going on more silently in the background, highlights the extent to which the analyst and the analysand have a mutual interest in recognizing, coming to terms with, and ultimately celebrating their common humanity.

OVERCOMING THE ODDS

The defiant affirmation that we seek to create through the analytic relationship has to overcome all kinds of odds. We are up against childhood traumas of varying degrees of severity as well as new traumas that inevitably accompany or episodically punctuate our lives. Life does not stand still while we try to address and overcome the consequences of injuries incurred in our impressionable early years. As the essays in a recent volume, *The Therapist as a Person* (Gerson, 1996), so beautifully attest, it does not stand still for the analyst any more than it does for the analysand. We struggle to foster the patient's potential for new, more integrated, and more fulfilling ways of being at the same time that patient and therapist alike are continually bombarded with challenges, crises, and sometimes tragedies that are unprecedented. The work must go on under conditions that are not always conducive to it. The attempt to build new realities sometimes has to be made in the midst of great turbulence. To be sure, there are periods of relative tranquility, and the analyst's office can also serve as something of a sanctuary from the pressures of everyday life. But the shelter it affords is only partial and intermittent. Indeed, the structure itself is not without its own set of flaws and even deeply hurtful features. The work, for the patient and the analyst, entails coping with whatever life brings now, at the same time that the internal realities of the patient as they were constructed in the past are explored, more or less enacted, critically reviewed, and gradually revised.

What I hope comes through in these pages is my own sense of struggle to find a way to be with patients that gives them the greatest opportunity, despite the odds, to make better lives for themselves. There is respect here for a variety of theoretical perspectives regarding motivation and development, in effect, a kind of critical pluralism. With that openness comes a special kind of uncertainty as to what stance on the part of the analyst is optimal for any particular analytic dyad at any particular moment. But pluralism and a conviction about the value of uncertainty are themselves very definitive, key aspects of a point of view about the analytic process that I develop and advocate in this book. To say that a range of perspectives may apply to a particular situation or experience is itself a supraordinate perspective, and none of the specific perspectives that it allegedly encompasses is considered its equal in terms of general truth value. Each specific perspective, moreover, is modified by its interaction with the others and by its relocation within the broader dialectical framework that I am proposing. That framework has its own implications for a theory of development (made explicit especially in chapters 8 through 10). Most prominently, however, what this metaview encourages is a certain kind of analytic attitude, one that has a subtle but pervasive effect on the analyst's experience and behavior, including such things as his or her demeanor and tone of voice. Thus, in a particular analytic encounter, the attitude may well affect, not only what the analyst says, but his or her entire manner of relating to the patient.

Despite its integrative nature, practically speaking the perspective may not be right for every analyst or for every patient. Some patients may need the distance that is more likely, perhaps, in a therapist with a more classical point of view, some the level of self-subordination and devotion to "sustained empathic inquiry" that a self psychologist is more likely to have cultivated, some the specific content of reconstructive interpretation that a Kleinian or other therapist with a specific theoretical commitment is more likely to offer. There is a personality variable here too that may have some relation to one's theory of technique but also has standing in its own right, and has much bearing on how good the match will be between analyst and analysand (Kantrowitz, 1996). Nevertheless, neither theories of technique nor personality types are totally static or closed entities. Perhaps it is not too much to hope that some readers, people with a range of theoretical viewpoints and personality styles, will find the point of view presented here useful, will be open to being influenced by it, and will find their own individual, creative, and self-expressive ways to bring it to bear in their work. Through them the power and meaning of the perspective itself can grow as more of its therapeutic potentials can be discovered, articulated, and brought to life in the broad spectrum of relationships that develop between patients and analysts.

• 1 •

The Dialectic of Meaning
and Mortality in the
Psychoanalytic Process

SOURCES OF EMBARRASSMENT AND
DEFENSES AGAINST THEM

The occupation of psychoanalyst or psychoanalytic therapist is a rather peculiar one. What the analyst offers is complex, but to the extent that it includes some kind of caring involvement at its core, it can feel a little too close for comfort to what other personal relationships offer. To have people come and pay for one's time, attention, understanding, and concern can even be something of an embarrassment to both participants: to the patient for needing this kind of service, and to the analyst for making a living offering it.

The situation is somewhat less embarrassing to the extent that what one offers can be attributed readily to one's special expertise. The traditional "technical skills" of the analyst are most prominent when his or her personal participation is minimized as a factor in the process. Historically, such was the case when the therapeutic action of psychoanalysis could be seen as limited primarily to the development of insight, with the analyst's main contribution consisting of interpreting the dynamics of the neurosis and of the transference. Change was promoted, allegedly, when insight into the origins of symptoms was combined with a realization by the patient that, as an adult, he or she had more resources and options than were available in childhood.

1

Repression and other maladaptive defenses became less necessary, not because conditions were created to compensate for early environmental failure, but because the patient's mature ego could now be brought to bear upon internally based conflict. In this model, the analyst attempted to provide a neutral presence, designed, allegedly, to have little or no impact on the patient's associations and unfolding transferences. Such an orientation reflected the classical Freudian ideal, one Freud (1912) himself felt had to be compromised because of the powerful influence of the "unobjectionable positive transference," according to which the analyst is invested with powers like those possessed by the parents in the patient's early life. Freud felt this aspect of the transference was unobjectionable, not so much because it was realistic as because the analyst could put it to good use (Friedman, 1969).

Building upon Freud's acknowledgment that such an interpersonal factor contributes to the therapeutic action of the process, Strachey (1934) offered the view that, coinciding with interpreting a forbidden wish in the transference, the analyst conveys an accepting attitude toward that very wish, an attitude that the patient internalizes, thereby mitigating the archaic, punitive aspects of his or her own conscience. More austerely, Macalpine (1950) proposed that the knowhow of the analyst includes a method for systematically inducing a regression by depriving the patient of an object relationship. In these accounts of the process, the emotional involvement of the analyst, the engagement of his or her personality, is largely a regrettable contaminant, creating a danger, in Strachey's view, that the influence of the archaic objects and of the current analyst will be indistinguishable or, in Macalpine's view, that the induction of the regressive transference neurosis will be impeded. These theorists seem to be emphasizing opposite factors, with Strachey identifying a positive aspect of what the interpersonal interaction offers the patient and Macalpine identifying the factor of systematic deprivation. What they have in common, however, is the idea that the analyst abstain from any personally expressive behavior. Strachey (1934) says, for example, "the analyst must avoid any real behaviour that is likely to confirm the patient's view of him as a 'bad' or a 'good' phantasy object," and further, "It is a paradoxical fact that the best way of ensuring that his [the patient's] ego shall be able to distinguish between phantasy and reality is to withhold reality from him as much as possible" (pp. 146–147). And Macalpine (1950) writes, "The continual denial of all gratification and object relations mobilizes libido for the recovery of memories, but its significance lies also in the fact that frustration as such is a repetition of infantile situations, and most likely the most important single factor" (p. 525). In both these conceptions of the process, the analyst and the patient are spared the sense that the service the analyst offers bears uncomfortable similarities to what people normally seek from family and from other loved ones.

In the last several decades, however, we've seen increasing attention to the role of the relationship itself as a factor, even as the crucial factor, in the therapeutic action of the analytic process. As recognition of the patient's legitimate developmental needs has grown, the aversion to the dangers of "transference cure" have decreased. That the analyst is a source of love is no longer unacceptable from the point of view of theory, since love in the analytic situation has lost at least some of the implication of inevitable incestuousness. But while gaining acceptance theoretically, the role of the relationship can be an awkward factor to acknowledge in practice. Even Macalpine (1950), whose focus was entirely on the influence of the analytic "setting," not on the analyst's personal contribution, said, in effect, let's admit *to each other* that we are not merely providing a neutral background for "free" associations, but that we are subjecting our patients to conditions of deprivation in order to make them regress. Nowhere does she go so far as to suggest that we admit this to the patients themselves. On the contrary, the "hoodwinking" of the patient (p. 527), the conveying of a double message (the analyst is there to help, the analyst is totally unavailable), is part of what may promote the regression, and it is not clear how being open about one's intentions would affect that objective.

Analogously, many contemporary analysts also often have something up their sleeves, although opposite to what Macalpine had in mind, that they may find awkward to share with their patients. If a naive patient asks in an early session for an account of how the process works, it is not easy, nor would it necessarily be wise, to say outright, "Assuming you attend sessions regularly and pay your bills, I will offer you a special kind of love and recognition to help compensate for what you did not get from your parents (or other caregivers) as a child." Doubts arise immediately as to the authenticity of "love and recognition" when they are offered as part of the "treatment plan." But regardless of that, the patient might find the idea that he or she is seeking love of some kind and is willing to pay for it abhorrent. It's more comfortable for both parties to talk about the more classical factors, the opportunity for the patient to speak freely and to explore and understand, with the aid of the analyst's interpretive skills, whatever has been unconscious and has interfered with the patient's chance to live a more fulfilling life.

Although awkward to acknowledge to our patients, it has nevertheless become relatively commonplace for us to admit to each other that some kind of nurturance is a big part of what we offer those who come to us for help. In keeping with what Mitchell (1993) has referred to as the revolution in "what the patient needs," a strong chorus of voices has spoken in favor of the analyst's availability as a "good object," offering an interpersonal experience that promises to compensate, in part, for whatever was lacking in the patient's childhood. Instead of defensively protecting the illusion of noninvolvement, we are inclined now to protect our sense of confidence that the "reparenting" that we offer is "good enough" to have therapeutic impact. So we start with the feeling that what we offer is basically good—an atmosphere of safety, a good holding environment, an empathic self-selfobject tie—and that the negative transference is either irrational or a result of hypersensitivity due to early traumas or deprivation. The fee itself, it is argued, contributes to the safety of the situation by ensuring consistent, unconditional compensation for the analyst and reducing his or her need for other kinds of interpersonal rewards. At the same time, however, it's hard to deny that the money also casts doubt upon the sincerity of the analyst's personal involvement and concern. We tend not to dwell on the fact that the integrity of our efforts is always on the verge of being compromised, or is actually compromised, in our patients' eyes as well as our own, simply by virtue of the fact that we are being paid for them. The exchange of money for therapy, which includes an intensely personal relationship, is usually a source of discomfort for both parties (Aron and Hirsch, 1992). As Muriel Dimen (1994) has written:

> When money is exchanged in a capitalist economy, both buyer and seller—patient and analyst—come to be like commodities, or things, to one another because they enter into relation with each other through the mediation of a third thing (money) that, simultaneously, separates them. As money wedges them apart, so it estranges them from themselves, a distancing that creates anxiety in both [p. 81].[1]

---

1. Slavin and Kriegman (1992) have cogently argued that an element of conflict between the self-interest of the analyst and the self-interest of the patient is inevitable, as is the conflict between the interests of parents and children. While there is room for criticism of particular cultural arrangements, it would be naively utopian to think that any transformation of society, including a Marxist one, would expunge such conflict from what Slavin and Kriegman call the "adaptive design of the human psyche."

I suspect that at some level, for both participants, the association to prostitution is hard to escape. I once supervised a resident who had a high-class, expensive call girl among his patients. She was continually confronting him on the parallels between her profession and his. She said she had genuine interest in her johns and felt quite proud of the quality of her work. She failed to see how what she was doing with her life was any more demeaning to herself than what the therapist was doing with his, a perspective that made it a bit difficult for him to challenge her adaptation.

In addition to the money, the idea of the analyst as one who is sytematically implementing a certain treatment strategy or method detracts from the patient's sense of the analyst's interpersonal authenticity. This problem would not occur in dentistry, medicine, or other service professions in the same way, because there the treatment procedures and their effects are relatively independent of the treator's personal involvement. Whether or not one's dental cavities are filled properly has little or nothing to do, intrinsically, with the genuineness of the dentist's personal attitudes. Similarly, it is unlikely that those who minimize the importance of the analyst's personal involvement, and who (defensively in my view) continue to see insight as the sole or predominant basis for the therapeutic action of the process, would be particularly concerned with the problem of authenticity. For them, little about the relationship per se is critical to the therapeutic action of the process. But for those who see the quality of the relationship as *at the core* of the therapeutic action, considerations of authenticity become implicitly, if not explicitly, critical. It follows that factors that may compromise it also become more threatening to consider.

FROM DIVINE AUTHORITY TO ANALYTIC AUTHORITY: IRONIC AFFIRMATION

Yet the nature of the service the analyst offers may be more embarrassing still than its association with everyday interpersonal influences, even with love in ordinary personal relationships. Freud (1926b) identified the role of the analyst as that of a "secular pastoral worker," someone who serves as a guide to people as they struggle to find their way in life on the basis of personal, individual experience. The importance of such experience is relatively new historically. Nietzsche's announcement of the "death of God" called attention to a moral vacuum in Western society and to a need for a new kind of authority in the culture, one with the power to serve as a catalyst for individual self-fulfillment. Philip Rieff (1966) contends that the psychoanalytic therapist, more than any other figure in society, assumed that role. But such a mantle is hardly a comfortable one to bear. To be a source of love is one thing, but to inherit the psychological functions of a supernatural power is quite another. It is a particularly difficult position in an era that is so dubious about authority altogether.[2]

Freud's answer to the question of how can we find a way to live without divine sanction and without hope for an afterlife centered on the valuing of truth and the overcoming of self-deception. He held, as an ideal, that a person strive for an integrated awareness of self and of "Reality" or "Necessity" and for an adaptation that reflects that awareness. Reality, both internal and external, was considered relatively fixed and essentially knowable. The highest virtue was to come to grips with the truth about both. As I said earlier, the analyst, according to Freud, may be seen as a moral authority whose power stems from an unobjectionable positive transference that is not entirely rational, but the aim remains to discover and integrate truths that have a fixed quality. The end justifies the means, which may entail a certain element of manipulation, a benign though paradoxical use of aspects of the very transference that is the object of critical analytic scrutiny (Friedman, 1969). So, from a Freudian perspective, if the analyst is a moral guide, the values that he or she tries to instill in the patient remain the values of the objectivistic scientist, namely, to seek the truth about one's self and one's world and live in a way that is "true to oneself" within the constraints of Reality (Freud, 1927a, 1933; Wallerstein, 1983).

Although he recognizes the moral dimension of the analyst's role in the culture, Rieff (1966) seems uncritical of the classical Freudian claims to the effect that truth-seeking and the expansion of the individual's range of freedom are the only moral imperatives underlying the analyst's endeavors. Rieff's modernist leanings in this regard come across in much of his writing, including his sharp separation of "commitment therapies" and "analytic therapies" and a corresponding dichotomizing of "priestly" and "analytic"

---

2. Donald Palmer (1988), in his overview of Western philosophy, writes, "of course, there can be no single correct answer to the question, 'what did Nietzsche mean by 'the Death of God'?'. . . but surely [he] at least meant to announce the end of traditional forms of authority: historical, political, religious, moral and textual" (pp. 288–289).

authority (pp. 74–78). Much in the spirit of an enlightenment sensibility, Rieff writes:

> Earlier therapists, being sacralists, guarded the cultural super-ego, communicating to the individual the particular signs and symbols in which the super-ego was embodied or personified. In this sense, earlier therapists assumed priestly powers. The *modern* therapist, however, is without priestly powers, precisely because he guards *against* the cultural super-ego and, unlike the sacralist, is free to *criticize* the moral demand system. Rather, he speaks for the individual buried alive, as it were, in the culture [p. 77, italics added].[3]

The values of truth seeking, coupled with those of individual freedom and self-realization, are not limited to Freudian theory, but are foundational for most psychoanalytic theory and practice. For example, in some respects, the place occupied by the id in classical theory is occupied by the "true self" in Winnicott. In Freud, however, unlike Winnicott, the "true self" is itself conflicted, a feature of Freud's thought that lends a tragic character to his view of humankind. In that regard, Freud is what I would call a "tragic objectivist," one who believes that what is discovered as a result of the investigation of mind is actually the impossibility of self-fulfillment, since the realization of one core wish or potential is inevitably achieved at the expense of another. Indeed, there is a bridge from Freud to postmodern moral uncertainty, since the structure of Freud's thought encourages consideration of multiple sources of conflict with no clear basis for their resolution.[4] Also, for Freud the fact of irreducible conflict among the primary instinctual aims of the id precludes the possibility of anything approaching a utopian transformation of society. The implicit Freudian view that any socially constructed

---

3. In an essay written twenty years after the publication of the *Triumph of the Therapeutic*, Rieff (1987) was dismayed by the collapse of moral order, of any sense of "the sacred," in "therapeutic culture." He writes: "Because the instinctual unconscious contains no either-or, it is worse than immoral: amoral, positively transgressive. Therapeutic neutrality in this matter is more than mistaken: it has been a tragedy for our, or any other, culture and for anyone alive to its deadly condition" (p. 364).

4. Freudian thought contains powerful precursors of recent discussions of the "decentered" self as represented, for example, in Mitchell (1993), Slavin and Kriegman (1992), and in the symposium in *Contemporary Psychoanalysis* entitled "The Multiplicity of Self and Analytic Technique," which includes Pizer (1996), Bromberg (1996), Harris (1996), Davies (1996), and Flax (1996).

reality favors the realization of some aspects of the self while abandoning others contrasts with perspectives—like those of Winnicott, Kohut, and Loewald—in which a unified self becomes a guide that analyst and patient can find, and happily follow. These theorists might be termed "romantic objectivists" since they believe in the possibility not only of a harmony of ascertainable internal and external realities, but also in the ultimate harmony within the true self of the individual. Consider the following statement by Loewald (1960), one that I think captures the essence of romantic objectivism:

> If the analyst keeps his central focus on [the] emerging core [of the patient] he avoids moulding the patient in the analyst's own image or imposing on the patient his own concept of what the patient should become. It requires an objectivity and neutrality the essence of which is love and respect for the individual and for individual development. This love and respect represent that counterpart in "reality," in interaction with which the organization and reorganization of ego and psychic apparatus take place.
>
> The parent-child relationship can serve as a model here. The parent ideally is in an empathic relationship of understanding the child's particular stage in development, yet ahead in his vision of the child's future and mediating this vision to the child in his dealing with him. This vision, informed by the parent's own experience and knowledge of growth and future, is, ideally, a more articulate and more integrated version of the core of being that the child presents to the parent [p. 20].

Although Loewald elsewhere (e.g., 1979) conveys a position that is more cognizant of the inevitability of conflict and uncertainty in mental life, in this particular statement we can see how the analyst can foster the patient's self-realization without concerns about inevitable extraneous sources of influence (intruding, for example, from the analyst's unconscious) or about anything within the patient's "emerging core" being left dormant and unrealized. Similarly, the parents can offer the child conditions for such full and relatively "uncontaminated" development (cf. Cooper, 1997).

The general project of promoting self-realization in some form, what Rieff (1966) calls the "gospel of self-fulfillment" (p. 252), becomes highly problematic when the patient's internal and external realities are understood to be, at least partially, historically, culturally, and individually relative constructions. The analyst emerges as a moral authority in a new and potentially more powerful sense the moment that preexisting realities are no longer considered adequate as moorings for analytic explorations. Now choices have to be made about what to *make* of one's life, past and present, and it is understood that these choices are not made in a social vacuum. Contrary to Rieff's view, which perpetuates the notion of analytic neutrality as both an ideal and as a real possibility, in a constructivist perspective the analyst becomes an immediate partner in the process through which those choices are made, choices that entail resolutions of the ambiguities that are intrinsic to the nature of experience. (See Introduction, fn. 1, on the term "choice.") Ambiguity encompasses what happened in the past as well as the potentials for action and experience now. We are faced with existential choice as an issue that cannot be settled via mere conformity to fixed psychic, social, or material realities and with a proportional expansion of the analyst's role as preceptor. The analyst's authority is, indeed, not "priestly" in the sacral sense that Rieff had in mind; but neither is it limited to impartially and antiseptically promoting development of the analysand's self-awareness and freedom. It reemerges in a manner that reflects neither scientific nor religious optimism but that acknowledges a universal human need. Ernest Becker (1973), struck by the way in which human affirmation of worth is under constant siege by awareness of mortality, appreciates the necessity for such affirmation, and the need to find a source for it outside of oneself. Thus, regarding the transference, Becker writes, "[T]he transference object contains its own natural awesomeness, its own miraculousness, which infects us with the significance of *our* own lives if we give in to it. . . . [T]ransference is a universal passion. It represents a natural attempt to be healed and to be whole" (p. 157).

The form, however, that the analyst's authority takes can only be ironic, because it lacks traditional sanction in our era and because, more than ever, it is vigorously challenged in the analytic situation itself. The heightened sense of the moral nature of analytic discourse is accompanied by a heightened sense of the absence of a solid foundation to support it. The analyst participates as a moral preceptor, even while both participants come to appreciate how much the role is a social construction designed to meet a universal human need. The authority of the analyst, even an element of mystique, survives and even feeds upon two sources of challenge to it, both of which are cultivated in what I am calling a dialectical-constructivist view. One is a process of joint critical reflection on its place in the patient's mental life, including its infantile prototypes, in other words, the analysis of the transference. The second is the analyst's personal participation in the interaction in a spirit of mutuality, the kind of participation that exposes the analyst's fallibility and vulnerability. The dialectical interplay of the emergence of the analyst's subjectivity and its relative submergence in the context of analytic discipline generates a position of "intimate and ironic authority" for the analyst (see chapter 3; and for a discussion of irony in psychoanalysis, see Stein, 1985).

I believe there is a tendency in the work of some relational theorists, as an overreaction to the scientistic authoritarianism to which classical technique was prone, to denigrate the irrational aspects of the authority of the analyst to a degree that denies what is implicitly built into the analytic arrangement. In my view, unless the fundamental asymmetry of the analytic situation were to be dismantled, the analyst is likely to retain a certain residue of special power that cannot be undone by analysis, by interpersonal negotiation, or even by personally revealing behavior if it is consistent with the maintenance of the analytic frame.[5] Instead, it remains the responsibility of the analyst to make use of the authority with which he or she is invested in a way that is as wise, as compassionate, and as empowering of the analysand as possible. To deny that the analyst's influence is likely to include, for most patients, an irrational or even magical component is to court a reversion back, ironically, to the rationalist ideal of modernism, to an enlightenment perspective, although one more democratized than it had been in classical theory. Meanwhile, the bridge between Freud's grudging concession to an irreducible, irrational substratum underlying the therapeutic action of psychoanalysis, on the one hand, and postmodern insight into the limitations of human freedom and reason, on the other, is jeopardized or lost.

A NEW PSYCHOBIOLOGICAL BEDROCK AND ASSOCIATED EMERGING VALUES

The freedom to choose is a mixed blessing when the subject feels neither empowered to choose nor convinced of the value of whatever options are available. Rieff (1966) states the predicament, with some hyperbole, as follows:

> This is one way of stating the difference between gods and men. Gods choose; men are chosen. What men lose when they become as free as

---

5. The basic features of the frame are not self-evident, of course. I would include among them that one person consistently comes to the other for help and that the person in the helping role, the analyst, tries consistently to give priority to the analysand's long term interests, subordinating—but by no means burying—his or her own immediate personal desires to that end.

gods is precisely that sense of being chosen, which encourages them,
in their gratitude, to take their subsequent choices seriously [p. 93].

To be chosen is to be empowered to choose and to have one's
choices recognized as significant and worthwhile. Parents, the
"gods" of infancy and childhood, have the power to give children a
sense of being "chosen," that is, of being valued as creative centers
of experience and choice in their own right. But of course the parents
themselves were and are the children of their parents, and so on ad
infinitum. So those who are chosen (i.e., affirmed) become those who
"choose" (i.e., affirm others).

As adults in a secular world we come to understand that this
process cannot begin "at the top" with some kind of divine authority but rather must be forged and sustained by people in their relationships with others. We come to recognize, in other words, that it's
always a "bootstrap operation."[6] But the blueprint for the ongoing
success of that operation is created in the beginning by the relationship of parents to infants and young children, a relationship that
could hardly be more hierarchical. Functionally, to their small, relatively helpless offspring, the parents are omnipotent and omniscient
figures, colossal giants. Their relative size alone is awesome, not to
mention their amazing capabilities. To a child two feet tall, a five-foot
six-inch parent would be like a fifteen-foot giant to that parent or to
anyone of the parent's height. Whatever these huge figures say, goes.
Whatever they convey is absorbed as the truth, including their sense
of the child's worth and of the child's right to be an agent, a choosing
subject, in the world. Such innocent absorption of "reality" occurs in
something akin to a "critical period," a time of illusion before the
child's reflective consciousness has developed enough to illuminate
the parents' and the child's own severe limitations. In that age of
innocence something can be taken in and secured in such a way that
it can withstand the potentially devastating impact of later realizations. What is cultivated in the beginning cushions the inevitable fall.
Of that launching in infancy, Winnicott (1968) says, "From this initial *experience of omnipotence* the baby is able to begin to experience
frustration and even to arrive one day at the other extreme from
omnipotence, that is to say, having a sense of being a mere speck in a

6. Mitchell (1997, p. 47) has used the term "bootstrapping" to refer to
the attempt of analyst and analysand to transcend an enactment of a transference-countertransference pattern when the attempt itself is embedded in
that very pattern.

universe. . . . Is it not from *being* God that human beings arrive at the humility proper to human individuality?" (p. 101).[7]

It seems likely, moreover, that beyond this early period any experience of interpersonal affirmation not only resonates with the original, hierarchically organized version, but also draws upon it for its power. To the extent that the original template is flawed (as it always is in some measure), the individual's capacity to find, create, and utilize opportunities for interpersonal validation will be proportionately impaired. The analytic situation is an arrangement conducive, among other things, to addressing and at least partially repairing the cracks in that foundation. As one who is consistently there as a caregiver, and whose defects are relatively hidden, the analyst becomes a magnet for the universal human appetite to reestablish the earliest conditions for the absorption of love. That appetite, as Freud (1927a) argued, is the great generator of religious, theistic belief systems. To the extent that, with the help of such figures as Nietzsche, Darwin, and Freud himself, those systems weakened or collapsed, the analyst was in a position to inherit some of their function, to be an anchor, a source of meaning, a powerful source of affirmation.

But to what extent can we expect a paid relationship with an analyst with limited scheduled hours to compensate for early emotional deprivations? It would seem, indeed, a poor substitute for a good, intimate relationship with another person in the real world, not to mention a trusting relationship with God. And surely there are aspects of the analytic situation, in which the party that pays is likely to be more needy and vulnerable than the party that is paid, that can legitimately be construed as nonoptimal, even as hurtful or exploitative (see chapters 9 and 10). Yet the patient who is entirely consumed by that grievance may well be handicapped by a parallel grievance in attempts to establish close relationships outside. They too, after all, could be experienced as poor substitutes insofar as they fail to match the fantasy of an ideal early tie to a parental figure. Thus the patient who finds a way to appreciate and cultivate the value of the analytic relationship, despite its glaring limitations, may well create a model for his or her being able to embrace and make the most of other relationships as well.

Loving, mutual relationships always entail a dialectic of use of the other as a need-satisfying object and appreciation of the other as a

7. I am indebted to Carolyn Clement (personal communication) for calling my attention to this statement by Winnicott.

separate subject. In some measure, each participant tolerates, forgives, even caters to the narcissistic and autoerotic tendencies of the other. In childhood, one should have the opportunity to experience oneself as more at the center of another person's concern than is possible later, and it behooves the caregivers to indulge this need, to foster this "illusion" through an optimal degree of self-subordination (Winnicott, 1971; Benjamin, 1988). The individual who has been cheated out of this opportunity, who has been, instead, more exploited than recognized as a child, often cannot readily tolerate the factor of self-interest that he or she must encounter in every other person in adult life. That factor may become toxic while a sense of entitlement to an impossible, selfless love generates depressive rage at the world for offering so little of what the person feels he or she needs.

In saying that the discrepancy between the imagined ideal and the real is inevitable I do not mean to imply that particular relationships should escape critical scrutiny. Some object choices are egregiously bad and should be dropped. Others, including the analytic relationship, may need a lot of work to stand a chance of moving in a healthy direction, and some significant share of the responsibility for change may fall on the other person (the analyst, for example) rather than the patient. Along with current relationships, the patient's experience with original caregivers must come under scrutiny, and to the extent that parental figures seemed to be inattentive, abandoning, abusive, or exploitative, their behavior should be identified as such, and the patient's grief and rage at not having a better, or even a decent start in life should be acknowledged and understood. At the same time, however, it is often important for the patient to take into account that *any* actual relationship in adult life cannot substitute for the creation of an optimal early childhood situation in which the capacity and opportunity for innocent absorption of love could be reinstated. To state the issue in another way, for many troubled patients, any current relationship is a poor substitute for being reborn under more optimal conditions. In this respect, it's not a matter of current potential love objects not being good enough. The fact is that the patient cannot transform himself or herself into that innocent, small child, the one who can uncritically absorb whatever good the environment seems to offer.

The traumas of childhood can mask, not only the inevitability of the limits of current relationships, but also the fact that even the best parents are never caregivers whose love, in terms of quality and power, is so perfect and permanent as to escape the fate of the child's disillusionment. The parents are ultimately exposed as poor substitutes for "the gods," even though, in the best circumstances, that exposure emerges gradually and is offset by the gains growing out of the child's emerging capacity for a more mature and realistic kind of love. But beyond the limitations of other human beings as sources of love, there is a sense in which life itself, human life as we know it, is a "poor substitute" for an imagined life that does not get ripped away from us at a time and in a way not of our choosing, and one in which others whom we love are not similarly taken from us. We weren't consulted about being conceived and born, first physically and then psychologically, into a life that leads to our own deaths and the deaths of every person to whom we become attached. We were, as Macalpine says of the analysand's plight, virtually "hoodwinked" into it, were we not? And yet it was an offer we had no opportunity to refuse, nor would most of us imagine refusing it if we had the choice. Better to have loved and lost than not to have loved at all; and better to have lived and died than not to have lived at all. We, the Slaves—that is, humankind—will take what we can from the Mistress-Master, that is, from Nature, even though we know that Nature, ultimately, brutally disregards our needs and wishes, ravages us with illness and old age, abuses us, forces on our bodies the most grotesque kinds of physical deterioration, kills us in unspeakably horrifying and unexpected ways. We are not all, to be sure, adult survivors of childhood sexual, physical, or psychological abuse; but we are all adult endurers of the ongoing abuse of the human condition.

And yet, we feel, most of us, emphatically, that it's worth it. Although the whole challenge of living might be described as the challenge of making the best of poor substitutes, "the best," after all, can be something quite wonderful, inspiring, and miraculous, even if also quite terrible. This perspective requires of mature love that it withstand and encompass the self-love of the other, along with the inevitability of death and loss. Put another way, it requires of such love that it absorb and survive the chilling currents of indifference and nonrecognition that emanate from the object and, ultimately, from the universe. If the love object reciprocates that tolerant attitude, mutual love and respect can grow and can subordinate "ruthless" (Winnicott) self-centered desire in oneself and in the other.

At the core of the generic bad object is some form of obliviousness to our experience as human beings. Awareness of mortality in a godless world brings with it the sheer horror of being infinitesimal specks in an indifferent universe. This is what humans realize when they assume what the philosopher Thomas Nagel (1986) refers to as the "objective standpoint." At the same time, what matters to people in their everyday lives is equally powerful and undeniable. Relationships, interests, appetites, ideals, ambitions, sensual pleasures, aesthetic experiences impress themselves on human consciousness in a way that can be extremely compelling. This sense of the importance of the particulars of our lives emerges from what Nagel refers to as the "subjective standpoint." Despite the irreducibility of our subjective sense of reality, our sense of its value is at least partially subverted by the impact of the objective standpoint. Thus, Nagel writes, "[t]he most general effect of the objective stance ought to be a form of humility: the recognition that you are no more important than you are" (p. 222).

What emerges from the interaction of the two standpoints is a sense of irony and of the absurd:

> The absurd is part of human life. I do not think this can be basically regretted, because it is a consequence of our existence as particular creatures with a capacity for objectivity. . . . It is better to be simultaneously engaged and detached, and therefore absurd, for this is the opposite of self-denial and the result of full awareness [p. 223].

Paradoxically, however, it is a part of full awareness that full awareness is unbearable. So Nagel also declares:

> The objective standpoint can't really be domesticated. Not only does it threaten to leave us behind, but it gives us more than we can take-on in real life. When we acknowledge our containment in the world, it becomes clear that we are incapable of living in the full light of that acknowledgment. Our problem has in this sense no solution, but to recognize that is to come as near as we can to living in light of the truth [p. 231].

Ernest Becker (1973) offers his own version of the dialectic between the objective and the subjective standpoints. Like Nagel, he feels it is virtually impossible for human beings to sustain in awareness the full comprehension of their mortality. The social construction of reality always entails a narrowing of awareness and can never be free of an element of fetishistic passion since it is partly driven by denial of the ultimate "lack," the ultimate castration, which is death:

> [Man] literally drives himself into a blind obliviousness with social games, psychological tricks, personal preoccupations so far removed from the reality of his situation that they are forms of madness—agreed madness, shared madness, disguised and dignified madness, but madness all the same [pp. 26–28].

The line between neurotic suffering and normal human misery now becomes blurred, indeed, if it is detectable at all, because the construction of any reality always requires blinders; it is always, partially at least, a defensive operation:

> In order to function normally, man has to achieve, from the beginning, a serious constriction of the world and of himself. We can say that the essence of reality is the refusal of reality. What we call neurosis enters precisely at this point: Some people have more trouble with their lies than others [p. 178].

A value begins to emerge from the writings of these contemporary thinkers whose existentialist leanings are tempered—in keeping with a postmodern sensibility—by recognition of the severe limitations of human self-awareness and freedom. Once again, as in Freud, what is valued is a courageous facing up to the truth about one's self and one's world. But the nature of that truth is quite different than it was for Freud. The truth that emerges now is that, paradoxically, much of reality is ambiguous and indeterminate. Whereas death is an absolute certainty, taxes, in fact, are not. The specific features of social reality are, largely, socially constructed.[8] The nature of the reality we create is not fully predictable and its sources not fully knowable. What emerges as a kind of "psychobiological bedrock," as the immutable, transcultural, transhistorical truth, is that human beings create their worlds and their sense of meaning in the teeth of the constant threat of nonbeing and meaninglessness. The story of Genesis, of Creation, becomes the story of humankind, forging, against a background of chaos, a sense of significance and order. As Paul Tillich (1956) put it, "[E]xistentially expressed, the symbol of creation shows the source of the courage to affirm one's own being in terms of power and meaning in spite of the ever-present threat of non-being" (p. 287). And further, "God . . . is the power of being itself, prevailing over against non-being, overcoming estrangement, providing us the courage to take the anxiety of finitude, guilt, and doubt upon ourselves" (p. 291). The sociologists Berger and Luckmann (1967) express a similar perspective, without the religious overtones, when they say, "death . . . posits the most terrifying threat

---

8. Many aspects of social reality, like taxes, exist unequivocally and objectively as facts, even though they are culturally contingent; that is, they don't exist *apart* from the collective activity of human subjects. In that sense they are not "necessary" features of the natural world. But *with* human constructive activity, their objective existence is indisputable.

to the taken-for-granted . . . realities of everyday life" (p. 101). Thus, "*All* social reality is precarious. *All* societies are constructions in the face of chaos" (p. 103). And finally, we have this expression of defiance from Charles Taylor (1989):

> [W]hat happens when, as in modern humanist views, we no longer have anything like a constitutive good external to man? What can we say when the notion of the higher is a form of human life which consists precisely in facing a disenchanted universe with courage and lucidity? . . .
>
> Man can be annihilated by the universe, but his greatness in relation to it consists in his going down knowingly. Something inspires our respect here, and this respect empowers [pp. 93–95].

There is a connection between finding ways to live with the dreadful realities and absurdities of the human condition and finding ways to make maximum constructive use of the analytic situation, despite its own highly peculiar and even absurd features, including the exchange of money for love. Louis Sass (1997), in a discussion of an earlier version of this chapter, suggested the following way of putting a central implication of this perspective:

> Indeed, it is the absurdity of the human condition that redeems and justifies the absurdity of psychoanalysis. Thus we might say that it is precisely the absurdity of therapy that allows us to accomplish the therapy of the absurd. For example, to recognize the absurdity of paying someone for intimacy can eventually play a role in helping us understand the unacceptable fact that other people always have their own agendas and their own needs, that they are never fully and selflessly devoted to us. So it seems that what at first sight is the weakness of the psychotherapeutic situation can be turned into its greatest strength.

So to confront the mercenary aspect of the analyst's self-interest is metaphoric for confronting the ruthless self-interest of every love object, which, in turn, echoes the ultimate indifference of the universe to one's well-being, even to one's very existence. As stated earlier, in mature, realistic love the autoerotic and narcissistic tendencies of the other are not only encompassed but nurtured in exchange for the same generous acceptance that the other extends toward one's own selfish inclinations. The resulting reciprocity can subordinate and transcend the egocentric propensities of both parties and allow a deeper level of gratifying and empowering mutuality to emerge.

DIALECTICAL CONSTRUCTIVISM

The Dialectic of Meaning and Mortality

As devastating as our awareness of our mortality may be, it is hard to imagine life without it. Even those who believe in an afterlife recognize that death marks the end of our being as we know it. Could we do *without* that anticipated ending? Imagine, if you will, subtracting it from our consciousness. Substitute for it an anticipation of, not a thousand years, or a billion, but infinite years of good health with no further aging or deterioration of physical well-being. What more could one wish for? Yet, what would happen then to our sense of time? What would happen then to our sense of the importance of any particular moment, of any particular experience, of any particular activity? We are so accustomed to appreciating the way in which the anticipation of death, of endless nonbeing, undermines our sense of meaningful selfhood, that we fail, perhaps, to sense that the prospect of *endlessness itself* is anxiety provoking, whether we imagine ourselves forever alive or forever dead. Conversely, perhaps, it is not easy to see how integral our mortality is to our sense of self. There is after all, a certain wisdom in Freud's (1916a) reflection (discussed in some detail in the next chapter) that "transience value is scarcity value in time" (p. 305). The very annihilation that jeopardizes our sense that anything we care about matters, paradoxically, is what infuses caring with the meaning that it has (cf. Peltz, 1998). Indeed, it permeates the experience of caring so thoroughly that we may not notice it, except, perhaps, in those extreme circumstances when a loved one is close to death or has died. Martha Nussbaum (1994), philosopher and literary theorist, puts it eloquently:

> The structure of human experience, and therefore of the empirical human sense of value, is inseparable from the finite temporal structure within which human life is actually lived. Our finitude, and in particular our mortality, which is a particularly central case of our finitude, and which conditions all our awareness of other limits, is a constitutive factor in all valuable things, having for us the value that in fact they have. In these constraints we see whatever we see, cherish whatever we cherish, as beings moving in the way we actually move, from birth through time to a necessary death. The activities we love and cherish would not, as such, be available to a godlike unlimited being. . . . [T]he removal of all finitude in general, mortality in particular, would not so much enable these values to survive eternally as bring about the death of value as we know it [pp. 225–226].

Becoming immortal is more like being reincarnated as another species than it is like living, as human beings, forever. The latter is a contradiction in terms, because our being as we know it is fully saturated with our mortality. This is the ironic and agonizing paradox of human life:

> Human beings want to be immortal and ageless. And, perhaps, even more clearly, they want the human beings they love never to age, never to die. There seems to be little doubt of this. Who, given the chance to make a spouse or child or parent or friend immortal, would not take it? (I would grab it hungrily, I confess at the outset.) And yet we don't seem to know very clearly what it is we are wishing when we wish that. And we may well suspect that there is an incoherence lurking somewhere in the wish; that what we actually love and prize would not survive such translations. That we may be doomed or fortunate to be human beings simply, beings for whom the valuable things in life don't come apart so neatly from the fearful and the terrible [Nussbaum, 1990, p. 368].

The relationship between our sense of being and our anticipation of nonbeing is an example of a dialectic. There is a tension between the two types of experience and yet neither could exist without the other. When one is figure, the other is ground, but together they comprise a whole that is incorporated into our sense of self. A related dialectic is that between subjectivity and objectivity as described earlier. The two standpoints may seem to conflict, and yet each can be understood as an aspect of the other. A variety of dialectical relationships explored in this book shape the psychoanalytic situation, among them: patient and analyst, transference and countertransference, the intrapsychic and the interpersonal, authority and mutuality, ritual and spontaneity, repetition and new experience, existential anxiety and neurotic anxiety, analytic frame as good holding environment and analytic frame as cultural symptom, conviction and uncertainty, construction and discovery. But the dialectic of our sense of being and our sense of our mortality is superordinate to all the others because it is the paradoxical foundation for our sense of meaning. There are links here to Lacan and Heidegger. Charles Shepardson (1996) writes that, for Lacan,

> death is not a simple "event," a moment "in" chronological time, but rather the very opening of time, its condition of possibility. Instead of being placed at the end of a temporal sequence, as a final moment in biological time, the relation-to-death is placed at the origin, and understood as the "giving" of human time, the opening of possibility,

of time as a finite relation to the future and the past, structured by anticipation and memory. Death thus involves a peculiar link between the symbolic and the real, presenting us with a sort of hole or void in the structure of meaning—a void that is not a deficiency, but virtually the opposite, an absolute condition of meaning. The human relation-to-death (discussed in such detail by Heidegger) is thus in some sense at the "origin" of the symbolic order—not represented "in" language, or entirely captured by the symbolic rituals that seek to contain it, but rather "primordial" to language [citing Lacan, 1977, p. 105]: "So when we wish to attain in the subject . . . what is primordial to the birth of symbols, we find it in death" [discussion point No. 6].

Ambiguity and the Dialectic of the Given and the Created

Awareness of mortality is a universal given in human experience, which bears upon the meaning of "constructivism" as I am using that term. It refers, not to a perspective in which reality is seen as entirely the product of human activity or cognition, but rather to one in which human agency is seen as interacting with more or less ambiguous givens in the environment and in experience. Those givens are there to be discovered, one might say. And yet, even their "discovery" is a creative act since it requires selecting and lifting out of the sea of experience this or that "fact" and bringing it into relation with other such discovered givens in reality, as well as with interpretive constructions. Conversely, constructions that resolve ambiguities in one direction or another are also discoveries, because through them certain potentials in the individual's experience can be retrospectively identified. What is realized sheds light, in retrospect, on the potential that was embedded in the experience to begin with. Potentials in experience that are not realized, like fertile ground for a seeding that has not occurred and that no one has even thought of, remain largely undeveloped and unknown.

I am approaching the term "constructivism" itself with a constructivist attitude. This means, in effect, that I regard the concept as having some sense that I am not free to ignore at the same time that it is ambiguous enough so that there is latitude for shaping its significance. The term, after all, has gained currency in many fields, so it is associated with a range of specific meanings. Regarding its use in psychoanalysis, Donnel Stern (1985), in a symposium on constructivism, wrote:

Today we are most concerned with the emergence of meaning in experience that did not have meaning before, less and less concerned with
what Bollas has aptly referred to as "official psychoanalytic decoding."
  This epistemological shift is by no means unique to psychoanalysis. In fact, psychoanalysis is in the process of importing it from a
motley consortium of overlapping disciplines including the philosophy
of science, literary criticism, history, hermeneutics, the study of language, cognitive psychology . . . and the arts [pp. 202–203].

Thus, clearly, there are choices to be made as this "importing" goes
on, and there is tailoring that is required in a psychoanalytic context.
Moreover, even within that context, those adopting a constructivist
view may differ in terms of the nuances of meaning that they would
attach to the term.

  By contrast, an objectivist attitude stipulates that constructivism
has only one correct meaning and that it should not be used unless
that meaning is the one intended. Some critiques that are allegedly of
perspectives like my own (e.g., Orange, 1992) seem tantamount to
critiques of constructivism defined exclusively as a kind of solipsistic relativism. Michael Mahoney (1991), the cognitive theorist, distinguishes between such "radical constructivism," typified by von
Glaserfeld (1984), in which "knowledge does not reflect an 'objective' ontological reality, but exclusively an order and organization of
a world constituted by our experience" (von Glaserfeld, 1984, p. 24;
quoted by Mahoney, 1991, p. 111) and what Mahoney calls "critical constructivism," according to which "the individual is not a self-
sufficient, sole producer of his or her own experience. Rather, the
individual is conceived as a 'co-creator' or 'co-constructor' of personal realities, with the prefix *co-* emphasizing an interactive interdependence with their social and physical environments" (p. 111). I
would locate myself much more with the critical constructivists.
Indeed, I feel I have no more in common with the radical group than
I do with the objectivist camp.[9]

  Let me elaborate a bit more on the way I think of constructivism
as applied to one's own experience. We can take our experience

---

  9. To further illustrate that the term "constructivism" does not automatically connote, much less denote, a radical relativism that leaves no room
for an independent reality, consider the following definition offered by Jones
(1975) in his glossary: "Constructivism: The view that what we experience
is not a world *wholly* independent of ourselves, but one to which the activity of mind contributes *certain* features" (p. 422, italics added).

during, say, a certain period of time and consider what it entails and what can be said about it. To attend to our own experience as a whole in that way, rather than to particular objects within it, is to take what Taylor (1989) calls "a stance of radical reflexivity" (p. 130), a stance in which we acrobatically attempt to include our own agency in our field of observation. I believe experience can be thought of as composed, *first*, of symbolically well-developed, indisputable, relatively unambiguous features, *second*, of symbolically underdeveloped, ambiguous attitudes, feeling states, and frames of mind, and *third*, of totally untapped potentials.

If we think of the analyst and the patient in the analytic setting, there are countless things going on that are unambiguous and indisputable in themselves, although the relationships among them and other aspects of experience may be open to interpretation. Some of the unambiguous aspects are undoubtedly shared in common by analyst and analysand. Among the more commonplace and, perhaps, trivial examples are facts such as these: that the two people are meeting in the analyst's office at a certain hour in a certain town, that they are meeting for the purpose of psychoanalytic therapy or psychoanalysis, and that there is a fee set for the hour. Notice that it makes no difference that such facts are entirely dependent on the activity of human beings. They exist no less "objectively" for being functions of human construction and perception than do facts that are relatively independent of such activity, for example, that it is a daytime or nighttime hour.

There are also countless unambiguous and indisputable aspects of the experiences of the participants that are more emotionally charged and, perhaps, resisted. To pick an example that is particularly relevant to a central theme of this chapter, both parties are aware, even if only preconsciously, of their mortality. It is an objective fact in the background at every moment, regardless of the respective eschatological beliefs of the participants. Both parties are also aware, at least preconsciously, of their bodies. They may not be thinking of their physical being, but if a major body part were removed, even if magically and painlessly—an arm, a leg, an eye, a nose, a genital—they would undoubtedly notice the change.

In the realm of the more ambiguous facets of the experiences of the participants, there are all their "unformulated" (Stern, 1997) emotional states. To say that these experiences are ambiguous is not to say that they are amorphous. They have "properties," which have the status, partly, of *potentials* relative to the possibility of development through language and other forms of expression.[10] Which potentials are developed and in what way is an open question. There is not any one single set of words, for example, that will make explicit what is there in what Gendlin (1973) calls "implicit experiencing," but neither is it the case that any words will do. In fact, while the number of expressions that will *not* fit is infinite, so is the number that *will*. To say otherwise would be like arguing that there is only a finite set of poems, paintings, or musical compositions that can reflect a person's experience at a given moment or during a given interval of time. There is a continuum, of course, between very good expressions of the experience and very poor ones. The movement from unformulated to formulated, from implicit to explicit, entails a dialectic between what is given and what is created. Charles Taylor (1985) refers to this movement as a process of "articulation":

> Our attempts to formulate what we hold important must, like descriptions, strive to be faithful to something. But what they strive to be faithful to is not an independent object with a fixed degree and manner of evidence, but rather a largely inarticulate sense of what is of decisive importance. An articulaton of this "object" tends to make it something different from what it was before [pp. 37–38].

Reflecting on experience is like searching for shapes in a cloud (or if you prefer, shapes in a Rorschach inkblot). No one would ever claim that every possible percept in the cloud has been identified. In fact, no one would claim that the cloud has only a certain finite set of percepts that are even hypothetically available for "discovery."

---

10. It is important to emphasize that what is unformulated should only be regarded *partly* in terms of its potential for symbolic expression, particularly via language. There are levels of organization of experience that are not accessible to verbal explication and that always exist as parallel currents to experience that is structured linguistically. Louis Fourcher (1992), in this vein, argues forcefully against the reduction of all nonverbal, unconscious modes of construction to the status of verbal, reflective modes in nascent form. He writes: "We can thus speak of the 'relativity' to linguistic consciousness of these other facets of experience to the extent that they are available to be assimilated to reflection. We can also, however, speak of their formal otherness, their 'absolute' quality of unconsciousness, to the extent that in the first-person immediacy of experience they are structurally distinct from linguistic consciousness" (p. 327). Sue Grand (1997) recently discussed the importance of maintaining respect for untranslatable, "nonlinguistic testimony" to childhood sexual traumas.

The sense of infinite possibilities demonstrates that, in terms of shape, the cloud is not merely complex but irreducibly *ambiguous* (Mitchell, 1993; Sass, 1998). Also, just as there are infinite possible percepts that conform to features in the cloud, so too are there infinite percepts that don't (like good and poor form responses on the Rorschach). We are making a "choice," however passively, when we resolve that ambiguity in one way rather than another, a choice that, as Charles Taylor says, is partially "constitutive" of the experience. Here is where the analogy to the cloud actually begins to break down. The analogy *may* apply to experience that has already occurred, experience that we are recalling and construing in one way or another, but it doesn't apply to experience as it is happening, as we are moving through it and partially creating it. One might say that viewing the cloud is more akin to *studying* history than to *making* it.

This brings me to the untapped potentials in experience, the sense in which it is like fertile ground for "seedings" that have not occurred. Imagine turning on your car radio while driving home from work. Maybe you're looking for the news. But some music[11] is playing, classical or jazz or whatever, and you find yourself moved by it, resonating to it, completely caught up in it. Now what was *there* in your experience before you turned on the radio that had anything to do with that music? Presumably you were not a blank slate. The music interacted with something that was fertile ground for it, a readiness of some sort for its impact. But is there any way that readiness could be noticed *before* you heard the music? Usually, I would say not. The fact that that music was playing was a serendipitous event that realized a potential in your experience that would not have been realized or even known about otherwise. Now consider all the serendipitous events that did *not* occur. There is no way to begin imagining what all of them could be. And yet all of those events correspond with infinite unrealized potentials in one's experience at any given time. The potentials are "properties" of the experience, even though there is something indeterminate about them, and even though the only ones that are discovered are the ones that are realized. If we think of the analytic situation and substitute the patient for the driver in the car, and an unanticipated action on the analyst's part for the music, we get a sense of the indeterminate nature of what the situation "holds" for the participants and of the

---

11. The expressive nature of music is useful to consider as counterpoint to the idea that experience is organized entirely according to language (Fourcher, 1992; Norris, 1990).

creative potentials of the interaction. It's important, of course, to remember that the patient may often be the source of the unanticipated "music," with the analyst in the position of the one who may be more or less responsive.

All of this is to emphasize that our experience is shaped by what we make of it, by how we construct it, and that whatever we do with it is *always* necessarily at the expense of innumerable other possibilities. To choose is to absorb sacrifice, loss, and the relentless flow of time. "Decisions," as Irvin Yalom (1980) puts it, "are painful because they signify the limitation of possibilities; and the more one's possibilities are limited, the closer one is brought to death" (p. 318).

So, in the analytic situation, whatever is known or guessed about the patient's experience cannot *solely* determine what the participants should say or do to maximize understanding or to promote the most desirable kind of change. First, experience is heterogeneous, reflecting the heterogeneity of the patient's self (Mitchell, 1993) and leading us simultaneously in multiple directions. Second, we can never know, particularly in light of all the contingencies that are beyond our control, what it would have been like to follow the paths not taken. Third, other ingredients in the *analyst's* experience, including cultural, moral, aesthetic, and personal factors, some aspects of which undoubtedly lie outside of awareness, affect the analyst's actions. The result of all these factors, is, inescapably, a sense of more or less acknowledged uncertainty that accompanies whatever course is chosen, with whatever degree of passion and conviction.

The responsibility to choose in the context of profound, irreducible uncertainty is frightening. I believe we are probably defending against that dreadful responsibility when, as analysts, we latch on to external sources of direction, setting them up as guides to doing the right thing. But neither the patient's unconscious desires, nor his or her "true self," nor the analyst's countertransference, nor any research "finding," nor a technically "correct" stance of any kind can wring the disturbing element of choice out of our actions, choice that lacks the kind of foundation we so crave. Again, quoting Yalom (1980): "To be fully aware of one's existential situation means that one becomes aware of self-creation. To be aware of the fact that one constitutes oneself, that there are no absolute external referents, that one assigns an arbitrary meaning to the world, means to become aware of one's fundamental groundlessness" (p. 319). From a critical constructivist view, combining modern and postmodern attitudes, we might amend that and say that one's fundamental groundlessness stands in a dialectical relationship with one's fundamental embeddedness. In this perspective, the aim is to come to grips with the analyst's and the patient's responsibility for coconstructing the reality of their immediate interaction as well as major facets of the patient's life, while at the same time wrestling with the given known and unknown constraints that limit the freedom of the participants.

BEING AN ANALYST

What can we say, finally, about what all this adds up to with respect to what it means to be an analyst or analytic therapist? Whereas I used to think of the great divide in psychoanalysis as that between objectivist and constructivist thinking, I now believe it is more to the point to say that it is between dichotomous and dialectical thinking. These two divides are very closely related, however, because dichotomous thinking is as integral to objectivism as dialectical thinking is to constructivism. To think dichotomously, for example, about what comes from the analyst and what comes from the patient (a special instance of thinking dichotomously of subject and object) is part and parcel of the objectivist view that, in principle, the analyst can discover precisely where his or her contribution and the influence of the current interaction leave off and where the patient's contribution and the influence of intrapsychic dynamics begin. By contrast, to view transference and countertransference as in a dialectical relationship creates a zone of irreducible ambiguity and indeterminacy as to the nature of their interaction and reciprocal influence, a zone that is open to multiple possible interpretive constructions.

Similarly, to think dichotomously about neurotic and existential anxiety is part and parcel of the objectivist view that it is possible for the analyst (and the patient as well, for that matter) to know what it is about the patient's way of being that should be changed and how. By contrast, to view the two types of anxiety as in a dialectical relationship generates uncertainty as to what is best for the patient, what aspects of himself or herself warrant further development as opposed to aspects that might best be left dormant. The dialectic necessitates judgments that have moral and aesthetic dimensions. Because of the simultaneous dialectic of the internal and external sources of self-realization, moreover, the analyst cannot stay out of it. He or she inevitably makes some personal, value-laden contribution to the patient's resolution of neurotic conflicts, interwoven as they inevitably are with existential predicaments.

What I have in mind are conflicts that entail meaningful options that are within reach, practically and psychologically. I'm thinking of patients struggling with difficult, real choices, such as whether to stay with or leave a companion with whom serious difficulties have arisen; whether to pursue an uncertain but somewhat promising career as an artist or stick with a secure professional job that is less personally fulfilling; whether to stay in town for the sake of a newly blossoming relationship with an aging parent or move to a much preferred city where a circle of friends resides and where a wonderful job opportunity has just presented itself. It's easy, of course, to "dismiss" options that are entirely foreign to the patient or that are totally impractical. Most of these never even occur to either participant. It's also easy, in principle at least, to dismiss, or at least identify as undesirable, options that are clearly symptomatic, perhaps self-destructive in an unmistakable way. Options that are totally foreign, impractical, or symptomatic are to the reality of the patient's sense of self and immediate experience as "poor form" responses are to the reality of the stimulus properties of a Rorschach inkblot. In my experience, however, patients are often struggling with alternatives that are quite within their grasp, that are very compelling, and that reflect ambiguous mixtures of neurotic and healthy motives. Even after extensive exploration, often the conflict stubbornly resists being broken down neatly into one between pathology and health. In regard to the brief examples given above, the patient who has the inclination to leave the companion may be in danger of enacting the latest version of a pattern of flight from intimacy and commitment, but it also may be that this particular "object choice" is not a good-enough one for the patient and that to stay would amount to an unfortunate, panicky flight from the repeating pattern itself. The patient considering staying in town to spend time with his or her aging parent may be governed, in the wish to stay, by lifelong debilitating separation anxiety stemming from early abandonments, but the desire to leave may be driven by terror of the parent dying and by a wish to escape dealing with that final separation. There is a danger, moreover, that such a flight will interrupt a connection with the parent that is deepening for the first time in terms of the development of mutual understanding and respect. In the case of the aspiring artist, perhaps throwing himself or herself into painting and sculpturing would be the long-overdue attempt to defy conventional and family expectations and, finally, to give neglected talents a chance. But if we envision dependents at home who would suddenly lose a primary provider who had previously committed himself or herself to their care, how enthusiastic can we be about his or her new venture? The plot would thicken, of course, if we found that the patient was devastated as a child when his or her father abandoned the family altogether to pursue a career in writing, an experiment that never amounted to anything and that left the family destitute. The specter of repetition via identification with the aggressor would certainly loom large in that case. Even then, of course, it would not follow like night does day what path would be healthiest to pursue. Maybe the son or daughter is more talented than the father. Certainly, a course driven by zealous counteridentificaton would be as dubious as one driven by zealous identification.

What is out of the question from a dialectical-constructivist view is that analysts can avoid any involvement with questions such as these and devote themselves exclusively to latent meanings having to do with intrapsychic dynamics, with archaic representations of self and other, with internal object relations, and the like. Events are transpiring and choices are being made right under the analyst's nose. To be silent about them at certain moments might inadvertantly be to speak volumes favoring one course of action or another. Moreover, the chances are high that through whatever he or she does say, and even through his or her tone of voice, the analyst will influence the patient in some way. If the analyst is invested in being a neutral presence, fostering only the patient's self-awareness and freedom, that influence is likely to be disclaimed and left unexamined.

Although the analyst cannot avoid making a personal contribution when these kinds of predicaments arise, he or she can also work hard with the patient to interpret unconscious factors that operate on either side of a conflict, colored as they may be by the immediate relational context. Also, the analyst's involvement need not take the form of an opinion as to what the patient should do. In my own experience, it is often the case that I simply do not know which of the courses under consideration would be best. I can struggle with the patient in weighing the options, but I'm not withholding anything as a matter of analytic principle when I say "I don't know." There are other occasions when I find myself leaning one way or another. Depending upon the strength of my conviction, I will encourage the patient to take my viewpoint with more or less of a grain of salt, sometimes assisting in that regard by revealing, if I can find it, some aspect of my own life that bears upon my bias. In some cases I've been able to help the patient arrive at a reasonable compromise, although such compromises usually entail sacrifice of important constituent elements of both sides of the conflict.

Fuller examples of the analyst's authority and personal influence can be found in ensuing chapters (see especially chapters 3, and 6 through 10). Returning to my central focus here, to think dialectically about the subordination of the analyst's subjectivity, desire, and moral perspective, on the one hand, and their emergence into the foreground in the analytic field, on the other, is to recognize that adherence to analytic discipline, whatever "book" one goes by, is personally expressive, and that conversely, it is possible for spontaneous self expression to be informed by theoretical wisdom and by a sense of what is in the patient's best long-term interest.

The analytic situation remains, nevertheless, highly peculiar and contrived as a context for promoting trustworthy mentorship, understanding, and affirmation. Analytic therapy can be viewed both as a cultural instrument of healing and as a cultural symptom, a symptom in which we are so fully absorbed that we cannot discern its shape, its impact, or its etiology. When the patient rages that he or she feels seduced by our explicit and implicit promises and then abandoned by the impersonal realities of time and money that define the arrangement, the analyst who thinks dialectically knows that he or she may be the last person to be able unilaterally to correctly assess the validity of the patient's grievances. So much of the meaning of what the analytic therapist is doing is deeply buried in his or her unconscious, which partakes partly of the collective unconscious of the culture. Dimen (1994) touches on the irony and complexity of this issue when she writes, "I think of psychoanalysis as the perfect therapy for a culture of alienation, for in it you pay a stranger to recover yourself. Paradoxically, psychotherapy that is bought and sold under conditions of alienation generates a 'dis-ease' in both the person who pays the stranger and the stranger who is paid, and that needs treatment too" (pp. 81–82). In a manner that echoes the dialectic of repetition and new experience (chapters 6 through 10), the exploitative potentials of the analytic process can be partially transcended and transformed through the analyst's owning of those features of the frame while still doing his or her best to overcome them. That effort is complemented by recognition of the connection between the peculiarities and absurdities of the analytic situation and those of human life itself, regardless of culture or historical period.

To be an analyst means not only tolerating but embracing multiple dialectics and the element of uncertainty that they entail. It means accepting one's daunting responsibility as the inheritor of functions that used to be reserved for the omniscient parents, for "the gods," at the same time that one interprets and participates in a spirit of mutuality with the patient, a spirit that exposes one's personal vulnerability, fallibility, and even one's possible exploitativeness. It means allowing oneself to get caught up in various forms of transference-countertransference enactments while still striving, often against mutual resistance, but also often with the patient's help, to create something new in the relationship that could open new ways of being for the patient and, perhaps, for oneself. It means continually working temporarily to reverse figure and ground in order to get in touch with as much of the potential afforded by the analytic situation as one can within the constraints of one's role and personal limitations. The challenge is to see and bring into the open many such figure-ground reversals: the analyst within the patient and the patient within oneself, the personal in the technical and the technical in the personal, the resonance of the past in the present and the impact of the present upon one's reading of the past, one's influence as it bears upon the patient's initiative and one's responsiveness to the patient as it bears on one's own initiative, the analytic arrangement as emotionally deadening and the analytic arrangement as the framework for liberating understanding and affirmation. In regard to the last, being an analytic therapist means accepting the challenge of struggling, creatively and collaboratively, to find forms of engagement through which the patient's own capacity for love, and for courageous, honest, and creative living—despite, and because of, full awareness of mortality—can be newly discovered and inspired.

◆ 2 ◆

Death Anxiety and Adaptation to Mortality in Psychoanalytic Theory

Whereas, historically, the subject of adaptation and mourning in relation to object loss has been the focus of considerable attention in the psychoanalytic literature (Pollock, 1961; Siggins, 1966; Miller, 1971),[1] relatively little attention has been paid to the process by which the individual anticipates, reacts to, and comes to terms with his or her own death. The discrepancy is less extreme when the comparison is limited, as perhaps it should be, to writings about *anticipation* of object loss in contradistinction to those dealing with the anticipation of one's own mortality (the loss of the self), because the literature on anticipatory mourning in general is relatively sparse (Futterman, Hoffman, and Sabshin, 1972). Nevertheless, of the three topics—adaptation following object loss, adaptation in anticipation of object loss, and adaptation in anticipation of the loss of the self— the last has undoubtedly been investigated and discussed least.[2]

Those psychoanalytically oriented authors who were contributors in the 60s and 70s to the dramatic groundswell of scientific interest in the psychology of death and dying, or "thanatology," generally agreed that psychoanalysis had not accumulated a body of clinical

---

An earlier version of this chapter appeared in 1979 in *The Annual of Psychoanalysis*, 7:233–267 (New York: International Universities Press).

1. For a more recent review see Hagman, 1995.

2. This assertion regarding the relative neglect of this subject in psychoanalysis was made in the late 1970s, but I believe it is true to this day.

observations in this area and had given the subject relatively little emphasis theoretically. Eissler (1955), for example, foreshadowing the movement, was struck by the failure of psychoanalysis to build upon Freud's original formulations:

> Since Freud has made death a central concept of his psychological system one would have expected that psychoanalysis would devote more effort to the study of death itself. Strangely enough, this has not happened. In general, death is still viewed as a purely biological phenomenon unless it is consciously or unconsciously induced by man himself [p. 39].

More than 20 years later, Avery Weissman (1977) observed that along with psychiatry as a whole, psychoanalysts had avoided the subject:

> Schur's contemporary study of Freud's thoughts about death and extinction underscores this anomaly. Suffering as he did from incurable cancer, Freud wrote much that would be useful for analysts. However, the clues that Freud offered have virtually been ignored. Psychoanalysts have preferred to revise the inexorability of death into a more acceptable form, which can then be "analyzed" as a symptom of something else, and whisked away. Like other people, psychiatrists are afraid of death [p. 112].

Eissler and Weissman emphasize psychological and sociological factors that may inhibit exploration of the psychological implications of mortality. However, in directing attention to the provocative germinal aspects of Freud's contribution, they gloss over those aspects of Freud's theoretical position which are themselves discouraging of further investigation—to some extent because the ideas are unclear or confusing but, more importantly, because their overall thrust is in the direction of discounting awareness of death as a psychologically important variable in human development and psychopathology.[3]

The present chapter begins with a critical review of Freud's attitudes on the subject of death. The survey is not intended to be comprehensive with respect to all of Freud's statements on the topic, but I believe that it does deal with the main points of view and theoretical positions that he adopted. Some ideas of later authors that have their origins in Freud are interpolated; in some instances the perpet-

---

3. Regrettably, this article was first published before I became aware of Ernest Becker's (1973) profound exploration of this subject, complete with a systematic critique of Freudian theory for its "denial of death."

uation in the later contributions of points of confusion or internal inconsistency in Freud's thinking is demonstrated. It is shown that the beginnings of an existential perspective—one in which awareness of mortality is viewed as a major factor in human adaptation—can be discerned in some of Freud's writings. These ideas, however, are not enlarged upon theoretically, in part because Freud adhered to certain questionable assumptions about cognitive development and its psychological significance.

The second section is a review of the perspectives of three post-Freudian theorists: Hartmann, Erikson, and Kohut. On the one hand, it includes some speculation on possible characteristics of Hartmann's ego psychology, which tend to thwart the development of a theory of adaptation to mortality, as contrasted with the characteristics of Erikson's and Kohut's "whole self" psychologies, which lend themselves to it more readily. On the other hand, Erikson and Kohut are also faulted for failing to capitalize upon Freud's notion of a hierarchy of anxiety experiences with conflict and ambivalence at every level, and for favoring, instead, an idealized, even mystical concept of healthy adaptation to mortality. The result is that the opportunity to construct a much needed bridge between the psychoanalytic and existential perspectives on the psychological impact of awareness of death is missed.

In the third section I present some of my own findings on the adaptation of parents to the loss of a child, focusing especially upon the heightened awareness of their own mortality that parents experienced following the child's death. The findings are consistent with a developmental perspective on adaptation in which coming to terms with the boundaries of the self in time is viewed as analogous to self-differentiation in physical and social space.[4]

The final section of the chapter points to two areas requiring further study. In the field of cognitive psychology, it addresses the relative paucity of data on the emergence of concepts of death in the course of development and the effects of anxiety upon this process. In the field of clinical psychoanalysis and psychoanalytic psychotherapy, it addresses the relative lack of data on the issue of adaptation to mortality as it presents itself in the clinical situation, especially with middle-aged and older patients.

---

4. When this paper was originally written I was much less sensitive than I am today to the culturally relative aspects of the Western conception of an autonomous, bounded, unified self (see Cushman, 1995; Flax, 1996; Mitchell, 1993).

FREUD'S POSITION ON AWARENESS OF
DEATH AND DEATH ANXIETY

Freud presents no single, coherent theoretical position on the issue of adaptation to mortality. I believe the various statements that Freud made and the attitudes that he expressed can be usefully classified in relation to four distinct, only partially developed positions or points of view. These are: (1) the point of view associated with the topographic model of the mind; (2) the point of view associated with the concept of the death instinct; (3) the point of view associated with the development of the structural model; and (4) the "existential" point of view stated succinctly and informally in "On Transience" (1916a).

The Point of View Associated with
the Topographic Model

Freud's statements about death prior to the publication of "The Ego and the Id" in 1923 centered upon the attributes of the unconscious. Among the most frequently cited of all Freud's (1915) remarks on the subject is the following:

> It is indeed impossible to imagine our own death; and whenever we attempt to do so we can perceive that we are in fact still present as spectators. Hence the psycho-analytic school could venture on the assertion that at bottom no one believes in his own death, or, to put the same thing in another way, that in the unconscious every one of us is convinced of his own immortality [p. 289].

Here Freud is emphatic in asserting that the difficulty in conceiving of death is derived from a fundamental cognitive limitation. The statement, however, has two parts, which Freud offers as essentially equivalent. The first part has to do with what we might "attempt" to "imagine" and with what we can "perceive." Presumably, this is the language of consciousness and constitutes the idea of cognitive limitation proper. The second half of the statement refers to a universal belief in the unconscious in immortality. How or why the second part of the statement is merely a paraphrase of the first part, as Freud claims ("to put the same thing in another way"), is far from obvious. The proposition, moreover, that "in the unconscious every one of us is convinced of his own immortality" is problematic in itself, since, allegedly, the unconscious is totally oblivious to time:

> The processes of the system *Ucs.* are *timeless*; i.e. they are not ordered temporally, are not altered by the passage of time; they have no reference to time at all. Reference to time is bound up, once again, with the work of the system *Cs.* [Freud, 1914b, p. 187].

Obliviousness to time would seem to preclude belief in either mortality or immortality in the unconscious. Moreover, to the extent that what people believe is determined by what they can concretely imagine, they can believe in their immortality no more than they can believe in their mortality. Eissler (1955) is mistaken in this respect when, following Freud's lead, he says, "Man's eternal life can be the content of a thought and can also be imagined in conformity with man's incapacity to imagine death" (p. 71). Both concepts, of mortality and immortality, require a notion of time extending endlessly, to infinity. As Kafka (1972) puts it, "the idea of immortality refers to the wish for the infinite extension into time of the self" (p. 666). People can no more imagine—again in the concrete sense of picturing it—time extended forever in their presence than they can imagine time extended forever in their absence.

Thus, on the one hand, Freud attributes to the unconscious a belief that it cannot hold because of the alleged timelessness of its processes. On the other hand, beginning with the dubious assumption that what can be meaningfully comprehended, what can "at bottom" be believed, derives entirely from what can be concretely imagined (cf. Schimek, 1975), he makes an erroneous assumption that the prospect of mortality defies imagination, whereas the prospect of immortality does not.

During this period, Freud is also unclear on another point. We find, along with the notion of cognitive limitation, a recognition, before the development of the structural model, of an inevitable tendency to avoid facing death because of the narcissistic injury that knowledge of its reality inflicts. In "On Narcissism" Freud (1914a) says, "At the most touchy point in the narcissistic system, the immortality of the ego, which is so hard pressed by reality, security is achieved by taking refuge in the child" (p. 91). But how can the "immortality of the ego" be so threatened if death cannot be grasped in any meaningful sense in awareness and if the unconscious holds nothing but a belief in immortality? Freud's (1915) lack of conceptual clarity on this issue is also striking in the following statements, in which the language of cognitive limitation is hopelessly entangled with the language of defensive avoidance of a painful and, if anything, all too well-comprehended reality:

His own death was just as *unimaginable and unreal* for primaeval man as it is for any one of us to-day. But there was for him one case in which the two opposite attitudes towards death collided and came into conflict with each other; and this case became highly important and productive of far-reaching consequences. It occurred when primaeval man saw somebody who belonged to him die—his wife, his child, his friend—whom he undoubtedly loved as we love ours, for love cannot be much younger than the lust to kill. Then, in his pain, *he was forced to learn that one can die, too, oneself, and his whole being revolted against the admission;* for each of these loved ones was, after all, a part of his own beloved self [p. 293; italics added].

And further:

Man could no longer keep death at a distance, for he had tasted it in his pain about the dead; but he was nevertheless *unwilling to acknowledge it*, for he *could not conceive* of himself as dead. So he devised a compromise: he conceded the fact of his own death as well, but *denied it the significance of annihilation*—a significance which he had no motive for denying where the death of his enemy was concerned [p. 294; italics added].

Once again, how can it be that a human being's "whole being revolted against the admission" of something that to begin with cannot be a content of subjective experience in any profound sense—something that is, rather, "unimaginable and unreal"? How can a danger that is a priori inconceivable be one that a person is unwilling to acknowledge? The language of defense grants implicitly (or even explicitly, as in "he was forced to learn that one can die, too, oneself") that awareness of death is a very real dimension of experience and one that is threatening in a unique and devastating way. Indeed, it would seem to follow from the point of view of defense that it is the admission of death and/or its significance that is relegated to the unconscious, whereas denial prevails in consciousness. Thus, in the defensive formulation, the relation between what is conscious and what is unconscious is the reverse of what Freud claimed. Instead of an unconscious belief in immortality, the defensive formulation suggests an idea of mortality that is fended off in favor of a conscious belief in immortality, one that is more compatible with the "narcissistic system."

Even as Freud's theory of defense evolved and crystallized with the development of the structural model, the signal theory of anxiety, and the concepts of disavowal and splitting of the ego, he clung to and reiterated the idea that awareness of death and death anxiety were impossible as such because one's own death defied imagination. Nevertheless, it is this most naive of Freud's various points of view about death which is often reflexively and uncritically cited by subsequent authors as though it were the ultimate expression of wisdom on the subject. And it is this idea in Freud, either selectively seized upon or thrown together with the other attitudes he expressed, which became a part of his legacy, and which may be one of the factors that has contributed to the relative silence of psychoanalysis on this issue. Fenichel's (1945) position epitomizes the common psychoanalytic view of awareness of death and anxiety about death as, essentially, epiphenomena:

> It is questionable whether there is any such thing as a normal fear of death; actually the idea of death is subjectively inconceivable [cites Freud, 1915], and therefore probably every fear of death covers other unconscious ideas [pp. 208–209].

In Eissler (1955), we find the conceptual wavering and inconsistency that we find in Freud perpetuated and elaborated. Addressing the issue of the child's development of awareness of death he writes:

> As Freud has shown, the problem of death is beyond the child's mental capacity. The utmost he can comprehend is the concept of absence. . . . Refined research into this matter might show that the child's inquiry into the generative processes is a secondary edition of an earlier and short-lasting inquiry into death. Possibly the child turns away from such an inquiry because of the accompanying horror and because of the utter hopelessness and ensuing despair about any possible progress in his investigation [p. 62].

The idea that the child "turns away" because of his "horror" is, in effect, the defensive formulation, and amounts to an admission that at some point the child's comprehension of mortality, like that of Freud's primeval man, may be profound indeed. This idea overrides the notion that the child turns away simply because of the "utter hopelessness" of the inquiry, that is, because of cognitive limitation. If anything, the latter claim could well be understood as a protestation of ignorance, which itself has a defensive function. Even though Eissler does take pains to point out that "man cannot imagine [death] although he knows it" (p. 62), the litanous reiteration of the truism that the state of death cannot be pictured, and the associated claim that death has no representation in the unconscious (pp. 28, 36–37, 62) have a chilling effect on Eissler's own notion that knowledge of death is the source of a unique kind of anxiety with extensive implications for adaptation.

The Point of View Associated with the Concept of the Death Instinct

Although Eissler (1955) regards "Beyond the Pleasure Principle" (1920) as "the cornerstone of [Freud's] thanatological system" (p. 30), in important respects this essay does not deal with the issue of adaptation to mortality at all. Within the framework of the attempt to conceptualize behavior and development in terms, exclusively, of the interplay of biological instinctual forces, cognition—including cognitive appraisal of the meaning of death—has little or no importance. The life and death instincts are essentially blind organic forces. Even the ego's interest in self-preservation is conceptualized in instinctual terms, first as a component of the death instinct "whose function it is to assure that the organism shall follow its own path to death" (p. 29), and later as an expression of Eros and as libidinal in character (p. 52). In either case, the ego's relation to death is not portrayed in terms of an adaptation that has an appraisal of the meaning of death as its point of departure.

It is beyond the scope of this essay to evaluate the concept of the death instinct in terms of its validity or theoretical utility. What is relevant, however, is to consider how expressions of a hypothetical death instinct might impinge upon a reflective, self-conscious ego. In this regard, it is essential to differentiate a wish to be relieved of the tension or pain associated with consciousness from a wish to embrace death, fully comprehended as permanent nonbeing. Freud (1920) does not make this distinction, but it is clear that the death instinct is most directly represented in experience as an immediate longing for a loss of consciousness, which is oblivious to time and is, therefore, ignorant of the meaning of death:

> The dominating tendency of mental life, and perhaps of nervous life in general, is the effort to reduce, to keep constant or to remove internal tension due to stimuli . . . a tendency which finds expression in the pleasure principle; and our recognition of that fact is one of the strongest reasons for believing in the existence of death instincts [pp. 55–56].

The link described later by Freud between the death instinct and sexual gratification (p. 62) highlights the gulf that separates the former from a genuine wish to die. As Schur (1972) observes, Freud was not careful to distinguish instinctual aims from their possible *consequences* (p. 324). The wish to experience pleasure or reduction of pain, tension, or discomfort through loss of consciousness has little relation to a wish to embrace one's own permanent extinction. It is the permanence itself, the irreversibility of the loss, that neither the instinct nor its psychological representations take into account. It is possible, of course, that eagerness to escape pain could result in actions that are fatal, but this eventuality could be conceptualized as a breakdown either in the ego's capacity to assess the consequences of the act or in its ability to regulate behavior in accord with such an assessment.

I believe that one of the reasons that Eissler's (1955) discussion lacks conceptual consistency and precision is that he fails to make this important distinction. In one breath he seems to acknowledge the ego's special readiness to comprehend, dread, and recoil from permanent loss of consciousness (i.e., death):

> The ego must learn to integrate the biological function of sleep which is fully formed during the initial phases of development. Only the certainty that the ego will find the world of objects again makes sleep a pleasurable process. The slightest doubt about the prospect of reawakening actually results in grave sleeping disturbances in the adult [p. 73].

But in the next breath, taking off from Freud's linking of the aims of the death instinct with those of sexual drives, he is prepared to portray the ego as blithely welcoming its own demise:

> It is my impression that at the height of true orgasm, when for moments the ego is lost, and during the subsequent short time of complete satiation, when the ego is also inaccessible to external or internal stimulation, a person is ready to surrender to death without struggle [p. 76].

To what, exactly, is the person "ready to surrender" in such a state? Is it death, or rather a loss of consciousness that is assumed to be reversible? If Eissler is saying, in effect, that the ego's functioning is impaired at the height of orgasm, so that appraisal of reality is reduced or absent, it would follow that the person, under such circumstances, is simply unaware of danger and therefore unlikely to struggle against it. Saying this is not the same as saying that the person is "ready" to surrender to death. To equate the two is like equating the observation that it is easy to kill a person who is sleeping with the claim that such a helpless victim is "ready" to die.

Theoretically, one could posit an instinctually based wish to lose consciousness, which under certain circumstances would threaten to obliterate the ego's capacity to be aware of the full implications of death and would result, therefore, in suicidal actions that are essentially miscalculations. In the interest of achieving certain immediate aims, the ego is, as it were, seduced into ignoring or denying the ultimate, irreversible consequences of self-destructive actions. But, again, the ego's relation to the proximate aims of the wish to lose consciousness remains quite different from its relation to the prospect of death as such. Only the latter entails a relatively advanced level of cognitive development and of ego development generally.

It is noteworthy that Freud (1920) wondered whether the idea of a death instinct might not have some defensive purpose, guarding against the full impact of an ego-alien fate:

> Perhaps we have adopted the belief because there is some comfort in it. If we are to die ourselves, and first lose in death those who are dearest to us, it is easier to submit to a remorseless law of nature, to the sublime Ἀνάγχη [Necessity], than to a chance which might perhaps have been escaped. It may be, however, that this belief in the internal necessity of dying is only another one of those illusions which we have created *"um die Schwere des Daseins zu ertragen"* [to bear the burden of existence] [p. 45].

The Point of View Associated with the Development of the Structural Model

The structural model actually provided a theoretical framework within which Freud potentially could have organized his ideas about mortality into an internally consistent and coherent position. As the concepts of the ego and the id crystallized, the properties that were, in the topographic model, the defining characteristics of the unconscious (or the system Ucs.) were attributed to the id instead. This theoretical advance makes it possible to conceive of unconscious ideas that are mediated by the ego and have the stamp of its perceptual and cognitive capability. As Freud (1933) put it in the "New Introductory Lectures":

> We perceive that we have no right to name the mental region that is foreign to the ego "the system *Ucs.*," since the characteristic of being unconscious is not restricted to it. Very well; we will no longer use the

term "unconscious" in the systematic sense and we will give what we have hitherto so described a better name and one no longer open to misunderstanding . . . we will in the future call it the "id" [p. 72].

And of particular relevance to our purposes here he says:

There is nothing in the id that corresponds to the idea of time; there is no recognition of the passage of time, and—a thing that is most remarkable and awaits consideration in philosophical thought—no alteration in its mental processes is produced by the passage of time [p. 74].

This revised position attributing timelessness to the id rather than to the unconscious and allowing the quality of unconsciousness to characterize aspects of the ego is often not taken into account or capitalized upon by other writers on the subject of time and immortality. Like Fenichel (1945) in the statement quoted earlier, Bonaparte (1940, p. 445) and Eissler (1955, p. 28) cite Freud's earlier position rather than his later one. Pollock (1971a,b) is apparently alone in attending to the transition to the later formulation, but he speaks in terms of an *expansion* of Freud's ideas within the context of the structural model (1971a, p. 441), perhaps missing the full theoretical potential of the revision. That this may be the case is also suggested by the fact that he goes on to summarize Bonaparte's discussion of timelessness as an attribute of the *unconscious*, as though the reinterpretation in line with the structural model is not of particular importance.

Pollock's (1971a) account of human beings' relation to death is cast, unquestionably, in terms of anxiety and defense, although the specific details of the fit of his description with the structural model are not spelled out:

Unlike all other forms of life man has a foreknowledge of his own death, even if it is only at an intellectual level. This transitoriness has given rise to the religious notion of immortality and to the dichotomy of body and soul. . . . Thus the notion of immortality is a way of arresting or reversing the irreversible flow of time toward death. . . . This optimistic hope of a world to come, where time has stopped and there is reunion and everlasting continuity, is a defense against the total helplessness associated with the "nothingness" of nonlife, be it death or the earliest states of infancy [p. 441].

A total lack of any sense of time in the id, as Pollock does emphasize (1971b, pp. 237–238), has to do with the obliviousness to time that is associated with the seeking of immediate discharge of drive tension. The preemptory nature of instinctual demands, however, whether located in the id or, as was earlier the case, in the system Ucs., is not the equivalent of a belief in immortality. To the extent that the latter develops, it arises as a defensive, restitutive response to the impact of a cognitive and emotional appreciation of the meaning of death. Both the belief in mortality and the belief in immortality can only be contents within the ego. Consistent with Pollock's account, the former would be identified with the conscious sector of the ego, the latter with its unconscious sector. The simultaneous presence, at different levels, of both beliefs amounts to a special case of disavowal and "splitting of the ego" (Freud, 1927b; 1940a, pp. 202–204; 1940b), although, significantly, it was never explicitly considered as such by Freud.

It is noteworthy, however, that Pollock actually stops short of allowing for a cognitive development in the ego that would make death anxiety as such possible. In the above statement, he suggests that a human being's "foreknowledge of his own death" may exist "only at an intellectual level." It is difficult to imagine how an awareness that is merely "intellectual," assuming that the connotation of relative superficiality is intended, can be the instigator of such massive defensive strategies, cutting across cultures and historical epochs. That Pollock is aware of this incongruity is evident in the fact that he feels the need to find the point of contact of death anxiety with something that for him is deeper and more real. And he finds this deeper echo in the individual's anxiety about helplessness. Pollock (1971b), in keeping with what has been adopted as Freud's legacy, comes down on the side of denying that death as such is anything that a person can really sense and fear: "I would suggest that, viewed retrospectively, the anxiety may not be about death and nothingness, which *cannot be conceptualized*, but the fear of absolute helplessness that does characterize the very early state of existence" (p. 250; italics added).

In keeping with the terms of the structural model and those of the signal theory of anxiety (Freud, 1926a), it would be logical to propose that there is an aspect of the mind that is oblivious to time—the id—and another aspect that comprehends time and should be the exclusive domain of ideas about mortality as well as immortality, whether these ideas are conscious, preconscious, or unconscious. Signal anxiety in response to a glimmer of an appreciation of the permanent annihilatory significance of one's own death could instigate defensive operations that would interrupt the development of this germ of an idea and its accompanying affect, relegating both to unconscious status while fostering a narcissistically comforting belief in immortality in consciousness. The situation could be more complex, of course. For example, the affect alone could be disavowed, so that a conscious claim of disbelief in immortality could be, in fact, merely an intellectual defense. It could conceal a well-guarded unconscious fantasy of immortality held in defiance of a still more deeply buried acknowledgment of the painful inevitability of one's own death (much like an unconscious fantasy of oedipal triumph can guard against a still more deeply buried sense of oedipal defeat).

With the notion of developmental transformations of anxiety and the idea that "each period of the individual's life has its appropriate determinant of anxiety" (Freud, 1926a, p. 142), all the conceptual tools necessary for integrating death anxiety into psychoanalytic theory seem to be ready at hand. But Freud again stops short of granting the same psychologically meaningful status to death as a danger that he grants to the other types of dangers that are encountered in the course of development. In this connection it is important to distinguish two points in Freud's thinking: one applies to any form of anxiety in the series, the other Freud reserved only for anxiety about death. The first has to do with the fact that each form of anxiety has continuity with, and incorporates qualities of, all the forms of anxiety that precede it. Thus, for example, castration anxiety is comprehensible only with reference to its predecessor, separation anxiety:

> The significance of the loss of the object as a determinant of anxiety extends considerably further. For the next transformation of anxiety, viz. the castration anxiety belonging to the phallic phase, is also a fear of separation and is thus attached to the same determinant. In this case, the danger is of being separated from one's genitals [pp. 138–139].

Similarly, moral anxiety has certain properties in common with castration anxiety at the same time that it introduces something qualitatively new:

> With the depersonalization of the parental agency from which castration was feared, the danger becomes less defined. Castration anxiety develops into moral anxiety—social anxiety—and it is not so easy to know what the anxiety is about . . . what the ego regards as the danger and responds to with an anxiety-signal is that the super-ego should be angry with it or punish it or cease to love it [pp. 139–140].

Finally, the fear of death[5] grows out of the fear of the superego:

> The final transformation which the fear of the super-ego undergoes is, it seems to me, the fear of death (or fear for life) which is a fear of the super-ego projected on to the powers of destiny [p. 140].

The idea of developmental continuity is not at all incompatible with consideration of anxiety about death as a distinct phenomenon deserving investigation in its own right. The "final transformation which the fear of the super-ego undergoes" could introduce something that is qualitatively new and important psychologically. But this brings us to the second of the two points in Freud's thinking that I referred to before. This point is that fear of death, in Freud's view, does not merely have continuity with the fear that precedes it in the series, but is actually reducible to it. Although Freud acknowledges an intellectual awareness of death, it is an awareness that has no depth and that plays no part in the etiology of neuroses:

> In view of all that we know about the structure of the comparatively simple neuroses of everyday life, it would seem highly improbable that a neurosis could come into being merely because of the objective presence of danger, without any participation of the deeper levels of the mental apparatus. But the unconscious[6] seems to contain nothing that could give any content to our concept of annihilation of life. Castration can be *pictured* on the basis of the daily experience of the faeces being separated from the body or on the basis of losing the mother's breast at weaning. But nothing resembling death can ever have been experienced; or if it has, as in fainting, it has left no *observable traces* behind. I am therefore inclined to adhere to the view that the fear of death should be regarded as analogous to the fear of castration and that the situation to which the ego is reacting is one of being abandoned by the protecting super-ego—the powers of destiny—so that it no longer has any safeguard against all the dangers that surround it [pp. 129–130; italics added].

---

5. Although Freud (1920, pp. 12–13; 1926a, pp. 164–165) made a point of distinguishing between the affect of fear and the affect of anxiety, depending on whether or not the source was known, in his description of the genetic hierarchy of danger situations he seems to use the two terms interchangeably.

6. Here Freud slips back into treating the unconscious as a system with certain formal properties, despite his stated intention, with the development of the structural model, to reserve such characterization for the id, ego, and superego, and to allow aspects of any of these systems to be unconscious.

Here, as before, only what can be literally imagined as a function of a similar previous experience is thought to have representation in the "deeper levels of the mental apparatus," in the unconscious. Later in the same essay (pp. 146–147), Freud again summarizes the various danger situations, now with the particular purpose of demonstrating how each anxiety reaction is rational or justifiable given the associated level of ego development. This, of course, is precisely the kind of theoretical framework into which death anxiety can be readily incorporated. But the way in which the issue has been settled for Freud at this point is evident from the fact that death anxiety is omitted entirely from this account.

Freud's narrow conception of what can gain representation in the unconscious results in a theoretical dead end. Actually, the logical implication of his position is that even the notion of the permanent loss of objects (feces, breasts, whole objects, or whatever) cannot be represented in the unconscious because the permanence itself, the irreversibility of the change, is, strictly speaking, unimaginable. The most a person, child or adult, can "picture" is the absence of the object during a given finite period. The conclusion that the object will *never* be restored requires a kind of inductive leap beyond the concrete experience. I would argue that this leap brings with it a sense of the meaning of "never" that is quite real and anxiety provoking even though no concrete image is associated with it. Freud did not seem to question the capacity of the child or the adult to develop this kind of awareness relative to object loss. In fact, he takes note of a possible precursor of this awareness in the infant:

> Certain things seem to be joined together in it which will later be separated out. It cannot as yet distinguish between temporary absence and permanent loss. As soon as it loses sight of its mother it behaves as if it were *never* going to see her again; and repeated consoling experiences to the contrary are necessary before it learns that her disappearance is usually followed by her re-appearance [1926, p. 169; italics added].

Of mourning, Freud states: "Mourning occurs under the influence of reality-testing; for the latter demands categorically from the bereaved person that he should separate himself from the object, since it no longer exists" (p. 172).

But reality testing, in the sense of concrete perception, can only record the absence of the object (the object is not here *now*; the object has not returned *yet*), it cannot record the irreversibility of the absence. The latter can only be sensed as a function of the unfolding—in the context of interaction with the environment—of an endogenous cognitive structure. Because Freud seems not to have recognized the jump beyond immediate experience that mourning the death of an object entails, his theorizing about object loss was not aborted by the empiricist leaning that can be discerned in his writings on the subject of the individual anticipating his own death.[7]

In fact, children have not only had regular experiences of loss of consciousness in sleep (Freud's choice of the exceptional experience of fainting rather than that of sleep is a puzzling one), but are also aware that other objects die, disappear, or are consumed or destroyed. They have only to identify with the lost object, or more precisely, to reach that stage of development which would enable them to identify with the anticipated perspectives of other people (survivors) in relation to themselves as permanently lost objects, to sense the threat that death poses. Of course, it is impossible to literally picture a "state" of death or nonbeing. But such an image is hardly necessary in order for anxiety about death to have a profound and unique meaning at the same time that it has continuity with developmentally earlier forms of anxiety.[8]

The sense in which we grasp the meaning of irreversibility, of something going on "forever"—in other words, the sense in which we grasp the meaning of "infinity" as the background of our finite being—is neither a function of direct experience alone nor a function of reason alone. The meaning of infinity is sensed at an unconscious, visceral level. We have a profound sense of that meaning, which, although it eludes rational, verbal comprehension, is pervasively organizing of experience. It is implicit in all abstract thought, in that such uniquely human, self-conscious activity coincides with recognition that every particular in our experience is a minute instance of infinite possible instances that stretch beyond what we can possibly experience concretely. Consider these reflections on the subject by Merleau-Ponty (1964):

> To be aware of death and to think or reason are one and the same thing, since one thinks only by disregarding what is characteristic of life and thus by conceiving death.
> Man cannot be made unaware of death except by being reduced to the state of an animal, and then he would be a poor animal if he retained any part of his consciousness, since consciousness implies the

---

7. See Schimek (1975) for an extensive discussion of Freud's associationism and its impact upon psychoanalytic theory.

8. The rest of this section is an addition to the original article.

ability to step back from any given thing and to deny it. An animal can quietly find contentment in life and can seek salvation in reproduction; man's only access to the universal is the fact that he exists instead of merely living. This is the price he pays for his humanity. . . . Life can only be thought of as revealed to a consciousness of life which denies it.

All consciousness is therefore unhappy, since it knows it is a secondary form of life and misses the innocence from which it senses it came [p. 67].

So, awareness of the universal is wedded to awareness of death, just as awareness of the particular is wedded to awareness of being. But beyond those linkages, there is an *interdependence*, echoing the dialectical relationship discussed in chapter 1, between death and the universal on the one hand, and being and the particular on the other:

Death is the negation of all particular given beings, and consciousness of death is a synonym for consciousness of the universal, but it is only an empty or abstract universal as long as we remain at this point. We cannot in fact conceive nothingness except against a ground of being (or as Sartre says, against the world). Therefore, any notion of death which claims to hold our attention is deceiving us, since it is in fact surreptitiously using our consciousness of being. To plumb our awareness of death, we must transmute it into life, "interiorize" it, as Hegel said. The abstract universal which starts out opposed to life must be made concrete. There is no being without nothingness, but nothingness can exist only in the hollow of being, and so consciousness of death carries with it the means for going beyond it [pp. 67–68].

Anticipating what is to come in ensuing chapters (especially chapters 3, 5, 9, and 10), we can think of psychoanalysis as an institution that has just that underlying purpose: finding that means within consciousness for confronting and "going beyond" mortality, that is, the means for investing in the particulars of living in the context of— even through—awareness of their negation.

The Existential Point of View Expressed Informally in "On Transience"

In his brief essay "On Transience" (1916a), Freud conveys a perspective on mortality that he never crystallized into a formal theoretical position. Because it was not integrated into Freud's theoretical system, and because it serves as a bridge to the more existentially oriented "whole self" theorists to be discussed later, it is taken up here out of chronological sequence with Freud's other points of view. In this perspective, the transience of any experience is considered in terms of its impact upon the value and meaningfulness of that experience. This perspective can be considered "existential" insofar as it implies an effort, typical of existentialism, to grapple with the problem of value as it arises when the individual is confronted with his or her own finitude.

In point of fact, Freud does not explicitly deal with the impact of the individual's anticipation of his or her own death in this essay, but rather with the "foretaste of mourning" (p. 306) that is experienced in considering the transience of cherished objects. Nevertheless, his remarks are sufficiently general to be readily applied to both kinds of awareness. In fact, some of his statements are ambiguous enough to suggest that he might have intended both meanings.

Freud contrasts the attitude shared by his companions, the friend and the poet, with his own. For the friend and the poet, the transience of beautiful things diminishes their worth, whereas for Freud their worth is increased because "transience value is scarcity value in time" (p. 305). Freud explains the attitude of his companions as "a revolt in their minds against mourning" (p. 306). The implication seems to be that his own more sanguine view is made possible not by avoidance, but by a greater willingness to experience the "foretaste of mourning" without trying to defend against it by depreciating time-limited experience. However, this account is less than convincing since, after all, it would seem that the sadness of Freud's companions is a direct expression of their anticipatory mourning, not merely a revolt against it. And, in fact, Freud earlier described the poet's despondency as, in effect, the opposite of a defensive posture:

> The proneness to decay of all that is beautiful and perfect can, as we know, give rise to two different impulses in the mind. The one leads to the aching despondency felt by the young poet, while the other leads to rebellion against the act asserted. No! it is impossible that all this loveliness of Nature and Art, of the world of our sensations and of the world outside, will really fade away into nothing. It would be too senseless and too presumptuous to believe it. Somehow or other this loveliness must be able to persist and to escape all the powers of destruction [p. 305].

Freud then introduces his own attitude, which he does not, however, list as yet another of the possible "impulses in the mind." It is as though his own attitude, that of affirmation of worth and value, stands outside his theoretical propositions about mental life:

But this demand for immortality is a product of our wishes too unmistakable to lay claim to reality: what is painful may none the less be true. I could not see my way to dispute the transience of all things, nor could I insist upon an exception in favour of what is beautiful and perfect. But I did dispute the pessimistic poet's view that the transience of what is beautiful involves any loss of worth.

On the contrary, an increase! Transience value is scarcity value in time. Limitation of the possibility of an enjoyment raises the value of the enjoyment [p. 305].

In effect, three kinds of adaptations to the reality of temporal limitation are described: acknowledgment with despair, acknowledgment with affirmation, and denial. Freud does not take the step of regarding the two different kinds of affective responses to the acknowledgment of transience as two sides of a likely, or even inevitable, ambivalence *within* the individual. He does not take the step of formulating the issue in terms of a fundamental paradox, namely, that awareness of temporal limitation threatens to divest things of their value and lends them value at the same time. It follows from this paradox that death represents not only a danger, but also a kind of necessary boundary which gives impetus to the assignment of value and meaning to experience. In the language of the structural model and ego psychology, one might say that the confrontation with transience and mortality gives rise to an intrasystemic conflict in the ego (cf. Hartmann, 1964, pp. 135–139), both sides of which can be conscious. One side corresponds to the feeling that life derives meaning and value from the fact that it is destined to end, the other side to the feeling that life is rendered empty and meaningless by the anticipation of death. It may even be that because of the value-lending psychological function of death as a boundary, the ego senses a kind of "need" for death as an organizing influence and as the background necessary for purposeful action (see Nussbaum, 1994, quoted in chapter 1). Eissler (1955) seems to make essentially this point when he suggests that a sense of identity and the action that emanates from it are predicated not only upon a sense of stability, but also upon the expectation of change, including the ultimate change of death:

The experience of a world altered by the death of an object intensely loved, the knowledge—conscious or unconscious—of the future destruction of one's own ego, the fracture lines which discontinue the identity of the world, all these factors demonstrate to the mind the extent to which the world can be changed. Here the imagery of death sets an intensive stimulus for action. . . . If man's existence were not subject to death he possibly would become a completely inactive being [pp. 93–94].

Thus, the line of reasoning articulated informally and in a lyrical vein in "On Transience," but never developed systematically by Freud, contains the seeds of a strictly psychological theory of adaptation to mortality in which awareness of death is given central status in the understanding of the organization of experience. Moreover, the potential is there for an integration of the existential perspective with the classical psychoanalytic formulation of danger situations and transformations of the quality of anxiety in line with the development of the ego. In this regard, I would agree with Anthony and Benedek (1975) that "a confrontation of psychoanalysis and existentialism is long overdue" (p. xviii). However, when the same authors suggest that "one aspect of Freud was intuitively existential but that he moved beyond this" (p. xxi), they overstate Freud's contribution and fail to pinpoint that aspect of Freud's position which has served more as a barrier than as a bridge to existential thought. The failure to integrate awareness of mortality into his theoretical system, as a unique factor emerging in the course of development with unique implications for adaptation, represents one of the ways in which Freud's stance was decidedly reductionistic and, if anything, anti-existential.[9]

Freud's informal existential views regarding death can be identified with what Holt (1972) regards as Freud's "humanistic," as opposed to his "mechanistic," image of humankind. Holt makes the important observation that "unlike the mechanistic image, the humanistic conception was never differentiated and stated explicitly

---

9. Becker (1973), similarly, takes exception to Freud's reductionism and then proceeds to recast key Freudian theoretical propositions as, in effect, metaphors for existential issues. Becker writes: "Freud never abandoned his views because they were correct in their elemental suggestiveness about the human condition—but not quite in the sense that he thought, or rather, not in the framework that he offered. Today we realize that all the talk about blood and excrement, sex and guilt, is true not because of urges to patricide and incest and fears of actual physical castration, but because all these things reflect man's horror of his own basic animal condition, a condition that he cannot—especially as a child—understand and a condition that—as an adult—he cannot accept" (p. 35). It takes an extremely liberal reading of Freud (e.g., Thompson, 1994) to attribute existential purposes to his basic theoretical stance, a reading which I believe the evidence brought forth here refutes.

enough to be called a model; yet it comprises a fairly rich and cohesive body of assumptions about the nature of human beings, which functioned in Freud's mind as a corrective antagonist to his mechanistic leanings" (p. 6). Regrettably, with regard to adaptation to mortality, the theorizing in Freud that is incorporated into his mechanistic model has had, by itself, an adverse effect upon subsequent theory development, whereas his less formally stated, potentially seminal, existential views have been relatively neglected.

SOME POST-FREUDIAN THEORISTS: HARTMANN, ERIKSON, AND KOHUT

Given the logical potential of the structural model to accommodate awareness of death as a source of anxiety, one might expect that Hartmann's theoretical extension of the model, especially as it focuses upon the functions and capabilities of the ego, would at least address the issue, if not take it up as a central concern. In fact, however, awareness of death in the existential sense is not a subject of concern in Hartmann's work, despite the fact that his concept of adaptation is bound up with an ego that is always "mindful" of the problem of survival: "We may say that the entire development of these processes [of adaptation] brings about a relationship between the genotype and the environment which is favorable for survival" (Hartmann, 1958, p. 24).

Hartmann actually offers some refinement of some of the conceptual tools that have the potentiality for dealing with awareness of death as a significant psychological variable. In addition to the relative autonomy of the ego, there is the clarifying distinction between ego *interests* and the instincts of the id (1964, p. 135); the notion of ego interests centering on the self (p. 136); and the idea of the importance of intrasystemic conflicts within the ego. Of the latter, Hartmann (1964) says:

> The intrasystemic correlations and conflicts in the ego have hardly ever been consistently studied . . . many misunderstandings and unclarities are traceable to the fact that we have not trained ourselves to consider the ego from an intrasystemic point of view [pp. 138–139].

Such an emphasis would seem to be favorable to consideration of the kind of psychological, existential dilemma that is implicit in "On Transience." Hartmann's (1958) failure to make any further advance on the subject seems to derive from his biological and mechanistic orientation, his lack of a theory of cognitive development, and his relatively exclusive focus upon the development and the fate of the instrumental, mastery-oriented functions of the ego:

> Ego development is a differentiation in which these primitive regulating factors are increasingly replaced or supplemented by more effective ego regulations. What was originally anchored in instincts may subsequently be performed in the service of and by means of the ego. . . . The individual's drive constitution is not his only inborn equipment. . . . The human individual, at his birth, also has apparatuses which serve to master the external world. These mature in the course of development [pp. 49–50].

For Hartmann, ego development has to do with changes in methods of mastery of internal and external stimuli. Changes in the phenomenology of anxiety and associated cognitive developments are hardly considered.

Rapaport and Gill (1959) claim that for both Hartmann and Erikson "each developmental step *gives rise to* and solves problems in relation to external reality" (p. 160; italics added), but, actually, Hartmann pays far less attention to changes in the nature of the problems than does Erikson. For the latter, "each successive step . . . is a potential crisis because of a radical *change in perspective*" (Erikson, 1959, p. 55). And, in fact, it is only in Erikson that the challenge of a self-conscious, reflective adaptation to mortality achieves some status as a developmental task late in life. In connection with the crisis of "integrity versus despair," Erikson says:

> Lacking a clear definition [of integrity], I shall point to a few attributes of this state of mind. It is the acceptance of one's own and only life-cycle and of the people who have become significant to it as something that had to be and that, by necessity, permitted of no substitutions . . . the lack or loss of this accrued ego integration is signified by despair and an often unconscious fear of death: the one and only life cycle is not accepted as the ultimate of life [p. 98].

I believe that a general criticism that has been directed at Erikson is applicable here, namely, that he tends to hold up the attitude represented by the positive side of each of his bipolar crises as a criterion of health (Clayton, 1975; Kovel, 1974). By regarding fear of death as, in effect, a sign of developmental failure, Erikson denies the emotional maturity that may be represented in adaptations that include dread and anticipatory grief or even depression,[10] along with self-affirmation, and that are impressive precisely because they indicate a tolerance of the tension between diverging or even contradictory attitudes. Erikson's standard of a seemingly nonconflictual "acceptance of one's own and only life-cycle" as the only alternative to total despair in confronting death has an oversimplified, even Pollyannaish quality.

Nevertheless, it may be of value to consider further what it is about Erikson's ego psychology, as distinct from Hartmann's, that permits self-conscious adaptation to mortality to surface at all as a developmental task. In this connection, Harry Guntrip's (1969) comparative analysis of Hartmann's and Erikson's work is pertinent (pp. 390–406). Guntrip, citing Apfelbaum (1966) in support of his position, locates Erikson squarely in the camp of "whole person" and "whole self" theorists, in contrast to Hartmann, whose concern is primarily with the instrumental aspects of the personality, with the ego as a system of functions. Having drawn the line sharply between ego and self, Hartmann opts to explore the theoretical ramifications of the former to the virtual exclusion of the latter. Erikson, on the other hand, with his emphasis on identity, has, according to Guntrip, "an over-riding concern for the 'whole person,'" for "a whole personal self, not just an ensemble of apparatuses" (p. 403).

If, to borrow Freud's (1915) language, it is a person's "whole being" that revolts against the admission that he or she is destined to die (p. 293; see above, p. 36), it is, perhaps, most likely that those theories that have as a focal concern the evolution of the individual's sense of his or her "being"—whether it be in terms of ego, person, identity, or self—are those that will give weight to the psychological impact of the prospect of death. Only a differentiated sense of self can give rise to a fear of death in the full sense of the term. This point is expressed clearly by the sociologist Philip Slater (1964):

> Fear of death is not at all primitive, elemental or basic. Animals have no such fear, nor do small children. It depends upon the rather advanced and sophisticated awareness of the self as a separate entity,

---

10. According to Basch (1975, p. 527), depression, at the symbolic level of development, in contrast to mourning, involves an injury to the self which cannot be readily alleviated by investment in new objects. In depression the individual's self-concept is destroyed, and along with it, the capacity to invest experience with meaning. "Depression," in this sense, may be a more fitting term than "anticipatory grief" or "mourning" for the negative side of the individual's ambivalent and paradoxical relation to death.

altogether detached from the natural and social environment. For the individual who feels blended with the world and his society, his own death has little meaning. It is only when he comes to view himself as a unique differentiated entity, with an existence which is separable and apart from other men and objects, that he can begin to have anxiety about the termination of that existence [p. 19].

I would only amend Slater's position to say that the anticipation of death is itself a factor that contributes to self-differentiation, particularly as the latter process includes a developing appreciation of the boundaries of the self in time. To the degree that awareness of self and awareness of mortality are interdependent, a focus on one is likely to be associated with serious concern with the other.

Kohut (1966), like Erikson, views the process of coming to terms with transience as among the highest achievements of human development. The cognitive aspect of acknowledging one's mortality is seen as intertwined with progressive self-definition through acceptance of limitation. Just as a concept of the separateness of objects is involved in the articulation of the boundaries of the self in social and physical space, the idea of one's own death is not an inert, merely intellectual concept, but a dynamic factor involved in coming to know and accommodating to the boundaries of the self in time:

The essence of this proud achievement [of wisdom] is therefore a maximal relinquishment of narcissistic delusions, including the acceptance of the inevitability of death, without an abandonment of cognitive and emotional involvements. The ultimate act of cognition, i.e., the acknowledgment of the limits and the finiteness of the self, is not the result of an isolated intellectual process but is the victorious outcome of the life-work of the total personality in acquiring broadly based knowledge and in transforming archaic modes of narcissism into ideals, humor, and a supraindividual participation in the world [p. 269].

Kohut's (1977) central concern with the self goes hand in hand with special attention to the later years, and especially to the middle years, as critical periods in the life cycle. It is then that the individual is confronted with the question of the meaning and the value of his or her life in its totality:

I believe there is, later in life, a specific point that can be seen as crucially significant—a point in the life curve of the self at which a final crucial test determines whether the previous development had failed or had succeeded. . . . I am inclined to put the pivotal point . . . to late middle age, when, nearing the ultimate decline, we ask ourselves whether we have been true to our innermost design. This is the time of utmost helplessness for some, of utter lethargy, of that depression without guilt and self-directed aggression, which overtakes those who feel they have failed and cannot remedy the failure in time and with the energies still at their disposal [p. 241].

Of course, the threat of death upon mature reflection at this late stage resonates with earlier threats to the self in childhood. For Kohut, the ultimate danger is neither that of losing the object nor that of castration. The bedrock is, rather, "the threat of the destruction of the nuclear self" (p. 117). This threat is first encountered when narcissistic injury is inflicted upon the child through the imperfect empathy of an early selfobject and is experienced in the form of distintegration anxiety.

I believe that Kohut (1977) sacrifices theoretical clarity and power when he locates disintegration anxiety outside of Freud's genetic hierarchy of anxiety experiences (pp. 102–104) instead of integrating it within Freud's framework. As Kohut acknowledges, the threat of annihilation in the reflexive, preconceptual sense was not foreign to Freud's way of thinking. On the contrary, although conceptualized in the physicalistic terms of overwhelming drive stimulation, it does in fact constitute the content of the earliest type of anxiety in the infant prior to self-object differentiation (Freud, 1926, p. 137). Kohut (1977) regards this idea of the earliest form of anxiety as an attempt "to deal with disintegration anxiety within the framework of the classical mental apparatus psychology" (p. 104). He argues, however, "that these anxieties cannot be properly conceptualized outside the framework of a psychology of the self" (p. 104).

But even granting that a concept of a developing self is lost or obscured in Freud's mechanistic model of the mind, it does not follow that such a concept has to be located outside of the developmental continuum Freud proposed, and that it is necessary to set up "two basically different classes of anxiety experiences" (Kohut, 1977, p. 102). Since Freud's hierarchy is explicitly presented by him in terms of a cumulative series, it is clear that for Freud, too, the threat of annihilation has a logical place as the primary danger and is one that must be sensed as an aspect of every ensuing form of danger in the hierarchy.

It is an oversimplification to regard these ensuing dangers, even in the classical sense, as so specific and so well circumscribed as Kohut suggests in contrasting them with disintegration anxiety. Fear of loss of the object, fear of loss of the love of the object, castration anxiety, and moral anxiety could all be understood as developmental transformations of fear of annihilation, with fear of death, fully conceptualized in the context of human mortality, emerging last in the sequence. Given his separate lines of development for narcissism and for object relations, Kohut has no choice but to excise disintegration anxiety and fear of death from Freud's developmental series instead of including them at the lower and upper ends of the hierarchy respectively. This could be done with appropriate conceptual modifications, emphasizing the importance of the self throughout. Removing disintegration anxiety and fear of death from the sequence results in a contrived dichotomy that deprives Freud's danger situations of the narcissistic threat that they undoubtedly include, just as it leaves Kohut's expressions of disintegration anxiety artificially bereft of significant object-related and libidinal overtones.

Kohut's position regarding fear of death is also vulnerable to the same critique that Erikson's point of view invites. Like Erikson, Kohut leans toward an ideal of adaptation to mortality that is free of conflict, anticipatory grief, and anxiety. Kohut (1966) picks up on the attitude toward anticipated loss that Freud describes as his own in "On Transience," and offers it as the ultimate expression of psychological health (pp. 265–266). Like Freud, who saw in his poet-companion a despondency that was essentially unnecessary and irrational, Kohut (1977) dichotomizes healthy adaptation and pathological maladaptation along the lines of tranquil acceptance and utter nihilism (pp. 241–242). By doing so he fails to consider the advanced level of development associated with a tolerance of an *ambivalent* relation to death—one that includes existential "dread" and anticipatory mourning as well as self-affirmation. It may be that the ultimate wisdom lies not with a "cosmic narcissism" that transcends individual narcissism and results in a calm acceptance of mortality (Kohut, 1966, pp. 265–266), but with an ability to maintain in awareness both sides of the paradox posed by the prospect of death, namely that death renders life meaningful and meaningless, precious and valueless at the same time.

In this respect, how much richer and closer to the spirit of the psychoanalytic tradition than Erikson's or Kohut's ideal of adaptation is the existential view of man facing death. Neither simple despair nor simple self-assertion or self-transcendence, but a complex admixture of contradictory attitudes characterizes the height of reflective consciousness of mortality:

Whatever philosophers wish to do hereafter with this concept, they ought certainly to reckon with it. If the truth about human nature is revealed in relation to what Jaspers called "Grenzsituationen," boundary-situations, my death is the most dramatic—more than that, the essential and determining boundary situation. If, as Sartre prefers to stress, it is terrible that I am responsible for what I have become, it is always hopeful to reflect that tomorrow I may do better. But what is most terrible is that I cannot do so forever, that in fact if I have bungled and cheated and generally made a fool of myself, there is only a little while, perhaps not all of today even, in which to do it all over. Kierkegaard's favourite maxim: "over 70,000 fathoms, miles and miles from all human help, to be glad" is the core of existentialism. It is this that Heidegger, in the tortuous yet decisive argument of *Sein und Zeit,* challenges us to face. And, deprived of Kierkegaard's faith, we are compelled even more urgently to face it. For to the individual denied supernatural support, cast alone into his world, the dread of death is a haunting if suppressed theme that runs through life. What is more, if at all times communication between men is tattered and fragile, it is in the face of death that each man stands most strikingly and irrevocably alone. For this Everyman there is after all no guide in his most need to go by his side; more intensely than for his medieval counterpart, his relation to death marks as nothing else does the integrity and independence of his life [Grene, 1957, pp. 44–45].

In the existential perspective, individuals are most keenly aware of their own responsibility for their lives at those moments, paradoxically, when they are most acutely and painfully aware of their helplessness to control their own ultimate destiny. They discover their own selves more fully when they perceive most clearly that they will die (Koestenbaum, 1964). In existentialism, the anticipation of one's own death promotes a consolidation of self beyond that which, in a psychoanalytic framework, is achieved via the identifications of the oedipal period or those following object loss. But the dread or anxiety associated with the anticipation of the loss of the self and the exhilaration associated with the sense of ownership of one's life are inseparable aspects of the same experience and reflect human beings' inevitably ambivalent relation to time and to temporal limitation. The link between the psychoanalytic and the existential perspectives that Erikson and Kohut seem to obscure when they extol the virtues of tranquil acceptance of mortality is this very emphasis upon dualism and ambivalence and upon the emotional pain that attends psychological growth.

SOME FINDINGS FROM AN EMPIRICAL STUDY

My own research in this subject area centered upon the adaptation of parents to fatal illness (leukemia) in a child (Hoffman, 1972; Hoffman and Futterman, 1971; Futterman, Hoffman, and Sabshin, 1972; Futterman and Hoffman, 1973). There is reason to expect that the experience of parents who are thus bereaved would include changes in awareness of and adaptation to mortality. As Freud suggested (1915, p. 293), the event that most impresses the individual with the inevitability of his or her own death is the death of someone the person loves. Moreover, the child occupies a special place among a parent's close relationships. He or she represents the promise of some kind of continuity of the parent's own self or identity beyond his or her lifetime. As Freud (1914a) said, "at the most touchy point in the narcissistic system, the immortality of the ego . . . security is achieved by taking refuge in the child" (p. 91). To the extent that this is true, one would expect the death of a child—more, perhaps, than any other loss—to intensify the parents' sense of their own vulnerability and to heighten their awareness of their own mortality.

I will report only a brief overview of the research along with a few specific examples of findings that bear on the subject at hand. The work brings into focus some of the elements of healthy coping and suggests that successful adaptation may best be conceptualized as a developmental process or one which leads to developmental change.[11] Instead of simple defensive (i.e., self-deceptive) reactions like denial, in which avoidance of pain is the goal, or even simple mastery activities, in which overcoming or gaining control over an external threat is the goal, what we found, frequently, was a relatively conscious struggle to meet the implications of the child's fatal illness head on. We conceptualized the coping process in relation to several major "adaptational dilemmas": the dilemma of maintaining an attitude of hope while nevertheless acknowledging the fatal prognosis; the dilemma of maintaining normal life routines and emotional equilibrium while at the same time grieving the anticipated or the actual loss; and the dilemma of affirming confidence or faith in

---

11. Since the late 1970s, when this paper was written, my own awareness of the value-laden underpinnings of claims about developmental changes has grown. And yet the basic change identified here, intensified awareness of mortality leading to a reorganization of priorities and a deeper commitment to living, is consistent with the values of dialectical constructivism, for which a kind of universal validity is being claimed.

oneself and in the world while still allowing oneself to experience inevitably profound skepticism, doubt, and anger.

What impressed us was the ability of parents to live in and with agonizing contradiction and ambiguity and to hold simultaneously to both horns of each dilemma—to keep them both in mind. We traced certain modal shifts in the balance that characterized each dilemma during the course of the child's illness and following the death, finding one or the other adaptational task predominant, depending upon the condition of the child and the stage of illness. Rarely, however, did commitment to any one task obliterate some consciousness, some keeping-in-mind, of the one that stood in relative opposition to it. Acknowledgment, for example, was not obliterated by hope during remission, nor was hope obliterated by acknowledgment or resignation at points of relapse. The balance among adaptational tasks and dilemmas was generally regulated by considerations of the future as well as by cognitive appraisal of present circumstances. In three strikingly deviant cases in the sample of twenty-one families there was a rigid, persistent preoccupation with one side (or task) of an adaptational dilemma at the expense of the other; in other words, these cases represented failures of adaptive integration.[12]

It is within the context of the third of the dilemmas listed above— that of maintaining confidence while integrating self-doubts and inevitable bitterness—that we can locate the parents' struggle for meaning. At one level, this is a struggle to affirm the meaning of the child's life despite its unexpected brevity, and to affirm the worth of the parents' love and care for the child despite their helplessness to prevent the child's death. At another level, which surfaced primarily after the death of the child, we observed the parents' struggle to reaffirm the meaning and worth of their own lives, despite a heightened awareness of their own vulnerability and mortality, and more specifically, perhaps, despite an erosion of the hope for immortality through their offspring. Experientially, this latter process entailed a coming to terms with personal limits and a reorganization of self-concept, which parents described as a sense of growth. In a formal sense, as well, it qualifies as a developmental achievement, insofar as development is understood to mean progressive differentiation and

---

12. In effect, one could say that most of the parents were able to sustain multiple pairs of dialectically related attitudes, whereas in the three cases of "failure" the dialectical relationships collapsed into dichotomous organizations with one side excluding the other. The formulation here anticipates the dialectical-constructivist view of the analytic process.

integration (Werner, 1957). In this instance, such change is reflected in greater awareness of the boundaries of the self, stemming from a confrontation with mortality and with the limits of one's power to control the course of events.

In general, as the child's illness progressed, parents increasingly focused attention on the *quality* of the child's life and of the time spent with him or her in lieu of the *amount* of time that would be lost. This emphasis on quality of time in place of amount of time was, perhaps, the most fundamental of all the bases for coming to terms with the child's death and the one most conducive to subsequent developmental change in the parents. In this process, parents were able to affirm the intrinsic worth and wholeness of their relationship with the child and of his or her life experience.

Although religious belief in an afterlife provided some consolation to many of the parents, it did not seem to obviate their investment in establishing that the child's life in this world was meaningful in and of itself. Toward the end, communications with the child sometimes expressed conscious efforts to compensate for loss of time and to give the relationship with the child a sense of completeness. Expressions of guilt and bitterness were not uncommon in interviews conducted after the child's death. Such statements, however, were almost always balanced by statements of absolution of self, of others, or of life itself. A major dimension of the coping process in this period was a general granting of forgiveness. And, again, offsetting the pain of the loss was a focus on the quality of the child's life.

From a psychoanalytic point of view, it may be suspected that such attitudes reflect a degree of disavowal of negative feeling or a kind of rationalization. However, the fact that these attitudes were embedded in a long, complex coping process, which generally included profound grief as well as conscious struggles with guilt and bitterness, suggests that to conceptualize them as merely defensive would be an oversimplification. Even if they served some defensive function in mitigating the intensity of the pain of the loss, there is also reason to view them as reflecting an integrative process. In this process, without arresting or preventing the painful aspects of the work of mourning, the value of the life of the lost cherished object is affirmed. In fact, in this light, the work of mourning might best be conceptualized as including a change in the *quality* of investment in both the lost object and in potentially new objects, rather than as merely a matter of withdrawal and redirection of investment. This modification of the quality of investment in objects has to do with a new integration of the relation between value and temporal limitation, with a new appreciation of the fact that, as Freud (1916a) put it, "transience value is scarcity value in time" (p. 305).

In the course of coming to terms with the deaths of their children, many parents developed a heightened awareness of their own mortality. What began, moreover, as an emphasis on the quality of the child's life generalized and became a commitment to savor and appreciate the immediate and to live more fully in the present. As noted earlier, insofar as this change in temporal orientation involved a process of increased differentiation and integration of the boundaries of self in time, it can be understood as reflecting psychological growth. As one mother put it:

> I see things that I had never seen before. It sometimes takes a tragedy to open your eyes to life itself and to appreciate what you have instead of taking it for granted. Summing it all up, life itself means much more to me. I can't took forward to tomorrow and yesterday is gone. Today is the day I worry about and appreciate. It makes you think that life is very short no matter how old you are when you go. Whether you are five, or thirty-two, or sixty-five, life is very, very short. So you must make the best of it.

The experience of having a fatally ill child or of losing a child made parents more conscious of the limitations, strengths, and potential for suffering that they and other human beings shared. Although the need to find something or someone to blame posed a threat to interpersonal trust, in the long run most of the parents in the study experienced a sense of increased closeness to and empathy with people, especially within their own families.

Along with a deeper sense of their limitations as human beings, especially with regard to their capacity to control their own destinies, many parents reported a feeling of greater personal strength, resiliency, and capacity to endure suffering, as well as a general sense of increased maturity:

> *Mr. G:* It's a training you can't get out of books. It's an experience and it's not a pleasant one. Yet how to describe it? It's not a gruesome one because it's real life; that's what it is. It's genuine living. It's not false; it's the core of living, you might say. We're all so willing to accept the good things; the hard things we look at and say, "Gee, it's really tough." But actually those are the sorts of things that make a human being, make them what they are; not the pleasures.

> *Mr. H:* Your mind has to mature; and it's a little more than what you'd planned it to. There can be people eighty years old that never

have to face such tragedy where they would actually have to grow up. But yet they have room to grow. You always have room to grow. Sometimes you have to; and some people don't ever have to. But you've got to be able to if the time comes.

Mrs. C: I was shocked that when I was finally faced with the reality of the situation, I was able to endure it. I never thought I'd be able to and yet I didn't faint or I didn't—you know—I just took it. So I think a person can rise to tremendous capacity when they are forced to do so. You have to recognize it's a rough world any way you look at it. And I don't know anybody, rich or poor, well or ill, who does not have some heartache. And I think that enduring this is a mark of simply being an adult. I feel that I have gained a tremendous maturity; more than anything I have ever had. I believe that I can face death and stare it down.

In sum, the parents' sense of growth was reflected in a changed temporal orientation, in a greater empathic identification with and tolerance for the limitations of others, and in an enhanced sense of resiliency and capacity to endure suffering. All of these changes had at their root the experience of loss and the associated confrontation with mortality.

The intimate relationship between mourning and growth has been discussed in a variety of contexts in the psychoanalytic literature (e.g., Fleming and Altschul, 1963; Wetmore, 1963), beginning, of course, with Freud's (1917) classic formulation of the relation between mourning and ego formation. The findings of the study reported here are relevant to the development of psychoanalytic theory in several ways. They provide an empirical basis for describing relatively healthy forms of adaptation and the growth processes that they entail. They are drawn from individuals who neither expressed nor demonstrated evidence of need for professional help, thus supplementing what can be learned from data collected in a traditional clinical context. In addition, they are based on the report of persons who, although they had recently suffered a major loss, were not in the extreme situation of imminently facing death themselves.[13] Too often, research on death and dying is limited to the latter circumstance, thus conveying the impression that the prospect of one's own death is otherwise a remote intellectual idea. Studies of the relation between object loss and adaptation to mortality can serve as a bridge to empirical work with people in normal, nonstressful circumstances.

---

13. For an application of Kohut's concepts to clinical work with terminally ill patients, see Muslin, Levine, and Levine (1974).

The latter could be designed to explore ways in which preconscious awareness of mortality may act as a major organizing influence in daily life, in the establishment of values and priorities, and in the setting of short-term and long-term life goals.

SOME IMPLICATIONS FOR RESEARCH AND CLINICAL WORK

Implications for Studies of Cognitive Development

Any theory that regards human awareness of death as a variable with important emotional significance must be able to accommodate a notion of concept development that is neither stimulus or image bound nor merely a superficial intellectual process. It must have room for cognitive transformations that have thoroughgoing psychological implications for an individual's sense of self. Because of Freud's emphasis upon endogenous, unconscious instinctual influences, Rapaport (1960, p. 13) locates Freud's epistemology on the side of Kant rather than with Anglo-Saxon empiricism. Freud's perceiving ego, however, remains something of a tabula rasa with respect to the way in which it processes stimuli; it is not equipped with specific unfolding cognitive structures or schemata of its own. As Schimek (1975) notes, "for Freud, in line with the association theory of the 19th century, perception is essentially the passive, temporary registration of a specific external object. The perceptual apparatus functions like the receptive surface of a slate or the lens of a camera" (p. 172).

The problem of adaptation to mortality, moreover, was undoubtedly not the only area in which this aspect of Freud's epistemology handicapped his theory building. For example, once having dropped the trauma theory of the etiology of the neuroses, instead of exploring the limits of what could be explained by the interaction among infantile sexuality, more subtle environmental events, and a developing intellectual capability with which to comprehend and interpret those events (thereby constructing their meaning), Freud was drawn to the Lamarckian concept of inheritance of memories of patricide to explain the Oedipus complex (Freud, 1939, pp. 99–100; Hartmann and Kris, 1945, pp. 21–22; Schimek, 1975, p. 180).

Schimek (1975) and Basch (1977) have called our attention to the importance of integrating contemporary notions of cognitive development, especially the work of Piaget, into psychoanalytic theory. It is interesting in this connection that Piaget, whose entire system is indeed concerned with cognitive development, does not take up the issue of the development of a concept of death. His study of the differentiation of the animate and the inanimate world (1963) is not concerned with the evolution of a concept of human mortality as such. Perhaps Piaget's adherence to the paradigm of conservation in closed physical systems (Blasi and Hoeffel, 1974) and his emphasis on the development of "reversibility" limit the scope of his theory and stand in the way of making the idea of death, the ultimate irreversible event, a subject of inquiry.

Nevertheless, some work of a Piagetian nature has been done in this area. Nagy's classic study (1959) identified three stages in the development of the concept of death: in the first stage (before five years old), death is understood as a reversible separation; in the second stage (five to nine), it is viewed as a final but not universal fate that is inflicted by a personified force; in the third stage (after nine and ten), it is conceived of as final, inevitable, and universal.

Nagy's stage sequence is relatively crude. Kastenbaum (1977) questions the ubiquity of the personification tendency of Nagy's second stage. He also points out that it is possible that fleeting early glimmers of the meaning of death are pushed aside because they are painful psychologically[14]:

It is . . . likely that newly discovered death meanings seem to fade away because of their emotional impact. It is too much to live constantly with the feelings stirred up by early realizations of death. Adults have trouble enough in coming—and staying—to terms with death. Most children are likely to find the impact of death realizations too powerful to sustain in conscious thought on a thoroughgoing basis. This suggests that a child can show a keen grasp of death's essence from time to time—yet behave more typically as though death were reversible, a form of sleep, something that happens only to the aged, the wicked, or the unlucky [p. 30].

We need studies that are sensitive enough to pick up on glimpses of the meaning of death, on the anxiety that such glimpses arouse, and on the ensuing defensive strategies that are set in motion—not only in children but also in adults. Piaget's system provides the framework for such studies, although his own work does not consider the possibility of cognitive regression under the impact of anxiety. For Piaget, cognition always moves forward; the disequilibrium

14. These speculations are consistent with the consensus of psychoanalytic observers that, by and large, the mourning process in children is aborted by massive denial (Miller, 1971).

between stages of cognitive development always resolves itself in movement to the equilibrium of the next and higher stage. There is no concern with the possibility that the child or adult may back away from cognitive transformations that are threatening to the self.

In addition to the need for more data on the development of awareness of mortality, there is a lacuna in studies of cognitive development with regard to the emergence of a sense of the meaning of infinity. I know of one experiment by Piaget and Inhelder (1956) that deals with this issue in the context of space. At a certain stage, the child realizes that there is no limit to the number of times that a line segment can be subdivided (pp. 146–147). Further work is needed to explore the quality of the experience associated with contemplation of time and space extending endlessly. At what point do children realize, and what is the phenomenology of the discovery, that they cannot conceive of the end of time or space and that they are forced always to the conclusion that beyond every boundary they try to impose there must be still more time, and still more space, ad infinitum? As noted earlier in connection with Merleau-Ponty's viewpoint, the concept of infinity is no mere mathematical, intellectual idea, but a preconscious factor in all abstract thought and a major influence on the organization of experience. (For example, the abstract concept "chair" refers, implicitly, not to any finite set of actual chairs but to infinite possible chairs.)

The individual's sense of self, once the stage of formal operations is attained, is permeated by a preconscious awareness of the relativity of immediate experience against the background of infinite other possibilities. With respect to awareness of mortality, I would suggest that there is a preconscious (more or less disavowed) appreciation that one's own existence, or one's own "time," is only one instance of infinite possible existences, or "times," which are exclusive of oneself. This is a narcissistically devastating and uniquely human insight, the phenomenology of which deserves much more study.

Implications for Clinical Psychoanalysis and Psychoanalytic Psychotherapy

One of the criteria of exclusion from psychoanalytic treatment that Freud (1905b) set down was that of age:

> The age of patients has this much importance in determining their fitness for psycho-analytic treatment . . . on the one hand, near or above the age of fifty the elasticity of the mental processes, on which the

treatment depends, is as a rule lacking—old people are no longer edu-
cable—and, on the other hand, the mass of material to be dealt with
would prolong the duration of the treatment indefinitely [p. 264].

This criterion, however, is based largely on consideration of those
aspects of the personality that one might expect to be most settled
(least "elastic") by the time of middle age. Whatever the validity of
that expectation, the criterion does not take into consideration those
aspects of adaptation that one might expect to be unsettled or fluid
in the middle and later years. In particular, it does not consider the
psychological impact of the realization that less time remains to be
lived than the time that has already been lived. As Kohut (1977) suggests (see above, pp. 54–55) the midlife period is likely to bring into
focus the person's struggle to affirm self-worth in the teeth of his or
her recognition of mortality. Inevitably, if we think in terms of
Freud's hierarchy of danger situations, the heightened sense of "time
running out" is likely to resonate with all the previous kinds of
threats to the integrity of the self with which the individual has had
to deal. Contrary to Freud's stated position, one would expect that,
in many cases, residues of early developmental conflicts would also
be stirred up, so that even they would become more elastic and
amenable to analytic influence.

What literature there is on analytic work with older patients
sometimes is encumbered by Freud's reductionism, at least in its theoretical aspects. The result is a formal commitment to the classical
reductionistic position, which is then abandoned in favor of a more
existential perspective without any acknowledgment of the shift. For
example, Grotjahn (1955) first claims that "growing old is often felt
as a narcissistic trauma, for it represents and repeats a castration
threat. The neuroses of old age are defenses against castration anxiety" (p. 420). But he later says that

> the task of integrating one's life as it has been lived and the final
> acceptance of one's own death are problems of existence. To deal with
> them is the great task of old age. They are essentially different from
> the tasks of infancy, childhood, adolescence, and maturity. . . . The
> difference between the naïve, narcissistic megalomania of the healthy
> infant and the mature, consciously achieved self-acceptance of old age
> can be studied best in relation to the existential problem specific for
> the elderly; and that is the final mastery of problems concerning one's
> own end of life [pp. 420–421].

I would question Grotjahn's view that the existential problem is
specific to the elderly. Although there might be a tendency for it to

reach a certain level of prominence in the later years, it more than likely emerges as a developmental task as early as the first glimmers of awareness of mortality in childhood. The whole course of adaptation to mortality should be investigated clinically, with a perspective that integrates the existential point of view with the classical psychoanalytic hierarchy of danger situations. The findings of studies of cognitive development should be taken into account along with the influence of anxiety and the associated vicissitudes of acknowledgment and disavowal.

Along the same lines, it may be important to consider the role of adaptation to mortality in investigating transference-countertransference configurations that arise between therapists and patients of varying ages. Grotjahn discusses some of the countertransference problems that must be dealt with when young therapists work with elderly patients. He focuses especially on "the reversed oedipus situation," with the therapist in the position of the child or grandchild, and upon associated countertransference difficulties. It might also be important to consider the heightened sense of mortality that might develop, along with anxiety and various mechanisms of defense, in the therapist working with a patient who is significantly older.[15]

Whatever the age of the patient, the psychoanalytic situation provides a context in which the idiosyncratic meanings of death, including connections with specific earlier danger situations, can be explored. The data gathered from intensive work with neurotic and even with psychotic patients can illuminate possible relations between particular symptoms and reactions to the anticipation of death. Meyer (1975) has shown how our understanding of neurotic symptoms can be enhanced by considering the role of death anxiety in symptom formation. Similarly, Searles (1961) has attempted to describe schizophrenic adaptation as a type of desperate flight from awareness of the inevitability of death. Although these discussions by Meyer and Searles may exaggerate the role of fear of death while underemphasizing other kinds of anxiety, they serve as needed correctives to the tendency to virtually ignore the contribution of the former to psychopathology.

15. For an example of my own work with an elderly patient, see chapter 10.

◆ 3 ◆

The Intimate and Ironic Authority of the Psychoanalyst's Presence

A SESSION FROM *SESSIONS*

There was a program on cable TV called *Sessions*. Each episode was organized around a session of psychoanalysis or psychoanalytic therapy, depending on your point of view,[1] with various flashbacks to scenes from the patient's current life situation and childhood as the patient described them. In one episode the patient's mother has had a scare. She's been hospitalized with a heart condition, perhaps a mild heart attack. The patient is on the couch. The analyst or therapist, played by Elliot Gould, comes across as warm and engaging.

An earlier version of this chapter appeared in 1996 in *The Psychoanalytic Quarterly*, 65:102–136.

1. For a discussion of conceptual and terminological issues regarding the relationship between psychoanalytic psychotherapy and psychoanalysis, see Gill (1991). Throughout this book, as noted in the introduction, the terms "psychoanalysis" and "psychoanalytic therapy" and the terms "analyst" and "therapist" are used interchangeably. "Psychoanalytic therapy" is Gill's term for the modality utilizing psychoanalytic technique without the couch and without the conventional frequency of psychoanalysis proper. The modality that interests me, whatever it should be called, entails a dialectical interplay of suggestive influence and critical reflection on the interaction.

The patient, who appears to be between 35 and 40 years old, is estranged from his father. He complains to the analyst about how his father is so self-centered that even under these circumstances he can only think of himself. The patient describes his experience with his father when driving home from the hospital after visiting the mother. We see the flashback. In the car, the father goes on about his anxieties over handling household duties. He doesn't know where things are, he doesn't know how to cook, he feels helpless. In the session, the patient is irate because his father conveyed no concern about the mother's well-being. At some point the analyst asks, "Do you think he's scared?" Caught by surprise, after a pause the patient replies, "Yes, I suppose so." The analyst says, "Maybe he needs someone to talk to about it." The patient says, "My father? You mean talk to a shrink-type person like you? Are you kidding? He'd never do anything like that." The analyst says, "Actually I wasn't thinking of a shrink-type person like me. I was thinking of a son-type person like you." The patient exclaims, "Are you crazy? My father and I haven't had a real conversation my whole life. Why in the world would we start now? That's just ridiculous!" After a pause the analyst says, "It's not a suggestion, you know, just a thought."

In the ensuing scene the patient is with his father in the kitchen of the parents' home. Their backs are to the camera as they stand in front of the kitchen counter. The father is stocky and somewhat shorter than the patient. He seems to be in his 60s, maybe early 70s. They are preparing dinner. The father is fumbling around, looking for utensils and other things. He drops something and picks it up. He is chattering nervously about how impossible it is for him to get along. He seems weary and leans for a moment against the counter. The patient asks, quietly, "Dad, are you scared?" The father is silent. He nods yes, sighs, and says, "Yeah, I am." After a moment the two simultaneously lean toward each other, and the patient puts his arm around the father who leans his head on his son's shoulder. The scene fades and the program ends.

REVISITING THE MYTH OF ANALYTIC NEUTRALITY

For the sake of illustration, if we treat the episode as if it were one from a real analytic therapy, no doubt there are many other things the therapist might have done or said. He could have been silent, for example, with the idea that he needed to hear more before feeling that he had something pertinent to say. Alternatively, he might have expressed empathy with his patient's anger at his father for being so self-centered. In that context he might have encouraged associations to this experience with some special interest in its historical ante-cedents. Another possibility might have been to listen for and even-tually try to interpret the latent transference meanings of this particular set of associations. Is there something in the content that alludes to an aspect of the patient's experience of the relationship with the therapist, or is there a desire for something from the analyst that is implicit in the patient telling about this experience at this moment? Indeed, perhaps the analyst's knowledge of the patient's history and his awareness of various aspects of the transference would lead him to interpret a conflictual wish for guidance about how to respond to his father's behavior. In that context, presumably, the analyst would interpret without *actually* advising or suggesting anything, in keeping with what might commonly be recognized as a proper, relatively "neutral" analytic attitude.

In fact, all the alternatives I just mentioned have a decidedly more neutral *appearance* than what the analyst or therapist does in this instance, which is to offer, despite his transparent disclaimer ("just a thought," he says), a blatant suggestion of something the patient might do. Hypothetically, there could be enough in the background of such apparent "advice" for it to carry more implicitly interpretive meaning. For example, the patient and the analyst might have devel-oped an understanding that the patient shies away from opportuni-ties for emotional contact with his father. In such a context, the analyst's overt suggestion might imply a question, such as, "Is this another instance in which you are refusing to think in a more sym-pathetic way about what your father may be feeling?" Without that context, however (and maybe even with it), many would view the analyst's comments as appropriate, at best, for counseling or sup-portive psychotherapy rather than for psychoanalysis or for any rig-orous type of psychoanalytic psychotherapy. According to that perspective, the last thing a good analytic therapist wants to do is cross the boundary that separates him or her from direct involvement in the analysand's life. Instead, analysts aspire to help their patients become aware of the unconscious issues and conflicts that are affect-ing their adaptation, so that their choices can become more integrated and more informed. To meddle in the patient's affairs is to inject one's personal prejudices at the expense of elucidating the patient's uncon-scious motivations and internal object relations, his or her "intrapsy-chic life." In the end, if there are difficult choices to be made in "real life," it is the patient who has to make them on his or her own. The aim of analysis, to paraphrase Freud (Breuer and Freud, 1893–1895, p. 305), is to transform neurotic suffering into normal human misery. Our responsibility ends where the patient's begins.

But is this portrayal of the process accurate? Suppose the analyst in the situation I described *did* offer one of the more ostensibly neutral types of responses. Suppose he just listened, or empathized with the patient's anger, or tried to interpret the latent meaning in the transference. What might have been the result? Would the patient have asked his father whether he was scared? Would that poignant moment of closeness have occurred? Perhaps. But it seems reasonable to think that the probability of that happening might have been less. Of course, the analyst's presence as an immediate influence is unmistakable when the patient asks the very question the analyst posed in the hour. Indeed, we think immediately about the dangers of behavioral compliance and/or identification with the analyst at the expense of other aspects of the patient's experience. But if the analyst did *not* make that conspicuous suggestion, and the patient did *not* ask his father that question and did *not* thereby make himself available as someone the father might talk to about his fears, would we recognize the influence of the analyst in the *not*-asking and in the *non*-occurrence of that moment of closeness, with all its potential for further development? My guess is that we would not. Instead, we would think of the patient as simply doing what *he chose* to do in keeping with his characteristic way of relating to his father. The analyst, we would say, didn't have anything to do with it; his hands would be clean. All he did was follow the patient's lead and explore various aspects of the patient's conscious and unconscious experience.

That is all very neat but also quite illusory, in my view. Whatever the analyst does is invariably saturated with suggestion (Gill, 1991). To follow whatever one decides is the *patient's lead*, to choose to pick up on one or another of the patient's more or less ambiguous communications, is also to *lead the patient* in a particular direction (Hoffman, 1990). If the analyst empathizes with the patient's anger, for example, he might well be suggesting, consciously or unconsciously, that it would make sense for the patient to continue to keep his distance from his father, at least for the time being. It might be argued that that last qualification ("for the time being") is quite important. If there is an apparent tilt at the end of a session in one direction or another, that hardly means the last word on the subject has been spoken. There will be plenty of time, one might argue, to get to other aspects of the patient's experience and to explore them, including, perhaps, a disclaimed wish for closeness with the father, along with an unconscious fear of it. *There is never any hurry in psychoanalysis.* In due time, many more or less conflicting facets of the patient's experience will come to light, and we will be in a position to demonstrate how evenhanded we can be in according due respect to all of them.

The trouble with this reasoning is that it denies that analysis goes on in real time—time that really counts—and that the patient is continually making real choices under our suggestive influence both within and outside the analytic situation. A common illusion that I think we try to maintain is that analysis is a kind of *sanctuary* from the world of choice. We have the idea, in that regard, that people should postpone certain choices until they know more about what they mean in terms of the underlying unconscious conflicts that are involved. Undoubtedly, that delay may be possible and even invaluable in some instances, but even then, of course, the postponement itself is a real choice with real consequences.

I think that the idea of analysis as sanctuary, taken too literally, denies both the extent of our authority and the extent of our intimate involvement with our patients as they risk doing or not doing one thing or another, both inside and outside the analytic situation. In trying so hard to stay out of it, we can really *be* "out of it." Opportune moments for action come and go. They do not necessarily recur, and they certainly do not last forever. The analyst is right there in the patient's life as those moments pass by. There is no risk-free position to which he or she can retreat. In the example I presented from the TV program, if the analyst adhered to the relatively passive and seemingly "neutral" mode that I think is idealized in many of our theories, that father might have *died* before the patient stumbled upon his own desire for, and his capacity to create, that special moment of intimacy, not to mention the amount of precious time that might have been lost even if such a moment did eventually occur.

I do not think it is melodramatic to consider those possibilities. Although it is rather pervasively denied in psychoanalytic theory (chapter 2; Becker, 1973), death is a rather common interference with our best-laid plans. In a basketball game or a football game, a team can at least call time-out, and the game clock literally stops while the team members collect themselves, soul-search, and strategize with the assistance of their coach. But a person's lifetime keeps on going relentlessly through every analytic hour, week, and year. The clock keeps running, and more or less agonizing choices are being made continually, with the analyst's witting or unwitting participation, right under his or her nose. If the analyst chooses to be silent or detached, he or she is nevertheless responding and participating. The effect of that silence or detachment is not simply to bring out "the truth" regarding the nature of the patient's desires; rather, it is to affect and partially shape those desires and their expression at any given time, both within and outside the analytic situation itself.

COMING TO GRIPS WITH THE ANALYST'S AUTHORITY IN A CONSTRUCTIVIST PARADIGM

These days it is commonplace to acknowledge that we are not involved in the therapeutic process merely as objective scientists. We recognize instead that some benign aspect of our interpersonal involvement is intrinsic to the therapeutic action of the process (e.g., Bromberg, 1983; Kohut, 1984; Loewald, 1960; Strachey, 1934; Winnicott, 1971), that our theories inevitably affect the kinds of interpretations that we pursue (e.g., Schafer, 1992; Spence, 1982), that our countertransferential attitudes are more pervasive, consequential, and potentially useful than what has traditionally been considered to be the case (e.g., Bollas, 1987; Ehrenberg, 1992; Gill, 1982a, 1994; Greenberg, 1995; Hirsch, 1993; Jacobs, 1991; Levenson, 1983; McLaughlin, 1981; Mitchell, 1988, 1993; Racker, 1968; Renik, 1993; Sandler, 1976; Searles, 1978–1979; J. Slavin, 1994; D. B. Stern, 1989, 1997; Tansey and Burke, 1989), and that we have to keep an eye on the way in which our own personal values may result in our trying to influence the patient in one direction or another (e.g., Gedo, 1983; Hoffer, 1985; Lichtenberg, 1983; Meissner, 1983; *Psychoanalytic Inquiry,* 3[4], 1983).

But to what extent do we merely pay lip service to these realizations? Even when the ubiquity of suggestion is acknowledged, the emphasis usually falls almost entirely on analyzing its effects in order to minimize them. How much do we embrace the fact that, whether we like it or not, we are inevitably involved in some measure as *mentors* to our patients? To accept fully that aspect of our role is to appreciate that it is not enough to say that our actions should always be subjected to analytic scrutiny. We also have to try to *act wisely* even while recognizing that whatever wisdom we have is always highly personal and subjective. In fact, because of that recognition, we do not *like* to think that we influence patients in regard to life-shaping questions, such as what career to pursue, what sexual orientation or quality of gender identification to adopt, whether or not to marry or even whom to marry, whether or not to try to have or adopt children, whether to reach out to estranged parents or sever ties to them, whether to take a certain political risk or not, or even whether or not to say a particular thing to a particular person between one session and the next.

Within the analytic situation as well, we want the patient to be the one who shapes the atmosphere of the relationship with little or no "interference" from us. When we interpret the transference, we like to think that we are merely bringing to the surface what is already "there," rather than cultivating something in the patient and in the relationship that might not have developed in the same way otherwise. We still like to believe that our influence on our patients' choices is limited to helping them become aware of the various aspects of their own inner conflicts as they shape the alternatives they feel they have. Perhaps with our new sophistication we have increased conviction that we cannot take our neutrality for granted, even after we have formally terminated our own analyses. But I think we have clung to the idea that with continual hard work, analysis of transference and countertransference, and critical reflection, we can *neutralize* our personal and theoretical prejudices so that their effects will be negligible. Continual doing and undoing, that is the new solution. Our hands are *not* clean; we all know that now. But we figure that if we keep washing them, maybe we can still get rid of most of the dirt (or the blood), or at least enough so that what remains will not be detectable even by ourselves.

But this strategy simply will not work. Those of us, especially, who have turned away from an objectivist view of the analyst's role and replaced it with the view that the patient's experience is partially constituted interactively in the analytic situation—in other words, those of us who have been trying to work out a "constructivist" view of the analytic process—are faced with the necessity of coming to grips with the full implications of that perspective for the role of the analyst in the patient's life. If we believe that the analyst is involved in the construction rather than *merely* the discovery of the patient's psychic reality, we are confronted with the fact that, according to that view, there is no way to reduce one's involvement to being *merely* that of a facilitator of self-awareness, or even of integration. There is no objective interpretation and there is no affective attunement that is merely responsive to and reflective of what the patient brings to the situation (Cushman, 1991; Seligman, 1990). There is always something personal and theoretical (the theoretical being an aspect of the personal) that is coming from the side of the analyst. Moreover, there is always something about that that is unknown, either because it is resisted or because it is simply beyond the patient's and the therapist's frames of reference. Whatever we can become aware of regarding the cultural, theoretical, and personal-countertransferential contexts of our actions, some things are always left in the dark. One might say that one of the contexts of our actions is always *the context of ignorance of contexts*. And yet, act we must. We have no choice about that. So along with awareness of our inevitable partial blindness, we can also recognize that the analyst is positioned right in the middle of the action, struggling with patients as they decide what to *make* of their lives, past, present, and future.

Let me pause here to say something about the term "constructivism." I realize that the term has a variety of meanings in philosophy, in literary theory, in sociology, and in psychology. Mahoney (1991) distinguishes between "radical constructivism," which connotes a virtually solipsistic relativism, and "critical constructivism," which connotes an interaction between a partially independent reality and the activity of human subjects. My use of the term constructivism is probably closer to what Mahoney means by "critical constructivism."

Neither the patient's experience nor the analyst's is some kind of Silly Putty, amenable to any shape one might wish to impose on it, and, of course, even Silly Putty has properties that limit what can be done with it. Constructive activity goes on in relation to more or less ambiguous *givens* in the patient's and the analyst's experience. In fact, some of those givens are virtually indisputable elements in the experiences of the participants, and any plausible interpretation would have to take them into account or at least not contradict them.[2] This goes for interpretations by each of the participants of the

---

2. The givens fall into two broad categories: those that are contingent and particular (like taxes) and those that are necessary, that have to be, because they are built into the structure of experience (like death). When I make assertions about the way experience works from a constructivist perspective I am claiming universal truth value for those assertions. For example, if I say that social realities are culturally relative in ways that are not fully knowable to the constructors of those realities, I do not mean to say that that assertion itself is culturally relative. The idea may emerge because of cultural-historical influences, but the truth value that is being claimed for it is transcultural and transhistorical. What may seem to be a resulting internal contradiction is more apparent than real and can be resolved with

experiences of the other as well as for interpretations that each directs toward himself or herself. Moreover, even the *ambiguous* aspects of experience are not *amorphous*. They have properties that are amenable to a variety of interpretations, maybe even infinite interpretations, especially if we take into account all the nuances that language and tone make possible. But *infinite* does not mean *unlimited* in the sense that anything goes. There are infinite numerical values between the numbers 5 and 6, but that range excludes all other numerical values.

Having recognized that, we can return to consideration of the constructive aspect of conscious and unconscious human action. Because its root is a verb denoting shaping and creating, I prefer the term *constructivism* to *perspectivism*.[3] Let me add that I do not believe that constructivism in the context of studying human experience as such should carry the same meaning as constructivism in the physical sciences or in literary theory. Experience, taken as a whole, is partially constituted by what we make of it, retrospectively, in the context of interpretation, and prospectively, in the context of experience-shaping actions (see chapter 6 for elaboration of these two aspects of constructivism).[4] I do not believe that the same could be said reasonably of the motion of the planets or of the literal contents of a completed written text. The planets and the existing text have a different sort of independence from the organizing activity of human subjects than does the flow of those subjects' experience during any given interval of time (see Taylor, 1985).

Howard (1985), writing on the role of values in psychology, while taking due note of the effects of the observer on the observed in the physical sciences, argues that in the social sciences and in psychology in particular there is a further consideration:

---

more precise use of language. Only *some* aspects of reality are socially constructed, in the sense that they are manufactured by human beings. Among those that are excluded is the fact that humans, *by their nature*, are active agents in the social construction of their worlds.

3. For a discussion of the two terms, see my reply (Hoffman, 1992) to Orange (1992) who favors "perspectival realism."

4. One of the variety of things that we can do at any given moment is to reflect upon and interpret what has gone on in the recent or distant past. Of course, the experience in the past as it happened at the time cannot be changed by any retrospective view of it. Thus the term "constitute" has different meanings in the retrospective and prospective contexts (Eric Gillett, personal communication).

The form and characteristics of any creation are, in part, a reflection
of the creator. This is true even in the natural sciences, where the theory bears the mark of the theorist. But I am arguing that subjectivity
cuts yet a second way in psychological theory and research: Human
action, the explanandum of the theory, can also change in reaction to
the theory. Therefore, although the psychologist shares with the natural scientist the task of explaining the present action of his or her
object of study, the psychologist has a further injunction: to consider
what human beings might become in response to our research.

Viewed from this perspective, psychologists are seen as agents in
the formation of human beings . . . researchers should modify their
ambition to become disinterested parties or value-free agents. It seems
that a more adequate solution would involve acknowledging and
accepting the place of values in their endeavors [p. 262].

What Howard says of researchers applies in spades, of course, to
psychoanalysts in the clinical situation.

As part of our involvement with our patients in their struggle to
shape their lives, we do, of course, work hard at reflecting critically
on the nature of our participation in the process. There is an ongoing tension and oscillation between the conscious and unconscious
building up of "realities" in one sphere or another and reflection
upon how, why, and at what cost those particular constructions
arose and became more or less calcified. Within the analytic situation, one might say there is a tension between allowing ourselves to
get caught up in various kinds of interactions with our patients, on
the one hand, and disciplining ourselves, often with our patients'
help (chapter 4), to step back to reflect critically on the meaning of
our involvement, on the other. To some extent, free association, as
the central focus of analytic attention, is replaced in this model with
the free emergence of multiple transference-countertransference scenarios, a sample of which is more or less reflected upon and interpreted over time. To say this is not to deny the central place of the
patient's "psychic reality." The transference-countertransference patterns that emerge bear the stamp, in part, of the patient's internal
object relations as they are externalized in the analytic situation
(chapter 4; Bollas, 1987; Racker, 1968; Sandler, 1976; Searles,
1978–1979). One of the potentially useful functions of countertransference disclosure is that it can bring into the open particular
transference-countertransference tensions that may be hovering in
the atmosphere of the relationship at any given moment.

Beyond the difference, however, between an emphasis on free
association and an emphasis on the emergence of transference-

countertransference configurations there is also a difference between analytic experience understood as representational or figurative and analytic experience understood as "actual" or literal (cf. Schafer, 1985). Levenson (1989) has taken psychoanalysts to task for being exclusively preoccupied with the former in connection with the exploration of "psychic reality" at the expense of recognizing the "actuality" of events inside and outside the psychoanalytic situation. The net result amounts to an institutionalized avoidance of actuality (an avoidance that may be linked with the avoidance of death as a real issue [Becker, 1973]. Levenson, however, appears to swing to the other extreme, denying the value, psychoanalytically, of regarding those events as also representational or metaphoric and as intrinsically ambiguous (Hoffman, 1990). What I think is called for is an attitude that highlights the dialectic between the figurative or "as if" aspect of the analytic experience and its literal aspect. With regard to the analyst's involvement, the tension is between viewing it as creating *opportunities for understanding in other terms*, particularly in terms of the patient's externalization of internal conflict, and viewing it as *important and consequential in its own right*. It is important to recognize, moreover, that our participation is likely to be consequential before it is explicitly understood to the extent we might like.

More broadly, it is an aspect of normal human misery, after all, that we cannot wait to be "cured" of our neuroses before we are required to make choices that profoundly affect our lives and the lives of others. To believe that analytic therapists can create fully enlightened grounds for action in the context of their work with their patients is a pipe dream. Moreover, even after a conflict seems to have been explored extensively, how it should be resolved is often unclear. So I do not think we can wash our hands of responsibility at that juncture where neurotic suffering and normal human misery meet, because I see our intimate involvement with and commitment to our patients as requiring that we be partners with them in their struggles with often agonizing existential choices and predicaments.

SOURCES OF THE ANALYST'S POWER

Now I want to turn to the nature of the analyst's power and authority in the psychoanalytic situation. Psychoanalysis entails a complex combination of ritual and spontaneity in a unique form of human interaction. The methodical, ritual, relatively impersonal features of the process are associated most clearly with the maintenance of boundaries and the personal, spontaneous aspects with the cultivation of intimacy. But the two dimensions of the process are in a dialectical relationship, so that each can only be understood in the context of the other. Indeed, each is dependent on the other for its meaning. There can be no intimacy, of course, without boundaries in *any* relationship. The challenge is to try to conceptualize the particular nature of that dialectic as it is represented and played out in the psychoanalytic situation.

I am interested in exploring the idea that the analytic therapist is involved in the process as a kind of *moral authority* in the broad sense. There is an interesting precedent for this view in Freud. Along with the notion of the unobjectionable positive transference, Freud (1916b) considered and struggled with the educative functions of the analyst in the context of what he called "after education." He wrote of this aspect of the analyst's role:

> Under the doctor's guidance [the patient] is asked to make the advance from the pleasure principle to the reality principle by which the mature human being is distinguished from the child. In this educative process, the doctor's clearer insight can hardly be said to play a decisive part; as a rule, he can only tell his patient what the latter's own reason can tell him. But it is not the same to know a thing in one's own mind and to hear it from someone outside. The doctor plays the part of this effective outsider; he makes use of the influence which one human being exercises over another. Or—recalling that it is the habit of psycho-analysis to replace what is derivative and etiolated by what is original and basic—let us say that the doctor, in his educative work, makes use of one of the components of love. In this work of after-education, he is probably doing no more than repeat the process which made education of any kind possible in the first instance. Side by side with the exigencies of life, love is the great educator; and it is by the love of those nearest him that the incomplete human being is induced to respect the decrees of necessity and to spare himself the punishment that follows any infringement of them [p. 312].

So Freud recognized that the analyst is in the position of a particular kind of authority, an intimate, *loving* authority that has continuity with the kind of authority that parents have in the lives of their children. In this connection it is noteworthy that Freud (1926b) thought that the analyst's social role could best be described as that of a "secular pastoral worker" (p. 255). Even though Freud thought of the exercise of authority by the analyst as limited primarily to persuading patients to come to terms with the "truth" about their internal and external worlds, he was hardly comfortable with this aspect of the analyst's function and warned of its dangers. In the *Outline* (1940a) he expressed concern about crushing the patient's independence, insisting that "[i]n all his attempts at improving and educating the patient the analyst must respect his [the patient's] individuality" (p. 175). Nevertheless, it is clear that Freud recognized, perhaps grudgingly, that the analyst functions as more than just a neutral facilitator of the patient's own reflective rationality and insight. Indeed, in a late work, after discussing the psychological impact of "mystical practices," Freud (1933) went so far as to say that "it may be admitted that the therapeutic efforts of psycho-analysis have chosen a similar line of approach" (p. 80).

I think it is undeniable that the boundary between the analyst and the patient defines a relationship that is, in part, hierarchically organized. The psychoanalytic situation can be viewed as a unique kind of contemporary social institution in which one of the two people involved has a special kind of power to affect the other. The delicate *integration* of boundaries and intimacy, of ritualized asymmetry and mutuality (chapter 5; Aron, 1991; Burke, 1992; Modell, 1990) helps to promote the socially legitimized authority of the analyst's role. As a modality that has the ambitious aim of altering deeply entrenched patterns of self and object representations, psychoanalytic therapy has some of the properties of what the sociologists Berger and Luckmann (1967) call "secondary socialization." In this regard, psychoanalysis entails a type of "conversation" that in itself has the potential for a great deal of impact:

> Different conversations can be compared in terms of the density of the reality they produce or maintain. . . . One may see one's lover only once a month, but the conversation then engaged in is of sufficient intensity to make up for its relative infrequency. Certain conversations may also be explicitly defined and legitimized as having privileged status—such as conversations with one's confessor, one's psychoanalyst, or a similar "authority" figure. The "authority" here lies in the cognitively and normatively superior status that is assigned to these conversations [p. 154].

When there is an attempt to radically alter an individual's "subjective reality," analogous, perhaps, to what psychoanalysts would call "structural change," what is necessary is a kind of "resocialization." Of the latter, the authors write the following:

> These processes resemble [the] primary socialization [of childhood], because they have radically to reassign reality accents and, consequently,

must replicate to a considerable degree the strongly affective identification with the socializing personnel that was characteristic of childhood. . . .

No radical transformation of subjective reality (including, of course, identity) is possible without such [affective] identification, which inevitably replicates childhood experiences of emotional dependency on significant others. These significant others are the guides into the new reality [p. 157].

The idea that psychoanalysis could bear any similarity to a process of resocialization is abhorrent to our sensibilities as analytic therapists. It smacks too much of brainwashing and too little of helping people become more aware of themselves and more able to realize their true potentials. And it is true that psychoanalysis puts a premium on skepticism and critical reflection, which distinguishes it from the other types of resocialization that Berger and Luckmann have in mind. However, I believe it is an overreaction, both to the idea of brainwashing and to the dangers of unwitting and unexamined suggestion, to deny that psychoanalysis entails a complex kind of concentrated social influence that partakes of some of the ingredients that Berger and Luckmann attribute to "resocialization." Not the least of these ingredients is a culturally sanctioned power that is invested in the analyst and that is sustained and cultivated in an ongoing way by the ritual features of the psychoanalytic process itself.

DOMAINS OF THE ANALYST'S MORAL AUTHORITY

I am thinking about two interrelated ways in which this power is likely to be (or perhaps is inevitably) utilized by the participants. One has to do with the affirmation of the patient's *sense of self* and worth as an experiencing subject and as an agent. The other has to do with accompanying the patient through, and in some measure becoming implicated in, the patient's *choices* as they emerge and are wrestled with over time. Some version of the first is more commonly accepted in the psychoanalytic community, implicit in various concepts. Relevant theorists are Strachey, Winnicott, Kohut, and others. The second is more controversial on its face. I think the two, although they can be distinguished conceptually, are inseparable in practice. Nevertheless, for discussion purposes, I will organize my remarks around affirmation in a relatively abstract sense, and then turn to the way in which its expression in practice implicates the analyst in the patient's choices and patterns of adaptation.[5]

Although there may be unconscious factors in the transference and the countertransference that interfere with the patient's ability either to elicit or to assimilate the analyst's affection and respect, I believe there is something to the simple idea that the analyst is an authority whose regard for the patient matters in a special way, one that we do not try to analyze away, nor could we, perhaps, even if we did try. In some cases it may take a lot of work to get to the point where that regard can be conveyed by the analyst and be received and integrated by the patient. But I doubt many of us have felt, as patients or as therapists, that the process, when it has been helpful, has not included that factor of affirmation (cf. Schafer, 1983, pp. 43–48). The likelihood of that happening in an *authentic* way is increased, not only because the analyst is in a position conducive to eliciting a certain quality of regard, but also because the patient is in an analogous position. Regard for *the analyst* is fostered by the fact that the patient knows so much *less* about him or her than the analyst knows about the patient. The analyst is in a position that is likely to promote the most tolerant, understanding, and generous aspects of his or her personality. I think of "idealization" partly in interactional terms (as in "making the other more ideal") because the analytic situation and often the patient actually do nourish some of the analyst's more "ideal" qualities as a person, what Schafer (1983) has referred to as the analyst's "second self." Conversely, however, the analyst's regard for *the patient* is fostered by the fact that he or she knows *so much* about the patient, including the origins of the patient's difficulties and his or her struggles to deal with them. Moreover, of course, neither party has to live with the other or even engage the other outside of the circumscribed analytic situation, so that each is afforded quite a bit of protection from the other's more difficult qualities.

Corresponding, again, with what several authors have discussed in terms of an interplay between the "principle of mutuality" and the "principle of asymmetry" (chapter 5; Modell, 1990; Aron, 1991; Burke, 1992), there is an ongoing dialectic between the patient's perception of the analyst as *a person like himself or herself* and the

---

5. The two paragraphs that follow are largely repeated in chapter 8 (pp. 203–204), which was published originally (in 1994) before this chapter (in 1996), although it was written later.

patient's perception of the analyst as *a person with superior knowledge, wisdom, judgment, and power*. Each way of viewing the analyst is very much colored by the other. Whichever is in the foreground, the other is always in the background. What the balance should be for any particular analytic dyad, at any particular moment or over time, is very difficult to determine or control. Also, it must emerge from an authentic kind of participation by the analyst rather than from adherence to some technical formula. The patient may benefit, however, simply from his or her recognition of the sincerity of the analyst's struggle with the issue.

I believe that there is likely to be a special affirming power associated with the analyst's willingness to engage the patient in a way that is personally expressive and spontaneous. The source of that power is precisely in the ritualized asymmetry that promotes a view of the analyst as elevated in some sense and as beyond the patient's reach. In that context the analyst's emotional and personal availability can become a kind of magical gift that is assimilated in a manner that has continuity with (although it is hardly equivalent to) the way in which the love of parents is assimilated in childhood. It might be argued that there is something magical associated with one person's winning the love of another, no matter what the circumstances, and I would agree that what I am talking about is very closely related to the experience of love in other contexts. I am arguing, however, that the analyst's personal involvement in the analytic situation has, potentially, a particular kind of concentrated power because it is embedded in a ritual in which the analyst is set up to be a special kind of authority.

I realize that these are uncomfortable ideas to entertain because they seem to imply an element of manipulation, just the kind that we imagine we are trying to undo through the analysis of transference.[6]

---

6. The structure of the point I am making reminds me of Macalpine's (1950) when she said, in effect: Look, we have to face the fact that the analytic setting does not simply facilitate the flow of spontaneous associations. On the contrary, the setting generally creates a situation of loss and deprivation that induces regression. Moreover, that is something, she said, that we don't tell our patients about, nor was she sure that we should. I am saying, let's not deny the power that we use to affect how our patients feel about themselves and how they conduct their lives, a power that does depend, in part, on the asymmetrical aspect of the relationship. Unlike Macalpine, I think it would be best if this aspect of the process became an open subject for exploration in the analysis. Also, unlike Macalpine, I do not favor deliberately trying to induce a regressive transference neurosis by

However, while such analysis might diminish or partially "deconstruct" the magical aspect of the analyst's role, I do not think it is likely that it would eliminate it entirely, which is probably fortunate. The very fact that we usually maintain the analytic frame even after termination, to the extent that, for example, we do not become friends with or socialize with our patients in the usual sense, indicates that we want to preserve rather than undo the special kind of *presence* in our patients' lives that the analytic situation fosters. So those of us who are interested in developing more mutual and egalitarian relationships with our patients should not deny the extent to which we are drawing upon the ritualized asymmetry of the analytic situation to give that mutuality its power. The asymmetry makes our participation in the spirit of mutuality *matter* to our patients in an intensified way, one that helps to build or construct our patients' views of themselves as creative agents and as persons ultimately deserving of love.

Our responsibility becomes more daunting when we recognize that the process of affirmation is never content-free. I do not think it is possible to locate and respond to a pure potentiality for experience and choice within the patient. Our affirmative attitude inevitably gravitates toward some of the patient's potentials at the expense of others. In that sense, affirmation of a patient's sense of self and participation in his or her moments or patterns of choice become inseparable. The context of affirmation is always one in which our patients are in the midst of doing or saying *something* or just being a certain way or set of ways. If we must have responsibility for affecting a patient's sense of self and worth, we might wish that, with regard to content, the *patient's* experience would be the exclusive governing factor in the interaction. If we are there as empathic selfobjects (Kohut), or as responders to the spontaneous gestures of our patients' germinal or half-buried true selves (Winnicott), then we ourselves, as people with our own individual dispositions and values, can disappear just as effectively as we could behind the mantle of scientific objectivity in the classical model. But affective attunement and empathic responsiveness, no less than traditional interpretation, are colored by each therapist's cultural, theoretical, and personal bias. Whatever the commonalities, there are undoubtedly nuances in the nature of affective attunement that vary from one culture to another

---

depriving the patient of an object relationship (cf. Lipton, 1977a). I am advocating a more complex struggle within the dialectic of asymmetry and mutuality as discussed and illustrated throughout this volume.

and from one parent to another or one therapist to another within the same culture (see Cushman, 1991; Seligman, 1990). I am not for a moment questioning that there is a difference between impinging on our patients in an intrusive way and leaving room for their relatively spontaneous initiatives. But no matter how far we go in the direction of responsiveness, we never reach a point where our own personalities disappear from the field.

I am anticipating that some might argue that perfect empathy and attunement, like perfect objectivity, are merely ideals to strive for, with the understanding that we are always falling short of them despite our best efforts. My reply is that I do not think it is good to set up intrinsically irrational ideals that do violence to human nature. Aspiring to walk on water and striving to be able to do that are bound to *interfere* with learning to swim. Such a standard of locomotion is no less wrongheaded if we humbly "admit" that, since nobody is "perfect," those attempting to walk will surely get wet. The ideals of accurate empathy and perfect affective attunement, like the ideal of perfect neutrality, encourage the development of inappropriate ego ideals which in turn promote defensive illusions about what we have been able to accomplish, along with misleading acknowledgments of our "imperfection." All of that distracts us from the more relevant issue, which is to consider, not whether, but *how* we have been personally involved with our patients. Also, such reflection does not erase our participation and its effects. Talking about our suggestive influence may liberate the patient from some of its unconsciously controlling power, but we are kidding ourselves if we think we have thereby managed to remove ourselves from the field or even that we have managed to restrict our influence to what is in accord with the valuing in psychoanalysis of consciousness and individual freedom. Indeed, the very way in which we analyze one "suggestion" is likely to carry another with it that is unknown. This is not to say that the patient is simply putty in the analyst's hands. On the contrary, it is precisely respect for the patient's agency that opens the door to overcoming our *phobic* attitude toward our own personal influence on our patients' lives. But let me hasten to add that after we have overcome that phobia, there is plenty left in the realm of relatively normal anxiety that is warranted in light of the unique nature of our responsibility as participants in the patient's struggle for integration and self-definition.

With regard to cultural bias, Cushman (1995) has contributed a major work exploring, both historically and clinically, the way in which psychoanalytic therapy tends uncritically to adopt and support the values of competitive, materialistic individualism, even though it has the potential to be a more constructively critical institution. I agree with Cushman's thesis that psychoanalysis is inevitably a moral enterprise and that it behooves the analyst to include, within the analytic work itself, scrutiny of his or her own passive conformity to prevailing social expectations regarding what constitutes the good life. Cushman is loathe, however, to search for possible universals underlying the activities and roles of "healing" figures in various cultures and subcultures, a project that seems quite useful to me, and one which is actually implicit in Cushman's own approach, despite his emphasis on cultural differences. He writes:

> Each era has a predominant configuration of the self, a particular foundational set of beliefs about what it means to be human. . . . These selves and roles are not interchangeable or equivalent. Each embodies a kind of unique and local truth that should not be reduced to a universal law, because such reductions inevitably depend on a particular cultural frame of reference, which in turn inevitably involves an ideological agenda [p. 3].

Granting the factor of cultural relativity, is Cushman not pointing also to the universal need for some kind of belief system and are there not moral authorities in every culture who provide a special kind of support to whatever the local belief system might be? Put another way, is not the claim that social reality is socially constructed one that Cushman believes is true transculturally and transhistorically, amounting, therefore, to a "universal law?" It may be that, in keeping with our postmodern sensibility, this perspective emerges specifically in our era, but the origin of the view has no bearing on the truth value that is being claimed for it. Cushman, despite his stated aversion to universalizing, writes the following regarding the human condition:

> There is something *in the very nature of being human* that makes it extremely difficult to differentiate what we are from what we construct, or what we can be from what our horizon permits us to be. We construct the social world in such a way so that we can consider it, experience it, as reality itself—the one, true, concrete truth. To do otherwise would be to open up the existential abyss for us, to force us to confront our own lacks, absences, and emptiness, to challenge the taken-for-granted power relations, economic privileges, and status hierarchy of our era, and to acknowledge the relational rules, alliances, and secrets of our family of origin. For various reasons, an awareness of the constructed nature of our world appears to be too

difficult to acknowledge and too frightening to live with [p. 309; italics added].

And yet the psychotherapist is called upon to question the status quo, and thereby to open that dreaded "existential abyss." Cushman says, "It is precisely this conspiring, this unknowing, embodied collusion that psychotherapy is designed to reveal and undo" (p. 310). It is one thing, however, to expose hidden values and biases and quite another to reject them in favor of specific alternative ways of being. Psychoanalytic skepticism itself, potentially informed and shaped by the critical spirit of postmodernism, ensures a questioning attitude toward explicit and implicit value systems, old and new. It casts doubt upon the moral authority of the analyst, even as aspects of analytic ritual promote its influence. The authority that endures can only be an *ironic* one, given the extent to which it is challenged. When we are aware of "the constructed nature of our world," we can no longer live in it with the same faith and in the same taken-for-granted way that was open to us without that awareness. Indeed, the one absolute that may survive such exposure is the value of that very awareness and, with it, the value of critical reflection upon one's world and oneself.

SESSIONS WITHIN SESSIONS

Now I would like to go back to the anecdote from the TV program, the episode of *Sessions*. I have something more to add to the story. It so happens that I do not get cable TV in my home and that the way I learned about *Sessions* was from a patient of mine who watched it regularly and thought I would enjoy it. He said he could tape a couple of episodes for me if I was interested. I said I was, and he brought them in. Although once I took the tape I felt I should see the program, I did not feel undue pressure from the patient, who is not at all demanding in his manner. Actually, I thought of it as an opportunity to share an experience with him that was of mutual interest. It is the sort of thing that I will do sometimes: see a movie a patient recommends, read something he or she suggests, and so on. I am especially likely to do it if I feel that it might further the process, that it is in keeping with my own interests, and that it does not result in my feeling overextended.

Of course, my conscious experience in this respect is not always reliable. It is always possible that a seemingly "conflict-free" response to a patient's appeals entails repression of the conflictual elements in both parties. The patient's regressively devouring impulse may be denied, for example, along with the analyst's impulse to retaliate. Or the patient may be identified with a demanding, intrusive, or assaultive parent while the analyst may be in the position of the child who is rationalizing his or her compliance (cf. Frederickson, 1990; Tower, 1956). When the analyst can detect signs of being caught in the "grip" of such a transference-countertransference field (D. B. Stern, 1991), he or she can begin the work of extricating him- or herself and the patient from it through reflection, interpretation, "negotiation," and other kinds of actions (chapters 4 through 10; Ehrenberg, 1992; Gill, 1982, 1994; Mitchell, 1988, 1993; Pizer, 1992; Racker, 1968; D. B. Stern, 1989; Tansey and Burke, 1989). The relationship between repetition of pathological aspects of the past and relatively new experience is usually highly complex and paradoxical. In fact, it is generally useful to view their relationship as dialectical, that is, each not only serves as ground for the other but is actually on the brink of evolving into the other (chapters 7 and 8; Ghent, 1992).

The example I am presenting here is relatively uncomplicated, however, in that so far as I was aware at the time (and have been since), the work was going on in the context of a rather strong sense of relatively unobjectionable positive transference and counter-transference. There was a feeling that the analytic relationship contrasted with the pathogenic aspects of the past in a rather straightforward way. Although the prevalence of a manifestly benign atmosphere can be grounds for suspecting something latently malignant, I do not feel it is necessary to arrange the analytic situation to induce the emergence of the latter. Macalpine's (1950) conceptualization of the analytic process in terms of a systematic induction of a regressive transference neurosis was based upon the assumption that the patient's pathogenic desires could be reduced to obsolete wishes that had to be renounced. We currently have a much broader conception of the nature of those desires, which have come to encompass legitimate developmental needs.[7] Now, if anything, we are in danger of the opposite mistake, which is to reduce

---

7. In this regard, Steven Stern (1994) draws a useful distinction between "the repeated relationship" (in "Type I transference") and "the needed relationship" (in "Type II transference").

the patient's desires to legitimate needs and to omit consideration of less legitimate wishes (Mitchell, 1988). Either reduction can lead to a mechanical, objectivistic approach, one lacking spontaneity and personal expressiveness.

Components of an optimal analytic attitude include: recognition of the dialectical relationship between the authority enhancing aspects of analytic ritual and the elements of mutuality and spontaneity within the personal side of the relationship; a perspective in which the patient's experience is seen as involving a complex, fluctuating hierarchical arrangement of needs and wishes, the quality, intensity, and rank order of which are partially dependent on the nature of the analyst's participation (Hoffman, 1987; Mitchell, 1993); recognition of the dialectical and often paradoxical relationship between repetition and new experience in the psychoanalytic process (chapters 6 through 10; Ghent, 1992; Pizer, 1992); and appreciation of the fact that the analyst is always in a position of some uncertainty as to the nature of what has emerged in the patient and in himself or herself as wellsprings for action.

Ultimately, there is no escape from the responsibility that falls to the analyst to act with as much wisdom as possible, even while recognizing the action's subjective foundation. Sometimes, the sense of uncertainty is there in principle, but what is in the foreground is a sense of conviction about how a particular line of thought or a particular kind of responsiveness might help to develop the relationship in a creative and authentic way (chapters 6 and 7; Bader, 1995). Such was the case in the example I have begun to report.

So to return to the story, in this instance I was pleased to accept the videotape that the patient brought in. Watching the program at home was an experience that was embedded in the analytic process, although outside of its customary boundaries. I will not go into detail about the case, except to say that the patient is the son of Holocaust survivors who raised him in a manner that was very austere, almost as though they were identified with their persecutors and he and his siblings were their prisoners. In his whole life he could not recall ever getting a toy from either parent. Room and board were provided, but there were virtually no overt demonstrations of affection. He said his parents never played with him. In addition, he was raised in an ultraorthodox religious manner. His parents, especially his father, were extremely strict about observing Jewish law. I therefore experienced the sharing of the tape, immediately, in the context of this patient's life, as a form of *playing* (Ehrenberg, 1992; Feinsilver, 1989; Winnicott, 1971) that violated the orthodox observance of *psychoanalytic* rules in a way that I thought was good.

Now we cannot omit from what I felt about all of this the fact that I also attended a parochial grade school and high school, although a much more liberal and modern one than what this patient went through. Nevertheless, like the patient, I broke from the tradition that I was raised in and now bear an ambivalent relation to it. Perhaps, not coincidentally, I have also broken from certain aspects of *psychoanalytic* orthodoxy. How could those experiences not color my experience of this patient's efforts to escape what I thought of as the bondage of his austere upbringing and, more immediately, the constraints of the usual boundaries of the analysis?

So I watched the tape. I enjoyed it a lot and told the patient so in the next session. We chatted a bit about various aspects of the program, some of which were, and some of which were not, as far as I could tell, of any special interest analytically. Incidentally, that ostensibly "inconsequential" part, from the point of view of the analytic work, was actually a very important part of the experience, because it was spontaneous and informal and *not* explicitly analyzed. If you try to analyze everything, even all aspects of possible enactments, you are bound to suck the life out of the experience. Indeed, why the analyst and the patient would feel compelled to do that would be the next thing that probably should be analyzed.

In this instance we did touch on various aspects of the program. We talked about the analyst's specific suggestion with regard to the father, and together we mulled over the question of whether there was any way the patient could approach *his* father that might create the opportunity for a breakthrough in their relationship. The patient did not think so, and I felt he was right. He said he was moved when the son and the father hugged at the end. I said I had been moved, too, but that I understood that his feelings had special poignancy in light of the seemingly impenetrable barriers between himself and his own father.

With regard to the analyst's transparent disclaimer, "just a thought," it has become a standing joke between us, so that whenever I notice that I am tilting one way or another on some dilemma the patient is struggling with, either he or I will comment, "just a thought, of course." With regard to the sharing of the tape, I said something like, "Well, he walks around a lot in the office, but I didn't see him borrowing any of the patient's videotapes, so maybe I win in the competition for who is freer and more flexible." The patient laughed.[8] It certainly is part of the atmosphere that we enjoy each other's sense of humor. An important point here is that I feel that my borrowing the tape was embedded in an atmosphere of mutual understanding as to one of its *probable* meanings in the context of the patient's life story, so that it seemed *to go without saying* that the interaction contrasted with any the patient could ever have had with his parents. Some personal moments like that are preanalyzed and it is sometimes not worth laboriously searching anew for their unspoken or unconscious meanings, because then you risk spoiling the element of spontaneity in them. On the other hand, if there are subsequent dreams or other associations that seem to allude to the unconventional interaction, it would be important, of course, to try to interpret them in light of that event.

To locate this vignette further in relation to the central issues I am considering, my borrowing the tape and sharing the experience of viewing the program and discussing it later were all actions that were expressions of my special rapport with this patient. I admired his sensitivity, his humor, his courage in breaking from his anhedonic family's restrictive codes of conduct, and his active search for experiences of pleasure with other people. I also trusted this patient, in that I did not feel that his making this request would open the floodgates for all kinds of demands. I felt confident that he respected my boundaries and was not going to make a habit of asking that I violate them. At the same time, the contents of the session in the TV program and of the actual analytic hour bore on the patient's hunger for an affective connection with a parental figure. The key here is that my closeness with this patient and my enjoyment in working with him on what Ehrenberg (1992) calls "the intimate edge" drew special power from the fact that, after all, I was also his analyst. As his analyst I did not *have to* participate with him in this way. And as his analyst I had already acquired some of the regard and power that is inherent in the role, at least as a very strong potentiality.

Finally, the expressions of recognition and attunement and the affective tone that accompanied them included much that came from my own personality and history. I could have been an analyst who

---

8. Joking remarks of this sort are often implicitly interpretive of issues in the transference and the countertransference. In this instance, among other things, the comment touches on the patient's wish that the analyst be flexible, the possibility that the patient is intending to evoke some competitive feeling in him, and the element of competitiveness that the countertransference actually includes at a conscious level.

was either seriously committed to the tradition in which the patient was raised or who practiced psychoanalysis in a more traditional way, and I doubt that the same kind of interaction would have occurred. It is quite possible that if the approach were more traditional, the patient never would have suggested that the analyst borrow the tape to begin with, because the atmosphere might not have been conducive to such a proposal. Instead, the patient may have experienced more grief about the absence of a warm, playful, affectionate environment in the analysis, repeating, but also usefully bringing into focus, the deprivations of his childhood.

Similarly, surely something else would have happened with an analyst who was more valuing of traditional religious practices. As different as that might have been, would it necessarily have been any less empathic or attuned to this patient's needs? For example, perhaps in that setting and in that company what would have gained more force would have been the patient's missing the orthodox community that he had moved away from, and a stronger, although still conflictual wish to return to it. The patient and I certainly talked about that side of his conflict, but without the same *conviction* that was mobilized on the other side. It would be comforting to think that what emerged with me was something closer to what Winnicott would call the "true self" and that what would have emerged with this other, hypothetical therapist would have been something more like the "false," "compliant self." But I doubt that the difference is nearly that cut and dried.

The patient's experience always contains a variety of potentials, including multiple potential "selves" or aspects of self (see Mitchell, 1993). Which of those potentials develops further and is strengthened might have something to do with who we (the therapists) are as people, reflected in what we respond to, with what affect, and with what degree of conviction. Again, whatever our orientation in other respects, we have to recognize that we are intimately involved in our patients' struggles to make better lives for themselves, and we cannot ignore our own vision of the better life in our participation in those struggles.[9]

---

9. I realize that there are different *kinds* of values associated with a sense of freedom and playfulness on the one hand, and a wish to break away from a specific orthodox belief system on the other. The former is a more "universal" value, or at least one about which there is more consensus in our culture. The latter is grounded more in assumptions that apply to a particular subculture or individual. It might be argued that it is acceptable for

There are occasions when the patient, in order better to exercise his or her own judgment, deserves to know something about the personal factors that we sense may be affecting the nature of our participation. I shared quite a bit with the patient I have discussed regarding my background and my own attitudes and conflicts with regard to some of the issues that he was dealing with. Sometimes, having those things on the table gives the patient the chance to see the relativity of the analyst's point of view to the analyst's own experience and history. What should or should not be revealed is a difficult and personal matter. My point is that in a constructivist view of the process we have the responsibility to come to terms with, and find ways to manage, our personal influence, without the protections that are afforded by a model of scientific inquiry into "the facts" of the patient's experience.

FROM SOLITARY REFLECTION TO RELATIONAL STRUGGLE

If we think of the history of our sense of the analytic process, we can trace a movement—one that is decidedly nonlinear—from Freud's solitary reflection on his own dreams, which sets up self-analysis as the ideal, to the detached presence of the analyst as a scientific observer and facilitator of the transference and its interpretation, to a view of the analyst as responsive in a therapeutically corrective way to the patient's needs and deficits, to an appreciation of the usefulness of countertransference in the process, to an understanding that the analyst's interpretations do not simply map on to a prestructured reality but rather contribute something to the construction of that reality, to a recognition of the culturally relative and ironic aspects of the analyst's authority, to an appreciation of the full extent and implications of our personal involvement with our patients as they struggle to make sense of and modify their ways of experiencing and constructing their worlds. Stated succinctly, and

---

analysts to be biased in favor of the more universal values, but that they have no business exercising influence with respect to the more individual issues. In practice, however, I believe that even with respect to the more individual matters, analysts are more involved than is often recognized. Moreover, the more commonly accepted values may be tied to particular cultural practices and beliefs that also warrant critical examination (Cushman, 1991, 1995; Grey, 1993; Seligman, 1990).

summarizing the movement from the beginning until now, we have traversed the distance from analysis as *solitary reflection* to analysis as *relational struggle*. In the latter, against the backdrop of the ritualized asymmetry of the psychoanalytic situation from which we draw special moral power, we participate as intimate partners with our patients as they wrestle with conflict and as they choose from among, and struggle to realize, their multiple potentials for intimacy and autonomy, for identification and individuality, for work and play, and for continuity and change.

◆ 4 ◆

The Patient as Interpreter of the Analyst's Experience

This chapter presents a point of view on the psychoanalytic situation and on psychoanalytic technique, in part through a selective review of the literature. An important underlying assumption in this essay is that existing theoretical models inevitably influence and reflect practice. This is often true even of models that practitioners claim they do not take seriously or literally. Such models may continue to affect practice adversely as long as their features are not fully appreciated and as long as alternative models are not recognized or integrated. An example of such a lingering model is the one in which the analytic therapist is said to function like a blank screen in the psychoanalytic situation.

THE RESILIENCE OF THE BLANK-SCREEN CONCEPT

The psychoanalytic literature is replete with attacks on the blank-screen concept, the idea that the analyst is not accurately perceived by the patient as a real person, but that he or she serves rather as a screen or mirror to whom various attitudes, feelings, and motives can be attributed, depending upon the patient's particular neurosis and its transference expression. Critiques of this idea have come from within the ranks of classical Freudian analysts, as well as from

An earlier version of this chapter appeared in 1983 in *Contemporary Psychoanalysis*, 19:389–422.

Kleinians and Sullivanians. Even if one looks only at the classical literature, in one way or another the blank-screen concept seems to have been pronounced dead and laid to rest many times over the years. In 1950, Ida Macalpine, addressing only the implications for the patient's experience of classical psychoanalytic *technique* as she conceived of it (that is, not considering the analyst's personal contributions), said the following:

> It can *no longer be maintained* that the analysand's reactions in analysis occur spontaneously. His behavior is a response to the rigid infantile setting to which he is exposed. This poses many problems for further investigation. One of them is how does it react upon the patient? He must know it, consciously or unconsciously [p. 526; italics added].

Theresa Benedek said in 1953:

> As the history of psychoanalysis shows, the discussion of countertransference usually ended in a retreat to defensive positions. The argument to this end *used to be* [italics added] that the classical attitude affords the best guarantee that the *personality of the therapist* [italics in original] would not enter the action-field of the therapeutic process. By that one assumes that as long as the analyst does not reveal himself as a person, does not answer questions regarding his own personality, he remains unknown as if without individuality, that the transference process may unfold and be motivated only by the patient's resistances. The patient—although he is a sensitive, neurotic individual—is not supposed to sense and discern the therapist as a person [p. 202].

In 1956, Lucia Tower wrote:

> I have for a very long time speculated that in many—perhaps every—intensive analytic treatment there develops something in the nature of countertransference structures (perhaps even a "neurosis") which are essential and inevitable counterparts of the transference neurosis [p. 232].

In the 1960s, Loewald (1960), Stone (1961), and Greenson (1965) added their voices to the already large chorus of protest against this remarkably resilient concept. From varying theoretical perspectives, the critiques continued into the 1970s and 1980s as represented, for example, in the writings of Gill (1979, 1982a,b, 1983; Gill and Hoffman, 1982a,b), Sandler (1976, 1981), and Kohut (1977), among many others. In fact, the blank-screen idea has probably not been articulated as often or even as well by its proponents as it has been by its opponents, a situation which leads inevitably to the suspicion that the proponents have been straw men and that shooting them down became, at some point, a kind of popular psychoanalytic sport.[1]

I am persuaded, however, that the issue is a very important one and that it deserves repeated examination and discussion. The blank-screen view in psychoanalysis is only one instance of a much broader phenomenon that might be termed *asocial conceptions of the patient's experience in psychotherapy*. According to these conceptions, there is a stream of experience going on in the patient that is divorced to a significant extent from the immediate impact of the therapist's personal presence.[2] I say "personal presence" because, generally, certain theoretically prescribed facilitating aspects of the therapist's conduct are recognized fully as affecting the course of the patient's experience. But the paradigm is one in which proper or ideal conduct on the part of the therapist allows for a flow of experience that has an organic-like momentum of its own and that is free to follow a certain "natural" course. An intriguing example of this asocial paradigm *outside* of psychoanalysis can be found in client-centered therapy. Ideally, the classical client-centered therapist is so totally and literally self-effacing that his or her personality as such is effectively removed from the patient's purview. Carl Rogers (1951) stated:

> It is surprising how frequently the client uses the word "impersonal" in describing the therapeutic relationship after the conclusion of therapy. This is obviously not intended to mean that the relationship was cold or disinterested. It appears to be the client's attempt to describe this unique experience in which the person of the counselor—the counselor as an evaluating, reacting person with needs of his own—is

---

1. It is interesting that critics of the blank-screen concept have frequently been concerned that others would think they were beating a dead horse (see, for example, Sterba, 1934, p. 117; Stone, 1961, pp. 18–19; and Kohut, 1977, pp. 253–255).

2. The implication that such an independent current in the patient's experience does not exist could be misleading. Clearly the patient brings a myriad of internal structures (or schemas) to the encounter with the analyst (innate dispositions, internal object relations, intrapsychic dynamics, patterns of selective attention and responsiveness). Yet those structures emerge and are colored experientially in the context of the interaction with the analyst who, in turn, brings his or her own internal structures to the situation.

so clearly absent. In this sense it is "im"-personal . . . the whole relationship is composed of the self of the client, the counselor being depersonalized for the purposes of therapy into being "the client's other self" [p. 208].

In psychoanalysis, the blank-screen idea persists in more or less qualified and more or less openly acknowledged forms.[3] The counterpart of the notion that the analyst functions like a screen is the definition of transference as a distortion of current reality. As Szasz (1963) points out, this definition can serve a very important defensive function for the analyst, a function that may partly account for the persistence of the concept. I believe that another factor that has kept it alive has been the confusion of two issues. One has to do with the optimal level of spontaneity and personal involvement that the analyst should express in the analytic situation. The other has to do with the kind of credibility that is attributed to the patient's ideas about the analyst's experience. A theorist may repudiate the notion that the analyst should behave in an aloof, impersonal manner without addressing the question of the tenability of the patient's transference-based speculations about the analyst's experience. To anticipate what follows, such speculations may touch upon aspects of the analyst's response to the patient that are thought to be well concealed or of which the analyst is unaware. In general, recommendations pertaining to the analyst's personal conduct in the analytic situation may very well leave intact the basic model according to which the transference is understood and interpreted.

STANDARD QUALIFICATIONS OF
THE BLANK-SCREEN CONCEPT

The notion that ideally the analyst functions like a screen is always qualified in the sense that it applies to only a part of the patient's total experience of the interaction, the part that is conventionally regarded as neurotic transference. This is the aspect of the patient's experience which, allegedly, distorts reality because of the persisting influence of childhood events, wishes, conflicts, and adaptations. There are two kinds of experience that even the staunchest propo-

---

3. Dewald's (1972) depiction of his conduct of an analysis exemplifies, as Lipton (1982) has shown, a relatively pure, if implicit, blank-screen position.

nents of the screen or mirror function of the analyst recognize as likely to be responsive to something in the analyst's actual behavior rather than as expressions of pure fantasy. One is the patient's perception of the analyst as essentially trustworthy and competent, a part of the patient's experience that Freud (1912) subsumed under the rubric of the "unobjectionable" positive transference, but that others, most notably Sterba (1934), Greenson (1965), and Zetzel (1956) chose to exclude from the realm of transference, designating it as the experience of the working or therapeutic alliance.[4] The second is the patient's recognition of and response to relatively blatant expressions of the analyst's neurotic and anti-therapeutic countertransference. Both categories of experience are said to lie outside the realm of transference proper, which is where we find the patient's unfounded ideas, his or her neurotic, intrapsychically determined fantasies about the therapist. The point is well represented in the following statements (quoted here in reverse order), which are part of a classical definition of transference (Moore and Fine, 1968):

---

4. For discussions of the implications of Freud's position on this matter see Lipton (1977a) and Gill (1982a, pp. 9–15). One of the advantages of the notion of the unobjectionable positive transference is that it ackowledges a possible irrational component in the therapeutic action of the process. For Freud, this aspect of transference involves elements of dependency and idealization with origins in early childhood. It is "unobjectionable" not because it is realistic, but because, hopefully, the analyst will employ it to a good end (see Friedman, 1969, for discussion of this paradox). The 1983 article that is essentially republished here is focused on correcting the view of the analyst as a blank screen. Consequently, this chapter fails to give sufficient weight to the importance of the analyst's relative subordination of his or her own personal interest and desire. In certain respects the analyst *should be* less visible than the patient. That asymmetry promotes both rational and irrational aspects of the analyst's therapeutic authority. In general, the notion of a dialectic between the patient's sense of the analyst as a person like himself or herself and the patient's sense of the analyst as a person with superior, even magical power is not recognized, much less developed, in this chapter (the original version of which was written ten years before the original version of chapter 3 on the analyst's "ironic authority"). What is developed here is precisely one side of that polarity, namely the place of the patient's perception of the *symmetrical* aspects of the analyst's participation, rather than the asymmetrical aspects. Nevertheless, certain dialectical relationships *are* in the foreground here, such as those between transference and countertransference, between the patient as interpreter and the analyst as interpreter, and between interpretation and "association" in both parties.

(1) Transference should be carefully differentiated from the therapeutic alliance, a conscious aspect of the relationship between
analyst and patient. In this, each implicitly agrees and understands their working together to help the analysand to mature
through *insight*, progressive understanding, and control.
(2) One of the important reasons for the relative anonymity of the
analyst during the treatment process is the fact that a lack of
information about his real attributes in personal life facilitates a
transfer of the patient's revived early images on to his person. It
also lessens the distortion of fantasies from the past by present
perceptions. It must be recognized that there are situations or
circumstances where the actual behavior or attitudes of the analyst cause reactions in the patient; these are not considered part
of the transference reaction (See *countertransference*) [p. 93].⁵

TWO TYPES OF PARADIGMS AND CRITIQUES

In my view, critiques of the screen concept can be classified into two
major categories: conservative and radical. Conservative critiques, in
effect, always take the following form: they argue that one or both
of the standard qualifications of the blank-screen view noted above
have been underemphasized or insufficiently elaborated in terms of
their role in the analytic process. I call these critiques *conservative*
because they retain the notion that a crucial aspect of the patient's
experience of the analytic therapist has little or no relation to the
therapist's actual behavior or actual attitudes. The conservative critic
reserves the term transference for this aspect of the patient's experi-

---

5. If there have been significant changes in mainstream psychoanalytic
thought since 1968 when the Glossary edited by Moore and Fine was originally published, they are not reflected in the definition of transference that
appears in the third edition (1990). Although the editors tell us in the
Preface that it is "greatly revised" and that many definitions have been
"updated" (with the assistance of 195 listed contributors), with regard to
the transference we are told that "the relative anonymity of the analyst facilitates the transfer of revived early images onto his or her person. In the
absence of information about the analyst's attributes and personal life, the
patient generates fantasies relatively uncontaminated by perception of the
present." And further: "Not all the patient's reactions to the analyst are
transference. Some are based on the analyst's attitudes or actual behavior"
(p. 197). Clearly, the dichotomy of transference fantasy and the real relationship is as sharp here as it was 22 years earlier.

ence. At the same time, this critic objects to a failure to recognize sufficiently the importance of another aspect of the patient's experience, which is influenced by the "real" characteristics of the therapist, whether these real characteristics promote or interfere with an ideal analytic process. The dichotomy between realistic and unrealistic perception may be considered less sharp, but it is nevertheless retained. Although the realistic aspects of the patient's experience are now given more careful consideration and weight, in relation to transference proper the therapist is no less a blank screen than before. By not altering the standard paradigm for defining what is or is not realistic in the analytic situation, conservative critiques of the blank-screen fallacy always end up perpetuating that very fallacy.

In contrast to conservative critiques, radical critiques reject the dichotomy between transference as distortion and nontransference as reality based. They argue instead that the transference itself generally has a significant plausible basis in the here and now.[6] Radical critics of the blank-screen model deny that there is any aspect of the patient's experience that pertains to the analyst's *inner motives* that can be unequivocally designated as distorting of reality. Similarly, they deny that there is any aspect of that experience that can be unequivocally designated as faithful to reality. From the point of view of these critics it is best for the analyst to have as a working assumption that the perspective that the patient brings to bear in interpreting the therapist's inner attitudes is one among many perspectives that are relevant, each of which may highlight a facet of the analyst's involvement. This amounts to a different paradigm, not simply an elaboration of the standard paradigm, which is what the conservative critics propose.

In rejecting the proposition that transference-dominated experience and nontransference-dominated experience can be differentiated on the grounds that the former is represented by fantasy that is divorced from reality whereas the latter is reality based, the radical critics do not imply that the two types of experience cannot be

6. The word "generally" in this sentence replaces the word "always" that appeared in the original article. To say "always" is an an overcorrection and an overstatement. Room has to be left for perceptions and inferences on the patient's part that are very improbable, virtually "off the wall," although as soon as one says that one must immediately become concerned about the analyst's ability to make that judgment. I would stand by the claim of the radical critics, as stated in the next sentence, regarding definitive conclusions about the analyst's inner motives.

distinguished. Indeed, having rejected the criterion of distorted versus realistic perception, they are obliged to offer other criteria according to which this distinction can be made. For such critics, the distinguishing features of the neurotic transference have to do with the fact that the patient is selectively attentive to certain facets of the analyst's behavior and personality; that he or she is *compelled* to choose one set of interpretations rather than others; that his or her emotional life and adaptation are unconsciously governed by and governing of the particular viewpoint he or she has adopted; and, perhaps most importantly, that the patient has behaved in such a way as to actually elicit overt and covert responses that are consistent with his or her viewpoint and expectations. The transference represents a way, not only of construing, but also of constructing or shaping, interpersonal relations in general and the relationship with the analyst in particular. One could retain the term "distortion" only if it is defined in terms of the sense of *necessity* that patients attach to what they make happen, and to what they see as happening, between themselves and their analysts.

The radical critiques are opposed not merely to the blank-screen idea, but to any model that suggests that the "objective" or "real" impact of the therapist is equivalent to what he or she intends or to what the analyst thinks his or her overt behavior has conveyed or betrayed. What the radical critic refuses to do is to consign the patient's ideas about the analyst's hidden motives and attitudes to the realm of unfounded fantasy whenever those ideas depart from the analyst's judgment of his or her own intentions. In this respect, whether the analyst's manifest conduct is cold, or warm, or even self-disclosing is not the issue. What matters to the radical critic in determining whether a particular model is based on an asocial or truly social conception of the patient's experience is whether the patient is considered capable of understanding, if only preconsciously, that there is more to the therapist's experience than what meets the eye, even more than what meets the mind's eye of the therapist at any given moment. More than challenging the blank-screen fallacy, the radical critic challenges what might be termed *the naive patient fallacy*, the notion that the patient, insofar as he or she is rational, takes the analyst's behavior at face value, even while the patient's own is continually scrutinized for the most subtle indications of unspoken or unconscious meanings.

Although we now have a broad range of literature that embraces some kind of interactive view of the psychoanalytic situation (Ehrenberg, 1982; Greenberg and Mitchell, 1983), emphasis upon interaction per se does not guarantee that any particular theoretical statement or position qualifies as one that views the transference in perspectivistic-social terms.[7] Moreover, emphasis on interaction can obscure the fact that a particular theorist is holding fast, for the most part, to the traditional view of neurotic transference as a distortion of a given and ascertainable external reality.

CONSERVATIVE CRITIQUES: TRANSFERENCE IN THE ASOCIAL PARADIGM

Overview: Types of Conservative Critiques

Conservative critiques, as I said earlier, retain the dichotomy of transference and realistic perception, but argue that the standard qualifications of the screen function of the analyst require amplification. Some conservative critics, like Strachey (1934) and Loewald (1960), offer reconceptualizations of the real, benign interpersonal influence of the analyst in the process, without any recommendations for changes in prevailing practice. Others, like Stone (1961) and Kohut (1977), combine such reconceptualization with advocacy of less restraint and more friendly, spontaneous involvement than is customary. In this context, Freud is often cited as a practitioner who was extraordinarily free in his manner of relating to his patients and who was, in that sense, not "classical" (see Lipton, 1977a).

Strachey, Loewald, Stone, and Kohut have in common some kind of elaboration of the realistically benign and facilitating aspects of the therapist's influence, although, to be sure, what is benign and facilitating in Stone and Kohut includes a certain optimal element of frustration or disappointment. The other major subdivision of conservative critiques are those that emphasize the importance and prevalence of objective perceptions of countertransference, which, it is argued, fall outside the province of transference. Langs (1978)

---

7. The term *perspectivistic* here replaces the term *relativistic* that appeared in the original version of this paper. The latter term has encouraged the misunderstanding that my position is one of "radical relativism" or even solipsism (see, for example, Orange, 1992; Zucker, 1993). To say that experience is ambiguous, and therefore open to a variety of interpretations, does not mean that it is amorphous and that anything goes. The term perspectivistic foreshadows the emergence of a critical "constructivist" view of the psychoanalytic situation.

mounts the most systematic and thorough critique of this kind. Perhaps the clearest example of all the conservative critics is Greenson (1971), whose "real relationship" includes the patient's experience of both the working alliance and of countertransference and unequivocally excludes the experience of the transference.

Hans Loewald and James Strachey

A good example of a primarily conservative critique of the blank-screen fallacy that advocates a greater emphasis on the benign, facilitating aspects of the analyst as a real person (or object) without any suggestions for changes in technique is that of Loewald (1960). I say *primarily* conservative because there are ambiguous hints in Loewald's position of a more radical critique that would not dichotomize transference and reality, although I believe the overall thrust of his position is undeniably conservative. Loewald represents the classical position to which he objects as follows (and I quote it at some length because this is one of the clearest statements of the position):

> The theoretical bias is the view of the psychic apparatus as a closed system. Thus, the analyst is seen, not as a co-actor on the analytic stage on which the childhood development, culminating in the infantile neurosis, is restaged and reactivated in the development, crystallization and resolution of the transference neurosis, but as a reflecting mirror, albeit of the unconscious, and characterized by scrupulous neutrality.
>
> This neutrality of the analyst appears to be required (i) in the interest of scientific objectivity, in order to keep the field of observation from being contaminated by the analyst's own emotional intrusions; and (ii) to guarantee a *tabula rasa* for the patient's transferences. . . . The analyst is supposed to function not only as an observer of certain processes, but as a mirror which actively reflects back to the patient the latter's conscious and partially his unconscious processes through verbal communication. A specific aspect of this neutrality is that the analyst must avoid falling into the role of the environmental figure (or of his opposite) the relationship to whom the patient is transferring to the analyst [p. 17].

While not discarding this position entirely, Loewald is concerned about the fact that it leaves something out or lends itself to a lack of sufficient attention to the influence of the analyst as a real object:

> [The analyst's] objectivity cannot mean the avoidance of being available to the patient as an object. The objectivity of the analyst has ref-

erence to the patient's transference distortions. Increasingly, through the objective analysis of them, the analyst becomes not only potentially but actually available as a new object, by eliminating step by step impediments, represented by these transferences, to a new object-relationship. There is a tendency to consider the analyst's availability as an object merely as a device on his part to attract transferences onto himself. His availability is seen in terms of his being a screen or mirror onto which the patient projects his transferences, and which reflect them back to him in the form of interpretations. . . .

This is only a half truth. The analyst in actuality does not only reflect the transference distortions. In his interpretations he implies aspects of undistorted reality which the patient begins to grasp step by step as transferences are interpreted. This undistorted reality is mediated to the patient by the analyst, mostly by the process of chiseling away the transference distortions [p. 18].

Here it is clear that Loewald is dichotomizing transference and nontransference experience along the lines of neurotic distortion, on the one hand, and a new appreciation of the real, presumably health-promoting aspects of the analyst, on the other. He goes on to elaborate on the therapeutic effects associated with the experience of collaboration with the real analyst in the process of self-discovery.

Loewald's position has a forerunner in Strachey (1934) in that Strachey too emphasized the new, real interpersonal influence of the analyst in the analytic situation. Loewald sees this new real influence in terms of the patient's identification with the analyst's higher level of ego functioning, particularly with the analyst's mature, rational perspective as it is brought to bear upon the patient's own neurotic tendencies. Strachey saw a new real influence more in terms of the patient's identification with the analyst's acceptance of the patient's hitherto repressed impulses, so that the modification that occurs involves a softening of the punitive tendencies of the patient's super-ego, rather than, as in Loewald, a strengthening of the reflective integrative capacities of the ego. But Strachey (1934) could not be more emphatic about the importance of keeping the "real" analyst separate from, and uncontaminated by, the analyst as transference object:

The analytic situation is all the time threatening to degenerate into a "real" situation. But that actually means the opposite of what it appears to. It means the patient is all the time on the brink of turning the real external object (the analyst) into the archaic one; that is to say, he is on the brink of projecting his primitive introjected imagos on to him. . . . It is important, therefore, not to submit [the patient's sense of reality] to any unnecessary strain; and that is the fundamental reason why the analyst must avoid any real behavior that is likely to confirm the patient's view of him as a "bad" or a "good" phantasy object [p. 146].

As we shall see, there could not be a starker contrast with the radical critics, according to whom a certain current of transference-countertransference "enactment" is not only likely, but also potentially useful, when combined with critical reflection and interpretation, in contributing to the therapeutic action of the process.

Leo Stone and Heinz Kohut

Whereas Strachey and Loewald explicitly disclaim any intent to influence technique, Stone (1961), who also is interested in the patient's perceptions of the real, human qualities of the therapist, is concerned about the excessively impersonal, cold, stiff manner in which he believes many analysts approach their patients, and takes an unequivocal stance in favor of a more natural, friendly, and spontaneous attitude. Stone takes issue with the implication that scrupulous neutrality and nonresponsiveness will allow for the emergence of pure transference ideas uncontaminated by any interpersonal influence. Instead, certain kinds of frustrations associated with mechanically strict adherence to the so-called rule of abstinence, Stone believes, will amount to very powerful stimuli, inducing reactions that, if anything, will be less readily understood in terms of their roots in the individual (see, for example, pp. 45–46).

Stone is clear in his rejection of the notion that transference fantasies will crop up spontaneously if the analyst manages to keep his or her personal, human qualities or reactions out of the patient's purview, in keeping with what Stone believes is the prevailing understanding of proper analytic conduct. But what is Stone's view of the relationship between transference and reality when the analytic situation is modified in accord with his recommendations? In this respect, he is more ambiguous. At times he seems to be saying that the transference will include, under those circumstances, realistic perceptions of the analyst and that this is not only not regrettable but actually desirable:

> For *all* patients, to the degree that they are removed from the psychotic, have an important investment in their real and objective perceptions; and the interplay between these and the transference requires a certain minimal if variable *resemblance*, if the latter is to be effectively mobilized. When mobilized, it is in operational fact of experi-

ence, always an integrated phenomenon, in which actual perceptions, to varying degrees, must participate [p. 41].

However, in certain of his remarks, and despite many qualifications, Stone seems to adhere to the standard dichotomy of transference and reality. For this reason I believe I am justified in classifying him as a conservative critic of the screen function of the analyst. For example, consider this rather unequivocal stance:

> I should like to state that clarity both in principle and in everyday communication, is best served by confining the unqualified term "transference" to that aspect or fraction of a relationship which is motivated by persistent unmodified wishes (or other attitudes) toward an actual important personage of the past, which tend to invest a current individual in a sort of misidentification with the unconscious image of the past personage [p. 66].

Stone is sympathetic to the views advanced by Tower, Racker, and others which point to the usefulness of countertransference in understanding transference and which connote what Stone (1961) terms a "diminution of the rigid status barrier between analyst and analysand" (p. 80). His preoccupation, however, is decidedly with the question: how should the analyst behave? It is very much less with the question: how should the patient's experience of the analyst be understood? Whatever the virtues of Stone's position, what is obscured by his emphasis on the therapist's behavior is the patient's capability to understand that the analyst's manifest verbal and nonverbal behavior can conceal or carry myriad latent, more or less conscious attitudes and motives. I think Stone's position exemplifies a particular variant of those conservative critiques of the screen concept that stress the importance of the benign, human attributes of the analyst. Instead of arguing that in addition to transference, weight should be given to the patient's experience of the analyst's real, benign qualities, this variant argues that the analyst's humanness draws out the transference, especially the positive transference. In a sense, instead of the analyst functioning as a blank screen in relation to the transference, he or she is seen as a kind of magnet for it, albeit a very human one (pp. 108–109). Again, while the idea may not be wrong, it is not the whole story, and the part of the story that it leaves out or obscures is what lies at the core of the radical critiques, namely that the therapist's outward behavior, however it is consciously intended, does not and cannot control the patient's perceptions and interpretations of the analyst's inner experience. As I said earlier, what the radical critic challenges is the view of the patient as *a naive observer of the analyst's behavior*, thus arguing against the expectation that, to the degree that the patient is rational, he or she will take the analyst's outward behavior or conscious intent at face value. It is the taking of the analyst's outward behavior or conscious intention as the basis for defining reality in the analytic situation that is truly the hallmark of the standard view of transference as distortion. And it is in this sense that Stone, with all his emphasis on what is appropriate outward behavior on the part of the analyst, leans toward the standard paradigm and can be categorized as a conservative critic of the notion that, ideally, the analyst should function like a screen.

I believe that Kohut's position on the screen function of the analyst, although it is, of course, embedded in a different theoretical context, can be classed with that of Stone as a special type of conservative critique. Kohut (1977) makes it clear that while it is particularly important in the case of disorders of the self, it is also important in the case of the classical neuroses that the analyst not behave in an excessively cold and unfriendly manner. He believes that "analytic neutrality . . . should be defined as the responsiveness to be expected, on an average, from persons who have devoted their life to helping others with the aid of insights obtained via the empathic immersion into their inner life" (p. 252). But Kohut, like Stone, conveys the impression that a friendly, naturally responsive attitude on the part of the analyst will promote the unfolding of the transference, whether classical or narcissistic, without specific reference to other aspects of the analyst's personality. For example, he writes:

> The essential transference (or the sequence of the essential transferences) is defined by pre-analytically established internal factors in the analysand's personality structure, and the analyst's influence on the course of the analysis is therefore important only insofar as he—through interpretations made on the basis of correct or incorrect empathic closures—either promotes or impedes the patient's progress on his predetermined path [p. 217].

Especially in the case of the classical transference neuroses, Kohut is clear that the analyst does function as a screen for elaboration of transference ideas, although he or she also facilitates change through empathic responsiveness and interpretation. This model follows the line of conservative critics like Stone, because the encouragement that is given to the analyst to express his or her humanness does nothing to alter the notion that the analyst as a real person is not implicated in the unfolding of the neurotic transference proper.

In the case of transferences associated with the disorders of the self, which Kohut increasingly viewed as the underlying disturbance even in the classical neuroses, the analyst as a real person is implicated more directly, insofar as his or her empathy facilitates the self-selfobject tie that the patient's development requires. More precisely, the sequence of empathy, minor failures in empathy, and rectification of such failures promotes the "transmuting internalizations" that can repair deficits in the development of the self. It would seem, however, that the whole complexity of the analyst's personal response to the patient is not something the patient would attend to in a way that is associated with any special psychological importance. To the extent that the patient is suffering from a disorder of the self, or a narcissistic disorder, he or she presumably does not experience the analyst as a separate person with needs, motives, defenses, and interests of his or her own. One might say that the patient, although concerned about breaches in empathy and reacting strongly to them, does not necessarily account for such failures by attributing particular countertransference difficulties to the analyst which then become incorporated into the transference. In fact, to the degree that the patient is suffering from a disorder of the self, and therefore is experiencing the analyst as a selfobject, the patient is, by definition, a naive observer of the analyst as a separate, differentiated object. Thus, I believe there is reason to classify Kohut as a conservative critic of the screen function of the analyst, even taking into consideration his ideas about the narcissistic transferences.[8]

Robert Langs

Whereas Loewald, Strachey, Stone, and Kohut are concerned with the fact that the screen concept lends itself to deemphasizing the "real," therapeutic, interpersonal influence of the analyst, others have been concerned more with its tendency to obscure the importance and prevalence of real neurotogenic influences that the therapist exerts via his or her countertransference. Here again, the critique

---

8. The self psychology literature by the early 1980s certainly included discussion of likely countertransference reactions to particular kinds of narcissistic transferences (e.g., Kohut, 1971; Wolf, 1979), but these discussions omit consideration of the patient's specific ideas about the nature of the countertransference. In the 1990s some self psychologists (e.g. Newman, 1992) have gone further in an attempt to integrate ideas advanced by Racker and, more generally, by object relations theory.

is conservative in form, insofar as it merely expands upon one of the standard qualifications of the blank-screen concept. A carefully elaborated critique of this kind is that of Robert Langs. No psychoanalytic theorist has written more extensively about the implications of the patient's ability to interpret the analyst's manifest behavior as betraying latent countertransference. In Langs's (1978) view, the patient is constantly monitoring the analyst's countertransference attitudes and the patient's associations can often be understood as "commentaries" on those attitudes (p. 509).

Despite his interactional emphasis, however, Langs must be classified as a conservative critic of the blank-screen fallacy because he is unequivocal about reserving the term transference for *distorted perceptions* of the therapist, whereas accurate perceptions fall *outside* the realm of the transference. Thus, he writes:

> Within the bipersonal field the patient's relationship with the analyst has both transference and nontransference components. The former are essentially distorted and based on pathological, intrapsychic unconscious fantasies, memories, and introjects, while the latter are essentially non-distorted and based on valid unconscious perceptions and introjections of the analyst, his conscious and unconscious psychic state and communications, and his mode of interacting [p. 506].

For Langs, what is wrong with the classical position is that it overestimates the prevalence of relatively pure, uncontaminated transference. Because countertransference errors are relatively common in prevailing practice, and because the patient is preconsciously always on the lookout for them, what dominates most psychoanalytic transactions are unconscious attempts by the patient to adapt to this current reality and even to alter it by trying indirectly to "cure" the analyst of his or her interfering psychopathology. To be sure, even the patient's valid perceptions can be points of departure for "intrapsychic elaborations" that bear the stamp of the patient's psychopathology. Nevertheless, the main thrust of all of Langs's writings is that a certain environment can be established that will be relatively free of countertransference and in which the patient will therefore feel safe to engage in a very special kind of communication, one that can take place in this environment and nowhere else. This special kind of communication is, like dreams, a richly symbolic expression of deep unconscious wishes and fantasies that have little relation to the actual person of the analyst. These are the true transference wishes and fantasies. The patient is always on the verge of retreating from this kind of communication because it is experienced as potentially dangerous at a very primitive level to the patient or to the analyst, and betrayals of countertransference (whether seductive, or attacking, or whatever) invariably prevent, interrupt, or severely limit this unique kind of communication.

Langs's position is based upon the same absolute view of reality that is implicit in any position retaining the dichotomy between distorted and undistorted perception of interpersonal events. Langs believes, for example, that strict adherence to a prescribed set of rules constituting what he calls the "basic frame" *will not be* interpreted—at least not accurately—as any kind of expression of countertransference that could endanger the kind of communication he wants to foster. By the same token, violations of the frame *will* be perceived and responded to in this way by virtually all patients.[9]

Langs appears to believe that there is a certain universal language that always carries at least general unconscious meaning. He will not claim to know *specifically* what it means to a particular patient that the therapist allows him or her to use the phone, or changes the appointment time, or fails to charge for a cancelled appointment, or tape records a session. But he does claim to know that all patients are likely to see such behaviors correctly as reflecting some sort of deep, unresolved, pathological conflict in the analyst. Conversely, he believes it is possible for the analyst to behave in a way that will persuade the patient that no such issues are active in the analyst to any significant degree, that is, to a degree which, objectively speaking, would warrant anxiety that the analyst's attitudes are dominated by neurotic countertransference. Thus, the analyst, with help perhaps from a supervisor or from his or her own analyst, can decide with some degree of confidence when the patient is reading the analyst's own unconscious motives correctly, which would represent a nontransference response, and when the patient is merely fantasizing and distorting because of the influence of the transference.

The conservatism of Langs's critique of the screen model in psychoanalysis is particularly ironic given the enthusiasm with which he

---

9. According to Langs, by maintaining the frame and intervening in an optimal manner, the therapist provides the patient with a secure holding environment. Langs's account of the nature and importance of this kind of environment in the analytic process complements his account of the importance of countertransference errors, so that he, like Greenson, actually elaborates on both of the standard qualifications of the screen concept.

champions the more radical positions of other theorists such as Searles (1978–1979) and Racker (1968). Langs feels that these theorists (especially Searles) inspired many of his own ideas, and he conveys the impression that in some sense he is taking up where they left off; but because he actually retreats to the standard dichotomy of transference and nontransference experience on the basis of distorting and nondistorting perceptions of the reality of the analyst's attitudes, I believe he actually takes a step back from his own sources of inspiration rather than a step forward.

Ralph Greenson

Perhaps the theorist who best exemplifies a conservative critique of the blank-screen fallacy is Greenson (1965, 1971). Greenson's "real relationship" encompasses both the patient's accurate perceptions of the benign aspects of the analyst and his or her perceptions of the analyst's countertransference. Greenson's position is an emphatic objection to the tendency he sees to underestimate the inevitably important role of the real relationship in the analytic process. There is nothing in his view, however, that alters in the slightest the standard understanding of transference as distortion and the standard dichotomy of transference and undistorted perception of the analyst. Thus he writes (1971), "The two outstanding characteristics of a transference reaction are: (1) It is an undiscriminating, non-selective repetition of the past, and (2) It is inappropriate, it ignores or distorts reality" (p. 217). In contrast to the transference, "the meaning of 'real' in real relationship implies (1) the sense of being genuine and not synthetic or artificial and (2) it also means realistic and not inappropriate or fantastic" (p. 218).

The extent to which Greenson is wedded to this dichotomy is betrayed by the fact that he cannot find his way out of it even when it seems like he is trying to. Thus, for example, he says, "I must add that in all transference reactions there is some germ of reality, and in all real relationships there is some element of transference" (p. 218). Here he seems to be saying that transference *itself* is not completely lacking in some sort of realistic basis, although the word "germ" suggests a very common kind of lip-service to this idea: the element of reality is considered to be so slight as to be hardly worth mentioning, much less making an issue of in one's interpretive work. But even this concession is lost immediately in Greenson's very next sentence, which he has in italics and which is clearly intended as a restatement or paraphrase of the first: *"All object relations consist of different admixtures and blendings of real and transference components"* (p. 218). Now the idea that *transference* includes something real is superseded by the much blander, conventional notion that all *relationships* include something real as well as transference. In other words, the dichotomy of transference and realistic perception is retained.

RADICAL CRITIQUES: TRANSFERENCE IN THE SOCIAL OR INTERPERSONAL PARADIGM

Overview

Whereas conservative critics of the blank-screen concept are relatively abundant, radical critics are relatively scarce. I would number among the foremost of them Merton Gill (1979, 1982a,b; 1983; Gill and Hoffman, 1982a,b), a leading exponent of this perspective coming out of a classical Freudian orientation; Joseph Sandler (1976), another theorist with classical roots, who, however, conceptualizes the psychoanalytic situation in object-relations terms; Heinrich Racker (1968), who takes his cue from a landmark paper on countertransference by a fellow Kleinian, Paula Heimann (1950), but whose rich and detailed account of the inevitable reciprocity of transference and countertransference is unique in the literature; Lucia Tower, if only for her one remarkable paper on countertransference in 1956, the implications of which have never penetrated the mainstream of psychoanalytic thinking about the relationship between transference and reality; Levenson (1972, 1981), Feiner (1979, 1982), and Ehrenberg (1982), who are among the neo-Sullivanians whose work leans heavily in this direction; Harold Searles (1978–1979), a clear and powerful exponent of the radical perspective; and Paul Wachtel (1980), whose Piagetian conceptual framework for understanding transference I will be drawing on myself in what follows.[10]

10. Since the original publication of this essay, the number of radical critics has grown. They include Altman, 1995; Aron, 1996; Bromberg, 1994; Davies and Frawley, 1994; Ghent, 1992; Hirsch, 1987, 1993; Mitchell, 1988, 1993; Pizer, 1992; Renik, 1993; Donnel Stern, 1997; and Tansey and Burke, 1989. Hirsch's (1987) paper is of special interest in that the author takes the criteria proposed here for classifying theorists and extends them to Fairbairn, Klein, Winnicott, Sullivan, and Schwaber, showing the sense in

To digress for a moment, although I have counted Gill among the radical critics, within his work in the 1980s there is actually a *movement* from a somewhat inconsistent but generally conservative position to a more consistently radical one. Thus, in his 1982 monograph, Gill (1982a) criticizes those, like Anna Freud and Greenson, who define transference in terms of distortion of reality. His objection, however, is tied specifically to what he describes as "a lack of recognition that Freud's inclusion of the conscious, unobjectionable positive transference in his concept of transference is not an unfortunate lapse but an integral aspect of the concept" (p. 12). Throughout his discussion of the distinction between the unobjectionable "facilitating" transferences and the "obstructing" transferences (pp. 9–15), it is only the former that is considered to have realistic features. There is nothing about realistic elements in the "obstructing" transferences, not to mention any question being raised about the dimension "realistic-unrealistic" itself. Overall, in the first six chapters of the monograph, Gill apparently had not yet extricated himself from the traditional asocial paradigm for understanding transference (that is, neurotic or obstructing transference) although he was struggling to do so. His transitional, but still essentially conservative stand is exemplified by the following:

> Analysts have largely followed Freud in taking it for granted that the analyst's behavior is such that the patient's appropriate reaction to it will be cooperation in the joint work. But there are significant interactions between the patient and the analyst which are *not transference* but to which the patient's appropriate response would not be cooperation. If the analyst has given the patient cause to be angry, for example, and the patient is angry, at least some aspect of the anger is neither transference nor cooperation—unless the idea of cooperation is confusingly stretched to mean that any forthright appropriate reaction of the patient is cooperative since it is a necessary element in continuing an open and honest relationship. We do conceptualize inappropriate behavior on the analyst's part as countertransference, but what is our name for an analysand's realistic response to countertransference? [p. 94; italics added].

There is a noticeable shift in the book, beginning with chapter 7, to a more fully social and perspectivist position (see, for example, p. 118). Moreover, in subsequent writing in this period, Gill contin-

---

which they are conservative critics, subscribing, in that sense, to an asocial paradigm; the analyst in these theories is a participant-observer rather than, in Hirsch's terms, the "observing-participant" of the social paradigm.

ued to develop a view of transference within the social paradigm (Gill, 1982b, 1983; Gill and Hoffman, 1982a,b; Hoffman and Gill, 1988a,b).[11]

I believe that the various proponents of the radical perspective may have more in common with each other than each of them has with what would generally be recognized as their particular school or tradition. In effect, I believe *there is a kind of informal "school" of thought which cuts across the standard lines of Freudian, Kleinian, and Sullivanian schools.* For example, what Gill (in his later work), Racker, and Levenson have in common may be much more important than how they differ, because what they have in common is a perspective on the fundamental nature of the psychoanalytic situation.[12]

Radical critiques of the notion that the patient's neurotic transference experience is divorced from the actual nature of the analyst's participation—that is, that it distorts the actual nature of that participation—rest on two basic propositions, with one or the other or both emphasized, depending upon the particular theorist. The two propositions, for which I am partly indebted to Wachtel (1980), are:

1. The patient senses that the analyst's interpersonal *conduct* in the analytic situation, like all interpersonal conduct, is always ambiguous as an indicator of the full nature of the analyst's

---

11. Over the years, my own views departed, in terms of emphasis, from those of Gill in a number of ways (see Introduction, pp. xiv–xvi). Perhaps most importantly, Gill's focus was generally upon the analysis of the transference in the context of appreciating the inevitability of the analyst's continuous interpersonal influence. My focus has been increasingly upon the dialectic of noninterpretive interpersonal interactions and interpretive interactions. Whereas for Gill, like Strachey, the heart of therapeutic action is in the moment of interpretation, for me it is in the dialectic of spontaneous, personal involvement and critical reflection on the process. In my own perspective, the analyst has the responsibility not only to interpret but also to contribute creatively to the development of the relationship in other ways, to wisely exercise his or her inescapable moral authority in the process, and to struggle through the paradox of participating in enactments while trying to understand and transcend them. An overemphasis on analysis of transference gravitates towards objectivism and technical rationality (see notes 9 and 10 in my paper on Gill's intellectual history [Hoffman, 1996, pp. 48–49]).

12. Although I am grouping Levenson among the radical critics, there is a strong conservative, objectivist bent to his thinking, which I became aware of and took up well after the earlier version of this chapter was published (Hoffman, 1990).

experience and is always amenable to a variety of plausible interpretations.
2. The patient senses that the analyst's personal *experience* in the
    analytic situation is continuously affected by and responsive to
    the way in which the patient relates and participates in the process.

Implications of the Ambiguity of the Analyst's Conduct in the Analytic Situation

There is an underlying view of reality that the radical critics of the
screen concept share. This view is simply that reality is not comprised
merely of preestablished givens or absolutes. As Wachtel (1980) says,
arguing from the perspective of Piaget's theory of cognitive development, "neither as children or as adults do we respond directly to stimuli per se. We are always constructing reality every bit as much as we
are perceiving it" (p. 62). Moreover, the realm of interpersonal events
is distinguished from that of physical events in that "such events are
highly ambiguous, and consensus is much harder to obtain" (p. 69).

Keep in mind that we have as our principal concern one person's
ideas (which may or may not be conscious themselves) about
another person's experience. The other person's experience can only
be inferred; it is never directly visible as such. Although we may
believe we recognize signs of it in verbal and nonverbal behavior, the
relationship between such signs and actual experience is always
uncertain. When we think about patients, we know that there may
well be discrepancies between what they say and what they consciously think, as well as discrepancies between what they consciously think and what they vaguely sense but resist facing up to in
themselves. We know that the relation between what is manifest and
what is latent may be extraordinarily complex. We know this of our
patients and in a general way of ourselves. What we are prone to
ignore or deny, however, is that this ambiguity and complexity
applies to the way in which the therapist participates in the analytic
process. As Racker (1968) says:

> The first distortion of truth in "the myth of the analytic situation" is
> that analysis is an interaction between a sick person and a healthy
> one. The truth is that it is an interaction between two personalities, in
> both of which the ego is under pressure from the id, the superego, and
> the external world; each personality has its internal and external
> dependencies, anxieties, and pathological defenses; each is also a child
> with his internal parents; and each of these whole personalities—that

of the analysand and that of the analyst—responds to every event in the analytic situation [p. 132].

In a similar vein, Racker (1968) says, "The analyst's relation to his patient is a libidinal one and is a constant emotional experience" (p. 31).

The safeguards of the analytic situation do not prevent the analyst from having this "constant emotional experience." What is more, every patient senses this, consciously or preconsciously. Also, every patient brings to bear his or her own particular perspective in interpreting the meaning of the analyst's manifest behavior as it communicates, conveys, or inadvertently betrays something in the analyst's personal experience. The fact that a particular perspective may be charged with tremendous significance for the patient does not nullify its plausibility. If anything, the opposite may be the case. The patient's transference predisposition acts as a kind of geiger counter, picking up aspects of the analyst's personal response in the analytic situation that might otherwise remain hidden. As Benedek (1953) put it:

> Rarely does one realize that the patient, under the pressure of his emotional needs—needs which may be motivated by the frustration of transference—may grope for the therapist as a real person, may sense his reactions and will sometimes almost read his mind. . . . Yes, the patient . . . bores his way into the preconscious mind of the therapist and often emerges with surprising evidences of empathy—of preconscious awareness of the therapist's personality and even of his problems [p. 203].

What the patient's transference accounts for is not a distortion of reality but a selective attention and sensitivity to certain facets of the analyst's highly ambiguous response to the patient in the analysis. What one patient notices about the analyst another ignores. What matters to one may not matter to another, or may matter in a different way. One could make a case for using the term "distortion" for just this kind of selective attention and sensitivity, but that is not usually the way the term is used, and I do think it would be misleading. After all, it is not as though one could describe the "real analyst" or the true nature of the analyst's experience independently of any selective attention and sensitivity. As Wachtel (1980) says:

> To be sure, each patient's experience of the analyst is highly individual and shaped by personal needs and fantasies. But consider the enormous variation in perception of the analyst by those other than his

patients—the differences in how he is experienced by his spouse, his children, his teachers, his students, his friends, his rivals. Which is the "undistorted" standard from which the transference distortion varies? [pp. 66–67].[13]

There is no perception free of some kind of preexisting set, bias, or expectation, or, to borrow from Piaget's framework, no perception independent of "assimilation" to some preexisting schema. Such assimilation does not twist an absolute external reality into something it is not. Rather it gives meaning or shape to something "out there" that has among its "objective" properties a kind of amenability to being assimilated in just this way. Moreover, the schema itself is flexible and tends to "accommodate" to what is in the environment, even while it makes what is in the environment fit itself. Thus, turning to the clinical situation that concerns us, a patient who, for example, has a readiness to feel used, may detect and be selectively attentive and sensitive to whatever qualifies as a plausible indication of an exploitative motive on the part of the particular analyst he or she is seeing. With one analyst it might be a high fee, with another, use of a tape recorder for research purposes, with another, use of the therapy for training, with another, (allegedly) sadistic use of silence, with another, (allegedly) sadistic use of active interpretation.

The analytic situation is comprised of only two people, both of whom are *participating* in a charged interpersonal interaction that can result in either one of them resisting recognizing something in himself or herself that the other discerns. From the perspective of the radical critic, it behooves the analyst to operate with this skepticism in mind about what he or she knows at a particular moment and to regard the patient as a potentially astute interpreter of the analyst's own resisted internal motives. In fact, in some cases a patient with a particular "transference predisposition" (a phrase that Racker uses that is comparable to the notion of schema) may guess something about the countertransference that most other independent judges would not have picked up. As Gill and I (1982b) wrote:

> In some instances, a group of judges may agree that the therapist has behaved in a particular way, one which could be construed as seduc-

---

13. In what seems to me to be a non sequitur, Wachtel retreats from the implications of this position at the end of his article (p. 74) and accepts the term *distortion* in a manner that contradicts the heart of his argument.

tive, or disapproving or whatever, only after some subtle aspect of his behavior is called to their attention by another single observer. This observer might, of course, be none other than the patient [p. 140].

Not despite the influence of the transference, but because of it,

[the patient] may notice something about the therapist's behavior or suggest a possible interpretation of it that most judges would over-look. Nevertheless, once it is called to their attention, they may all agree that the patient's perceptions and inferences were quite plausible [p. 140].

Implications of the Responsiveness of the Analyst's Experience in the Psychoanalytic Situation

In what I have said so far I have deliberately contrived to deempha-size the second major consideration that addresses the implication of the analyst's personal presence for the transference. I have done this in order to take the argument associated with the ambiguous nature of the analyst's involvement as far as I could. But it is the second consideration, coupled with the first, that I think clinches the argu-ment of the radical critic that the patient's plausible interpretations of the analyst's experience be considered part of the transference and that the transference not be defined in terms of perceptual distortion.

This second consideration is simply that the analyst in the analytic situation is continuously having some sort of personal affective reac-tion that is a response to the patient's manner of relating. What is more, every patient knows that he or she is influencing the analyst's experience and that the freedom the analyst has to resist this influ-ence is limited. Patients create atmospheres in analysis—atmospheres that we sometimes actually speak of as though something were "in the air" between the participants. These atmospheres include the therapist's personal reaction to the patient, the patient guessing what the reaction is partly on the basis of what the patient thinks his or her own behavior is likely to have elicited, the analyst guessing what the patient is guessing, and so on.

Sandler (1976) puts it this way:

In the transference, in many subtle ways, the patient attempts to prod the analyst into behaving in a particular way and unconsciously scans and adapts to his perceptions of the analyst's reaction. The analyst may be able to "hold" his response to this "prodding" in his

consciousness as a reaction *of his own* which he perceives, and I
would make the link between certain countertransference responses
and transference via the behavioral (verbal and non-verbal) *interaction* between the patient and the analyst [p. 44].

Sandler's emphasis on the analyst's behavior as a basis upon which
patients conclude (preconsciously) that they have elicited the
response they are looking for underestimates the extent to which a
patient's ideas about the countertransference can flow directly and
plausibly from what the patient knows about the evocative nature of
his or her own behavior. However the analyst believes he or she has
behaved, if the patient thinks his or her own attitude has been continually depreciating, or harshly critical, the patient has reason to
believe that the analyst may experience a degree of injury, along with
a measure of irritation and a wish to retaliate. Such ideas do not
require perceptual confirmation in order for the patient to believe,
with reason, that they are plausible. The perceptual confirmation
might follow, nevertheless, in any number of ways. For example, if
the analyst keeps his or her cool and reveals not the slightest bit of
upset, the patient might well imagine that this is precisely the analyst's expression of revenge: to demonstrate imperviousness to the
patient's provocations. And, undoubtedly, ostensible adherence to
the more austere canons of "proper" analytic conduct can sometimes
function as a disguised vehicle for the expression of intense countertransference attitudes on the part of the analyst. The perceptual confirmation may be secondary, however, since from the patient's point
of view the die is cast and the outcome is highly likely, given his or
her own evocative behavior.

For a theorist like Racker the countertransference[14] is inevitable,
and his discussion of it carries none of the opprobrium that comes

---

14. I am in sympathy with Racker's (1968) use of the term "*countertransference*" to encompass the totality of the analyst's experience of the
patient, including his or her tendency toward understanding and empathy.
Racker refers to the latter as "concordant countertransference" as distinct
from "complementary countertransference," which refers to the analyst's
nonempathic emotional reactions to the transference (pp. 135–136). In this
chapter, I sometimes use the general term "countertransference" to refer to
what Racker calls "complementary countertransference." Similarly, the term
transference is used to refer to the neurotic or "obstructing" transference
rather than to the unobjectionable positive or "facilitating" transference
(Gill, 1982a).

across so heavily and oppressively in the work of Langs. Racker and Heimann take the same step forward with respect to countertransference that Freud took when he moved from thinking of the transference as an obstacle to thinking of transference as the principal vehicle of the analytic process. The countertransference in the social paradigm of the radical critics is likely to embody something resembling aspects of the patient's internal objects or aspects of the patient's self-representation. Heimann (1950) goes so far as to say, "The analyst's countertransference is not only part and parcel of the analytic relationship, but it is the patient's *creation*, it is part of the patient's personality" (p. 83).

The element of hyperbole in Heimann's position illustrates an error that often appears in discussions of the mechanism of projective identification. Instead of being a blank screen, the analyst becomes an empty "container" (Bion, 1962) into which the patient deposits various parts of himself or herself. Although the emphasis is on interaction, the metaphor of the container lends itself, ironically, to yet another asocial conception of the situation, since somehow the analyst's personality has once again been eliminated from the field (cf. Levenson, 1981, p. 492). Nevertheless, the concept of projective identification, with the hyperbolic metaphor removed, does help bridge the alleged gap between the intrapsychic and the interpersonal (Ogden, 1979). It should be evident that in this paper the terms "social" and "interpersonal" do not connote something superficial or readily observable from "outside," or something non-intrapsychic, the pejorative connotations that these terms have unfortunately acquired for many classical analysts. Experience that is conceptualized in the terms of the social paradigm is experience that is layered by reciprocal conscious, preconscious, and unconscious responses in each of the participants.[15] What is more, something can "unfold" in the course of the analysis that bears the stamp of the patient's transference predispositions. What is intrapsychic is realized in the patient's idea of the interaction of the transference and the countertransference, an idea that is likely to include a rough approximation of the quality, if not the quantity, of the actual countertransference, however ambiguous, inaccessible, or indeterminate the latter may be. It is in this element of correspondence between the

---

15. See Fourcher (1975) for a discussion of human experience as the expression of social reciprocity on multiple levels of psychological organization and consciousness.

patient's idea of the countertransference and the actual counter-transference that the elusive interface of the intrapsychic and inter-personal lies.

IMPLICATIONS OF THE SOCIAL
PARADIGM FOR TECHNIQUE

The Impact of the Countertransference on the Fate of the Relationship

Because analysts are human, they are likely to have in their reper-toire approximate blueprints for the emotional responses that their patients' transferences dictate, and those responses are likely to be elicited, whether consciously or unconsciously (Searles, 1978–1979, pp. 172–173). Ideally, this kind of response serves as a key—perhaps the best key the analyst has—to the nature of the interpersonal scene that the patient is driven by the transference to create. The patient as interpreter of the analyst's experience suspects that he or she has cre-ated something, the complement of the transference, in the analyst; that is, the patient suspects it at some level. What he or she does not know, and what remains to be decided, is what role the counter-transference experience of the analyst will have in determining the total nature of the analyst's response to the patient. In other words, the patient does not know the extent to which the countertransfer-ence will combine with the neurotic transference to determine the destiny of the relationship. The extent to which the analyst's "objec-tivity," the tendency that is inclined toward understanding more than enacting, the extent to which this tendency will prevail and success-fully resist the pull of the neurotic transference and countertransfer-ence is unknown at any given moment, not only to the patient but also to the analyst.[16]

---

16. The emphasis here on the tension between deleterious enactments, on the one hand, and interpretation of enactments, on the other, is somewhat misleading in that it fails to consider the subtle blending of old and new *within* virtually all interactions in the process, whether they are ostensibly interpretive, reflective, and exploratory, or noninterpretive and emotionally expressive. The paradoxical interplay of repetition and new experience, the way in which one can serve as necessary ground for the other, is obscured by the polarization here of regressive enactment and healthy understanding. My own sense of the complexity of the process, conveyed, hopefully, in other chapters, developed more fully some years after this chapter was pub-lished in its original form.

Within the transference itself, there is a kind of self-fulfilling prophecy, and with it, a kind of fatalism—a sense that the outcome is inevitable. The transference includes not just a sense of what has happened or is happening, but also a prediction, a conviction even, about what will happen. The attempt to disprove this prediction is an active, ongoing, mutual effort that is always accompanied by a real element of uncertainty. The analyst's uncertainty has as much, if not more, to do with his or her inability to know, in advance, how much the countertransference will govern his or her response to the patient as it has to do with the analyst's inability to measure, precisely, the patient's resistance and motivation for change. Moreover, the patient, as interpreter of the analyst's experience, has good reason to think and fear that the countertransference-evoking power of the neurotic transference may be the decisive factor in determining the course of the relationship. Or, to say the same thing in another way, the patient has good reason to fear that the analyst's constant susceptibility to complementary countertransference will doom the relationship to repeat, covertly if not overtly, the very patterns of interpersonal interaction that the patient came to analysis to change.

Pitted against the powerful alignment of neurotic transference and complementary countertransference is the interest that the patient and the analyst share in making something happen that will be new for the patient and will promote his or her ability to develop new kinds of interpersonal relationships. This is where the "objectivity" of the analyst enters and plays such an important role. It is not an objectivity that enables the analyst to demonstrate to the patient how his or her transference ideas and expectations distort reality in any simple sense. Instead it is an objectivity that enables the analyst to work to realize other potentials in the relationship and in the patient's experience, potentials that are at variance with the reality created by the interplay of the neurotic transference and the complementary countertransference. In this process, the patient comes to know that the analyst is not so consumed or threatened by the countertransference as to no longer be able to interpret the transference. For to be able to interpret the transference means interpreting, and in some measure being receptive to, the patient's interpretations of the countertransference (Racker, 1968, p. 131). What ensues is a subtle kind of rectification. The patient is, in some measure, freed of an unconscious sense of obligation to resist interpreting the analyst's experience in order to accommodate a reciprocal resistance in the analyst. Ironically, the resistance in the patient sometimes takes the form of an apparently fervent belief that, objectively speaking, the analyst must be the very neutral screen that, according to the standard model, he or she aspires to be (see Racker, 1968, p. 67). The patient takes the position, in effect, that his or her ideas about the analyst are nothing but fantasy, derived entirely from childhood experiences, nothing but transference, in the standard sense of the term. In such a case, the denial must be interpreted; the analyst must combat the resistance, not collude with it. To the extent that the analyst is objective, to the extent that he or she keeps from "drowning in the countertransference" (Racker, 1968, p. 132), which, of course, could take the form of repressing it, to that very extent is the analyst able actively to elicit the patient's preconscious and resisted interpretations of the countertransference and take them in stride.

Interpretation as Rectification

Whether the analyst's response will be dominated by complementary countertransference or not is a question that is raised again and again throughout the course of the therapy, probably in each hour with varying degrees of urgency. Also, it is a question that in many instances cannot begin to be resolved in a favorable direction unless or until a timely interpretation is offered by the analyst. At the very moment that he or she interprets, the analyst often extricates himself or herself as well as the patient from transference-countertransference enactment. When the analyst, who is experiencing something of the quality, if not the quantity, of the countertransference reaction that the patient anticipates, says to the patient, "I think you think I am feeling vulnerable," or "I think you have the impression that I am hiding or denying my hostility toward you" or "my attraction to you," at that moment, at least, he or she manages to cast doubt on the transference-based expectation that the countertransference will be consuming and will result in defensive adaptations in the analyst complementary to those in the transference. The interpretation is "mutative" (Strachey, 1934) partly because it has a certain reflexive impact on the analyst that the patient senses. Because it is implicitly self-interpretive it modifies something in the analyst's own experience of the patient. By making it apparent that the countertransference experience that the patient has attributed to the analyst occupies only a part of the analyst's response to the patient, the analyst also makes it apparent that he or she is finding something more in the patient to respond to than the transference-driven provocateur. Not to be minimized as a significant part of this "something more," for which the analyst is now implicitly showing a kind of appreciation, is the patient's capacity to understand, empathize with, and interpret the analyst's experience, especially his or her experience of the patient (cf. Searles, 1975).

As Gill (1979) has pointed out, the patient, through the analysis of the transference, has a new interpersonal experience that is inseparable from the collaborative development of insight into the transference itself. This new experience is most powerful when the insight into the transference includes a new understanding of what the patient has tried to evoke, and what he or she has plausibly construed as actually having been evoked, in the analyst. The rectification, mentioned earlier, of the patient's unconscious need to accommodate to a resistance that is attributed to the analyst is also more likely when the analyst is able to find the patient's interpretation of the countertransference in associations that are not manifestly about the psychoanalytic situation at all. In doing so, the analyst demonstrates to the patient that, rather than being defensive about the patient's ideas about the countertransference, the analyst actually has an appetite for them and is eager to seek them out.

Systematic use of the patient's associations as a guide to understanding the patient's resisted ideas about the countertransference is a critical element of the interpretive process in the social paradigm.[17] Without it, there is a danger that the analyst will rely excessively on his or her own subjective experience in constructing interpretations. The analyst then risks making the error of automatically assuming that what he or she feels corresponds with what the patient imagines to be the case. In fact, Racker (1968), whom I have cited so liberally, seems to invite this criticism at times, although he also warns against regarding the experience of the countertransference as oracular (p. 170). It is true that in many cases the most powerful interpretations are constructed out of a convergence of something in the analyst's personal response and a theme in the patient's associations. There are other instances, however, when the associations suggest a latent interpretation of the analyst's internal state that comes as a surprise to the analyst and that overrides what he or she might have guessed based upon his or her conscious experience. Thus, continually reading the patient's associations for their allusions to the countertransference via the mechanisms of displacement and identification (Lipton, 1977b; Gill, 1979, 1982a; Gill and Hoffman,

---

17. Encouraging "systematic use of the patient's associations" may promote an approach that leans too far to the side of the methodical in the dialectic of the methodical and the spontaneously personal.

1982a,b) is a necessary complement to the analyst's countertransference experience in constructing interpretations and ensures that the patient's perspective, as reflected in the content of his or her communications, is not overshadowed by what the analyst is aware of in himself or herself.

The Role of Enactment and
Disclosure of Countertransference

The new experience that the patient has is something that the participants make happen and that they are frequently either on the verge of failing to make happen or actually failing to make happen. That is, they are frequently either on the verge of enacting transference-countertransference patterns or actually in the midst of enacting them, even if in muted or disguised ways. Where Gill, Racker, Searles, and Levenson, among others (see fn. 10 for other recent contributors) differ from conservative critics like Strachey and Langs is in their acceptance of a certain thread of transference-countertransference enactment throughout the analysis, which stands in a kind of dialectical relationship with the process by which this enactment, as experienced by the patient, is analyzed.

I want to be clear that nothing I have said *requires* admission on the part of the analyst of actual countertransference experiences, On the contrary, I think the extra factor of "objectivity" that the analyst has to help combat the pull of the transference and the countertransference often rests precisely on the fact that the nature of his or her participation in the interaction is different from that of the patient. This is what increases the likelihood that the analyst will be able to subordinate his or her countertransference reactions to the purposes of the analysis. What Racker (1968) speaks of as "the myth of the analytic situation," namely that it is an interaction "between a sick person and a healthy one" (p. 132), may be perpetuated, ironically, by those who argue that regular countertransference confessions should be incorporated as part of psychoanalytic technique.[18]

---

18. Bollas (1983) has discussed and illustrated the usefulness of *occasional* judicious disclosures by the analyst of his or her countertransference predicament. See also Burke (1992) for an attempt to spell out the rationale for disclosure. In my view, any approach that is overly specific in terms of technical principles threatens to rob disclosure of the elements of spontaneity and authenticity that are among its main benefits. The principal dialectic, as I see it, is between the inclination to reveal and the inclination to

Such regular self-disclosure is likely to pull the therapist's total personality into the exchange in the same manner that it would be involved in other intimate social relationships. To think that the analyst will have any special capability in such circumstances to resist neurotic forms of reciprocal reenactment would have to be based on an assumption that his or her mental health is vastly superior to that of the patient. Revealing countertransference reactions also tends to imply an overestimation of the analyst's conscious experience at the expense of what is resisted and is preconscious or unconscious. Similarly, it implies an extraordinary ability on the part of the analyst to capture the essence of his or her experience of the patient in a few words, whereas the patient may grope for hours before finding words that seem to fit something in his or her experience of the analyst. Another way of saying this is that countertransference disclosures may encourage a shared illusion to the effect that the element of ambiguity that is associated with the analyst's conduct and that leaves it open to a variety of plausible interpretations has now been virtually eliminated. Once the analyst says what he or she feels, there is likely to be an increment of investment on the analyst's part in being taken at his or her word. This is an increment of investment that the patient may sense and try to accommodate, so that the reciprocal resistance to the patient's continuing interpretation of the therapist's inner experience can become very powerful.

Although countertransference disclosure may often be ill-advised, there are also times when a degree of personal, self-revealing expressiveness is not only inescapable but desirable (Ehrenberg, 1982; Bollas, 1983).[19] In fact, there are times when the only choices available

---

conceal aspects of one's personal experience in the analytic situation. Such an emphasis is less on discrete moments of choice as to whether to disclose or not to disclose and more on an ongoing dialectic between personally expressive and personally restrained behavior.

19. My views on this subject have been gradually changing away from the rather conservative position taken in this paper, published originally in 1983. Although restraint is called for in keeping with the asymmetrical arrangement, I now believe that it is often useful to be open with patients regarding one's personal reactions in the process. Such openness can facilitate identification and exploration of enactments as they occur; it can help the patient identify and take account of the analyst's biases as they affect his or her participation; and it offers the possibility for a level of spontaneous personal engagement which, in a dialectical relationship with psychoanalytic discipline, has great therapeutic potential. These considerations must be weighed against the reservations articulated in the text above.

to the analyst are a variety of emotionally expressive responses. Neither attentive listening nor interpretation of any kind is necessarily a way out of this predicament, because the patient may have created an atmosphere in which customary analytic distance is likely to be experienced by both participants as inordinately withholding, compulsive, or phony. As long as the ambiance is such that both patient and the analyst know that whatever is going on more than likely has meaning that is not yet being spoken of or explored, but eventually will be, openly expressive interpersonal interactions may do more good than harm and may continue for some time before it becomes possible to interpret them retrospectively in a spirit that holds any hope of benefit for the patient. In other words, it may be some time before the act of interpreting will become sufficiently free of destructive countertransference meaning for the patient to hear and make use of the content of the intervention.

Again, it is not that instead of interpreting in such circumstances one should merely wait silently, but rather that a certain specific kind of spontaneous interpersonal interaction may be the least of the various evils that the participants have to choose from, or, more positively, the healthiest of the various transference-countertransference possibilities that are in the air at a certain time. It may be that such "healthier" types of interpersonal interaction actually do have something relatively new in them, or maybe something with weak precursors in the patient's history that were not pathogenic but growth promoting. A safe working assumption for the analyst is that the interaction represents a complex alloy of repetition and new experience. It is crucial that the analyst not presume to know the value of his or her contributions and that he or she be guided by the patient's subsequent associations in determining how the patient experienced the interaction and what it may have repeated or continued from the past.

Exploration of History in the Social Paradigm

An important weapon that the patient and the therapist have against prolonged deleterious forms of transference-countertransference enactment, in addition to the therapist's relative distance, is an evolving understanding of the patient's history. This understanding locates the transference-countertransference themes that are enacted in the analysis in a broader context that touches on their origins and helps immeasurably to free the patient and the analyst from the sense of necessity and importance that can become attached to whatever is going on in the here and now. Analysts' distance and ability to reflect critically on the process is aided by the fact that they, unlike their patients, do not routinely reveal their private associations. The patient's ability to reflect on the process relies much more heavily on being able to explain what is happening on the basis of what has happened in the past. Such explanation, because it demonstrates how the patient's way of shaping and perceiving the relationship comes out of his or her particular history, also adds considerably to the patient's sense of conviction that alternative ways of relating to people are possible. Again, what is corrected is not a simple distortion of reality but the investment that the patient has in shaping and perceiving his or her interpersonal experience in particular ways. Moreover, the past too is not explored either in a spirit of finding out what really happened (as in the trauma theory) or in a spirit of finding out what the patient, for internal reasons only, imagined happened (the past understood as fantasy). The patient as a credible (not accurate necessarily, but credible) interpreter of the analyst's experience has as its precursor the child as a credible interpreter of his or her parents' experience, especially the parents' attitudes toward the child (see Hartmann and Kris, 1945, pp. 21–22; Schimek, 1975, p. 180; Levenson, 1981). The dichotomy of environmentally induced childhood trauma and internally motivated childhood fantasy in etiological theories has its exact parallel in the false dichotomy in the psychoanalytic situation between reactions to actual countertransference errors on the analyst's part and the unfolding of pure transference that has no basis or only a trivial basis in reality.

The Patient's Perception of Conflict in the Analyst

The analyst's participation, involving his or her tendency toward understanding on the one hand, and his or her complementary countertransference reactions on the other, often entails a sense of real conflict as part of the analyst's total experience of the relationship. I think this conflict is invariably a part of what the patient senses about the analyst's response. In fact, one subtle type of asocial conception of the patient's experience in psychoanalysis is one that implies that from the patient's point of view the analyst's experience is simple rather than complex, and unidimensional rather than multifaceted. The analyst is considered to be simply objective, or critical, or seductive, or threatened, or nurturant, or empathic. Any truly social conception of the patient's experience in psychoanalysis grants that the patient can plausibly infer a variety of more or less harmonious or conflictual tendencies in the analyst, some of which the patient would imagine are conscious and some of which he or she would think are unconscious. In such a model, the patient as interpreter understands that, however different it is, the analyst's experience is no less complex than his or her own.

• 5 •

Toward a Social-Constructivist
View of the
Psychoanalytic Situation

A common theme in papers by Aron (1991), Greenberg (1991), and Modell (1991), appearing in the inaugural issue of the journal *Psychoanalytic Dialogues*,[1] is an emphasis on the importance of the personal presence and participation of the analyst in the psychoanalytic process. A real, personal relationship of some kind is thought to develop inevitably. The only options have to do with whether or how the patient and the analyst attend to it, choices that will, in turn, affect the quality of the experience for both participants. These articles suggest that exploring the patient's perceptions of the analyst's immediate experience in the analytic situation, as well as perceptions of the analyst's general attributes, is at least in keeping with the value

---

An earlier version of this chapter appeared in 1991 in *Psychoanalytic Dialogues*, 1:74–105.

1. As stated in the introduction, although it appeared originally as a discussion of these three papers, I believe the chapter can stand on its own. Throughout, unless indicated otherwise, references to Aron, Greenberg, and Modell are to the papers in that inaugural issue, which were followed by this discussion.

of bringing resisted aspects of the patient's experience to consciousness. More boldly, there is the suggestion that such exploration, which entails an overcoming of reciprocal resistance, creates the opportunity for a special kind of affective contact with the analyst that is thought to have therapeutic potential.

All three authors recognize that increased attention to the patient's experience of the analyst's personal qualities must occur in a context in which the patient's mental life remains the supraordinate focus. Both Aron and Modell stress the importance of integrating the "asymmetrical" requirements of the process with the principles of "mutuality" (Aron) or "egalitarianism" (Modell). Greenberg seeks an integration framed in terms of exploring, in a balanced way, endogenous sources of the patient's desire and the patient's perceptions of the external world and of the analyst in particular. We can discern a rough parallel between the dual principles of Aron and Modell and Greenberg's view, in that the asymmetrical aspect of the analytic situation can be thought of as promoting the emergence and understanding of repressed, endogenous wishes whereas the mutual aspect could be considered as more conducive to illumination of denied or disavowed perceptions of the analyst.

Each author locates his ideas in the context of a movement that he identifies within psychoanalysis and/or related fields of inquiry. Modell feels that his idea of paradox is in keeping with contemporary developments in the physical sciences (p. 14). Moreover, he believes that there are broad social changes, including "critical consumerism," underlying the increased emphasis on the analyst's participation as a "real," fallible person (pp. 19–20). Aron sees his position as consistent with a broad movement in psychoanalytic theory that has been catalyzed recently by feminist social theory and by ideas emerging from research on mother-infant interaction (pp. 30–31). Greenberg regards his ideas as consistent with "a shift in the theoretical winds" (p. 58). He traces a movement in the direction of increased appreciation of the nuances of the influence of the environment to relatively late developments in Freud's thinking. In these developments, arising from Freud's ego psychology, the role of defense against anxiety-laden perception gains in importance. Greenberg feels that this emphasis has been further developed in the work of a variety of contemporary theorists.

Do these authors have in mind the same theoretical movement or different aspects of the same movement? If so, what are its essential features? Does it amount to a new paradigm? If it does, to what extent has it taken hold as the prevailing model that is guiding contemporary practice and theory building, including the ideas presented in these papers?

My own conviction is that there is a new paradigm struggling to emerge in the field, but it has not yet fully "arrived," much less been firmly established. These articles, and much of the theoretical work that the authors cite as consistent with their own positions, can be viewed as transitional from the old to the new paradigm. Because they are transitional, residues of the old paradigm are mixed together with indications of the new. In this discussion I take the liberty of regarding the authors of these three papers as "aiming" for the new paradigm. This view is my own construction, of course, and is open to debate. The authors themselves may not subscribe to my view of the nature of the new paradigm, not to mention its current status relative to their own work.[2]

Let me begin by immediately saying that the paradigm shift I have in mind is not the shift from the drive model to the relational model that Greenberg and Mitchell (1983) and Eagle (1984) have identified as central in the field. Put succinctly, the change that I regard as fundamental and still germinal in psychoanalytic theory and practice is from a positivist model for understanding the psychoanalytic situation to a constructivist model (Berger and Luckmann, 1967; Schön, 1983; Gill, 1983; Gergen, 1985; Stern, 1985; Protter, 1985; Hoffman, 1987; chapter 4). Moreover, the confounding of the two axes, drive-relational and positivist-constructivist, leads to a great deal of inconsistency and confusion. The move to the relational perspective may be conducive in some respects to the more basic change in epistemology, but it is not equivalent to it. In fact, there are aspects of classical theory that are also conducive to a shift to a constructivist point of view. One could even argue that they seem to just about pave the way for its emergence, a point that is hinted at in Greenberg's article. Unfortunately, for the most part, post-Freudian theories, whether relational or not according to the criteria of Greenberg and Mitchell (1983), have not taken that path. Instead, ego psychology, object relations theory, self psychology, and interpersonal theory, despite their varied and rich contributions, have perpetuated the positivist

---

2. Since this chapter's original publication, Greenberg (1995b), in his response to my review (Hoffman, 1995) of his book *Oedipus and Beyond*, has taken exception to having his ideas evaluated in terms of their consistency with some kind of constructivist ideal that is not his own. I believe, however, that identifying apparent internal inconsistencies in any theory can be useful and can lead to important clarifications.

aspect of Freudian theory, even while, in many instances, disclaiming it (see chapter 4; Hirsch, 1987).

What I have called in chapter 4 the "social paradigm," cited by Aron and Greenberg as influential in their thinking, is not, despite the apparently similar terms, the same as the relational model. It does more than emphasize the importance of the patient's awareness of the analyst as a person. Its features are not fully or perhaps even accurately described in terms of a move from a view of the transference as illusory to a view of it as also real (Modell), a move from a view of analysts as objects of their patients' desires to a view of them as also desiring subjects (Aron), or a move from exploration of endogenously based fantasy to exploration also of realistic perceptions of the analyst (Greenberg).

A different step is required, one that has to do specifically with the kind of knowledge that the participants are thought to have of themselves and of each other. The paradigm changes, in my view, only when the idea of the analyst's personal involvement is wedded to a constructivist or perspectivist epistemological position. Only in effecting that integration is the idea of the analyst's participation in the process taken fully into account. By this I mean, very specifically, that the personal participation of the analyst in the process is considered to have a continuous effect on what he or she understands about himself or herself and about the patient in the interaction. The general assumption in this model is that the analyst's understanding is always a function of his or her perspective at the moment. Moreover, because the participation of the analyst implicates all levels of the analyst's personality, it must include unconscious as well as conscious factors. Therefore, what the analyst seems to understand about his or her own experience and behavior as well as the patient's is always suspect, always susceptible to the vicissitudes of the analyst's own resistance, and always prone to being superseded by another point of view that may emerge.

A version of these principles applies to the patient, of course, just as much as one applies to the analyst. In the constructivist model, a proportion of the patient's perceptions of the analyst do not suddenly become simply objective or realistic in a reversal of the classical view that they merely reflect fantasies divorced from reality. I think Langs and Levenson are notable examples of theorists who, in very different ways, have fallen into this reversal (see chapter 4, and Gill, 1984b, on Langs; see Greenberg, 1987, and Hoffman, 1990, on Levenson). The idea is not that fantasy and reality have been redistributed but that we have moved into a world of mutual influence and constructed meaning. Experience is understood to be continually in the process of being formulated or explicated. Although not amorphous, unformulated experience is understood to be intrinsically ambiguous and open to a range of compelling interpretations and explications (Gendlin, 1962, 1964; Fourcher, 1975, 1978; Stern, 1983, 1989).

Finding a good term for the new paradigm is problematic. The term *constructivism* sometimes connotes the interpretation of reality, but not necessarily the shaping of it through reciprocal, interpersonal influence. This connotation of constructivism, often modeled upon the reading of texts (e.g., Hare-Mustin and Marecek, 1988), does not adequately take account of the fact that there is no preestablished text in the evolving interaction and dialogue between two people. Not only is the patient's life story a matter of historical reconstruction, it is also a piece of new history being made or constructed right now in the immediate interaction. The term *social* has the connotation of participation and interpersonal influence, but it does not necessarily have the additional connotation of giving particular meaning to an ambiguous reality. To capture both meanings and to avoid confusion with the relational model, the term *social-constructivist paradigm* seems useful. Also, although unwieldy, the term *participant-constructivist* might well describe the role of the analyst in this paradigm.[3]

Although psychoanalysis may be lagging behind developments in contemporary physics, philosophy, and literary theory with regard to the paradigm issue, it is not out of step within the world of professional

---

3. If it were not for their common connotations, either of these terms, *social* or *constructivist*, might be conceptually sufficient. No thoroughgoing application of the idea of social participation could omit taking account of the factor of selective construction of meaning, and no thoroughgoing application of constructivism to the analytic situation could omit taking account of the social factor as it relates to the past and the present. Accordingly, depending on the context, in this chapter (originally published in 1991) I sometimes use the terms *social* and *constructivist* as shorthand for social-constructivist paradigm.

For a debate about the relative merits of the terms *constructivism* and *perspectivism* or *perspectival realism* see Donna Orange's (1992) commentary on this discussion and my reply (Hoffman, 1992). Partly in light of the connotation of radical relativism that some, like Orange, associate with *social constructivism* I now believe that *critical constructivism* or *dialectical constructivism* may be less misleading and convey more of my intent.

practice. Schön (1983) argues persuasively that even when it is disclaimed, positivism[4] continues to be the dominant epistemology across a wide range of professions. The expression of positivism in these disciplines (ranging from architecture to city planning to psychotherapy) is an approach Schön calls "Technical Rationality." In this model, "professional activity consists in instrumental problem solving made rigorous by the application of scientific theory and technique" (p. 21). In the contrasting paradigm, which Schön calls "reflection-in-action," the practitioner engages in "reflective conversation with a situation that he treats as unique and uncertain. Through his transaction with the situation he shapes it and makes himself a part of it. Hence, the sense he makes of the situation must include his own contribution to it" (p. 163). I would add that analysts working in this model would assume not only that their contributions could be described and interpreted in various ways, but also that their own particular ways of understanding their contributions would be skewed in keeping with their personal participation in the process.

WHOLLY AND PARTIALLY INCOMPATIBLE
BEDFELLOWS FOR THE NEW PARADIGM

Although it may seem like a departure from my primary task of discussing the substantive points of these papers, I want to take a critical look at a sample of the literature cited by the authors as contributing to their own views and to the movement that they discern in the field. With respect to the paradigm issue, a good deal of confusion can result from grouping various theorists together as implicitly or explicitly constructivist when their positions vary considerably in terms of their adherence to that point of view.

In general, because the relational model is often loosely and incorrectly thought of as constructivist, theorists often overestimate the extent to which the positivist tradition in psychoanalysis is a dead relic of the past. Modell speaks as though the view of the transference as simple distortion and of the analyst as the arbiter of reality is virtually extinct. I think that the reports of the death of this notion are highly exaggerated. On the contrary, I agree with Greenberg that the asocial view of transference is "alive and well in contemporary

---

4. Schön uses the term *positivism* in a broad sense. See fn. 2, chapter 6, on "objectivism" versus "positivism."

psychoanalytic practice" (p. 60). Although Greenberg has elsewhere recognized the extent to which certain relational theorists, especially the interpersonalists, have been infected by some form of objectivism (e.g., Greenberg, 1981, pp. 251–252, on Sullivan and Thompson; Greenberg, 1987, on Levenson), in this paper he continues to leave the impression that classical drive theory is the primary, if not the only, culprit with regard to this issue. Some of the theorists whom he identifies here as sympathetic to the new paradigm are relational, but they are also positivist in one way or another. Thompson (1964a), for example, whom both Aron and Greenberg mention as an important contributor to the social paradigm, wrote: "Transference consists entirely of irrational attitudes toward another person" (p. 14), and "In psychoanalysis, the therapist has a different attitude toward the irrational trends in the patient from that of all other therapists. By persistently indicating to the patient that he does not wish to dominate, that he is not angry, that he does not feel contempt, nor, on the other hand, is he a paragon of all virtues, he aims at eventually destroying his unique position in the patient's eyes" (p. 17). In the same article, Thompson, like Greenson (1971) and other theorists, pays due respect to the patient's allegedly "realistic" perceptions of the analyst, but these are unequivocally distinguished from the patient's irrational ideas, and it is the analyst who decides which is which (see chapter 4).[5] Greenberg (1981) previously termed the idea of inevitable, partially blinding entanglement "a friendly and compatible extension of the interpersonal approach" (p. 254). I believe that, on the contrary, the idea that the analyst inevitably gets caught up in this way is a radical departure from that approach. Moreover, the idea is an essential aspect of the social-constructivist paradigm.

Similarly, Weiss and Sampson (1986) are cited by Greenberg because of the emphasis on perception in their theory. Consistent with the model of technical rationality, however, there is something remarkably formulaic and "prescriptive" (cf. Greenberg, 1981) about the way in which these theorists go about identifying "pathogenic beliefs" and the attitudes and behaviors that the analyst can adopt in order to disconfirm them. The control-mastery theory

---

5. In some later, less formal statements, Thompson's (1964b) description of the process has more the flavor of constructivism or "reflection-in-action." Such inconsistency is in keeping with Schön's (1983) observation that the way practitioners actually work, at least some of the time, may put them into conflict with their own theories.

developed by Weiss and Sampson does not encourage the analyst to expect to be caught up in complex patterns of interaction involving ambiguous integrations of repetition and new experience. Similarly, it does not encourage analysts to expect that their own understanding will inevitably be skewed by their personal participation in the process (see Hoffman and Gill, 1988b, for further discussion of Weiss and Sampson).

Schafer's work is especially interesting with respect to the paradigm issue because he has written so much about psychoanalysis from a constructivist point of view. Greenberg is particularly interested in Schafer's view of danger situations. It is noteworthy, however, that with respect to the psychoanalytic situation, Schafer's constructivism is focused primarily on the way the analyst's theoretical bias affects the patient's life story as it emerges in the process. With respect to the issue of personal participation, the analyst remains quite detached and objective. Schafer's "analytic attitude" is essentially purified of the analyst's personal influence through "*continuous* scrutiny of countertransferences" (p. 221; italics added). The intrusion of countertransference "results in analytic incoherence" (p. 228). The whole tenor of Schafer's book *The Analytic Attitude* is consistent with the classical view of countertransference as occasional, as undesirable, and as something to be overcome when it does intrude. There is no latitude in many of Schafer's statements, any more than there is in the statements quoted from Thompson, for the idea of an inevitable interplay of transference and countertransference with concomitant effects on understanding, including the inevitable undiscovered blind spots that Greenberg mentions. The very fact that Schafer seems to believe that "continuous scrutiny" of the countertransference is possible, not to mention what he implies such scrutiny can accomplish, gives his view of the process the stamp of positivism rather than constructivism.

Since the concept of intersubjectivity that Aron is trying to develop has been grounded at least partly in self psychology, it is important to underscore the extent to which that point of view in particular departs from the social-constructivist paradigm. In the first place, as Aron says, although there is a focus in self psychology on the analyst's subjectivity as a source of understanding, in another sense, in relation to the needs of the patient, the emphasis is entirely on the analyst as an object, as a person whose subjectivity is decidedly not "recognized" (Benjamin, 1988). If anything, the selfobject transference is associated with a need that I discuss later for a relatively selfless, idealized other, a need that conflicts with the patient's interest in discovering and exploring the analyst's subjectivity. In the second place, even the focus on the analyst's subjectivity in the process of "introspection and empathy" is of such a nature as to locate it outside the paradigm in which the analyst is a participant-constructivist. The discrepancy from that paradigm is evident from the fact that the self psychologist, as Eagle (1984, pp. 64–65), Mitchell (1988, p. 296), and Black (1987) have pointed out, ultimately lays no less claim to the possibility of an objective or accurate reading of the patient's experience than does the classical analyst. Such a view of the analyst's position is perpetuated in some instances by neo-self psychologists. Even Stolorow, a leading exponent of the theory of intersubjectivity, despite his determination to reject the positivist tradition (see especially, Stolorow, 1988), seems, at times, to end up squarely within it. Atwood and Stolorow (1984), for example, have written the following:

> Whether or not . . . intersubjective situations facilitate or obstruct the progress of analysis depends in large part on the extent of the analyst's reflective self-awareness and capacity to decenter [citing Piaget] from the organizing principles of his own subjective world and thereby to grasp empathically the *actual meaning* of the patient's experiences [p. 47; italics added].

This is old wine in new bottles, yet another search for an apprehension of the reality of the patient's inner life that is uncontaminated by countertransference (especially by potentially useful complementary countertransference) or any kind of perspective that the analyst may have. The idea of the analyst's participation is not taken seriously in this account.[6]

For the theory of intersubjectivity to be consistent with the social-constructivist paradigm, it must encompass interaction on multiple

---

6. Stolorow and his collaborators have identified their viewpoint with a "perspectivalist" epistemological position (Stolorow and Atwood, 1992, p. 123). Although the tendency toward objectivism in their thought is reflected in the centrality of key concepts such as "sustained empathic inquiry" (see, for example, Brandchaft and Stolorow, 1990, reprinted with revisions in Stolorow and Atwood, 1992, pp. 87–102), they have also struggled to extricate their intersubjective view from that paradigm, as reflected, for example, in their formulation of the stance of "empathic-introspective inquiry," which "does not seek to avert, minimize, or disavow the impact of the analyst's psychological organization on the patient's experience" (Stolorow and Atwood, 1997, p. 441).

levels of psychological organization and consciousness. Any divorc-
ing of the intrapsychic and the interpersonal is unacceptable in this
model. Thus, for example, Benjamin (1988), who Aron feels influenced his own view of intersubjectivity, takes a position that is contrary, in one respect, to the social-constructivist viewpoint. Her
strategy is to put aside the realm of the intrapsychic while developing theory addressed to what she feels is the relatively neglected
realm of the intersubjective (p. 21). To some extent, this strategy is a
temporary expedient. She recognizes that intersubjectivity theory is
"unidimensional" when separated from intrapsychic considerations
and that the two domains are "interdependent" (p. 21). The strategy
itself, however, as well as some of her specific statements, creates the
impression that she is prepared to accept the meanings of the terms
without the redefinitions that their synthesis would require. She
writes, for example: "The intersubjective foundation of erotic life . . .
emphasizes the tension *between interacting individuals* rather than
that within the individual. . . . [T]hese rival perspectives seem to me
not so much mutually exclusive as concerned simply with different
issues" (p. 29). This approach effectively succumbs to the traditional
polarization of the intrapsychic and the interpersonal. I think of
intersubjectivity as the interaction at all levels of two hierarchically
organized psychological systems.[7] The notion of interaction on multiple levels gives full meaning to the idea of participation in the analytic situation. Moreover, we certainly are not starting from scratch
when we attempt to integrate the interpersonal and intrapsychic
domains. Racker (1968), in a paper published originally in the *The
Psychoanalytic Quarterly* in 1957, was ahead of his time, and perhaps our own, when he wrote:

> The first distortion of truth in "the myth of the analytic situation" is
> that it is an interaction between a sick person and a healthy one. The
> truth is that it is an interaction between two personalities, in both of
> which the ego is under pressure from the id, the superego, and the
> external world; each personality has its internal and external depen-
> dencies, anxieties and pathological defenses; each is also a child with

---

7. Actually, Benjamin herself, despite her stated strategy, deals with patterns of interaction in terms that combine the intrapsychic and the intersubjective. For example, the dominated person, in her theory, is understood
to be unconsciously identified with the dominating one, and vice versa. For
a discussion of intersubjectivity in Benjamin's perspective compared to my
own see Benjamin's (1991) commentary on this discussion and my reply
(Hoffman, 1991).

his internal parents; and each of these whole personalities—that of the analysand and that of the analyst—responds to every event of the analytic situation [p. 132].

Racker's concept of the countertransference goes a long way toward synthesizing the idea of the analyst's subjectivity, considered in depth, with the idea of his or her responsiveness in the analytic situation. The countertransference for Racker is not simply reactive, the connotation of the term to which Aron objects.

I cannot discuss all the theorists who are cited in these articles as contributing to the "shift in the theoretical winds" (p. 58) that Greenberg detects. I agree with Aron, who, following Hirsch (1987) and me (chapter 4), points out that a variety of theorists, including Sullivan, Winnicott, and Kohut, continue to suggest that analysts can somehow manage to keep their own subjective experience from "contaminating" their patients' transferences. A corollary of this view is that analysts are in a position to assess accurately what they and their patients are doing and experiencing. That there is no advance here beyond Freud's positivism is obscured by Aron's emphasis on the progression from drive theory to relational perspectives. In fact, the most that could be said is that some of the internally contradictory features of the positions taken by some of these theorists lend themselves to a constructivist resolution. But, in the end, I am not sure that the gulf that separates Kohut, Winnicott, and Sullivan from the social-constructivist point of view is less wide than the gulf that separates Freud from that perspective.

BACK TO AND BEYOND FREUD:
ON THE VERGE OF SOCIAL CONSTRUCTIVISM

Returning to Greenberg, I want to examine his analysis of the historical origins of the tendency to focus on "endogenous" determinants of the transference at the expense of perceptions of external reality. Greenberg takes us back to Freud, a laudable approach, I think, because it so often yields either a rediscovery of lost insights or an awareness of obsolete foundations for aspects of current practice or theory that should be discarded or modified. I find his review of Freud's theorizing illuminating, although I missed reference to a few of Freud's writings that are especially relevant to the issue of Freud's recognition of the importance of unconscious perception. I am thinking, for example, of the "Postscript to Dora" (1905a), in which

Freud says he regrets having failed to inquire as to whether there was anything about himself that reminded Dora of Herr K (pp. 118–119). It is remarkable that this kind of inquiry and its theoretical implications are never developed further in Freud's writings. In addition, the paper on fetishism (1927b) is pertinent as Freud's paradigmatic example of nonpsychotic disavowal and splitting. It is interesting, too, that Freud (1940b) seems inadvertently to illustrate his own "splitting of the ego in the process of defense" when he opens the paper with that very title by remarking, "I find myself for a moment in the interesting position of not knowing whether what I have to say should be regarded as something long familiar and obvious or as something entirely new and puzzling. But I am inclined to think the latter" (p. 275). In light of the writings just mentioned, as well as other works (Freud, 1940b, Strachey's introductory note, pp. 273–274), Freud's musing here seems like an intriguing indication of his disavowal of the significance of disavowal in his own thinking!

These points, however, are merely in support of Greenberg's thesis that Freud failed to develop the idea of defense against perception of external reality and to give it the theoretical status of repression of impulses. More important for the purposes of this discussion, Greenberg's critique of Freud stops with this point and thereby implicitly accepts the dichotomy of endogenous instinctual pressures and perception of the external world. I recognize that Greenberg is interested in getting away from this dichotomy. He refers to the seemingly paradoxical dimension of Freud's thought with respect to the interdependence of drive and external danger. He writes that "at our best, we listen to our patients from a perspective that emphasizes the mutually interdependent matrix of their needs and the circumstances in which they live," and he speaks of "the elegant ambiguity" (p. 55) of this posture. In much of the paper, however, he seems to accept the classical notion of a tension between the two sources of influence, each of which seems to retain its integrity. By not thoroughly challenging Freud's dichotomy of realistic perception and drive-determined fantasy, Greenberg fails to identify a major additional impediment in Freudian thought to the development of a constructivist view of the analytic situation.

Freud's view of perception is consistent with naive realism rather than constructivism. As Holt (1989) has written, "Like his contemporaries in psychology and psychiatry alike, Freud assumed as a matter of course that perception is a simple matter of coming into contact with reality" (p. 285). And Schimek (1975), in a detailed discussion of this issue, writes the following:

Freud seems to have been hampered by his belief in the originally veridical nature of the contents of perception and memory and the dichotomy between factual and psychical reality. He retained the concept of immaculate perception rather than assuming that perception always involves the interaction between the "objective" features of the external stimuli and the "subjective" drive or schemata of the individual which selectively organize and give meaning to immediate experience [p. 180].

I have discussed this issue myself (chapter 2) in connection with Freud's failure to consider death anxiety as an emergent, irreducible danger situation. Freud (1926a) lamely argues that death cannot have psychodynamic significance because it cannot be "pictured" like "faeces being separated from the body" (pp. 129–130). Hartmann and Kris (1945, pp. 21–22) noted that Freud felt impelled to resort to phylogenetic explanations of castration anxiety, insofar as a boy may not encounter literal threats to his penis as he is growing up. They suggest that Freud failed to consider the possibility that the boy might construe and react to possible latent meanings of the parents' behavior rather than to its manifest content alone. In Freud's thought, the swing of the pendulum from literal seduction in childhood to drive-determined fantasy (complemented by phylogenetic memory) in the etiology of the neuroses seems like a thesis and an antithesis that are just begging for the synthesis that constructivism could offer. But Freud's return to consideration of perception and defenses against it within the ego does not translate into a constructivist paradigm, even though it may seem on the verge of doing so.

Throughout his paper, Greenberg himself seems too comfortable with the polarity of internal and external influence. For example, he says "not only *impulses* but *observations*, too, become subject to repression" (p. 59); he objects to the lack of evidence for Arlow's claim that his patient is "*wishing* rather than *seeing*" (p. 61); he says that "patients often try to protect us from the less palatable aspects of what they see" (p. 63); and he says that the patient and the analyst each brings to the analytic situation "a unique and *observable* personality" (p. 63; italics added).

I recognize that to some extent this is just a manner of speaking; that is, one could hold a perspectivist view and still speak of "seeing" and "observing" another person's qualities, with the understanding that what is meant is not simple observation, but rather a certain degree of inference or speculation regarding behavior that is ambiguous as to its meaning. In fact, I think that for most purposes it would be too confining to have to watch every word and too cumbersome continually to be putting one's terms in quotation marks. Also, at the extreme there are categories of experience that are so accepted as part of our consensually validated world that the sense in which they are "constructions" becomes somewhat academic. Greenberg, moreover, feels that "some of [the patient's] conclusions [about the analyst] may be elaborations of the most obvious, concrete observations that can be made" (p. 64). Nevertheless, in attempting to develop theory, I believe there is reason to try to be more rigorous about terminology, especially if there is an interest in shifting from one paradigm to another when the paradigm that is supposedly being superseded is still very entrenched. To speak of "observable personality" in this climate, and to organize an argument around the question of the relative weights of endogenous pressure and the influence of the external world without fully addressing the extent to which such terms and polarities are problematic, gives just too much fuel to the positivist fire, assuming, of course, that one has some interest in putting it out.[8]

Despite the residues of Freud's positivist dichotomies, there is a clear contribution in Greenberg's paper to the development of the social-constructivist paradigm. In bringing out the disequilibrium in Freud's theorizing, in particular the failure to integrate the importance of perception into the theory, Greenberg implicitly demonstrates the way in which Freud's model is virtually poised for a transformation that would not simply accommodate perception but would change its meaning. Similarly, in his insistence that transference is penetrated by reality, Greenberg separates himself from all the "conservative critics" of the blank-screen fallacy who emphasize the real relationship, but only as something apart from the transference (see chapter 4).

Greenberg's own valuable clinical vignettes illustrate the practical application of a perspectivist or constructivist attitude. He does not ask the patient who claimed to know nothing about him to report his "fantasies," nor does he simply ask for factual observations. Instead, he encourages the patient to "speculate" about him, and he listens with a sense of openness to the patient's conjectures (pp. 62–63). Not only is he interested in establishing that a patient noticed his

---

8. It should be noted that even "the most obvious, concrete observations that can be made" are selectively lifted out of the "chaos" of "unformulated experience" (Stern, 1983, 1989; cf. Gendlin, 1962, 1964). In another individual, in another culture, in another time, these "facts" might not matter in the same way or might not matter enough to be noticed at all.

messy waiting room, a perception he regards as important as a starting point, but he wants to go further by asking what the patient
"thought about the messiness" (p. 71). With the financially successful patient who "has every reason to assume, correctly as it happens,
that [Greenberg's] net worth is considerably less" (p. 64), Greenberg
is interested not only in this "observation" by the patient, but also
in what conclusions the patient might draw from this as to how he
should handle his own success in the therapist's presence, conclusions that would be guided, in part, by other impressions of the
analyst and, in part, by common sense.

Common sense is a very important factor in this process. It is
often common sense that tells patients that their own behavior is
likely to have elicited some kind of inner reaction from the analyst,
so that perceptual confirmation may be of secondary importance. In
the instance cited by Greenberg, the patient may plausibly imagine
that the analyst would be envious or annoyed if the patient allowed
himself to gloat. Greenberg says that "it will be a long time before
[the patient] will be able to express an emotion like gleefulness
about having more money than I do" (p. 64). Although he does not
spell it out in this example, it would be in the spirit of Greenberg's
paper to add that this "long time" may be partly associated with
the period that the analyst would require to struggle with his feelings about the matter and to come to terms with whatever resentful
envy he may be experiencing.

In general, might we not actually secretly appreciate the fact that
patients are considerate enough to give us the opportunity to interpret
their inhibitions about touching on our points of vulnerability? If that
is so, and if we interpret the inhibition with the implication that it has
not been necessary at all, we are being subtly dishonest. Grappling
with what we are experiencing and with our personal attributes as
they impinge on the patient is an important implication of the social-
constructivist position. But just how our experiences are formulated
and understood is a function of perspectives that are themselves more
or less formulated and that are subject to change. Moreover, the analyst struggles not only with anxiety and defense (as in Levenson,
1990, p. 300), but also with the intrinsic ambiguity of experience.

ON CALLING ATTENTION TO ONESELF

Both Greenberg and Aron want the analyst to work to overcome the
reciprocal resistance that interferes with exploration of what the

patient discerns about the analyst. One of the ideas that emerges
from Aron's application of the theory of intersubjectivity is that
patients are not only responsive to their impressions of their analysts'
mental lives, but are also actively interested in exploring their analysts' personal qualities as part of a basic tendency that has roots in
the infant's interest in the subjectivity of the mother. This idea is
challenging and opens the door to a very different orientation
toward the patient's curiosity. Now, instead of viewing that curiosity
only as an expression of a forbidden or unrealistic wish in the transference, we are invited to consider it also as a relatively healthy
search for meaningful contact with the analyst. Aron gives us a sense
of the way in which he actively encourages his patients to overcome
their resistance to this exploration, an exploration that might lead
the analyst to discover something new about himself. I do not think
the importance of this point can be overestimated. I would add that
if this discovery is not something completely new, it might be something familiar from one's private life that one never dreamed would
be apparent to any of one's patients. The attitude Aron recommends
entails a radical kind of openness. In working in this way, Aron,
courageously I think, removes or reduces that component of the
patient's resistance that is accommodating to what the patient might
otherwise plausibly attribute to him, namely, a wish to remain hidden or invisible, or at least a wish not to have his prevailing self-
image as an analyst disturbed.

Greenberg and Aron, following some of my own suggestions on
this issue in 1983 (chapter 4), articulate some of the arguments
against analysts actually disclosing their experience. Assuming that,
in keeping with the principle of asymmetry, analysts are going to listen much more than they talk and focus on their patients much more
than on themselves, there is a danger that whatever they do disclose
will be taken to imply that they, unlike their patients, have relatively
easy access to their own experience. Nevertheless, I agree with Aron
that there are often times when it makes sense for analysts to reveal
some aspects of their experience to patients, including, when it seems
pertinent, reference to their reservations about doing so. In that connection, when the patient asks a direct question, there can be much
honest self-disclosure, paradoxically, in the process of struggling out
loud with one's conflict about answering it. In fact, what might be a
need on the patient's part for more personal contact with the analyst
may be partially satisfied by such frankness, and the original question itself may become less pressing. However the analyst responds,
such exchanges should be explored retrospectively to understand

better the nature of the patient's need or wish and feelings about the analyst's response.[9]

It is important to recognize, however, that exploring our patients' perceptions of us frequently does make necessary some struggle with the issue of self-disclosure. Greenberg does not address this issue in the context of any of his vignettes, but it seems likely that inviting patients to formulate and speak of their impressions of the analyst would sometimes generate new dilemmas for the participants. Aron says that "once analysts express interest in the patient's perceptions of their subjectivity, they have tantalized the patient and will surely be pressured to disclose more of what is going on inside themselves" (p. 40). Although I prefer that this warning be restated in more qualified, perspectivist terms (e.g., "may be experienced as tantalizing" and "may feel pressured to disclose") it is, nevertheless, useful and raises important questions. I think, however, it is a mistake to add immediately that "self-revelation is not an option; it is an inevitability" (p. 40) because—contrary, perhaps, to Aron's intention—this view minimizes the likely differences among three possibilities: betraying something about ourselves without exploring the patient's perceptions, exploring the patient's perceptions, and deliberate self-disclosure. Just as showing interest in the patient's perceptions is an option, so is deliberate self-disclosure an option. In each case, in different ways, we are making a point of inviting attention to our subjectivity, and the repercussions for the patient's experience and our own have to be considered. Those repercussions are not fully predictable. Ferenczi (1931) found that his principles of "relaxation" and "indulgence" eventually led his patients to relive childhood traumas at a level of intensity far greater than what had been promoted by the principles of abstinence and frustration. Unfortunately, he died before he could give us a fuller sense of how things worked out for those patients. These were people, one might say, who felt seduced by the element of mutuality in their relationships with their analyst and abandoned when the principle of asymmetry was

---

9. The traditional idea that it is always better to explore the patient's wishes in this regard under conditions of abstinence and deprivation is another reflection of positivist thinking. The implication is that the "true" nature of the wish or need will be exposed if the analyst does not "contaminate" the field by yielding to the patient's pressures. In the constructivist model, whatever way the analyst responds is likely to affect what is then "found out" about the intensity and quality of the patient's desire (cf. Greenberg, 1986; Mitchell, 1991).

reasserted. Notwithstanding Ferenczi's conviction that such reliving of childhood traumas could serve the purposes of the analysis, the fact is that sometimes our patients may feel more drawn in by our accessibility and then more hurt or traumatized by the limits of the relationship than seems optimal. We ourselves may end up feeling more involved, exposed, or vulnerable than we had anticipated. Aron and Greenberg are talking about opening themselves up in a certain way, not about some kind of fully controllable, technical maneuver. The challenge is to recognize fully the complexities and problems of this approach and yet not shrink back into positions in which our own subjectivity is denied and in which any kind of spontaneous, personal participation is prohibited.[10]

The underlying paradigm is decisive with regard to this issue. If exploring the patient's perceptions is thought of as merely getting at something that is "there" anyway, so that the only choice is whether it is made conscious or left unconscious, then, assuming the value of self-awareness for the patient, there is generally only one reasonable course to take. Also, its consequences from this positivist viewpoint should not be especially problematic. The analyst, as a reader of the patient's unconscious, rather complacently feels sure that he or she is not going to be as disturbed by the patient's impressions as the patient might fear. If, instead, we think of such exploration, in the first place, as frequently explicating something that had never been formulated before and, in the second place, as affecting the experiences of the participants in ways that may be surprising, then we have to recognize that there is more risk and more responsibility involved than is connoted by the idea of merely making unconscious perceptions conscious. Instead, we are contributing to *shaping* the relationship in a particular way among many ways that are possible. Both the process of explication and the moment of interpersonal influence entail creation of meaning, not merely its discovery. And whatever is explicated by the patient and the analyst about themselves or about each other, out loud or in their private thoughts, affects what happens next within and between the two people in ways that were not known before that moment.

I think that in the past, Gill and I (e.g., Gill and Hoffman, 1982a,b) failed to take adequate account of this aspect of the analy-

---

10. It is important to remember that keeping our subjectivity in the background is also a choice that has repercussions that are not fully predictable, even though it may be more conducive to an illusion of control over the process.

sis of transference. Although we wrote about the transference repercussions of transference interpretations, especially, in fact, about the
effects of interpretations that refer to the analyst's contributions to
the patient's experience, I do not think we fully grappled with this
issue of opening up something that is not entirely captured through
extensions of the "technique" of analysis of transference. The term
technique itself suggests a degree of control that does not fit the fluid
movement of the process (cf. Schafer, 1983, p. 291). A more open
and flexible attitude is called for. The baseline to which the analyst
continually returns remains that of critical reflection on the way the
immediate interaction is being shaped by the participants, but a
deeper appreciation is required of the fact that the unformulated
aspects of the process necessarily and continually elude analytic closure. Gill and I may have progressed further had we considered more
fully the unexpected *countertransference* repercussions of exploring
the patient's experience of the relationship. That consideration would
have helped to free us of the particular kind of technical rationality
to which the analysis of the transference is prone.

In addition to the importance of the asymmetrical arrangement as
a means of ensuring that the patient's experience remains the center
of attention and as a means of reducing the chances that the analyst's
involvement could become excessive and ultimately traumatic for the
patient, I want to suggest one other important source of conflict and
legitimate reciprocal resistance to the emergence of the analyst's subjectivity in the process. Could it not be argued that the whole ritual
of psychoanalysis is designed, in part, to cultivate and protect a certain aura or mystique that accompanies the role of the analyst, and
is there not a residue of this aura that remains even after we have
analyzed it in many ways? I think this question touches on a fundamental conflict, both sides of which need to be both respected and
questioned as they emerge in the process: on the one hand, the interest in the emergence of the analyst as a subject and, on the other
hand, the interest in the submergence of the analyst's subjectivity.
This conflict undoubtedly has its precursors in childhood. The primal scene, both literally and as metaphor for the parents' private
experience, is aversive as well as magnetic, and the aversiveness is
surely not merely a defense to be overcome. In the analytic situation
there is an important tension between the desire *to know* and the
desire *not to know* more about the analyst's personal experience.[11]

---

11. Since the time of the symposium that included the paper by Aron
(1991) and this discussion, Aron (1996) has proposed that we distinguish

Moreover, I would argue that it is against the backdrop of idealization, promoted by the ritualized asymmetry of the psychoanalytic situation, that the analyst's willingness to participate in the spirit of mutuality can become so meaningful for the patient and so powerful.

CONSTRUCTIVISM AND PARADOX
IN THE PSYCHOANALYTIC SITUATION

Modell's paradox points to a central dimension of the analytic experience for both the patient and the analyst. From the point of view of the analyst it can be thought of as a tension between a relatively methodical clinical perspective and one that is relatively personal, spontaneous, and affectively responsive. Of course, what is, in the foreground, a part of psychoanalytic technique is also, in the background, personally expressive and vice versa. But with this caveat, the notion of a dialectic between these two ways of participating in the interaction is clinically useful. If the patient who has slighted or depreciated the analyst asks, "Did I annoy you or upset you?" the analyst's inner response, whether or not it is revealed, usually is more complex than even an elaboration of a "yes" or a "no" would capture. Even if the patient has reached the analyst in a very personal way, the analyst's experience usually includes a clinical perspective on this very interaction. Thus, in keeping with Modell's paradox, a relatively full answer would often include elaborations of both "yes" and "no." There is a good chance that the affective response that the patient is asking about, even if it is intense, will have been mitigated by the analyst's interest in its meanings in the context of the interplay of the transference and the countertransference. An awareness of the amalgam of personal and clinical-technical responses may be more likely in therapists who work implicitly or explicitly in accord with the social-constructivist paradigm, in which this mix is not only expected but welcomed.

The premise of such a direct question often denies that the analyst may have some personal experience associated with the role-

---

between the dialectics of mutuality and autonomy, on the one hand, and symmetry and asymmetry, on the other. With respect to analyst and analysand, he has emphasized the inevitability of their mutual influence as well as the importance of the asymmetry of their role-requirements. His recent book (1996) explores in depth the theoretical and clinical issues associated with these dimensions of the process.

determined aspects of the relationship. In some instances, analysts may buy into the implicit disallowing of this aspect of their experience so that they may have a vague sense that the only legitimate choices are to "confess" or to refuse to reply. In fact, the question itself may have aggressive connotations, in that it may be designed to "knock the analyst off his perch," as Modell puts it (p. 24). So if the analyst decided to respond directly, the reply might well include some account of his or her experience of the question itself.

Regardless of the emotional aspect, the clinical perspective is usually an organic part of the analyst's experience. It is not merely tacked on in a superficial way, nor is it necessarily defensive. In this regard, I think Modell is wrong to say that "one feels angry, guilty, sexually aroused, and so forth in *precisely* the same way as one does in everyday life" (p. 24; italics added). To say that the feeling is "precisely" the same and that "mental labor is required in order to transpose this experience back into the therapeutic frame" is to compartmentalize the personal and the technical aspects of the analyst's experience and to underestimate its immediate complexity.

Modell is somewhat inconsistent in the way that he refers to the role-related and the more idiosyncratically personal dimensions of the analytic exchange for both participants. He usually speaks in terms of "two levels of reality," but he sometimes refers to the affective aspect as illusory and to the role-determined aspect as real. Speaking of more disturbed patients, he says that "[the therapist] may be forced to remind the patient that this relationship is, after all, a treatment" (p. 23). What are the implications of the phrase "after all"? Could one not argue just as well that the situation is, "after all," a personal relationship between two people? The notion of paradox implies a contradiction, but the contradiction is too easily resolved if we slip into regarding the emotional connection between the patient and the analyst as somehow less real than the technical aspects of the relationship. The converse is also true. When Modell says that we respond affectively precisely as we do in everyday life and then have to work to bring back the relevance of the frame, he comes close to resolving the paradox in the opposite direction, that is, one that grants the personal exchange more "reality" than artificially imposed analytic discipline. In this regard, he speaks of "real affects within an 'unreal' context" (p. 24).

Modell's idea of the paradox of the therapeutic relationship is limited in that it is not clear how the paradox is representative of a general phenomenon in human experience. Modell does refer to it as an instance of "acceptance of contradictory phenomena without striving for a synthesis" (p. 14), and he refers to various thinkers, such as William James and Winnicott, who have discussed the issue in other contexts. However, the emphasis is so much on the peculiar nature of the therapeutic situation that more general implications are either missed or understated. In fact, Modell seems unclear as to why tolerance of the specific paradox of the analytic situation should be desirable in the long term. He says, rather vaguely, "It would seem that the acceptance of paradox may in some way be connected to mental health" (p. 23).

What is missing from Modell's conceptualization in this article is the universal relevance of the insight that however real and inevitable the forms of an individual's social life may seem, they can generally be shown to be constructions that reflect the capacities and potentialities of the human organism, but are not necessary or inevitable in terms of their specific features. Social reality is neither externally given nor created out of whole cloth by the individual. As Berger and Luckmann (1967) put it, with emphasis, *"Society is a human product. Society is an objective reality. Man is a social product"* (p. 61). The patient's "ordinary life," in Modell's terms, corresponds to what Berger and Luckmann refer to as the "taken-for-granted world." This world is itself a social construction. Mitchell (1988) has discussed the importance of the interplay of "narcissistic illusion" and more realistic appraisals of the worth of self and others. But these appraisals are themselves constructions that could be regarded as narcissistic illusions. The fact is that people, against a threatening and omnipresent, preconscious awareness of the potential meaninglessness of their existence, forge and sustain a sense that their lives do matter. All social realities are "sandcastles" (Mitchell, 1988, p. 195), jeopardized by awareness of mortality. In the terms of Berger and Luckmann (1967):

> The experience of the death of others and, subsequently, the anticipation of one's own death posit the marginal situation par excellence for the individual. Needless to elaborate, death also posits the most terrifying threat to the taken-for-granted realities of everyday life. . . . All legitimations of death must carry out the same essential task—they must enable the individual to go on living in society after the death of significant others and to anticipate his own death with, at the very least, terror sufficiently mitigated so as not to paralyze the continued performance of the routines of everyday life [p. 101]. . . . *All* social reality is precarious. *All* societies are constructions in the face of chaos. The constant possibility of anomic terror is actualized whenever legitimations that obscure the precariousness are threatened or collapse [p. 103].

We all live in innumerable, concentric worlds within worlds. At the outer limits there is the sense of our mortality in the context of infinite time and space. Moving rapidly inward, we find human history, the cultures and subcultures to which we belong, and then our family and individual histories. The psychoanalytic situation can be thought of as a special kind of interaction designed to expose the dialectic between the activity of patients in constructing certain problematic aspects of their lives, past and present, and the preestablished givens with which they have had to live and with which they have to live now in the immediacy of the relationship with the analyst.

On the one hand, this project has a very narrow focus. Only a minuscule proportion of the multiplicity of realities in which the patient's life is embedded and in which the patient is implicated is lifted out for exploration and critical reflection. The rest are likely to be unexamined, taken-for-granted values and conventions, many of which the patient and the analyst may share. On the other hand, the project is ambitious in two ways. First, the aim is to affect some of the most longstanding and deeply rooted ways in which patients experience themselves and others. For example, the attempt may be to affect even central aspects of the patient's sense of worth, established originally in childhood before there was any possibility of questioning the authority of caretakers. Second, the recognition of the ways in which the patient and the analyst are implicated in the repetitive patterns of the transference and the countertransference can generalize so that patients become aware, not only that these patterns are relative rather than absolute and inevitable, but also that all aspects of their lives can, in principle, be subject to the same analysis. In other words, patients are encouraged to develop an implicitly constructivist attitude toward their own experience (Schafer, 1983, pp. 125–127; Protter, 1985). One effect of such an attitude is to take oneself a little less seriously, to cultivate a sense of humor about oneself. Yet this attitude does not preclude living with passion and commitment. Modell begins his article by distinguishing between the love relation of the analyst and the patient and other love relations, on the grounds that in the case of the former, "the partners will inevitably separate when the aim of the treatment has been realized. . . . this separation is a fact that neither participant can forget" (p. 13). But this separation is analogous to the final and ultimate separation. In the context of the latter, the paradoxical effect is simultaneously to divest life of meaning and to promote people's responsibility for making their lives as meaningful and as rich as possible (see chapters 1 and 2).

The authority of the analyst plays an important role in the process by which the patient's fixed ways of experiencing himself or herself and the world are affected in analysis. The analytic situation is a setup, not only for deconstructing the sense of necessity that under-lies the transference, but also for constructing an alternative social reality involving modifications in the patient's sense of self and of others. The "ritualized arrangements," as Modell calls them, which include the ritualized asymmetry of the process, are likely to pro-mote the sense of the relationship as hierarchical. The authority of analysts rests not only on their professional expertise and not only on the fact that the situation tends to elicit, in relatively concentrated form, their capacity to offer a special kind of attentive presence, what Schafer (1983) refers to as an analytic "second self" (p. 291). I believe it usually also draws upon the power generated by the asym-metrical arrangement combined with the special, regular time and place. The frequency of meetings adds to the emotional intensity and to the transformative potential of the process. Psychoanalysis can be viewed as a psychologically complex kind of relearning, in which a major objective is to promote critical reflection on the way the patient's reality has been constructed in the past and is being con-structed interactively right now, with whatever amalgams of repeti-tion and new experience the current construction entails. Embedded in this process of critical reflection, however, there is something going on that is affirming to the patient in a general way. The ana-lyst's attitude conveys a variety of messages to the patient, including, for example: "Your subjective experience matters. Your responsibil-ity for your life is mitigated by these aspects of your history and cur-rent circumstances that have not been in your control. You have the power to significantly affect the quality of your life." The magical component in the analyst's authority, an extension of Freud's "unob-jectionable positive transference" with, undoubtedly, close connec-tions to the "idealizing transference" of self psychology, may be explored and partially understood, but it is not likely to be com-pletely undone. Moreover, that outcome would not necessarily be desirable.

If, as Greenberg and Aron suggest, there is a need on the part of both participants to protect the analyst from exposure, the need can-not be dismissed entirely as an irrational clinging to an unnecessary idealization. Some aspect of the idealization may be a necessary, jointly created and sustained construction. Here is an example of actions speaking louder than words. The fact is that from the begin-ning to the end, despite the possibility of temporary departures and modifications, basic ritual features of the analytic situation—the regular visits, the fee, the asymmetry of personal expression—generally remain intact. Indeed, they are likely to promote the special power that the analyst has in the patient's mental life even beyond the point of termination of the analysis.

FIGURE-GROUND RELATIONSHIPS, SIMULTANEITY, AND TERMINOLOGICAL ISSUES

Turning to a terminological issue that is also important theoretically, let us look at the suggestion by Aron that the term *countertransference* be discarded because of the connotation that the patient is responsible for the analyst's experience. When we try to develop a new model, it is very difficult to escape from the polarities that characterized the old ones that we are used to. And one of the most tempting and deceptive avenues of escape is always the one that reverses who has what while still retaining the old terms of discourse (or their equivalents). What happens, then, is a dramatic but superficial change. The difficulties of the old model will invariably come back to haunt us, a little like the return of the repressed. On the other hand, bringing in new terms like *constructivism* or *intersubjectivity* is not a panacea. These terms also usually require some sort of tailoring or redefinition.

With regard to the term *countertransference*, I would agree with Aron that it is stretched beyond recognition when used to refer to all aspects of the analyst's character to which the patient may be responsive in the analytic situation. To say, however, that the term necessarily implies that the analyst's experience is "reactive rather than subjective, emanating from the center of the analyst's psychic self" (p. 33) is implicitly to accept the very polarization of responsiveness and subjectivity that I think Aron wants to reject. We want a model in which responsiveness is understood to be simultaneously self-expressive, just as self-expressive initiative is understood to be simultaneously responsive to the other person in the interaction. Aron and the classical analyst do not mean the same thing, even when they both speak of wanting to emphasize the "subjective" component in the analyst's experience of the countertransference. Aron suggests that what is essential in the new model is to recognize that both patient and analyst are simultaneously both subject and object. But that which is simultaneously both subject and object is, in a certain sense, neither, because the meanings of those terms have been established primarily in the context of their polarization. So we have to consider that we have moved into new territory where the boundaries among various categories have been altered. In effect, we have new terms of discourse, even if we continue to use the old ones. As noted earlier in connection with the polarity of endogenous pressures and perception, if it would not make our writing and speaking ridiculously cumbersome, we would and should be saying or writing "quote, unquote" all the time, for example, in conjunction with the terms *transference, countertransference, reality, fantasy, intrapsychic, interpersonal, subject, object, individual,* and *social.*

My own preference would be to hold on to many of the traditional terms and try to redefine them (or assimilate redefinitions of them that have been offered) rather than change them. This is what Gill and I, in fact, tried to do with the term *transference,* and it is what I would suggest we try to do with the term *countertransference.*[12] In fact—and this is the substantive issue that is at stake—the redefinition of the terms is crucial. Without redefinition—if, for example, we call the analyst's experience "transference," as McLaughlin (1981) suggests—we are in danger of making the same mistake that is associated with the use of that term for the patient. In this case, in our zeal to recognize the analyst as an agent, we might neglect the extent to which the analyst is responsive to what the patient is doing. Also, as Aron suggests, this strategy would put us well on the road toward mind-boggling terminological confusion. There is, in fact, just as much reason to call the patient's experience "countertransference" to emphasize responsiveness to the analyst as there is to call the analyst's experience "transference" to emphasize the extent to which the analyst is "the initiator of interactional sequences." In the interest of preserving our sanity, in light of the fact that the terms have to be redefined anyway, and perhaps most importantly, in deference to the principle of asymmetry that governs the analytic situation, I think keeping the terms *transference* and *countertransference*

---

12. Racker (1968) made a great advance in the 1950s in reconceptualizing countertransference, combining the notion of externalization of internal object relations with appreciation of the personal involvement of the analyst on multiple levels. A number of authors, particularly the "radical critics" of the blank-screen fallacy (chapter 4), have taken a similar position in conceptualizing countertransference without the implication that it is merely reactive. And yet Racker himself may fall short of the social-constructivist paradigm because of the kind of certainty that he has about the nature of the countertransference and what it indicates about the patient's experience.

for the patient and the analyst, respectively, is by far the least of the various evils among which we have to choose.

In the model to which Aron is objecting, although the analyst is seen as participating in a sequence of interactional events, the claim would be that it was the patient who "started it." The whole tenor of the evolving interaction would essentially reflect the patient's influence, with analysts only playing out roles or positions (presumably experienced as foreign to themselves) into which they are cast by the patient. This model is the one to which both Aron and Greenberg object, correctly I think, to the extent that it understates the analyst's responsibility for what is going on and the way in which the personality of the analyst affects the nature of the interactions and the transferences that emerge.

I do think, however, that there is much to be said for a modified version of this model, one that does not make this error. In this modified version, the two directions of influence are understood to be simultaneous (although usually unequal) from the beginning. As Benjamin (1988, p. 26) points out, simultaneity is much more difficult to grasp than sequences of events. If, for example, we try to look at the origins of the interaction between a patient and a therapist, it may seem obvious that the patient made the first move when he or she called for an appointment. But one could argue that, at the same time, the patient is responding to the fact that analysts have advertised themselves as available for this kind of relationship, a version, one might say, of "creation of consumer demand." From that point of view, it is the analyst (as a representative of the whole culture or institution of psychotherapy) who "started it." Racker (1968) makes this point in a hyperbolic way when he says:

> The analyst communicates certain associations of a personal nature even when he does not seem to do so. These communications begin, one might say, with the plate on the front door that says "Psychoanalyst" or "Doctor." What motive (in terms of the unconscious) would the analyst have for wanting to cure if it were not he who made the patient ill? In this way the patient is already, simply by being a patient, the creditor, the accuser, the "superego" of the analyst; and the analyst is his debtor [p. 146].

So the analyst is calling the patient in to ask for the opportunity to atone for past crimes and failures. Here we have the basis for a redefinition of the "presenting complaint"!

Nevertheless, as I have said, I believe there is still wisdom to the traditional allocation of the terms. As a participant-constructivist, the analyst sets himself or herself up to be, not the detached observer, but the relatively malleable one, whereas the patient comes with a story to tell and to enact. But we can capture the asymmetrical nature of the process by speaking in terms of the patient's transference and the analyst's countertransference, even while recognizing that by reversing figure and ground we can find a current in the process in which it is the patient who is responding to the impact of the analyst's influence.

The notion of figure-ground relationships is central to the transition to the social-constructivist paradigm. Often the change in the way things are viewed has the general form that what had been polarized between analyst and patient is now understood in terms of multiple, fluctuating, complementary figure-ground relationships within each of the participants. For example, when we reverse figure and ground, the patient's associations become interpretations, and the analyst's interpretations become personally expressive associations. Searles (1975) reverses figure and ground when he writes about "the patient as therapist to the analyst." We name our professional conferences as gatherings of psychoanalytic therapists and psychoanalysts. That aspect is in the foreground. But in the background, the fact is that there are few, if any, places where one could find a greater concentration of psychoanalytic patients. In general, it is a good idea to call things by whatever aspects are usually in the foreground, with the understanding that the resulting terms often connote complementary aspects that are in the background.

CONCLUSION: ONE-PERSON AND
TWO-PERSON THEORIES IN THE
SOCIAL-CONSTRUCTIVIST PARADIGM

The paradigm issue is independent of questions regarding the content of the primary issues in human development and the specific needs, wishes, and conflicts that are central in governing human experience and behavior. To be sure, a constructivist position is, by definition, wary of overly confident assertions about human nature. There is, however, no obstacle to theory building if framed in terms of heuristic working assumptions and corollary propositions and hypotheses.[13]

---

13. I would amend this now to say that dialectical constructivism has its own theoretical implications regarding human development as it applies to

Although the terms *social-constructivist* and *participant-constructivist* refer to the continuous interaction in the psychoanalytic situation, they do not preclude consideration of aspects of experience and motivation that are not primarily social, even though they inevitably take on additional meanings in a social context. In each of the articles discussed, despite what I regard as the misleading status given to the shift from drive theory to relational theory or from a one-person to a two-person perspective, there is an emphasis on not losing sight of the patient as an individual. Modell underscores the requirement of asymmetry in the analytic situation in order to allow for the emergence of the patient's desire. Aron also writes about this asymmetry and about the importance of the analyst's finding the right balance between being responsive and giving patients the "space" they need for self-expression. Greenberg is emphatic about the importance of not discarding attention to "endogenous" factors, even while exploring the patient's perceptions of the analyst.

The constructivist paradigm actually demands taking account of both relatively social aspects of experience and relatively individual aspects. Berger and Luckmann (1967) take pains to emphasize that "subjective biography is not fully social" (p. 134), and they discuss the dialectic between the individual and the social in experience (cf. Ghent, 1989; and, since the first appearance of this essay in 1991, Benjamin, 1995; Seligman and Shanook, 1995). Whichever aspect is in the foreground can be understood only in the context of its complement in the background. Neither has to be conceptualized exclusively as a derivative of the other. Sexuality can have primary autoerotic as well as primary object-related facets. The experience of love has both a self-centered, narcissistic dimension and a dimension that recognizes the other as a subject. The exercise of motor or cognitive functions can be understood in terms of the immediate intrinsic gratification that it affords as well as in terms of the social meanings and rewards that become attached to it. Even if we think of language as necessarily social, so that no symbolic experience as such can be considered as purely individual, experience that is not yet formulated, whether in the molar sense of the preverbal life of the child or the molecular sense of moment-to-moment implicit

---

the adult analysand as well as the child. In a nutshell—always a risky condensation—it points to a fundamental need for balance between freedom to shape one's own experience, on the one hand, and responsiveness to external influence, on the other. See the conclusion of chapter 8 for an attempt to articulate these implications more fully (also see Hoffman, 1995).

experiencing, can be thought of as having a relatively nonsocial aspect that is not merely reducible to biology. An integrative theory would take account of both sources of the quality of experience, recognizing that neither will be manifested in pure form but that both would be reflected in a continuous dialectical interplay of figure and ground in human experience (Flax, 1996; Fourcher, 1975, 1978; Ghent, 1989; Gill, 1994; Greenberg and Mitchell, 1983, pp. 400–408; Slavin and Kriegman, 1992; Stern, 1983, 1989).

With respect to the issues that are the focus of these papers, the interest that the patient has in making fuller contact with the analyst as a person places the two-person, relational aspect of motivation in the foreground while the one-person, individual aspect recedes to the background. But the interest patients have in denying or ignoring their analysts as desiring subjects, as people like themselves, does just the opposite. It highlights the individual, one-person dimension of experience while throwing the relational dimension into the background. The meaning and power of whichever aspect is in the foreground are partly dependent on the aspect that is in the background. In our zeal to correct the overemphasis in classical psychoanalytic theory on the individual dimension, it is important that we not swing to an overemphasis on the relational dimension, thereby isolating each from the other. The shift to a social-constructivist paradigm for understanding the psychoanalytic situation certainly does not require such a reversal. If anything, it requires a synthesis of the two perspectives with appropriate redefinitions of each in the light of their interdependence.

◆ 6 ◆

Conviction and Uncertainty in Psychoanalytic Interactions

FROM OBJECTIVISM TO SOCIAL CONSTRUCTIVISM

The epistemology of psychoanalytic practice may be thought of by
some as a philosophical subject that lies in the realm of metatheory
far removed from clinical application. In fact, however, it bears
directly upon the way analysts work, on their attitudes toward their
patients and toward themselves in the process, and on what they feel
free or obliged to do or not to do within the compass of their roles.
In this chapter, in addition to defining some of the main features of
a constructivist view of reality as applied to the psychoanalytic situation, I will try to convey some of the practical implications of that
point of view.

In chapter 5, I suggested that there are two major competing models or paradigms for conceptualizing the nature of the interaction of
the analyst and the patient in the psychoanalytic process.[1] I have
called these the positivist or objectivist and the social-constructivist
paradigms. These terms may or may not be the best for what I want

---

An earlier version of this chapter, with the title "Some Practical Implications of a Social-Constructivist View of the Psychoanalytic Situation,"
appeared in 1992 in *Psychoanalytic Dialogues*, 2:287–304.

1. I am using the term *paradigm* in its informal sense, synonymous with
"model" or "point of view," not in the formal sense associated with Kuhn's
thesis on scientific revolutions.

to describe, considering their various connotations within the philosophical literature. In a recent article, Donnel Stern (1991) has
suggested that the model I am interested in has its clearest foundation in the hermeneutic thought of Gadamer and that it is less compatible with the hermeneutic view of Habermas. In keeping with
Fourcher's (1992) view, however, I believe that the constructivist perspective must take account of unconscious processes that are nonverbal and that resist transformation into words, an issue that
Gadamer may not address adequately. In general, Stern's and
Fourcher's writings on the interface of philosophy and clinical psychoanalytic theory have been influential in my own thinking. I hope
that the foreignness of some of the terms that I use, or what some
may feel is an unfamiliar use of a term, will not distract the reader
from the substantive issues. In this connection, it may be important
to recognize that my interest in this subject derives primarily from a
way of working in the psychoanalytic situation. The epistemological
discussion represents an attempt to explicate the underlying assumptions of that way of working and of being with patients. Of course,
hopefully, that explication feeds back into the clinical orientation
and helps to shape and support it.

What I mean by the positivist or objectivist paradigm[2] is a view of
the process in which analysts or psychoanalytic therapists[3] are
thought to be capable of standing outside the interaction with the
patient, so that they can generate rather confident hypotheses and
judgments about the patient's history, dynamics, and transference
and about what they themselves should do from moment to
moment. In this model, a version of what Schön (1983) calls "technical rationality" and what Fourcher (1996), following Bourdieu
(1990), refers to as "intellectualism," the analyst applies what he or
she knows on the basis of theory, research, and previous clinical
experience in a systematic way to achieve certain immediate and

---

2. The term *positivism* is used somewhat loosely here. It corresponds
roughly with the way Bernstein (1983) uses the term *objectivism* and with
the way Protter (1985) uses *correspondence-essentialism,* that is, to refer
both to literal positivism in the natural sciences and to what Protter calls the
"hidden essentialism of Neo-Kantian Interpretation" (p. 212; also see
Bernstein, 1983, pp. 8–16).

3. I believe that the points that I will develop here are applicable to the
conventional arrangements of both psychoanalytic psychotherapy and psychoanalysis. The relevance of the distinction between those modalities fades
from a dialectical-constructivist viewpoint. See discussion of this issue in the
introduction to this volume.

long-term results. The approach is implicitly diagnostic and pre-scriptive. Having assessed the nature of the patient's psychological disturbance or immediate state of mind, the analyst implements a prescribed approach or specific intervention within one or another theoretical framework. The positivist view does not preclude a certain kind of openness. If one approach or intervention does not "work" or is not fruitful, another may be tried (cf. Pine, 1990). This is a very different kind of openness, however, from what is encouraged in the social-constructivist viewpoint. I will return to this issue a little later. At this point I want to emphasize that a central feature of the positivist view, as it applies to psychoanalytic interactions, is the implication that analysts, as a function of their knowledge of theory and of accepted principles of technique, can be confident, not only about their sense of what their patients are doing and experiencing, but also about the nature of their own participation at any moment.

A relatively well established critique of positivism in psychoanalysis, exemplified by Schafer (1983), applies to the kind of truth that is sought in developing a picture of the patient's history and dynamics. In the positivist model, it is argued, interpretations are judged in relation to the relatively hard facts of the patient's experience, past and present. In the alternative model, which I will refer to as the *limited constructivist view*, the patient's experience is thought to be more ambiguous and malleable. Interpretations suggest ways of organizing the patient's experience among the many ways that are possible. Suggestion, that bugaboo of the process in a positivist framework, becomes an intrinsic aspect of any interpretation in the alternative framework. Indeed, in an important sense, within this framework interpretations *are* suggestions.[4] This is not to say that one cannot speak of one interpretation fitting the patient's experience more than another. But there is more leeway for a range of interpretations that are persuasive, and it is understood that, inescapably, there is some influence coming from the side of the analyst in deciding what line of interpretation to pursue. The "data," that is, the patient's associations and other aspects of the patient's behavior, cannot decide the issue by themselves. In this limited application of constructivism to psychoanalysis, there is particular interest in the way in which the analyst's theoretical perspective selectively

---

4. While this essay in its original form was awaiting publication, I came across the same statement, with emphasis, in a paper by Stolorow (1990, p. 124).

shapes the narratives encompassing the patient's history and current experience in the process.

Although I think it is valid in its own right, this limited constructivist critique leaves undisturbed what I think of as the heart of positivist thinking in psychoanalytic practice. In particular, it does not challenge the notion that analysts can know the personal meaning of their own actions on a moment-to-moment basis in the process. The attitudes that analysts maintain toward their own actions have a retrospective aspect and a prospective aspect. Retrospectively, the issue has to do with the kind of confidence analysts have in what they know about their own personal contribution to their patients' experience up to a certain time. The limited constructivist critique is riveted upon the nature of the relationship between the theoretical bias of interpretation, on one hand, and the "reality" of what the patient's experience has been, on the other. That focus, however, modifies nothing in the classical view of the analyst's personal involvement in the process. For example, Schafer's (1983) "analytic attitude" is allegedly purified of personal factors through "*continuous* scrutiny of countertransference" (p. 221; italics added). As in the classical model, such countertransferences are considered by Schafer to be occasional and, in principle, avoidable intrusions (see chapter 5; and Stern, 1991, pp. 74–76). But, in what I am calling the "social-constructivist" view, it is the current of countertransference that is continuous, not its scrutiny. It is simply impossible to keep up, reflectively, with the stream of what Stern (1983, 1989) has called "unformulated experience." Only a small fraction of the potentials in that experience can be attended to and developed through symbolic thought at any given moment (Fourcher, 1975, 1978). Moreover, whatever is selected out of that stream reflects the influence of specific currents of more or less unconscious countertransference resistance at the time. In this model, just as the analyst may see something in the patient that the patient resists, the patient may see something, consciously or unconsciously, that the analyst resists. One of the practical implications of the social-constructivist view is that the analyst is encouraged to take a special interest in the patient's conscious and unconscious interpretations of the analyst's influence (see chapter 4).

What I have just said pertains to the *retrospective* aspect of the analyst's attitude, the part of it that has to do with what he or she has already done, that is, to the way in which the analyst's personal participation has affected the patient's experience up to a given moment. The second arena that is left undisturbed by the limited constructivist critique in psychoanalysis is the personal dimension of *prospective* action. In this respect, the issue has to do with the analyst deciding how to act at any given moment, in other words, with the analyst contributing to *making* a bit of the patient's (and his or her own) history rather than merely interpreting it. The positivist and the limited constuctivist models share the view that the analyst can comfortably adopt the position of the relatively detached listener and interpreter because it is assumed that that stance is favorable for the emergence of transference, for the development of insight, and also, perhaps, for the promotion of new experience as a by-product. In the more thoroughgoing social-constructivist model, although the sense of the possible value of the relatively detached stance is retained, there is also a sense of uncertainty as to its meaning to one-self as well as to the patient at any given moment, along with recognition that other kinds of interaction might be possible and useful. It is important to emphasize, however, that other kinds of participation, for example, those that seem to reflect more emotional involvement, are no more transparent in terms of their meanings to the participants than is the relatively detached position. Working within this perspective confronts the analyst with a new sense of risk and personal responsibility regarding whatever he or she chooses to do from moment to moment.

PSYCHOANALYTIC AUTHENTICITY IN THE SOCIAL-CONSTRUCTIVIST PARADIGM

Do these features of the social-constructivist paradigm imply that the analyst can never speak with any sense of conviction to a patient? Do they require that the analyst always be riddled with self-doubt or that the analyst always adopt the patient's point of view? What is left of the analyst's authority in such a model?

Paradoxically, the analyst is freer in this model to speak his or her mind. With the elimination of the standard of doing just the "right" thing according to some external criterion, there is more leeway for a spontaneous kind of expressiveness than there was before, and that spontaneity might well include expression of conviction about one's point of view. In the social-constructivist model there is a dialectical movement between the personal and the technical; neither exists in pure form, isolated from the other. On the one hand, the analyst's interpretations are reflective of countertransference; in other words, they are personally expressive (Jacobs, 1986; Gill, 1982a, 1991). On the other hand, personal, emotional reactions can be utilized in the development of interpretations; in other words, they become incorporated into technique (Racker, 1968; Ehrenberg, 1984; Tansey and Burke, 1989). What is not possible in this point of view is a total transcendence by analytic therapists of their own subjectivity. The resulting special kind of "uncertainty" frees analysts to "be themselves," that is, to be the people they are within their analytic role. That role constrains the analyst to regular critical reflection on the nature of his or her participation. The conviction with which an analyst may speak to the patient at certain times does not preclude questions remaining in the analyst's mind regarding possible, as yet undiscovered meanings of such interactions, including the part the analyst has played in them.[5]

The fact that the analyst working in this model neither claims nor aspires to the objective kind of knowledge that a positivist model offers does not mean that he or she does not make use of accumulated understanding from many sources, ranging from personal life experience to common sense, to specific clinical experience, to a grasp of varous theories. Ideally, these theories are cut loose of their positivist moorings and then adapted to suit the analyst with a particular patient at a particular moment.

A way of putting the central, practical implication of the shift from a positivist to a constructivist model is to say that as conviction based on objective knowledge is reduced, conviction based on the analyst's subjective experience is increased (cf. Mitchell, 1991, p. 153). With this shift, what had been "known" before on the basis of theory, research, or cumulative clinical experience is not discarded; rather, the authority of that knowledge is subtly diminished in proportion to a subtle increase in respect for the analyst's personal, subjective experience as a basis for what the analyst does or says. That experience includes, but is not reducible to, the various sources of understanding just mentioned. Ideally, a new kind of uncertainty and a new kind of openness accompany this change. In the positivist

---

5. It is a very short step from a claim that one knows one's own mind to authoritarianism. Adam Phillips (1996) contrasts the "Enlightenment Freud" who "can help us remind ourselves of who we are, of what we once and always knew (and wanted)," with the "post-Freudian Freud" who was "the ironist of exactly this enlightenment project. He was an expert on the impossibility of self-knowledge, on the limits of expertise, and particularly on that version of self-knowledge that plays into the hands of instrumental reason and social control. Knowing who you are means telling people what to do" (p. 6).

framework, uncertainty and openness pertain primarily to trying a certain approach with the expectation that it may or may not "work" and with the understanding that if it fails, another approach could be attempted. This kind of openness presupposes particular assumptions about one's ends as well as the equal accessibility of various means to achieve them. Thus, to promote the process, the therapist could try one mode of response—say, an empathic one—and perhaps eventually move on to a more confrontational or aggressively interpretive one if the first was not fruitful, according to whatever criteria were applied. With the kind of eclectic virtuosity that Pine (1990) recommends, the analyst could move freely among various theoretical perspectives in trying to achieve understanding or to affect the patient's mental state, a little like trying a series of medications to combat a set of symptoms.[6] More broadly, open-minded positivism promotes the idea that the analyst is in the position of the scientist who is uncertain about the correctness of his or her hypotheses and is prepared to see them disconfirmed. But in the social-constructivist model there is another source of uncertainty that derives from questions such as, on the retrospective side, What is not yet understood about the meaning of what I have said or done? And, on the prospective side, What qualities of relating are available to the patient and to me at this moment? Can I relate to the patient now in a way that is authentically expressive at the same time that it promotes new understanding or the realization of new potentials in the patient's experience? Now the analyst's uncertainty has to do with how the reality that he or she creates with the patient is selected at the expense of other possibilities that are unrecognized or that are inaccessible to the analyst and the patient for various reasons, including the whole gamut of possible unconscious motives. Even if, for all practical purposes, the long-range goals of the analysis are fairly well established (and, of course, even those are subject to revi-

---

6. Greenberg (1995a) sees Pine as exemplifying the second of three stages in the evolution of psychoanalytic technique. The first, the classical Freudian, is entirely prescriptive. The rules are specified in advance and are the same for all patients. The second allows for more flexibility on the analyst's part, but "the variations depend exclusively upon the needs of the patient" (pp. 11–12). Furthermore, "the particular analyst's hopes, fears, and beliefs are not taken into account as legitimate determinants of technical choices" (p. 12). Only in the third stage are the implications of a fully interactive model realized, so that it is understood that "everything that happens in an analysis reflects the personal contribution of each participant" (p. 13).

sion), the immediate means and ends are not fully knowable in the constructivist context, and both may be regarded, at least partially, as in the process of being created by the participants.

With regard to what is available to the analyst, among the limiting factors are the temperaments and resources of the participants as well as the analyst's and the patient's unconscious interest in particular kinds of interactions and associated unconscious resistance to other forms. Whether the therapist is empathic or confrontational at a certain moment, for example, has much to do with what inner response the therapist has available, not merely with the needs of the patient construed in isolation from the analyst's experience. Given a combination of what the patient is eliciting, the analyst's affective dispositions, the analyst's resistance, and the analyst's understanding of the process at the moment, the analyst "decides" to act in some way, to speak or not speak, or to say one thing rather than another. We know how long even certain recognized patterns may continue without being spoken of and how common it is for therapists to kick themselves (or each other) for failing to do or say the "obvious." What this kind of reproachful attitude does not consider and respect enough (depreciating it usually as merely unfortunate countertransference) is the possible element of wisdom in the analyst's behavior, given the nature of the experience that it reflects.

I said the analyst "decides" to do or say something, but usually there is no linear, temporal relationship between thought and action. The action occurs largely as an immediate expression of myriad considerations within the analyst's "unformulated experience" (Stern, 1983, 1989). Although the analyst may feel a good deal of conviction on the basis of that experience, the very fact that the analyst's subjectivity is implicated on multiple levels brings with it a measure of uncertainty about the meaning and wisdom of whatever he or she may choose to say or do.

For example, if the analyst feels that he or she has been repeatedly depreciated by the patient and that, despite various attempts at interpretation and understanding, the depreciation has continued relentlessly, the analyst may feel a surge of anger and a conviction that it is justified and that it warrants expression. In a recent article, Frederickson (1990) gives an example of a moment in which he suddenly exploded at a patient who had been standing over him and yelling at him, the latest of a long series of provocations. In Frederickson's words, "I quickly stood up with my face only three inches from his. In as loud a voice as I could muster I yelled, 'Shut up!'" (p. 483). The analyst cannot make a judgment about what to do at such a moment simply on the basis of some dispassionate understanding of the patient. The strength of the analyst's affect has to be taken into account. For the sake of the health of the *relationship*, which certainly includes the analyst's well-being, it may be important that the analyst react emotionally. Winnicott (1949), whose paper on hate in the countertransference Frederickson cites as background for his own work, states that the analyst must determine whether the "hate" that he or she is experiencing is "objective" or not. Only when it is objective is it legitimate for the analyst to express what he or she feels. Although he is not entirely consistent about it, Winnicott's formulation of the issue is, for the most part, a positivist one. It gives the analyst the authority to make such an assessment on the basis of "objective" criteria. At the same time, it denies him or her the right to act to a greater extent on the basis of his or her subjective experience. Of course, that experience will probably implicitly include consideration of how outrageous the patient's behavior has been, a consideration that could be reframed as the extent to which it seems likely that most people in the culture, even most therapists, would react emotionally in the way the analyst finds himself or herself reacting. In this context, known patterns in the patient's relationships with others could also be taken into account (Tansey and Burke, 1989). Such an assessment, however, could hardly be truly objective. Moreover, in the social-constructivist model the analyst can take the position that no matter how others may respond, his or her own particular, individual response has its place in the process. Displacing objectivity as the ideal to which the analyst aspires is a special kind of authenticity. Unlike the authenticity that is encouraged in a humanist-existentialist orientation, however, authenticity in the social-constructivist model is continually the object of psychoanalytic skepticism and critical reflection (Sass, 1988).

In Frederickson's (1990) example, after the patient and the analyst sat down and after the analyst elaborated a bit more on his feelings, and told the patient he just could not take the screaming anymore, the patient said, "Good, the first human response I've gotten from you" (p. 483).[7] The ensuing exploration suggested that the analyst was in the position the patient had been in with his abusive

---

7. The course of the process is very much like that in a vignette reported by Tower (1956) in which the analyst's anger was expressed unconsciously by her forgetting an appointment with a patient who had been relentlessly abusive for months. In the next session, the analyst says simply: "I'm sorry, I forgot," to which the patient replies, "Well, you know, Dr. Tower, really I can't say that I blame you" (p. 238). Tower reports that that episode marked "the first break in this obstinate resistance" (p. 238).

father, with whom the patient was now identified. When he yelled "Shut up," in effect, the analyst was speaking up for, and indirectly empathizing with, the patient as a child. As the incident is presented, it seems clear that this meaning of the analyst's response crystalized *after* the yelling episode. Yet, in his discussion, the author conveys the impression that his outburst was, to begin with, based on an awareness that he was speaking in the voice of the child. Indeed, he suggests that one can decide that the expression of such anger is appropriate when one feels identified with the abused child rather than the abusing father (pp. 489–490). I think this formulation amounts to a post hoc explanation for what seems to have been a more spontaneous personal reaction. Such personal reactions may include inklings of where they fit in relation to the patient's history and intrapsychic world, but those inklings may be rather faint at the moment of action. At that moment, the analyst feels impelled to speak up for himself or herself, knowing that the action may turn out to mean any number of things and also that what follows is not fully predictable.

Frederickson's example turned out extremely well, not a surprising result in a published vignette. Still, I admire the author's courage in reporting it. But how many published accounts are we likely to have of instances in which, following such an expression of anger on the therapist's part, the patient walks out and never returns? Reticence to publish such accounts is understandable, I think. How quick would many of us be then to point the finger at the analyst for his or her "unprofessional" behavior? It is misleading, however, to judge an action in an absolute way on the basis of what happens after it. The fact is that at the moment of action there is always more than one kind of handwriting on the wall. At that moment the emotional authenticity of the analyst has to count for something in its own right. What that authenticity banks on, as a general rationale within the context of the analysis, is the hope that there will be enough common emotional ground between the patient and the analyst so that when the dust settles, the participants will be able to locate some aspect of the analyst's response somewhere within the patient's patterns of interpersonal relationships and somewhere in the patient's intrapsychic world.

Frederickson's account is an instance of the more general situation in which the conscious perspective of the analyst and the conscious perspective of the patient clash. The analyst may have a particular idea about what the patient is expressing unconsciously. It may be something the patient is very invested in not knowing or recognizing.

If the patient is in a fury about the analyst's inaccessibility between sessions, is repeatedly calling the analyst at home at ungodly hours, and believes that there is nothing unreasonable about his or her demands, some kind of dispute may ensue. The key here is that the analyst speaks out of a personal, subjective sense of conviction that derives partly from the countertransference. In this instance, for example, it may be a sense of being encroached upon in a way that is personally unacceptable. Instead of simply trying to do the "right" thing according to some external criterion, the analyst in this model tries to do the thing that is integrative of multiple aspects of his or her experience, including, but not restricted to, consideration of his or her complementary reactions to the patient's behavior, what Racker (1968) refers to as "complementary identifications." These emotional reactions usually comprise only a portion of the analyst's total response to the patient (p. 67). Included in the rest of that total response is the analyst's sense of his or her professional purpose and responsibility, which is to promote understanding and to try to offer the opportunity for a relationship that promotes change.

Integral to the analyst's professional position is knowledge based on theory and previous clinical experience. The sense of being encroached upon, to continue with that example, may be accompanied by all kinds of more or less developed ideas about possible meanings of the patient's behavior. Maybe there is some kind of role reversal going on, as in Frederickson's example, or maybe the patient is angrily objecting to the analyst having a separate life. The complementary countertransference is experienced along with these particular, theoretically informed ideas about its significance or, at least, along with the expectation that such possibilities will be explored. The conviction of the analyst is qualified in that the particular nuances of his or her experience are understood to be reflective of the analyst's own personality and history, not only of the patient's. Also, it is understood that the patient is not only driven by internal pressures, but is also responding to ways in which the analyst has participated in the interaction. For example, the analyst may have behaved in such a way as to encourage the patient to think that the analyst is more available than is actually the case. The analysand and the analyst are both responding to and influencing the experience of the other. In a clash of points of view, what is in the foreground for one of the participants may be in the background for the other, and vice versa. Moreover, what is in the background may correspond with what is unconsciously resisted in each participant. The constructivist position, however, does not require that the analyst always identify with the patient's conscious or preconscious point of view or with the view that emphasizes the analyst's culpability in affecting the patient's experience and behavior. Such a requirement exaggerates the analyst's responsibility for transference-countertransference patterns at the expense of the patient's responsibility for them in a simple reversal of the relationship between the two that is promoted in the classical model. In the constructivist view, the analyst can take a position based on his or her experience without "pulling rank" by claiming the position of the objective scientist.

A FEW EVERYDAY EXAMPLES

I would like to say a word about the difficulties associated with trying to illustrate this way of working with patients. In a roundabout way, these difficulties may tell you as much about what I am trying to say as any particular examples. The moments selected for illustration, like the one from Frederickson, tend to be relatively dramatic. Consequently, they fail to capture the sense in which that way of being with patients is routine. What I am talking about, in part, is a kind of naturalness, and it seems a little odd to give examples of how one behaved naturally, partly because the public presentation of such experiences can compromise one's sense of their personal, spontaneous quality. It transforms the moment of personal engagement with the patient into something much more systematic and methodical than what one intended; it becomes an "approach," an aspect of "technique," even a "manipulation." Whereas in the positivist framework one was concerned about protecting the patient's confidentiality in presenting such examples, in the social-constructivist framework one's concern shifts to protecting the integrity, the mutual sense of privacy, and the intimacy of one's engagement with the patient. There is no question, however, that to think of the relationship merely as spontaneous and personal is to misrepresent it by ignoring its more methodical and purposeful aspects.

Despite the stated reservations, therefore, I will present a few general examples of the kinds of everyday things that I think this model allows or encourages. I will touch on a few examples briefly to convey the idea in an impressionistic way.

To begin with an example a step removed from direct clinical experience, as a supervisor, I have found that the way problems are formulated by supervisees is often pretty close to what I suggest they consider conveying to the patient. Frequently, there is a predicament involved for the supervisee that is communicated to me in roughly this form: "I'd like to say X, but I'm concerned about Y." So, for example, I might end up recommending that the therapist consider saying to the patient something like, "You know I feel a pull from you to understand your complaint about your friend or spouse and to take your side, but I have to admit I feel some sympathy with this other person because similar things have happened between us and I have felt that I was in his or her position." Of course, in constructing such a statement for presentation, I am removing all the pauses and other irregularities that accompany—and are essential to—natural speech.

It is important, on the other hand, not to force the issue. Sometimes it is better for the therapist not to say anything about a certain matter, not only because of concern about the patient's reactions, but also because of concern about his or her own anticipated feelings. The outside consultant is usually well-advised to suggest only that at some time it might be good if the therapist and the patient could find a way to talk about the subject. The issue is not reducible to a diagnostic question regarding what the patient is ready for. It certainly *includes* what the patient is ready for, but it also includes what the therapist is ready for, or comfortable with or, more broadly, what this particular relationship can accommodate at a certain moment.

A general and common kind of dilemma that therapists usually take upon themselves to resolve, instead of discussing it with the patient, involves a question as to whether the patient's desire for something reflects a developmental deficit and need or a conflictual wish (cf. Mitchell, 1991). Often I think it is OK to say something like, "You know when you ask for reassurance or guidance, I'm sometimes inclined to give it to you because we've developed this idea that it's something you've never had and that you really need from me. But sometimes I worry that that premise is wrong and that I'm participating with you in a way that perpetuates a kind of unnecessary dependency." I cannot recall any time when saying this kind of thing has done any harm. Discussing such dilemmas and conflicts with patients often helps to engage them in a collaborative exploration of the various patterns of relating (rooted in various kinds of internal object relations) that are either being enacted or that are potential at any given time.

If the patient begins an hour by saying that he or she is not sure where to begin, nine times out of ten it probably makes sense just to wait and see what comes to the patient's mind or to explore the meaning of the difficulty starting. But once in a while it is not a bad idea to get things going by initiating something, especially if the therapist has something in mind that he or she would really like to pursue. The analyst might be interested in picking up on something that was interrupted at the end of the last session; or the therapist might have thought of a possible meaning of something between sessions that he or she could bring up now. Patients are usually quite appreciative when the analyst is willing to depart from the customary ritual in this way or other ways once in a while. Such departures often convey a willingness on the analyst's part to break out of his or her own set patterns. My impression has been that patients often reciprocate by overcoming resistances and bringing up new issues. To be sure, because there may be some enactment going on that the analyst is participating in unconsciously, it is important to look continually for such possibilities, a point Gill made in many of his writings (see, especially, Gill, 1991). But such enactments are going on all the time anyway. Adhering to customary routines religiously can be an unconscious enactment also (Jacobs, 1986). Occasional departures from the routines have the side benefit of demonstrating to the patient (and oneself) that although those routines are important, they are not fetishes and have not buried the analyst's sense of the personal aspect of the relationship.

It may seem that these examples are rather banal and that the implicit foil for them is a straw man. As I prepared this essay, I was comforted in that regard by an old article I had read years ago, one that I had saved and that I was lucky enough to be able to dig up. It is a remarkable, little-known paper by Schafer (1974) in which he advances the idea that there is a particular way of relating that psychoanalytic therapists commonly do not employ, one the author calls "talking to patients." Schafer suggests that it is something we ought to try. Instead, he alleges, "for too long we have been content automatically to use a fundamentally impersonal diction: it seems so safe and effective, so tried and true" (p. 511). Schafer gives many everyday examples of the contrast between this "impersonal diction" and the alternative, which he refers to as "speaking freely" and as "self-expressive." Here are just a few: "You must have felt awful," instead of "How awful"; "You must be very proud of yourself," instead of "Congratulations"; "Your life does not seem very satisfying or easy," instead of "That's a helluva way to live" (pp. 511–513). In concluding, Schafer writes:

> I must at last face the question that has been hanging over this entire discussion—whether or not my suggestions are banal. To many of you

they might seem so. You might judge that I have merely described and recommended what is done naturally by any psychotherapist who is experienced, relaxed, and humane rather than constrained by the pseudoanalytic model I mentioned earlier. It will not surprise you to find that I disagree with that judgment [p. 514].

Unfortunately, despite his extensive contributions to psychoanalytic theory, Schafer never gave the ideas expressed in this article the grounding they needed in a revised theory of countertransference and in a thoroughly constructivist view of the interaction. Instead, as noted earlier, he has been an advocate of the limited constructivist view that perpetuates the positivist attitude toward the analyst's personal participation. That attitude, in turn, provides the foundation for the very scientistic, impersonal diction to which Schafer objected in this relatively early article.[8]

AUTHENTICITY, SOCIAL CONSTRUCTIVISM, AND PSYCHOANALYTIC DISCIPLINE

I want to emphasize, in conclusion, that all I have said takes for granted that the analyst has in his or her bones a sense of certain fundamental features of the psychoanalytic situation. The bare essentials include, I think, a circumscribed time and place; the asymmetry of personal expression in the process; a primary interest in exploring the patient's experience, conscious and unconscious, past and present; a commitment by the analyst to critical reflection on his or her own participation; and a sense of the relationship as a whole as a means to promote the patient's development. Every interaction in this context is experienced by the analyst as a *psychoanalytic* interaction. There are no exceptions. Whether the analyst is reacting emotionally, talking about the weather, or talking about the patient's childhood, the stamp of the analytic situation should never be lost on the participants.

Finally, as noted in chapter 5, though a central purpose of analysis in the social-constructivist paradigm can be described as the

---

8. The title of the article, "Talking to Patients in Psychotherapy," is associated with a good deal of ambiguity in the paper itself as to whether and how the point Schafer is making applies to psychoanalysis proper as opposed to psychotherapy. It is difficult, however, to imagine that Schafer would advocate "impersonal diction" for psychoanalysts.

deconstruction of the analyst's authority as it is represented in the transference (Protter, 1985), the goal is also the construction of an alternative social reality in which the patient's sense of self and others is altered. In this aspect of the therapeutic action of the process, the analyst's authority has a powerful and paradoxical role to play. The ritualized asymmetry of the psychoanalytic situation (Modell, 1991; Aron, 1991; also see chapter 5), however much its repercussions are analyzed, is likely to promote an element of idealization, an extension of Freud's "unobjectionable positive transference." Along with the dialectical interplay of the personal and the technical, the role of the analyst entails another dialectic between, on the one hand, the combination of personal presence and technical expertise and, on the other hand, an element of mystique derived largely from the ritual aspects of the psychoanalytic situation. In some respects, that irrational component in the analyst's authority, embedded in psychoanalysis as a social institution, may lie beyond the grasp of the participants. This statement by the German romantic Schlegel, quoted in an article by Sass (1988), makes the point: "Every system depends in the last analysis . . . on some . . . point of strength that must be left in the dark, but that nonetheless shores up and supports the whole burden and would crumble the moment one subjected it to rational analysis" (p. 258). Although I do not believe that a critical exploration of the issue by the analyst and the patient is likely either to fully illuminate or to jeopardize the special power that accompanies the analyst's role, actions that damage the fundamental asymmetry of the analytic situation might well have that unfortunate effect. The kind of authenticity that I have been talking about should not be confused with such damaging actions. On the contrary, that authenticity actually incorporates the special kind of discipline that the psychoanalytic situation requires of the analyst.

7

Expressive Participation and
Psychoanalytic Discipline

Imagine, if you will, the following scenes. A patient lingers at the end
of an hour. I think he is about to reach a point of closure; it seems as
though it will be any second. But he continues. He is in the middle
of something that seems important. With what gestures and words
do I interrupt him? I feel that he is very vulnerable. Should I try to
explore his obliviousness to the time or his opposition to it? If I wait
until the next session, I may not find an opportunity to bring it up.
In principle, I should be able to say something like, "I'm finding it
hard to interrupt you, but we do have to stop now. You know I
think the way it goes between us at the ends of sessions may have
some meaning that we should explore." But within the situation
itself, to say that seems very difficult.

Another patient gets up to leave two or three minutes before the
end of her session. There has been no readily identifiable provoca-
tion. This is one way that she frequently deals with the separation.
Should I just let her go or should I say, "You know we still have a
few minutes?" or, "Oh sit down will you!" or, "Excuse me. Is my
time up?" Maybe I should try to offer a more straightforward interpretation, accompanied, perhaps, by an attempt to articulate the
feelings her behavior has elicited in me. If, however, the only interpretation that occurs to me is one that I have offered many times
before, should I repeat it?

An earlier version of this chapter appeared in 1992 in *Contemporary
Psychoanalysis*, 28:1–15.

In another instance, a patient speaks, parenthetically, of a stance she has regarding a certain political matter. It so happens that I am quite strongly opposed to her position and am tempted to tell her this and to explain why. The rapport between us is good, but we don't usually chat informally about things of this nature. I know from comments the patient has made that she is conflicted about getting to know more about me. Should I take the opportunity to interpret a possible expression of this conflict at this moment? On the one hand, it seems like it would be simple enough to ask, "I wonder whether you are interested in knowing what *I* think about this matter?" On the other hand, given my interest in registering my opinion, I have the feeling that such a question would be manipulative.

THE DIALECTIC OF ACTION AND UNDERSTANDING IN THE PSYCHOANALYTIC PROCESS

Are a therapist's choices at moments such as these adequately described as matters of technique? Is there a correct thing for the analyst to do? Many would say, "it depends." More needs to be known about the patient's history and dynamics, the history of the analytic relationship, the status of the transference, and the nature of the process in the session, to mention just some of the relevant considerations. I have told you, after all, so little of what I knew—so little, as one might say, of what was "going through my mind." In fact, there may have been no explicit thoughts at all between the moment of feeling some inclination to act and the moment of action. It was all "unformulated experience," as Donnel Stern (1989) would say, or "implicit experiencing," in Gendlin's (1964) terms, or the "unthought known," as Bollas (1987) would put it. But even if I could explicate much of what I knew about the patient, would we be in a position to decide, with confidence, what I should have done? Is an accurate assessment of the patient's state of mind possible? And if it were possible, would it be enough to establish the ideal way for the analyst to behave? Is the conceptualization of such an ideal independent of what a particular analyst may be experiencing? Do we say, in effect, "based on an assessment of the patient's developmental level and current state of mind, this is the best thing to do"? Or do we say, in effect, "given that the analyst is experiencing such and such, perhaps the analyst could do or say this or that?

I believe that what a therapist does at such moments, although it may reflect a great deal of clinical and theoretical sophistication, is also invariably personally expressive and cannot be understood merely as the application of a principle of technique in any simple sense. Moreover, the full nature of what is expressed by the action is not transparent to the therapist, to the patient, or to anyone else. In the first place, behavior and the experience it reflects are intrinsically ambiguous and subject to myriad compelling explications and interpretations. In the second place, as a participant in an interaction, the analyst's ways of construing his or her own behavior and experience are bound to be influenced to some degree by unconscious factors. Such factors and their effects certainly cannot be prescribed. So what is not possible is that the therapist at such a moment will simply treat the patient with an appropriate intervention of some sort on the basis of a correct diagnostic assessment of the patient's general condition or even of his or her immediate state of mind.

If what the therapist does is so personally expressive, how is it any different from how anyone might respond in an ordinary social situation? The difference resides, of course, in the therapist's attitude toward the interaction and toward his or her own emotional experience. In the model I have in mind, one that I have identified as a "social-constructivist view" of the psychoanalytic situation (chapter 5) —a term later superseded by "dialectical constructivism"—that attitude entails a combination of personal openness and a particular kind of perspective on the process. Indeed, what I described about my experience in the examples I gave is incomplete in that it leaves out, among other things, the fact that in each case an integral aspect of the experience for me was at least some curiosity about the significance of my reactions within the context of the analytic work. I retained the sense that the scene in which I was participating had meaning in the process that was likely to reflect some aspect of the patient's motivation and personality structure as well as my own. So, whether I was awkwardly apologizing for interrupting a patient at the end of a session, or imploring a patient to stay to the end of her hour, or injecting my political views in the course of a session, in the context of the analytic purpose of the relationship, I felt some confidence that with the patient's cooperation, I would be able to transform these moments into parts of the process of exploration of the patient's experience and relational patterns.

In his article on Freud's approach in the case of the Rat Man, Lipton (1977a) argues that it is an error to subsume the personally expressive aspects of the analyst's behavior under the rubric of technique. Using the example of Freud's offering the Rat Man a meal,

Lipton differs both with those who would object to such behavior on the grounds that it is technically *incorrect* (because it may have unanalyzable transference repercussions) and with those like Alexander, and perhaps certain deficit theorists, who, depending on the diagnosis of the patient, might regard it as technically *correct*, and might even consider incorporating it into a systematic program to provide the patient with a corrective emotional experience. Instead, in keeping with an attitude he attributes to Freud, Lipton favors regarding such behavior as merely personal and spontaneous, with no major technical implications unless transference repercussions surface subsequently in the patient's associations (p. 268).

Lipton fails to consider the more integrative possibility in which the analyst's action is immediately experienced by the analyst as both a genuine expression of some aspect of his or her personal experience and as theoretically informed. Sometimes analysts working in this model, one that Donald Schön (1983) refers to as "reflection-in-action," are aware of specific hypotheses about the meaning of their own personal involvement at a certain moment. In other instances, they may have less developed ideas about the possible implications of their participation. Nevertheless, they usually will have the general sense that there is probably something in their response that has been promoted by the patient and that has some meaning that bears upon the patient's relational patterns as well as their own. In other words, in keeping with what Heinrich Racker (1968) originally described in a series of articles published in the 1950s, the analyst has an ongoing sense of the embeddedness of his or her actions in a relational field in which transference and countertransference continually shape and partially illuminate each other. In this approach, a therapist's readiness to participate in a personally revealing and expressive way could be understood as an adjunct to, if not an intrinsic part of, a special kind of psychoanalytic discipline.

The position I have in mind entails an integration of Lipton's and Racker's attitudes. In accord with Racker, the analyst who works with this perspective is likely to generate hypotheses about the transference on the basis of his or her experience of the countertransference. In contrast to Racker and in accord with Lipton, the analyst would also be very open to surprising possibilities emerging from the patient's subsequent associations. These possibilities may not have occurred to the analyst or may actually violate expectations developed by the analyst based on whatever he or she was conscious of in the countertransference (cf. Stern, 1990).

Let there be no mistake about the relentless continuity of the flow of the process. Although my focus here is on moments of expressive action that depart from customary analytic routines, those routines themselves provide little or no sanctuary from the more or less turbulent currents of interpersonal responsiveness and self-expression that run through every analytic encounter. In the first place, the very fact that one has elected to be in this peculiar role of the analyst is probably saturated with personal meaning. And then, within that role, the conventionally expected acts such as listening and interpreting are invariably self-expressive in terms of their timing, manner, and—in the case of interpretation—their content (Jacobs, 1986). Even when analysts find themselves and their patients in the relatively calm waters of critical reflection on what has transpired between them, they are also in the midst of new, personally expressive actions that are eluding critical scrutiny at that moment. Thus, on the one hand, a conspicuously self-revealing act can be part of the development of an interpretation, while, on the other hand, the act of interpretation itself is always embedded in the flow of relational "scenarios" (Gergen, 1988) or "configurations" (Mitchell, 1988, 1991) governed partly by unconscious factors in the transference and the countertransference.

WAYS OF CLASSIFYING TYPES OF PARTICIPATION

I think it is useful to try to classify types of overtly expressive participation on the part of the analyst, because such classification makes it possible to recognize, collate, and learn from certain kinds of clinical experience. As a beginning effort in that direction, it has struck me that the various types of expressive participation could be described in relation to at least four independent issues: (1) the content of the participation (e.g., is it hostile or affectionate, serious or playful, dominant or submissive); (2) the extent to which the participation is immediate and unanticipated versus the extent to which it is more planful and deliberate, even though it may have begun in a more spontaneous way; (3) the extent to which the participation is experienced by the analyst as a response to pressure from the patient, as compared to an inclination that the analyst experiences as coming more from within himself or herself; and (4) the extent to which, taken in isolation, the participation feels to the analyst like it is probably repeating something from the patient's past or like it may be part of a relatively new experience for the patient.

It should be noted, again, that everything the analyst does represents some kind of participation that can be located in relation to these issues. I am not thinking only of the kinds of interactions that stand out because they are experienced immediately as deviating from convention. Such interactions may be of special interest because of their more obviously personal nature, but conformity to conventions cannot be devoid of personal meanings either, many of which cannot be accessible to the analyst from moment-to-moment.

Although I will say a few things about each of these four issues, I will devote most of my attention here to just the last of them, that is, to the continuum from repetition to new experience.

Content

With regard to the issue of content, some types of participation have gained more common acceptance than others. For example, it is probably more acceptable to be serious than to be playful, and if playful, it is probably more acceptable to be subtly humorous than to be giddy or silly. Ehrenberg's (1990) paper on the role of playfulness in analysis and Feiner's (1990) discussion of it break new ground in demonstrating how even a kind of whimsical frivolity can be analytically useful in the long run. Expressions of anger are also generally thought to be unacceptable, but Frederickson (1990), as discussed in chapter 6, demonstrates how even a momentary expression of rage on the part of the analyst can be incorporated into an enlightening and therapeutic experience for the patient.[1]

Anticipation

With respect to the issue of anticipation, at one extreme there are immediate reactions that are not anticipated, although the analyst may have more or less readiness for such responsiveness. The analyst winces as an extremely painful event is described, laughs at a joke, expresses shock, dismay, pleasure, appreciation, or anger in reaction to some unexpected development. At the other extreme, the analyst may "actively seek" a certain attitude or posture that seems best for

---

1. An important new frontier is that of erotic transference and countertransference as reflected in a recent surge of literature on the subject, including a groundbreaking symposium in *Psychoanalytic Dialogues* on "Passion in the Countertransference" (Tansey, 1994; Davies, 1994a,b; Hirsch, 1994; Benjamin, 1994; Gabbard, 1994a,b. Also see Gabbard, 1996).

a particular patient (Goldberg, 1989). Sometimes what begins as an unanticipated, spontaneous response may be converted into a way of interacting that becomes part of the routine of a particular analysis. To overcome an impasse, for example, the analyst may decide to talk more or less, to reveal more or less, to greet the patient in a particular way, or to end sessions in a certain way. He or she may decide to chat more with a patient about a subject of mutual interest, to read something the patient has read or written, to change the seating arrangement or even what he or she wears on the day that a certain patient is scheduled. Unlike the planned actions of Alexander, the kind I have in mind are genuine, responsive, sometimes creative expressions of certain inclinations that arise within the analyst in the course of the interaction, inclinations that might otherwise be inhibited (cf. Bader, 1995). Although the analyst or the patient may have some more or less formulated hunch about how the behavior might further the process, the action is much more personally expressive and responsive and less tied to a claim of an objective assessment of what the patient "needs" than any relatively systematic effort to provide the patient with a corrective experience on a moment-to-moment basis (cf. Mitchell, 1991). In this approach, unlike those that entail rigorous implementation of diagnostically based treatment plans, the analyst maintains a sense of uncertainty about the full meaning of his or her participation and an openness to the various ways that the patient may experience the behavior, consciously and unconsciously.

Each of the poles of this continuum of deliberateness can, potentially, have features that are associated with the other. Responses of the moment, even when they appear to be entirely spontaneous, may be theoretically and technically informed. Conversely, those that seem to be planned and to have explicit rationales may be expressive simultaneously of powerful countertransference attitudes of which the analyst is not aware.

Sense of Initiative versus Response to Pressure from the Patient

With regard to the issue of initiative versus response to pressure from the patient, if you think about the examples with which I began, the patient who went overtime and the patient who got up to leave early put me under more pressure for some sort of immediate response than did the patient who spoke of her political point of view. But here again, the relationship between the two poles of the continuum is that of figure and ground. What appears to be responsive to pressure from the patient is also, in the background, expressive of something within the analyst, and what appears to be the analyst's spontaneous initiative is also, in the background, responsive to something in the patient (see chapter 5).

Repetition Versus New Experience

Each of the poles of this continuum can also have features that are associated with the other. What seems, at first glance, to be part of something old may also turn out to be part of something new, just as what seems, on the surface, to be part of something new may also turn out to be part of something old. There are at least two ways in which what seems to be part of a repetition can, nevertheless, further the differentiation of the past from the present. One is by making palpable, vivid, and accessible for reflection a relational pattern that is rooted in the past and that the patient is pulling for in the analytic situation. In this regard, Racker (1968), in a paper published originally in 1958, speaks of "a transitory performance of the role induced by the patient followed by an analysis of what had happened and what had been enacted." Through such an interaction, he continues, "we can . . . show the patient, more vividly, the role he desires the analyst to play and why he desires it" (p. 69). From the overall context, I think it is clear that Racker is thinking of this process as less deliberate or contrived than what the language of role-playing might connote. In any case, the momentary appearance of repetition is likely to be at least partially undone by the subjection of that very moment to scrutiny (Gill, 1991), or sometimes, just by the mutual understanding that, potentially, such critical reflection *could* be brought to bear on whatever has transpired. When the patient develops a sense of trust in the analyst's overall commitment to the purposes of the analysis and to the patient's long-term well-being, even the moment of apparent repetition may be permeated by a sense of its difference from the past.

The second major way in which such moments can be facilitating of differentiation is simply through the fact that the content of the alleged repetition itself, when looked at closely, is probably not the equivalent of an interaction in the past, but bears only some kind of analogous relationship to it. Indeed, the most useful and powerful differentiations that can be promoted in any psychoanalytic therapy are not those between pathogenic types of interactions and their literal opposites, but those between such interactions and relatively healthy variants of them. The believable and generalizable differentiations are not between an intrusive parent and an analyst who never impinges on the patient at all, but between one kind and degree of intrusion and another; not between a pathologically narcissistic parent and a totally selfless analyst, but between such a parent and an analyst with narcissistic qualities that seem to be integrated with sincere interest in the patient's growth; not between a sexually abusive parent and an analyst who shows no evidence of sexuality, but between that parent and an analyst who, for example, compliments a patient on his or her appearance in a way that could be construed as flirtatious, but who also seems to be consistently respectful of the patient, attentive to his or her other qualities, and invested in the patient's development.[2]

Only these more subtle differentiations are generalizable, not only from the analyst to others in the patient's life, but also from the analyst to the patient himself or herself. Generally, the patient and the analyst have many culturally derived attributes in common. Their respective personality structures are unlikely to be so different that aspects of the patient's internal objects, rooted in the patient's experience with primary caregivers, will not have some reflections in the personal qualities of the analyst, especially when the patient is trying to elicit them. For the analyst to aspire to be virtually untainted by the shadow of the patient's past object ties, as many authors have suggested is desirable (see chapter 4 for review and discussion of this issue) is not only a futile project, but is likely to make the analyst less accessible to the patient as an object for new and healthier identifications. As Mitchell (1988) has written, "Unless the analyst affectively enters the patient's relational matrix or, rather, discovers himself within it—unless the analyst is in some sense charmed by the patient's entreaties, shaped by the patient's projections, antagonized

---

2. The whole area of erotic transference and countertransference is a very complicated and difficult one that is not explored in any depth in this volume (see previous footnote). I will say only that from a constructivist view, psychoanalytic interactions involving sexual feeling must often draw on the art of understatement. What is said by the participants does not merely reflect what exists, but also creates what exists and what will exist in the experiences of both people. The associated risks and potential benefits must be reckoned with. See Davies, 1998a,b; and Hoffman, 1998, for my own recent attempt to apply a constructivist perspective to this subject.

and frustrated by the patient's defenses—the treatment is never fully engaged, and a certain depth within the analytic experience is lost" (p. 293).

The issues become especially complex when the patient enacts a relational pattern with a parental figure or other significant object by identifying with that figure and casting the analyst in the position the patient was in as a child. Often, one of the purposes of the analysis is to free the patient from the grip of such identifications or, alternatively, from the feeling that even a partial identification of this kind is completely defining of the patient's being. Thus, on the one hand, the patient often has an interest in seeing that the therapist does react, to some degree, the way the patient reacted to a parental figure in the past. On the other hand, the patient may be asking implicitly whether the analyst's response will reflect recognition of the difference between the patient and the original object with whom the patient is identified.

THE DIALECTIC OF REPETITION AND NEW EXPERIENCE: SOME ILLUSTRATIONS

To illustrate some aspects of the complex interplay of repetition and new experience I'd like to return to two of my opening vignettes.

With regard to the patient who made a habit of jumping up to leave several minutes early, of course the mood each time was somewhat different, and I said and did different things at different times. One understanding we developed of this pattern was that the patient was not only protecting herself from the humiliation of being cut off by me by beating me to the punch, but also that she was identifying with her father who often put her in the position of a supplicant for his time and attention, a position that I was now in with her. The sheer complexity of the opportunities for repetition and differentiation that such an enactment creates should not be underestimated. I would say that at the simplest level, the patient wants to see that I am not indifferent to her leaving early and that I want to spend time with her more than her father did. Beyond that, she is curious about how I cope with her identification with her father. Do I sometimes feel a little devalued as she did? Do I experience any frustration or annoyance? Do I try to prove myself? If I said, "You know we do have a few minutes," she might say something like, "What are we going to say in a few minutes that will make any difference?" or "Well, I'm through, so is there something you want to say? I mean what good would it do to just sit here and stare at each other?" At this point she would shrug and look at me expectantly, as if to say "Well?" Sometimes it seemed like she wanted some confirmation that her own feelings with her father were "normal," confirmation that she could not get if the analyst behaved mechanically according to some prescribed rule. But I think she also wanted me to notice that despite the similarity I recognized that she was very different from her portrayal of her father, that she was much warmer, more generous overall, and much more self-critical. In addition to the obvious advantages of my position over that of the patient as a child, on a personal level, the difference between the patient now and her father in the past was another factor that made it possible and desirable for me to respond to her with more humor, openness, and acceptance than she could mobilize in her relationship with him.[3]

With regard to the patient with whom I had the inclination to register my political views, the denouement is also interesting with regard to the interplay of repetition and new experience. I did, in fact, interject my opinion, which led to a brief debate, but one that I felt was friendly in its tone. In the next session, the patient reported the following dream: "I met up with you somewhere, a public place. I sensed that I was going to wind up being intimate with you. We got back to your room, but then you had to leave because of an emergency. I did sleep in your bed although you were not there. Then I realized that because of what had gone on I would have to drop out of therapy."

With some amusement, the patient said she felt it was an advance for her to have had a dream that even hinted at sexual feeling in the transference, and an even greater advance to have had the courage to tell me about it. She laughed about the fact that nothing sexual actually happens, joking about her inhibitions; she thought it was funny that even in her dream she had to have me called away for an emergency to keep things from going too far. I asked her if she had any other associations regarding our doing something forbidden that could threaten the therapy. Needless to say, I was fishing for her

---

3. What I am describing is related to the dynamics of projective identification. That concept, however, when applied to the psychoanalytic process, often connotes an adaptation by the analyst superior to that of the patient as a child (or to that of the patient's self in relation to the internalized object) without credit to the patient for being different, often, from the parental figures with whom the patient is also identified as the provocateur within the analytic situation.

thoughts regarding the conversation about politics. She drew a blank, so I asked, "What about the talk about politics?" She was stunned and began to laugh. Of course, that must have been it. The proof of it was that not only had she forgotten about it at this moment, but on the very day of the conversation, she had, at some point later in the day, found herself with the distinct memory of having had a discussion with "someone" about those political issues, but for the life of her she could not remember who that person was! This was remarkable to her now as she realized that unconsciously she must have felt that the discussion with me was equated with some kind of forbidden, dangerous involvement. It was especially striking because, although she had some feeling in the midst of the political discussion that it was a bit "weird," she also felt good about it and left the session feeling fine. Although we had differed sharply, she thought she had held her own and that the whole thing had been enjoyable. Also, here she was reporting this dream, which suggested that she was actually feeling freer and more expansive than ever with me, as though the unconscious anxiety and guilt were outweighed by a stronger sense of both my acceptance of her and her inner acceptance of herself.

I now jump to the last session with this patient, which took place several months later. As we were reflecting on the ways in which the therapy had helped her, she said, to my surprise, that if she had to select one event in the whole therapy that she thought had had the most impact, it was probably that time when we discussed politics. She said it was hard to explain just how that worked, but she thought it had something to do with allowing herself and being allowed by me to step out of the role of the patient, if only momentarily—something to do with regarding herself and being regarded by me as a peer.

In the historical background there was the fact that the patient had grown up in the shadow of her older brother. He had been worshipped by her parents and by her. Indeed, she had always felt vastly inferior to him and never felt she could hold her own with him in an argument. So whatever else it may have meant, our discussion about politics, to the extent that I was identified with this brother, seemed to foster, on the one hand, a differentiation of him and me and, on the other hand, a differentiation of the patient's self-image as the intimidated kid sister and her sense of herself as an intelligent adult who commanded respect. The process as a whole, including the dream-inspired reflections on the moment of deviation from analytic routine, also contributed to the differentiation of forbidden, incestuous wishes and ambitions and the patient's desire to consolidate her sense of identity as a woman.

What about the last thought in the dream, in which the patient has the idea that she will have to quit therapy because of what had transpired? An apparently excellent termination several months later suggests that the patient did not quit prematurely and that the danger hinted at in the dream did not become a reality. Of course, such an optimistic understanding of the ending is not necessarily the last word on it, even in a literal sense. Sometimes a patient will return after several months or years and tell the therapist something that had been withheld or that the patient or the analyst had resisted recognizing at the time of the termination. In this case, such a return could lead to a view of the end of the dream as prophetic of a termination in which aspects of the transference might have been acted out, through flight, rather than more fully worked through. The point is that although a certain perspective can create a sense of considerable conviction and closure and be associated with important practical decisions, it is also always susceptible to more or less radical revision.

CONCLUSION

Ultimately, what determines whether a particular moment of interaction in the psychoanalytic situation will have the potential to facilitate differentiation, instead of promoting pathological repetitions that perpetuate old self and object representations, is the analyst's commitment to the long-range goals of the analytic process. There is a lot of leeway for interludes of spontaneous interaction of various kinds when the patient's and the analyst's convictions about that long-range commitment are strong. Needless to say, there are many types of interaction that, even if transient, would destroy or throw serious doubt on the analyst's credibility in working with a particular patient. Indeed, certain basic ritual features of the psychoanalytic situation usually protect an element of necessary idealization of the analyst and probably should not be compromised, a point discussed earlier (chapters 1, 3, and 5). Short of the extremes, however, the analyst's openly expressive participation, integrated with a sense of the continuous interplay of transference and countertransference, and ultimately subordinated to a disciplined interest in the patient's experience, can be a great boon to the analytic work.

◆ 8 ◆

Dialectical Thinking and
Therapeutic Action

ON THROWING AWAY THE BOOK

Momentum has been gathering toward a full appreciation of the inevitability and usefulness of the analyst's personal involvement in the analytic process. With or without knowledge of each other's work, many analysts, going back to Racker and others in the 1950s, have reported the ways in which they were able to use their emotional experience or countertransference, broadly defined, to enhance their understanding of their patients and to open up new therapeutic potentials in the process. It is important to recognize that the contributions to this movement have come from analysts with diverse backgrounds that cut across many of the major psychoanalytic schools: classical Freudian, Kleinian, object relations, and interpersonal. To be sure, there are many important and interesting differences among the authors who have contributed to this current of thought. One of the commonalities among them that has struck me, however, is the extent to which the clinical experiences they report include, at some juncture, implicitly or explicitly, a feeling of *deviation* from a way of working that they view as more commonly

An earlier version of this chapter appeared in 1994 in *The Psychoanalytic Quarterly*, 63:187–218.

accepted, more a part of their own training, more traditional in one sense or another. There is a feeling of "throwing away the book" that Jacobs (e.g., 1990, pp. 450–451; 1991), Natterson (1991), Ehrenberg (1992), Mitchell (1991), and others mention or allude to in a number of their articles. Moreover, that feeling is not restricted to the analyst. One gets the impression that patients are often aware that there is a good deal of tension between the analyst's more customary attitude, or the one the analyst may regard as more acceptable within his or her particular analytic community, and the moments of deviation from it.

So I began to wonder to what extent a sense of deviation from tradition or from a stance that seemed more "psychoanalytically correct" was an important or even essential part of the therapeutic action of the experience. If it was, it seemed to me that those of us who were part of the movement were in for trouble. How often could we throw away, retrieve, and throw away the same book? One would imagine that over time the vividness, if not the credibility, of our sense of defiance and liberation would be eroded. After all, it is not as if we are keeping our own iconoclastic ideas hidden. On the contrary, a new composite Book on the process seems to be emerging, made up of such works as *Collected Papers on Schizophrenia and Related Subjects* by Searles (1965), *Transference and Countertransference* by Racker (1968), *Analysis of Transference* by Gill (1982a), *The Ambiguity of Change* by Levenson (1983), *The Matrix of the Mind* by Ogden (1986), *The Shadow of the Object* by Bollas (1987), *Relational Concepts in Psychoanalysis* by Mitchell (1988), *Understanding Countertransference* by Tansey and Burke (1989), *Other Times, Other Realities* by Modell (1990), *The Use of the Self* by Jacobs (1991), *Beyond Countertransference* by Natterson (1991), *The Intimate Edge* by Ehrenberg (1992), *Contexts of Being* by Stolorow and Atwood (1992), and *Affect in Psychoanalysis* by Spezzano (1993).[1] When the general spirit of these books becomes The Book, what Book shall we discard? How can we spontaneously and creatively defy tradition once a new tradition emerges that seems to require at least a modicum of defiance as a matter of principle?

---

1. Since the original version of this chaper went to press in 1994, many more books have appeared that focus on the place of the analyst's subjectivity in the process. These works, by authors not represented in the text above, include, among many others: Aron, 1996; Benjamin, 1995; Cushman, 1995; Davies and Frawley, 1994; Frankel, 1995; Gabbard, 1996; Kantrowitz, 1996; Stern, 1997; and Winer, 1994.

Then to defy the old would be to conform to the new, a conformity that might well diminish the flavor of creative rebellion, spontaneity, and discovery that an important sector of our community has managed to sustain for 30 or 40 years.

There are good theoretical and commonsense reasons, moreover, to think that a sense of spontaneous deviation, shared by patient and analyst, may be a central or even crucial feature of whatever corrective experience may be afforded by the emergence of the analyst's subjectivity in the process. When the patient senses that the analyst, in becoming more personally expressive and involved, is departing from an internalized convention of some kind, the patient has reason to feel recognized in a special way. The deviation, whatever its content and whatever the nature of the pressure from the patient, may reflect an emotional engagement on the analyst's part that is responsive in a unique way to this particular patient. It is not that the content is irrelevant. Certainly each instance of use or expression of countertransference would have to be examined individually to weigh the relative contributions of therapeutic, nontherapeutic, and antitherapeutic factors. But I would argue that there is something about the deviation itself, regardless of content, that has therapeutic potential. Indeed, it is possible that even when the affective reactions of the analyst seem to implicate him or her in the enactment of old, pathogenic object ties, meeting what Ghent (1992) has referred to as malignant as opposed to benign needs, the context of *deviation* from a standard technical stance, in favor of immediate responsiveness to the patient, can transform one's apparent participation as the "bad object" into that of a "good object" in the current situation. Conversely, when the analyst adheres religiously to a particular stance, ostensibly in order to ensure contrast with the patient's bad objects, the context of *conformity* to the technical stance, at the expense of immediate responsiveness to the patient, can transform one's apparent participation as the good object into that of the bad object in the present.

It is commonplace to recognize the narcissistic, exhibitionistic, and exploitative potential of overtly self-revealing behavior. But any automatic routine might also be viewed, plausibly, by the patient as a resistance on the analyst's part to an individualized engagement with the patient and as a form of self-indulgence of one sort or another. The patient might view the analyst as content to sit back and pat him- or herself on the back for doing "the right thing," according to whatever the Book requires, at the expense of attending in a creative way to the patient's needs. Alternatively, or simultaneously, the patient might view the analyst as fearful of any kind of personal engagement. Thus, for example, if the patient felt overburdened or exploited by needy parents, a line of correspondence might be drawn between that history and an analyst who never openly conveys anything at all about his or her own needs. The common factor in that case could be the patient's sense that the behavior of the parent or the analyst is propelled by fixed, predetermined, internal pressures rather than by responsiveness to the patient's immediate experience and communications. So, again, to be the good-enough object, the analyst sometimes has to show a willingness, on a manifest level, to be pulled somewhat in the direction of the bad object, whereas a determined effort to avoid any behavior that might be similar in its content to that of the bad object might be precisely what constitutes the bad object in the analytic situation.

Regarding adherence to the rituals of classical technique, here is what Searles wrote in 1949 in a paper, twice rejected for publication, that Robert Langs (1978–1979) finally discovered and published:

> The analyst who attempts to adhere to the classical behavior of unvarying "dispassionate interest" toward his patients regularly finds the patients to be irritated by such behavior which, after all, they have to cope with in everyday life only in so far as they may deal with schizoid other persons. It seems that such dispassionate behavior all too often merely repeats the patient's discouraging childhood relationship with one or another schizoid parent, and lends itself to unconscious employment by the analyst as a way of expressing hostility to the patient. For the analyst to reveal, always in a controlled way, his own feelings toward the patient would thus do away with what is often the source of our patients' strongest resistance: the need to force the analyst to admit that the patient is having an emotional effect on him [Searles, 1978–1979, p. 183].

But classical technique, especially when practiced in a rigid way, is a familiar target of criticism for its seeming coldness. I would say it is actually a scapegoat, a whipping boy, for a problem that cuts across most of the major theoretical positions, sort of like the identified patient in a disturbed family. It is more difficult but equally important to locate the expression of disturbance in points of view that advertise themselves explicitly as warmer or more "human" alternatives to the classical position. Self psychology is one such point of view. The central principle of technique in self psychology is "sustained empathic inquiry." Can conformity to such a "benign" principle cast the shadow of the bad object on the analyst? I think it can. Consider the argument of Slavin and Kriegman (1992):

[I]t is quite possible for empathy to be practiced with a fair degree of verisimilitude, as a technique, rather than as the genuine intimate act and sign of mutuality that is so profoundly, intrinsically valued. Indeed, patients know, or come to know, that another human being whose only substantial utterances take the form of validating affirmations of the patient's own subjective world and developmental strivings are likely, themselves, to be engaged in one or another form of self-deception and deception [p. 250].

The attempt to remain exclusively attuned to what appear to the therapist to be the dominant themes and meanings in the patient's subjective world is, in fact, sensed by many patients as a self-protective strategy on the part of the therapist. . . . Over and above any particular individual defensiveness that we may attribute to the therapist, the overly consistent use of the empathic mode will, for some patients, be sensed as the therapist's hiding some aspect of him- or herself, or pursuit of his or her own interests—interests that, as the patient well knows but therapists are loath to face, indeed, diverge in some significant ways from those of the patient. We must, thus, clearly face the fact that an immersion in the patient's subjective world . . . must be complemented, at times, by what is, in effect, the open expression of the analyst's reality [pp. 252–253].

Even such "open expression" is hardly exempt from falling prey to the tendency toward standardization and mechanization. The analyst's self-disclosure is no more a panacea for inauthenticity than is empathic inquiry. Bromberg (1994) writes:

[I]f the analyst's choice is motivated by his need to be seen in a certain way by his patient (such as honest, accommodating, unsadistic, or innovatively "free" as an analyst) then self-disclosure becomes a technique and as a technique is as instrumentally linear as any other intervention based on an "if I do this, then the patient will do that" model. Like any human quality that is "packaged," self-disclosure too can lose its primary relational ingredient (mutuality) and become what Greenberg (1981) has called "prescriptive." When it fails in its purpose, it is usually for that reason. It lacks the authenticity, spontaneity, and unpredictable impact on the future, that makes analytic growth possible [p. 541].

Some patients more than others are particularly sensitive to and intolerant of anything that smacks of psychoanalytic clichés, or of going by the Book in one way or another, or even of a measured, unvarying psychoanalytic tone of voice, whether it is coolly detached or warmly "empathic." Those patients often have a therapeutic effect on me because they do not let me get away with the party line or tone. Instead, they challenge me to think things through in a fresh way, to be myself, and to respond to them as unique individuals. Of course, intolerance of stereotypic behavior can sometimes be excessive and defensive. Some acceptance by the patient of the recognizably technical aspects of the analyst's behavior is essential for the viability of the relationship and of the process; but the conspicuously formal, role-related aspects of the analyst's participation, however much they may contribute to a safe analytic environment, can also be powerful magnets for the patient's mistrust. And, of course, for every patient who complains explicitly about something artificial in the analyst's behavior there are countless patients who would not say a word about it or who would deny it. With them, one would have to look for disguised references to the issue in dreams and other associations (see chapter 4). In some cases, the patient might simply identify with the aggressor (as perceived) and go through the motions for a long time, sometimes years, without feeling touched or reached. In this connection, Lipton (1977a) has suggested that there may be some patients who are thought to have narcissistic personality disorders who are actually identifying defensively and unconsciously with analysts who do not make themselves available for a personal relationship.

PSYCHOANALYTIC DISCIPLINE IN A NEW KEY

So the question arises: If we appreciate the dangers inherent in uncritical systematic application of psychoanalytic technical stances and rules of conduct and the potential benefits that can come from spontaneous personal engagement with the patient, why not simply get rid of the former and cultivate the latter to the hilt? Well of course, that will not do at all. We would then simply be entering personal relationships with our patients with the arrogant claim, masked as egalitarianism, that to spend time with us will somehow be therapeutic. Also, we would be promoting allegedly "authentic" personal involvement as an encompassing technique, an approach that would be just as suspect in terms of its genuineness as any fanatically ascetic stance. No, clearly there is much wisdom in the requirement that the analyst abstain from the kind of personal involvement with patients that might develop in an ordinary social situation.

How then, in light of the current emphasis on the importance of acknowledging and making constructive use of the analyst's emotional participation, should we conceptualize the special sense of analytic restraint that undoubtedly remains indispensable to practice? Perhaps a key abstract principle to which we would all subscribe can be stated as follows: Analysts, assuming adequate monetary (or other) compensation, must try, in a relatively consistent way, to subordinate their own personal responsiveness and immediate desires to the long-term interests of their patients. Such consistent subordination can be optimized only in the context of the analyst's ongoing critical scrutiny of his or her participation in the process. Well, even if the money is good, that is a lot to ask, perhaps more than what we would expect of good-enough parents (Slavin and Kriegman, 1992, p. 243). Fortunately, the principle has to be qualified as stated, because we now have more conviction about the interdependence of the patient's and the analyst's needs. If the analyst is too abstinent or too self-negating, the patient's healthy need for the analyst to survive, and even to benefit from, the patient's impact (Winnicott, 1971; Searles, 1975) will not be met. So, on the one hand, a sense of psychoanalytic discipline, which includes restrictions on the extent and nature of the analyst's involvement, provides the backdrop for whatever spontaneous, personal interactions are engaged in by the participants. On the other hand, given our current understanding of how important it is that analysts allow themselves to be affected and known to some significant degree by their patients, the restrictions themselves are more qualified than they once were. Thus, the moment in which the analyst allows himself or herself to surface as a desiring subject (Benjamin, 1988) is not experienced with the same sharp edge of deviation that characterized it before. Now, instead of *throwing away* the Book, we place it temporarily in the background while the analyst's distinctive self-expression moves into the foreground. The opposite holds as well. When the analyst's more standard, formal, detached, reflective, and interpretive stance is in the foreground, the aspect of the relationship that reflects his or her more personal engagement can still be sensed in the background.

DIALECTICAL THINKING

What I have just said amounts to a dialectical way of thinking about the analyst's participation in the process, one that others, including Benjamin (1988), Ghent (1989), Mitchell (1988), Ogden (1986), Pizer (1992), and Stern (1983), have been trying to articulate and develop. The term *dialectic* has a long history in philosophy, involving a variety of meanings.[2] For my purposes, the following definition by Ogden (1986) has been useful: "A dialectic is a process in which each of two opposing concepts creates, informs, preserves, and negates the other, each standing in a dynamic (ever changing) relationship with the other" (p. 208).

To think and speak in a dialectical way is difficult and sometimes confusing. Many of our concepts in psychoanalysis imply dichotomous thinking: fantasy versus reality, repetition versus new experience, self-expression versus responsiveness to others, technique versus personal relationship, interpretation versus enactment, individual versus social, intrapsychic versus interpersonal, construction versus discovery, even analyst versus patient. There is a sense that these polarities constitute a series of mutually exclusive opposites. But when we think about the poles within each pairing in dialectical terms, we are challenged not only to recognize their obviously contrasting features, but also to find the effects of each pole on the other, and even aspects of each pole represented within the other. One might think in terms of two mirrors positioned opposite each other, so that we can see the endless series of reflections of the two within each. The relationship between psychoanalytic discipline and expressive participation is dialectical in that sense.

On the side of analytic discipline, first, however much it is learned and internalized in a process of professional socialization, such an attitude gets into the analyst's bones, so that it expresses a very important aspect of him- or herself. Second, that discipline, to begin with, is not simply imposed from outside but represents a special kind of development of the analyst's potential for attention to the experience of others. And third, although the analyst speaks partly in the context of the role of disciplined expert, his or her *voice* can and should remain personally expressive. The effect of the dialectic, as noted in chapter 6, is to encourage what Schafer (1974) called "talking to patients," as opposed to the "impersonal diction" that he found to be so pervasive among analytic therapists following a "pseudoanalytic model." With regard to the other pole in the dialectic, moments of personal self-revelation or spontaneous action on the

---

2. At one point, Ghent (1992, p. 156) decided to eschew the term *dialectic* because of the connotation of a movement toward synthesis in which tensions are dissolved. He preferred the term *paradox*. I think dialectic has the advantage, however, of implying an interactive dynamic between opposites, whereas paradox seems more static. In any case, I intend the connotation of tension, not resolution.

part of the analyst can be located within, and intuitively guided by, a sense of their place in the process as a whole. The latter involves a complex mosaic of interdependent, overtly interpretive, and overtly noninterpretive interactions (Pizer, 1992). So, as discussed in chapter 7, on the one hand, psychoanalytic discipline can be self-expressive and, on the other hand, the analyst's self-expression may reflect a complex, intuitive kind of psychoanalytic discipline.

The analyst's personal, emotional response to the patient, when expressed, may or may not entail some form of gratification of the patient's needs or wishes. Because of the valuing of abstinence in classical psychoanalytic theory of technique, a withholding attitude tends to be associated with a more "correct" posture, whereas "giving in" to pressures from the patient tends to be associated with the unfortunate intrusion of something from within the analyst. Deficit theories, such as those of Kohut and Winnicott, have legitimized certain kinds of gratification as an intrinsic part of the psychoanalytic process. At the same time they have introduced a new kind of institutionalized disguise for personal, countertransferential tendencies. Mitchell (1991) has discussed the influence of the analyst's personal attitudes on the classification of the patient's desires into those that qualify as "needs" for responses that are developmentally necessary and those that amount to "wishes" for gratifications that have forbidden, incestuous meaning. He argues that such assessments are never simply "diagnostic" of what is objectively true of the patient. Instead, they express complex organizations of transference and countertransference that can often be explored usefully only in retrospect, that is, after certain enactments have occurred. Elsewhere, Mitchell (1988) provides us with an excellent example of dialectical thinking in his account of the optimal posture of the analyst dealing with narcissistic issues in the transference. With respect to the patient's invitation to the analyst to participate in a "mutually admiring relationship," Mitchell writes:

> Responding to such an invitation in a way that is analytically constructive is tricky, and difficult to capture in a simple formula. What is most useful frequently is not the words, but the tone in which they are spoken. The most useful response entails a subtle dialectic between joining the analysand in the narcissistic integration and simultaneously questioning the nature and purpose of that integration, both a playful participation in the analysand's illusions and a puzzled curiosity about how and why they came to be so serious, the sine qua non of the analysand's sense of security and involvement with others [p. 205].

It is important to emphasize that my interest in this chapter is in the dialectic between the analyst's personal emotional presence and the analyst's role-determined behavior, whatever their respective contents. Either could be ostensibly gratifying or frustrating with respect to the patient's desires. In the broad sense, one could think of the tension as that between a pull that both participants are likely to feel, in varying degrees, toward a quality of interaction akin to what they would experience (or imagine they would experience) outside of the analytic situation and the sense that both may have, in varying degrees, of the need for a special kind of restraint that is peculiar to the analytic situation itself (cf. Modell, 1990). To the extent that the patient wants a personal relationship with the analyst, one could think of a pressure from the patient for a generic kind of "gratification" (Searles, 1978–1979, see above, p. 196). When I speak of analysts participating in a "self-expressive" or "personally responsive" way, I have in mind their own inclinations to respond to the patient, in part, as they might imagine they would outside of the analytic situation. The point, however, of appreciating the dialectic between personal responsiveness and analytic discipline is to recognize that despite the tension between them, each tendency is also reflected in a substantial way in the other. Thus, the analyst who behaves "naturally" would be incorporating in his or her actions the sense of discipline that is intrinsic to his or her sense of identity as an analyst. The possibility of such integrative action does not do away with potential tensions arising from discrepancies between types of reactions that antedate psychoanalytic training (in the broad sense) and those that directly reflect its influence.

PSYCHOANALYTIC AUTHORITY, MUTUALITY, AND AUTHENTICITY

The analytic situation is a unique setup, a ritual, in which the analyst is invested by society and by the patient with a special kind of power, one that the analyst accepts as part of his or her role. I believe that power has psychological continuity with the power of parents to shape their children's sense of themselves and their worlds. The magical aspect of the analyst's authority is enhanced by his or her relative inaccessibility and anonymity. There is a kind of mystique about the analyst that I doubt we want to dispel completely. It is noteworthy in that regard that however much we, as analysts, may interpret and attempt to deconstruct our authority through the analysis of transference, we do not generally dismantle the analytic frame during the analysis or even after it. We do not usually invite our patients to our homes for dinner or visit them in theirs. Instead, we take pains to protect the special kind of moral presence that we have in our patients' lives.

With regard to therapeutic action, I think there is something to the simple idea that the analyst is an authority whose regard for the patient matters in a special way, one that, again, we do not try to analyze away, nor could we, perhaps, even if we did try. In some cases it may take a lot of work to get to the point where that regard can be conveyed by the analyst and received and integrated by the patient. But I doubt many of us have felt, as patients or as therapists, that the process, when it has been helpful, has not included that factor of affirmation (Bromberg, 1983; Schafer, 1983, pp. 43–48). I think the likelihood of that happening in an authentic way is increased not only because the analyst is in a position conducive to eliciting a certain quality of regard, but also because the patient is in an analogous position. Regard for *the analyst* is fostered partly by the fact that the patient knows so much *less* about him or her than the analyst knows about the patient. The factor of relative anonymity contributes not only to the irrational aspect of the analyst's power, but also to a more rational aspect. The analyst is in a relatively protected position, after all, one that is likely to promote the most tolerant, understanding, and generous aspects of his or her personality. I think of "idealization" partly in interactional terms (as in "making the other more ideal") because the analytic situation and often the patient actually do nourish some of the analyst's more "ideal" qualities as a person—what Schafer (1983) has referred to as the analyst's "second self." Conversely, however, the analyst's regard for *the patient* is fostered by the fact that he or she knows so *much* about the patient, including the origins of the patient's difficulties and his or her struggles to deal with them. Moreover, of course, neither party has to live with the other or even engage the other outside of the circumscribed analytic situation, so that each is afforded quite a bit of protection from the other's more difficult qualities.

Corresponding with what several authors have discussed in terms of an interplay between the "principle of mutuality" and the "principle of asymmetry" (Aron, 1991; Burke, 1992; Modell, 1991), there is an ongoing dialectic between the patient's perception of the analyst as *a person like himself or herself* and the patient's perception of the analyst as *a person with superior knowledge, wisdom, judgment, and power.* Each way of viewing the analyst is very much colored by the other. Whichever is in the foreground, the other is always in the background. So, those of us who are interested in developing more mutual and egalitarian relationships with our patients should not deny or forget the extent to which we are drawing upon the ritualized asymmetry of the analytic situation to give that mutuality its power. The asymmetry, the hierarchical arrangement, makes our participation in the spirit of mutuality *matter* to our patients in an intensified way, one that helps to build or construct our patients' views of themselves as creative agents and as persons ultimately deserving of their own and other people's love. What the balance should be between asymmetry and mutuality for any particular analytic dyad, at any particular moment or over time, is very difficult to determine or control. Also, it must emerge from an authentic kind of participation by the analyst rather than from adherence to a technical formula. To affect the patient's representations of self and other, what is necessary is that the analyst's authority be sufficiently authentic, on the one hand, and that his or her authenticity be sufficiently authoritative, on the other. The fact that analysts cannot know exactly how they should position themselves with respect to the dialectic of overtly expressive participation and relatively standard authority-enhancing technique is precisely the wellspring for an overarchingly authentic way of being with the patient, one that is marked by a sense of struggle with uncertainty, by a willingness to "play it both ways," and by an openness to consideration of the unconscious meanings, for the analyst and patient, of whatever course has been taken.

CLINICAL ILLUSTRATION

Now let's look at these ideas as they bear upon a piece of clinical experience. I was seeing Diane, a single medical student in her late twenties. We were in the midst of an analysis that I was conducting as a candidate at the local Institute for Psychoanalysis. The Institute was there with us in the process, like a concrete representation (and externalization) of a somewhat forbidding psychoanalytic superego. Since sometime in the second year, Diane had refused to lie on the couch, sitting up on it instead. Ordinarily, I sit in a chair opposite the couch when patients sit up. But in this case, I dutifully sat in the chair behind the couch (actually at a 45° angle), as if to say, "You're the one who is violating the rules, not me. I've got nothing to do with it." I am not sure how it came about that she started sitting up.

I remember it being a gradual and insidious change, one that I was against. At least I claimed I was against it and told her so. I cannot deny, however, that even as I stated my objections, her mischievous smile, when she began turning around, sometimes elicited a slight smile in return. And when she asked me point blank, "Are you sure the couch is necessary for the process? I think the eye contact is more important for me," I bluntly replied, "Well, I don't know about the process, but it might be necessary for me to graduate."[3] My conviction about that was somewhat diminished by the fact that the supervisor, one I had chosen, had a propensity for independent thinking. (The supervisor, of course, does not always have the last word on such matters.) Although he thought it was preferable that Diane lie down, he did not think her sitting up was a major problem. The important thing, he thought, was that we try to explore the meaning of whatever was going on. But for reasons that were undoubtedly related to those that accounted for Diane not lying on the couch, she was not always enthused about analyzing things either. She had real troubles in her life, and she wanted to talk about them and have me understand their importance. She did not think of herself as offering associations as grist for my psychoanalytic mill. She thought of herself as talking to me about things that really mattered in their own right, things that she wanted me to take at face value and help her deal with in a direct way.

So, maybe she was "unanalyzable," a candidate for psychotherapy at best, not for psychoanalysis. (See Gill, 1991, for a discussion of the distinction between psychotherapy and psychoanalysis, and Bromberg, 1983, Gill, 1991, and Ehrenberg, 1992, for challenges to traditional views of "analyzability.") This, however, was not the whole story. What I discovered, and what was so important for the analytic process, was that if I met the patient "halfway" (that is, what seemed to her to be a quarter of the way and to me three quarters of the way), she could do a lot of very hard work in the standard analytic sense. If I showed genuine and extended interest in the manifest issues first, joint exploration of latent meaning would often come later. Not only that, but whatever was learned was always lived out in a very vivid way. Interpretations had to stew with other

---

3. Over time I conveyed to her the various rationales for the use of the couch. I also admitted that my convictions about it were hardly absolute. Nevertheless, I said that I had a serious interest in gaining experience with that arrangement and that I considered such experience to be one of the benefits of the Institute training program.

kinds of interactions or the patient would not chew on them at all, much less swallow or digest them.

About the not lying down, we came gradually to appreciate how much humiliating submission[4] there already was in Diane just getting herself to the office for her appointments. Lying down while I sat up added too much insult to injury. Her father, a Holocaust survivor, had been compulsive and tyrannical about all kinds of trivial matters in the home. Things had to be in place, wife and children (two older brothers and a younger sister) had to be on time, the waiter or waitress in the restaurant had to provide quick service or he would get enraged. At times he seemed identified with his Nazi persecutors in his rigid, authoritarian ways. He was also a very charismatic, energetic man, successful in his business and a dedicated athlete and outdoorsman. Diane, seeing him as a powerful and exciting figure, worshiped him in her early years, only to become bitterly disappointed and disillusioned as she came to regard him as extraordinarily self-centered and stingy with his time, his money, and his demonstrations of affection. In my nonverbal acceptance of Diane's sitting up, I was consciously disidentifying with her father. The presence of the Institute made the departure from convention both harder and easier for me to accept and participate in: harder because of a fear of real consequences for my training, easier because I was able defensively to externalize my own real interest in doing it the conventional way. If I did not really care, I did not have to feel cheated by the patient or angry with her. Instead, I could restrict my attention to enjoying being a renegade with the patient's appreciation and approval.

To say that I was disidentifying with the patient's father is not precisely correct, in that, needless to say, there were other aspects to the father's personality. It would be more precise to say that I was disidentifying with the father's persecutory superego, one that rather mercilessly governed his behavior and that of the people around him, and also one that was internalized to a significant degree by the patient herself. But there was another side to the father that was also in evidence at times, however faintly. The father had great difficulty, as I said, showing affection. At moments of greeting or parting, for example, he would position himself near the patient in a way that would suggest interest in some contact, but he could not initiate it

---

4. Ghent (1990) draws a useful distinction between "surrender" as a benign form of yielding and "submission" as a malignant subjugation of self.

himself. It was always she who had to take the lead. Sometimes the patient felt that her father had a lot of feeling bottled up inside that he just could not express. So with her gradual move from lying down to sitting up, in an attenuated way, the patient and I enacted this aspect of the patient's experience with her father. It was her initiative to have face-to-face contact, and I was the one, like her father, complying in an inhibited, ambivalent manner.

When I say the enactment was attenuated, I have in mind subtle but crucial differences between the original scene and the analytic one. In the first place, although these things are impossible to quantify, I am fairly sure (or I like to think) that my conflict was less intense than that of the father and that there was more pleasure than pain and more playfulness than fear in "succumbing" to the patient's will.[5] The fact that we could laugh about it at times—I at the patient for her intolerance of analytic rituals and she at me for my interest in them—was evidence of that. In the second place, the enactment itself was embedded in a context in which it was generally recognized as an object for reflection. Whether we were actually reflecting on it at any given time or not, just the fact that the atmosphere was one in which it was understood that what was going on had more meanings than what we might be seeing or acknowledging, and the fact that I was actively curious about those meanings, made the whole situation very different from its prototype in the patient's history. All in all, I would say that there was enough sense of similarity between the patient's psychological situation and my own to foster strong mutual identifications, and enough differences so that subtly new ways of being and relating could be explored.

In saying that I was disidentifying with the father's persecutory superego there is another imprecision that amounts to a kind of shorthand. I could only identify with the father to begin with to the extent that he had qualities akin to some objects of identification in my own life. Similarly, of course, the disidentification could only occur in my own experience relative to those internalized objects. No externalization (Sandler et al., 1969) of internal object relations in the patient can occur unless it finds a "mate" in the internal object relations of the analyst. I recognize that this is the juncture at which some authors, like Jacobs (1991) or McLaughlin (1981, 1988),

---

5. In the background the enactment may well have had the reverse meaning. The patient might have been identified with the father, demanding that I, in the position she was in as a child, submit to her will.

might become aware of stories in their lives that dovetail with the patient's story. While I have the conviction, one that I hope I convey to my patients, that my experience in the analytic process reflects directly on my own history, even as it may shed light on something in theirs, my attention does not necessarily gravitate toward specific details in my childhood that complement or parallel those in the patient's experience. Instead, my focus, to the extent that it is on myself, often stays on my own immediate experience as it relates to the patient's immediate experience and to the patient's history. Of course, my experience outside of the analytic situation is often affected by the patient, and that part of my life automatically comes under scrutiny as an aspect of the countertransference (Feinsilver, 1983, 1990). In this instance, the Institute affiliation, whatever its intrapsychic-historical meanings for me, parallels the patient's relationship with her father.

There is a difference here that surely has as much to do with personality as it does with a chosen approach (cf. Jacobs, 1991, p. 44). Nevertheless, whatever its benefits, I think that attention to the specific historical bases for the countertransference may sometimes detract from struggling with the nuances of the immediate experience with the patient, particularly in a way that involves the patient directly. It is important to remember that within a given psychoanalytic hour, the process is continuous and the analyst is continuously called upon to respond without the benefit of being able to call "time out" to reflect on his or her past. The clinical experiences reported by Racker back in the 1950s, and in recent years by Gill, Ehrenberg, Donnel Stern, Mitchell, and others, illustrate intensive work on the transference and the countertransference with the patient in the here and now, without reference to particulars in the analyst's personal history. Over the course of an analysis, however, an integration of the kind of reflection that these authors describe in their work and the kind described by Jacobs and McLaughlin would probably be ideal.

All that I have said serves partly as introduction to the following episode in my work with Diane. I think the episode further illustrates the way therapeutic action can be born of the dialectical interplay between analytic discipline and personal participation, and between formal analytic authority (which operates silently in the background) and an atmosphere of spontaneity and mutuality.

We were in the third year of the analysis. An aspect of the transference that was becoming increasingly prominent was the patient's demand for a kind of maternal preoccupation with her needs, one the patient felt her mother reserved for the patient's younger sister Louise at the patient's expense. In fact, it was possible to understand some things that happened in the analysis as a demand that I be consumed with anxious worry about the patient's well-being to the point of being frantic, "hysterical," or "crazy," just as the patient's mother had seemed to be about Louise from the time of her birth when the patient was about two years old. Allegedly, Louise was an abnormally small, sickly, and vulnerable infant. Implied suggestions by me that Diane could function at a high level without feeling overwhelmed when she was hurt or disappointed about something were often associated in Diane's mind with the mother's underestimation of Diane's difficulties and overestimation of Louise's needs. The problem was compounded by the fact that because Diane felt she had been so intensely jealous of Louise and so hostile toward both her and her mother, she also felt that she herself had been an unlovable, greedy, ungrateful, and even hateful child, and she hated herself for it. The derivative of this in the analysis was that she often felt she was an impossibly difficult patient and that I wanted to be rid of her.

After a recent move to a new apartment, the patient became obsessed with a noise she could hear from a garbage chute adjacent to her new residence. An advanced medical student going through a stressful rotation, Diane suddenly could not sleep or study. She was beside herself with anger and anxiety. In addition to recognizing the manifestly disturbing nature of the noise, we explored various meanings that it may have had within and outside of the transference. Among other things, we understood that the patient was reacting to it just the way she thought her father would under similar circumstances, with total, half-crazed preoccupation and furious intolerance.

One morning the patient called, asking for an appointment early in the day rather than her regular late afternoon time. I could not arrange it, however. When she came in at her regular time, she announced in the waiting room, as soon as I opened the door, "I'm here for one reason and one reason only, and that is to get some Valium. If you can't help me get some, I might as well leave right now!" Nevertheless, she grudgingly trudged in. She knew, of course, that I am a psychologist, but thought there must be someone I knew to whom I could refer her for medication, if not get it directly from that person myself. She much preferred the latter alternative, because she did not want to go through the ordeal of having to see someone for an evaluation, a solution that I also thought would be too burdensome under these circumstances. She was just so agitated that she had to have something now to help her relax, to help her sleep. We could worry about what it all meant later. In the meantime she had to go to work, she had to attend classes, she had to study. What did I care about more, her well-being or my analytic purity? Was I worried about what people would think, or about what she really needed? I tried to maintain a "proper" analytic attitude toward all this, pointing out, among other things, that even if it were true that some sort of tranquilizer might help right now, the idea that she had to get it from *me* was irrational, considering the many other resources she had. So the demand that I give it to her must represent something else, something very important, but to get her a pill might obscure more than it would clarify what that need was. She would have none of this, except in the most intellectual sense, and persisted relentlessly in her demand that I address the issue at face value.

Now let us consider the position of the analyst at this juncture. What kinds of options do I have and how should they be conceptualized? Do we take for granted that as an analyst I am restricted to trying to explore the meaning of the patient's behavior? I think that most of our theories of the process do take this position. If the patient reacts with frustration and anger, so be it. Those are precisely the affects that need to be understood analytically. Those are the states, allegedly, that are most clearly reflective of the patient's internal dynamics, without excessive influence from the analyst. If we take the view, however, that the analyst is always implicated in "constructing" whatever the patient experiences, and that insisting on playing it by the rules can be as provocative as deviating from them, the door is opened to consider other ways of interacting. Also, now the analyst has to struggle with a sense of uncertainty, risk, and responsibility for whatever he or she elects to do (Hoffman, 1987; Mitchell, 1988, 1991; Moraitis, 1981, 1987; Stern, 1983, 1989). I believe that this struggle, one that is located within the dialectic of spontaneous expressiveness and technical rigor, has, in itself, great therapeutic potential. It is at the heart of what it means to be a new, good object because it is the most open to the multiple potentials within the patient and the analyst.

So what ensued with Diane was the following. Under the patient's pressure and out of my own need and, perhaps, intuition, however "implicit" (Gendlin, 1973), "unthought" (Bollas, 1987), or "unformulated" (Donnel Stern, 1983), I asked Diane whether she had an internist whom she could ask for a prescription. She said she did, but was not so sure how he would feel about it because she had not been in for a check-up in a long time. I said, "Well, if you give me his number, I'll call him right now." She replied, "Really?!" sort of delighted and floored at the same time. She gave me the number, and I called. While I waited for the doctor to come to the phone, Diane began whispering in an animated way, "This is crazy; I could get a friend to do this; I could do this myself." She was smiling but seemed somewhat embarrassed. I thought of hanging up just as her doctor picked up the receiver, but decided to go through with it. I identified myself and said I thought it would be okay, if the patient called, that she be given some mild tranquilizer. He said, essentially, that it was no problem and that Diane should call him. After I hung up, Diane and I started to talk, and she was receptive for the first time to exploring the meaning of the whole transaction.

Now let us stop again and think about what went on. Why is the patient suddenly freed of the grip of her own compulsion to force our interaction into a particular mold? Why is she suddenly able to get out of the prisonhouse of projective identification? Ogden (1986) has described projective identification and the alternative to it in terms of dialectics:

> Interpersonally, projective identification is the negative of playing; it is the coercive enlistment of another person to perform a role in the projector's externalized unconscious fantasy. The effect of this process on the recipient is to threaten his ability to experience his subjective state as psychic reality. Instead, his perceptions are experienced as "reality" as opposed to a personal construction. This process represents a limitation of the recipient's psychological dialectical processes by which symbolic meanings are generated and understood. Neither the projector nor the recipient of the projective identification is able to experience a range of personal meanings. On the contrary, there is only a powerful sense of inevitability. Neither party can conceive of himself or of the other, any differently or less intensely than he does at present [p. 228].

In the work with Diane, I believe that the key is to think, again, in terms of reversal of figure and ground. What is in the foreground is the way the patient, as she enters the office, is aggressively and unreflectively shaping the interaction. She is saying, in effect, "This is who I am and this is who you are when you are with me. It's the bottom line and there are no options." What is in the background, however, is a projective identification that originates with *me*. Because to the extent that I am uncritically committed to exploring the meaning of the patient's experiences at every turn, it is I who am saying to her: "This is who I am and this is who you must be when you are with me. Me analyst, you analysand! Those are the terms. Take them or leave them." It is a case of tyrannical father locking horns with tyrannical father. So when I say, "I'll call your internist right now," I am saying, "Look, there is nothing sacrosanct about this way of being in the relationship. You and I together have other potentials that we can realize."[6] I am also saying, "I may *resist* your demands and I may not be sure what is in your best interests, but I'm confident that for me to yield to *some* of those demands will not kill me. I can find a way to yield that is also expressive of my own will." In this instance, my "yielding" involves an initiative on my part that has an aggressive component, a kind of calling the patient's bluff that takes her by surprise. The patient, in turn, is out from under her sense of submission to the requirement that she do it my way and can now freely find *within herself* an interest in doing it that very way, that is, in reflecting and analyzing and seeing her role in shaping the interaction. The episode conforms to the formula stated simply by Benjamin (1988), drawing on Winnicott: "When I act upon the other it is vital that he be affected, so that I know that I exist—but not completely destroyed, so that I know that he also exists" (p. 38; see also Fourcher, 1975, p. 417).

All this is happening with the ritually based power of the analyst operating silently in the background to give the moment of mutual recognition and responsiveness the intensified impact it must have to stand any chance of overcoming the profoundly damaging effects of those early object relations in which domination of the other or masochistic submission seemed like the only alternatives available (Benjamin, 1988; Ghent, 1990). When the patient reacts to my getting on the phone, it matters that it is I, the analyst, who is doing this, a person who occupies a special position in the patient's mental life. Again, the asymmetrical and hierarchical aspects of the arrangement provide the backdrop, the element of idealization, that gives such moments of mutuality, cumulatively, their power to affect deeply entrenched and longstanding patterns of internal and external object relations (cf. Berger and Luckmann, 1967).

When the patient starts whispering while I am waiting for her doctor to come to the phone, "This is crazy, I could do this myself,"

---

6. To say that there is "nothing sacrosanct about this way of being in the relationship" is not to deny that there are aspects of the analytic arrangement, including its fundamental asymmetry, that are, indeed, sacrosanct relative to the goals of the analysis. Not *everything*, moreover, can be decided on an individual basis. The standardization of certain parameters is partly what contributes to an atmosphere of safety in the analytic situation.

I go through with the call. Why? Maybe it is a bit of playful tit for tat, as if to say, "You tortured me for a half hour, now it's your turn." The aggression on my part borders on a frame violation, a piece of acting out, perhaps, retaliating for the patient's challenges to the frame, challenges that may have carried particularly aggressive implications in light of Diane's knowledge of my status as a candidate (Elizabeth Perl, personal communication).[7] Nevertheless, the playful aspect of the exchange reflects our entry into a new kind of transitional space. Also, the shift that I make reflects my movement from one stance to the other, which, it turn, demonstrates the element of uncertainty and struggle that I am suggesting is a central component of the therapeutic action.

So, to continue with the story in the clinical situation, exploration of the meaning of this episode continued sporadically over several weeks of work, and a number of important insights emerged. In the first place, Diane acknowledged that she had been very angry because I could not see her earlier in the day. She said, smiling, "Really, I don't ask for that much. Was that too much to ask?" I said, it was one thing to ask and another to be enraged if I could not arrange it, something she undoubtedly recognized herself; otherwise, I said, she would have come in angry about *that* rather than about my anticipated reluctance to get her Valium. She needed something to help legitimize what she recognized as childish: the demand that I see her whenever she wanted to see me.

This demand was linked to another very important issue, another bit of enactment that we had not sufficiently examined because it had been so emphatically presented as a reality issue. I pointed out

---

7. The question arises (posed by Judy Kantrowitz, personal communication, among others) as to whether, in retrospect, my own behavior should be regarded as regrettable. I would say that some kind of "deviation" was probably called for, but it would have been better had I not gone as far as I did. For example, I could have encouraged the patient to call the internist herself, even during the hour, or as things went, I could have hung up as soon as the patient said "this is crazy. . . ." A critical perspective on the analyst's participation has to be maintained along with the paradoxical recognition of the way in which a "mistake" may often get woven into the fabric of therapeutic action. The place of nontraumatizing empathic errors in self psychology, which can lead to "transmuting internalizations," or more recently, the effects of sequences of "disruption" and "repair" (Beebe and Lachmann, 1994), may be analogous to "participation errors" in the dialectical-constructivist point of view. One does not aim to make them, but recognizes their inevitability and the importance of making constructive use of them when they occur.

that the obsessional preoccupation with the noise in her apartment had, in fact, been associated with quite a few phone calls, not just the one mentioned. This was interesting in light of the fact that during that month we had been meeting only three times per week because the patient insisted she could not make the fourth hour due to her hectic schedule. I had agreed to this most reluctantly and "under protest," with the understanding that we would continue to search for a mutually agreeable fourth hour. Now the patient admitted, much to my surprise, that she actually felt that I had given in "too easily." She expected me to put up more of a fight. Here, as in the case of the demand for Valium, the sense of necessity that characterized the transference demand (we must cut down to three times per week) is undone when the sense of necessity in the countertransference (we must meet four times per week) is undone. She agreed that it was a no-win situation for me (and her), in that if I had been more rigid about it, she would have thought I was doing merely what was best for *me*, at her expense. But the fact was that now she thought I was just relieved to not have to spend so much time with her. She figured that she was as annoying to me as the garbage noise in her apartment was to her; or from another point of view, she felt deserted, left alone to cope with all her miseries, condensed symbolically into the sound of the garbage in the chute. The whole sequence recreated the patient's experience with her mother who, for example, was all *too* ready, the patient felt, to stay home (in a distant suburb) and not come to visit if the patient said that she was busy and that it was not a convenient time. Shortly after this, incidentally (and for the record), we resumed meeting four times per week and continued on that basis to the end of the analysis, about three years later.

With regard to my calling the internist, the patient said she really liked that and appreciated it, because it meant I had become "a little crazy," which somehow meant I understood something about her own sense of desperation at times. This meant both that I sensed her desperation and wanted to do something for her and that I felt desperate myself and was willing to show it, if only temporarily. The enactment helped me and the patient to begin to see how much she wanted me to be frantic about her in a way similar to how she thought her mother was frantic about Louise, the difference being that my "getting hysterical" was also an object of curiosity and critical reflection. Thus there was reason to believe that the quality of my attention, taken as a whole, was better than what either the patient or Louise got from their mother.

CONCLUSION: OEDIPAL AND PREOEDIPAL
DIALECTICS AND THERAPEUTIC ACTION

When the patient makes her aggressive demands for an earlier session, for Valium, for cutting back the frequency of our meetings, and for direct "help" with her life, one might say that she is threatening to "destroy" the analyst-object, and I am in a position of having to decide how far I should go in defending that part of myself that is under fire. It is, of course, only a part of myself. It is not even the part of myself that I would designate as my "true self," not entirely anyway. In working with this patient, some part of my "true self," I would say, wants to abandon the standard analytic position even while another part wants to hold on to it. Conversely, despite her protests to the contrary, there is a part of the patient that does not want to lose me as her analyst, as the person with a unique, encompassing perspective, special expertise, and special power to affect her life.

One could translate this situation into oedipal terms and say that the patient (like any patient?) has an investment in my remaining "wedded" to the Institute, to the Book, and to analytic principles, including the principle of abstinence that helps protect my capacity to subordinate my own personal responsiveness and immediate desire to the patient's long-term interests in the course of the work. Even as she attempts to lure me away from that marriage, capitalizing, perhaps, on points of vulnerability in it that she detects, she knows at some level that such an oedipal triumph would be a pyrrhic victory. In that respect, in the long run she would rather that her assaults on that part of me not succeed. She would like to win a few battles, perhaps, but not the war. In the last analysis, the child wants to love and be loved by both parents (or their surrogates) and to feel that the parents love each other. Similarly, the patient's deepest need is for the synergy of my personal involvement and the relatively detached, theoretically informed, and interpretive aspect of my analytic attitude.[8]

Abstracting further, to a level that encompasses preoedipal as well as oedipal issues, the "triangle" consists of the patient, the analyst as one who is preoccupied with responding to the patient's immediately

---

8. The opportunities afforded by the psychoanalytic situation for corrective resolution of oedipal rivalries are relatively weak because those in the position of rival love objects (which applies to siblings as well as oedipal rivals) are not available to the patient as sources or objects of love (see chapter 10 for further discussion of this issue).

expressed desires, and the analyst as one who has other narcissistic and object-related investments. Just as a parent's investments in other objects of interest are inextricably linked to the parent's abstaining from engulfing emotional or incestuous involvement with the child, so too is the analyst's attachment to other objects, including psychoanalytic theories and the "Book of Abstinence" itself, linked to the analyst's avoidance of excessive, suffocating personal involvement with his or her patients. The patient, in turn, although he or she may seem to try to destroy the analyst as a separate subject—which means forcing a collapse of the analyst's internal dialectic—also has a vital interest in the analyst's survival. Here we return to the patient's ambivalence. The tension within the analyst has its counterpart in a similar tension within the patient. The patient, like the analyst, has an aspect of self that is preoccupied with the other and a side that excludes him or her and has other interests, narcissistic and object related. In effect, the patient as a whole person cannot survive, much less grow, unless both of these aspects survive and grow together in a dialectical relationship, one that has its counterpart in a complementary, living dynamic tension within the analyst. The tolerance of the tension within each participant goes hand-in-hand with tolerating and nourishing the creative potentials of the tension in the other (cf. Benjamin, 1988).

As the analyst, I cannot know just what balance I should strike at any given moment between my own conflicting allegiances and inclinations. Indeed, relevant aspects of my own conflicts at any given time are likely to be unconscious. In fact, analytic therapists in general can safely assume that they do not have privileged access to their own motives, nor are they able, despite their advantageous position, to know exactly what is best for their patients. That is why the attitude that is the most integrative and authentic must be an alloy of doubt and openness (Hoffman, 1987). At any given moment, the sense of uncertainty might be in the background, as the analyst engages in one or another mode of relating with a good deal of conviction. Moreover, whatever the analyst does, we must not forget, in our enthusiasm about "the meanings and uses of countertransference" (Racker, 1968), that his or her influence has real impact in real time. It is not merely a bit of manifest content, like that of a dream (cf. Kern, 1987), that stands in need of interpretation (although it certainly is that too). As discussed in chapter 3, there is a dialectic between the analyst's participation understood as figurative (or symbolic) and the same participation understood as literal (or actual) and as consequential in the patient's life. In either case, the work requires an underlying tolerance of uncertainty and with it a radical, yet critical kind of openness that is conveyed over time in various ways, including a readiness to soul-search, to negotiate, and to change.

The bad object that is lurking in every analytic situation is the one that pulls either of the participants into absolute commitment to one side of his or her conflict (for example, the side that wants to analyze), with the result that the other side (for example, the side that wants to respond in a more spontaneous, personal way) must be abandoned and repressed. The good-enough parent maintains a balance among investments in each child, in spouse (or others), and in self. He or she recognizes the inevitable tensions among these interdependent yet rivalrous attachments but does not abandon any of them. The quality of the attention to the child (and to each of the others), moreover, respects and fosters the same kind of balance and tolerance of tension within him or her. Similarly, analysts, through their capacity to uphold both sides of multiple polarities, can combat the threat of the "single-minded" bad object in themselves and in their patients and create the basis for new experience. Thinking dialectically can be a powerful expression, in itself, of the analyst's struggle to come to grips with the complexity of the patient's multiple aims and potentials as they interface with the analyst's own. Potentiated by the ritually based mystique and authority of the analyst's role, that struggle assumes a position that is at the heart of therapeutic action in the psychoanalytic process.

◆ 9 ◆

Ritual and Spontaneity in the Psychoanalytic Process

PSYCHOANALYTIC RITUALS

There is a fixed routine in the psychoanalytic process, a routine with the kind of symbolic, evocative, and transforming potential that gives it the aura of a ritual.[1] There are fixed times, a fixed place, and a fixed fee. Each appointment is usually 45 or 50 minutes long. Commonly the seating arrangement is the same every time, whether or not it entails the use of the couch. The couch itself, when it is used, adds to the peculiarity of the situation, to its foreignness, and perhaps to the mystique of the now seemingly disembodied analyst's voice.

In addition to these "extrinsic" factors (Gill, 1954, 1984a), within the process itself there is a fundamental asymmetry. The patient is invited to "free associate," and thereby, presumably, to expose the structure of his or her emotional life. The analyst remains strangely hidden or anonymous, strangely, that is, relative to the norms of ordinary social conduct. Although analysts vary considerably in the ways that they conceptualize the role of their own subjective, personal

---

1. Catherine Bell (1992) writes that "ritualization is a way of acting that specifically establishes a privileged contrast, differentiating itself as more important or powerful. Such privileged distinctions may be drawn in a variety of culturally specific ways that render the ritualized acts dominant in status" (p. 90).

reactions in the process, few if any—notwithstanding Ferenczi's experiments late in his life—would advocate the complete break-down of this asymmetry. If there is room in our culture for that kind of process, it is certainly difficult to imagine what it could mean in the context of a professional service in which one party pays the other for confidential psychological help. Indeed, we are in Ferenczi's debt for exposing the untenability of anything approaching a fully mutual analysis. One of the problems Ferenczi (1932) ran into very quickly was that he couldn't possibly speak freely to RN about what came to his mind and still honor the confidentiality of his experiences with other patients, because those experiences were often precisely what came to his mind (p. 34).

The analytic frame, of course, provides the general boundaries for the relationship, a multifaceted scaffolding of protection for both the patient and the analyst. It sets up the special "potential space" in which the "play" of psychoanalysis can go on (Winnicott, 1971; Modell, 1990). As Modell says, "Despite the spontaneity and unpredictability of the affective relationship between the analyst and the analysand, there are also certain affective constants that are institutionalized as part of technique and contribute to the frame or the rules of the game" (p. 30). We usually think of these institutionalized constants, combined with the fixed aspects of the setting, as contributing to a safe environment, one that provides the context for the real analytic work (as in the working alliance) or is in itself the vehicle for a good deal of therapeutic action (as in the holding environment). From this point of view, deviations from psychoanalytic rituals might be thought to endanger the atmosphere of safety that they are designed to foster and their nurturant, development-facilitating potential.

DOES THE FRAME CREATE A SANCTUARY?

There are, however, important counterpoints to the view that the analytic frame establishes a standard, safe environment. First of all, the extent to which the setting can be standardized is limited. Psychoanalytic rituals leave a great deal of room for variations in the manner in which they are carried out. Thus, if the rituals *were* adhered to by an analyst in a very rigid way, that in itself would be experienced by the patient as a choice by the analyst, one that would be highly suspect in terms of its motivation. This goes without saying, of course, for the interactions that go on within the context of the frame but are not themselves conspicuously defining of it. What the analyst will say, for example, between 9:00 A.M., when he or she opens the door and says "come in," and 9:50, when he or she says "it's time to stop," is (or should be) clearly less predictable than those starting points and end points themselves. But it is also the case that even the start of the hour and its conclusion leave much latitude for the analyst to convey a range of personal attitudes and moods. Is the analyst smiling, or frowning, or neither? Does he or she say "Hi, Bob. C'mon in," or just "hello," or nothing—maybe just a slight nod of the head? At the end, does the analyst say, "Our time is up" or "we have to stop now" or "I know this is a difficult moment to stop, but we are out of time for today"?

The conclusion of a session is of special interest. Because it is the last moment, it has special weight. Whatever taste it leaves is apt to linger at least until the next session, which is not to say the taste has to be pleasant. Sometimes it might seem "best" for a session to end on a sour note: depressed or angry or whatever. But it's important to recognize that there is an element of choice, uncertainty, and responsibility associated with the analyst's contribution to the ending. As much as we might like to feel that what we do at the end of a session merely conforms to a standard routine for which we are not personally responsible—a little like merely "following orders"—the conclusion of every session is a joint construction, one that is chosen, in part, by us, however much it is organized around a given, objective boundary.

Suppose a patient says, with about a minute to go, "I feel like I'm going in circles today and not getting anywhere. Frankly, I don't think I've changed much since I started seeing you," and suppose he or she then falls silent. Now there is a half minute or less left. As the analyst, I could wait 20 seconds or so in what might feel like a heavy silence and then simply say, "it's time to stop." We would be ending then on a certain kind of note. I could tell myself that, after all, it's the note the *patient* chose to end on. The patient's action and the clock created that ending, not I. Because it's the ending created by the patient and the standard time limit, it's the "right" one for the patient and me to live with and, perhaps, to explore the next time we meet. Certainly the patient is a major architect of the session's conclusion. To leave it at that, however, would be to deny that in being silent for those last seconds I was *choosing* a course of action and thereby cocreating that ending. First of all, in all likelihood I would not, in fact, know what the time was to the second, but even if I did, I could have said it was time to stop just a few seconds after the patient spoke, or I could have waited about 20 seconds more than I did. These are options that are likely to create three very different endings with very different affective colorations. And then, there is the alternative of actually responding directly to the patient's comment. There are innumerable possibilities of course.[2] On the side of combatting the mood set by the patient, if it seemed to fit, I could say, "I think it means something that you say that right at the end. In fact, I think that it's your way of expressing your anger about having to leave"; or maybe, "Really? I thought that was a good session and that we accomplished a lot. Aren't you doing that number on yourself and on me that we've talked about many times?" Whatever I said, I would then have the option of saying "it's time to stop" right after I made my comment, or waiting a few seconds to give the patient a chance to respond. The latter might be a risk, because I'd be running over and I'd be concerned about inviting a response and then having to cut the patient off. So maybe I'd say, "Unfortunately, it looks like I'm going to have the last word today, because we do have to stop." The point is that each of these options, the various lengths of silence and the various comments that I might make, constructs a different ending and a different reality. Moreover, in that moment, in that split second which is the moment of choice and of action, there is no way to know what is the "right thing" to do. Indeed, there can be no single "right thing" for the patient or for the relationship. The moment is shot through with uncertainty. First, I don't know just what it means that the patient has said what he or she has said. Second, I don't know the full meaning of whatever inclinations I may have to be silent or to speak. And third, whatever I choose to do, I don't know what opportunities are being lost and what would have happened if I had chosen a different course. The safety afforded by the analytic frame is a qualified one in that it cannot spare the patient or the analyst these uncertainties and the anxieties that attend them.

Ultimately, constructing a "good-enough ending" is the challenge of termination, a separation process that can be decisive in terms of the outcome of the entire analysis. And yet the boundary situations

---

2. Of course this is a hypothetical example, so the possibilities of what I might say are relatively unconstrained. But even with a real case, there would be infinite possibilities, although they would be encompassed within a narrower range. "Infinite" does not mean "unlimited." As noted in chapter 3 (p. 77), "there are infinite numerical values between the numbers 5 and 6, but that range excludes all other numerical values."

associated with the endings of sessions and with the ending of the analysis as a whole are also like any moment within every session, which is always both structured by analytic ritual and left to the participants to create. Thus in every moment there is a kind of ricocheting going on, a dialectical interplay between ritual and spontaneity, between what is given and what is created, between what is role-determined and what is personal, between constraint and freedom.

In fact, in a general way, it could be said that in our neuroses we suffer from the dichotomous organization of these polarities, a feeling that the choice is between a suffocating submission to internal and external constraints, on the one hand, and a loss of control in which "all hell breaks loose," on the other. We hope that through analysis it will be possible for us to replace such dichotomous thinking with dialectical thinking, with an integrative sense of the interdependence of apparent opposites. In that light, perhaps, we can reaffirm Freud's aphorism, in somewhat revised form: "where id [and superego were, split off from each other,] there ego shall be, [mediating their dialectical relationship]" (cf. Freud, 1933, p. 80).

Before moving to a fuller clinical illustration, I'd like to discuss another counterpoint to the view of the frame as a kind of sanctuary. Not only is it not possible for the analyst's behavior to be fully standardized, but also the intrinsic features of the frame are not simply benign. Racker (1968) says that no encounter with the actual person of the analyst is necessary in order for the patient to begin speculating about the complementary countertransference. He says:

> [T]he analyst communicates certain associations of a personal nature even when he does not seem to do so. These communications begin, one might say, with the plate on the front door that says 'Psychoanalyst' or 'Doctor.' What motive (in terms of the unconscious) would the analyst have for wanting to cure if it were not he who made the patient ill? In this way the patient is already, simply by being a patient, the creditor, the accuser, the 'superego' of the analyst; and the analyst is his debtor [pp. 145–146].

But is a reparative motive, which is, after all, relatively benign, the only kind that the patient can plausibly attribute to the analyst for assuming this rather peculiar role? It seems to me there are others that are much more threatening to the patient's sense of safety. Is the analyst not the person who has detected a certain need in the society for understanding, for love, for an idealized object; the one who has scanned the culture (usually with special attention to the white, urban middle class and upper class) and thought, "why shouldn't I take advantage of this hunger, this craving that a lot of people have for this kind of attachment"? Is the analyst not also the one who has found a way to feed his or her narcissism without being subjected to very much personal risk, or, perhaps, one who fears and craves intimacy and has found a way to have it while still maintaining a good deal of control and distance, or one who enjoys his or her sense of power over the people (if business is good, the *many* people) who want to be his or her special or favorite one? Finally, what could be better than to have all of this hidden under the guise of being the "good-enough parent" who provides, "objectively," a secure holding environment, armed against whatever protests might arise with knowing interpretations of the "neurotic transference"?

These motives, and others like them, comprise the dark, malignant underside of the analytic frame. It is a side that I think we commonly deny. It's rather astonishing, I think, how ready we are to compare ourselves to rather ideal parents, not perfect perhaps, but surely "good enough," and how prepared we are to see the influence of the pathogenic aspects of the patient's past upon the entry into the analytic space of the so-called "bad object" (cf. Slavin and Kriegman, 1992).

The rituals that constitute the frame are undoubtedly essential to the process, and deviations from them are certainly as open, if not more open, to suspicion regarding their self-serving nature as is their religious observance. What I'm questioning is the *neatness of the dichotomy*: adherence to the frame creates safety, deviation from the frame creates danger. Even if the frame is mostly beneficial, it does not create a perfect sanctuary because, as I have said, it cannot eliminate the analyst's personal participation as a coconstructor of reality in the process and because its defining features are, in themselves, suspect.

Psychoanalytic rituals provide usefully ambiguous grounds, not only for new experience and development, but also for neurotic repetition.[3] Acknowledging this reality has at least two important clinical implications. First, the patient's conscious and unconscious objections to analytic routines, even his or her rage about them, must be taken seriously. By that I mean *more* than that we have to get into the patient's world and see it from his or her point of view. That attitude can be subtly patronizing, to the extent that we consider the patient's perspective to stem from deficits or even from unresolved conflicts originating in childhood, and to the extent that

_____

3. See this volume, pp. 2–3, on Macalpine, 1950.

we hope that the patient will eventually come to see things from a more developmentally advanced perspective. Instead, I mean that we recognize what may be objectionable about the frame, even from the point of view of a mature, "healthy" adult, so much so that we may wonder what kind of pathology would result in a person being willing to go along with it at all! The one in need is the one who may be driven to accept an invitation to be exploited, and the analytic arrangement can be construed, quite plausibly, as extending such an invitation. A second clinical implication of acknowledging the malignant aspects of the frame, in addition to recognizing a place for an unobjectionable *negative* transference (cf. Guidi, 1993) and for reasonable resistance, is that such acknowledgment provides theoretical grounds for considering the benign potentials of momentary deviations from the standard routine. A readiness to deviate in certain limited ways may offset the exploitative meanings that can get attached to maintaining the frame in an inflexible manner. There is no way for the analyst to know, with certainty, what course to pursue with respect to the balance between spontaneous, personal responsiveness and adherence to psychoanalytic rituals at any given moment, nor can the balance that is struck be one that the analyst can completely control. The basis for the patient's trust is often best established through evidence of the analyst's struggle with the issue and through his or her openness to reflect critically on whatever paths he or she has taken, prompted more or less by the patient's reactions and direct and indirect communications.

With these ideas as background, let's take a closer look at a piece of clinical experience.

CONFRONTING A PHOBIA WITHIN
THE ANALYTIC SETTING:
A SERENDIPITOUS OPPORTUNITY

A patient, Ken, is in my private, downtown office on the 21st floor for the first time. For about three years we had met four times per week at my office at the university, which was on the seventh floor. In that office there was one small window at the foot of the couch. Here, there are two enormous windows on the wall across from the couch to the patient's right, about 6 or 7 feet away. The patient is terrified of heights. The theme of high places is at the center of a complex knot of symptoms, an amalgam of depression, anxiety, obsessional tendencies, and phobia. Ken has had full-blown panic attacks just contemplating certain situations that involve heights, not to mention being in them. On one occasion, he traveled to another city for a meeting where he was to make a presentation on a subject of great interest to him. At the last moment, to his dismay and embarrassment, he had to back out, because to get to the room where the meeting took place he would have had to walk across a corridor with a railing overlooking an atrium. But his reactions are variable, and sometimes he has managed very well in situations that could have been disabling. In general, he is a very competent, resourceful person, a mental-health professional himself and a psychotherapist.[4] Ken is also a devoted husband and father of three young children.

At the university office, Ken had generally felt comfortable. He had rarely felt anxious during a session. Sometimes he would get anxious after a session while waiting for the elevator, which was next to a window. Often he would take the stairs rather than wait. He had told me of a fantasy of coming back to the office to ask for some ill-defined help. He had thought of my comforting him or perhaps waiting with him at the elevator, but he never acted on that impulse. In general, he had always been respectful of the conventional limits of the analytic situation and had made good use of it as a context for expressing and exploring the things that troubled him. In many ways he was an ideal analysand, reporting many dreams and experiencing and reflecting upon transference issues in the here and now and in terms of genetics.

Changes in my schedule and Ken's made it more convenient to have first one, then two of our four sessions in my downtown office. The idea of meeting there was broached for the first time by me, anticipating a day when the university would be closed because of a holiday but when I would be working in my practice. Ken actually declined that invitation, but he subsequently brought up the possibility himself because he wanted to take advantage of the opportunity to tackle his fear of heights within the context of the analysis. We did, however, discuss the fact that once the option was made available, Ken felt some internal pressure to try it, along with a sense that I might want him to. And it is true that I thought this might be a serendipitous development. The combination of the two locations

---

4. In an earlier draft of this chapter, this information was disguised. After reading it, the patient said he felt that the disguise took too much away from the atmosphere of the process and that it was not necessary.

could provide the opportunity to confront the phobia directly, as Freud (1919) suggested was necessary with such symptoms, but with the advantage of having that confrontation woven into the analytic routine itself. The latter would include alternation between the "safer" and the more "dangerous" settings.

So, here we are at the end of this first session on the 21st floor. Ken has managed to get through this hour without a major attack of anxiety or vertigo. He was quite anxious at the beginning, although it was not as bad as he had anticipated, especially with the window shades pulled down, something I had done in advance at Ken's request. He said, "I was afraid I would be drawn to the windows and I would become like a robot or an automaton, unable to control myself. And then what would you do? Would you stop me? Of course, I feel that you would." I say that he may have a wish for an experience in which I stop him physically from doing something self-destructive. He says he feels that would be a demonstration of will and strength for his benefit. He reports a dream. "There is a truck with long boards of wood. Somehow I go underneath all the wood boards. They started to slide out of the truck on top of me and I realized I could be crushed. But I got out and I didn't panic. I don't remember whether there was anyone else helping. I think I just got out myself." He spontaneously thinks of the unloading of a truck as a metaphor for the analysis. Then he associates to his father. He thought of him as husky and strong physically, but he always felt threatened by him rather than comforted. He says his father "always wanted to win," whereas he, as a father himself, enjoys roughhousing in a playful way with his own children. I say, "Meeting with me here has a lot of meaning for you I think. It's probably not just the height as such that is affecting you." The patient says, "I could get into resenting it, having to put myself through this. But I do have a sense that we are in this room *together* and that in general we are in the process together, and that helps." Now this much-anticipated and dreaded first time is over. I say it's time to stop. Ken sits up. He seems a bit shaky. Then he looks at me and, rather to my surprise, he says, "I don't feel *too* bad, but I wonder if you'd mind walking to the elevator with me?"

MOMENT OF TRUTH: THOUGHT IN ACTION

I think it's good to stop at points like this to consider the analyst's position, because, as an exercise, it's useful to consider the kinds of attitudes the analyst may have toward the patient's request without the benefit of hindsight.

The instant the patient's question is posed I am called upon to act. There is no way that I can "call time" to think it over. If I hesitate or if I say, "Well, wait, let's think about this for a moment," or "maybe you could say a little more about what you're feeling," I am of course *acting* in a particular way. There is no way to just think about it without acting, and however I act will have some sort of complex meaning to myself and to the patient. The commonsense idea, one that is highly valued psychoanalytically, that I should think *before* I act is of little or no help in this respect. It certainly will not do to say "let's think about it and talk about it more tomorrow and then we'll see." The moment of truth is now. What I do will express *something* about me, about our relationship, and about the patient. While it cannot be action following thought in a linear way, it might, nevertheless, be action that is saturated with thought or thought-full.

Does it make any sense to ask what is the right thing or the best thing for the analyst to do? Many would say, "it depends." More needs to be known about the patient, his history, his dynamics, the status of the transference, and the nature of the process in this very session. I have told you so little, after all, of what I know or knew, so little, one might say, of what was "going through my mind." But even if I could explicate all of the issues pertaining to that list of considerations about the patient, to what extent would that put us in a better position to decide what I should have done and with what attitude? Is an accurate assessment of the patient's state of mind possible? And if it were possible, would it be enough?

The alternative to the view that the analyst should act simply in accord with an assessment of the patient takes it for granted that the analyst acts in relation to a complex, only partially conscious, organization of his or her own thoughts and feelings. In the moment of action there is no sharp split between what is personally expressive and what is in keeping with one's technical principles or diagnostic assessment. Expressive participation and psychoanalytic discipline are intertwined (chapter 7). If there is a "right" or best thing for the analyst to do, it might be something that is *integrative* of as many considerations about the *relationship* as possible. From the point of view of a supervisor or consultant, for example, the information that is relevant would have to include the nature of the analyst's experience. And the suggestions that a supervisor would make would take account of the analyst's involvement in the process. The supervisor might say, "Given that the patient was apparently experiencing such and such and that you [the analyst-supervisee] were experiencing such and such, might it have been useful to do or say this or that?" Let me emphasize that I'm not saying that this "given" in the analyst's experience should be immune from criticism. After all, there are certain attitudes and perspectives that we try to cultivate so that the probability will be higher that our experience will at least include certain properties: empathic listening, for example, theoretically informed understanding, critical reflection on our own participation, and so on. In fact, part of my purpose in this paper is to convey my own sense of the optimal analytic attitude, one that allows for a range of countertransference experiences that can be used constructively to promote the process.

SOME BACKGROUND: A CHILDHOOD
OF SCARCE LOVE AND DREADED IMPULSE

Certainly, as I said, I have conveyed only a small fraction of the information about the patient that was relevant to my action at that moment. In fact, what I could formulate to myself at that time, not to mention what I can recapture from memory, is probably only a fraction of the information I was processing. Considerations of confidentiality limit even further what I can convey to you accurately. Finally, whatever information is selected and however it is organized constructs a story line of some kind, a particular narrative account among the many that might be pertinent and even compelling (Schafer, 1992). With those qualifications, here are a few more highlights from the patient's history.

Ken was an only child. His mother was alcoholic, estranged from her unsympathetic, self-centered husband, painfully lonely, and often depressed. When the patient was 15 years old she killed herself, using a combination of drugs, a plastic bag over her head, and gas sucked in from a Bunsen burner from the patient's chemistry set. The patient came home from school one day and found the house locked. A note on the door suggested he go to a neighbor's house until his father came home. Later, the father and the patient descended the winding stairs to the basement where they found the mother's body. There was a note addressed to the patient that read: "I had to do this. I couldn't take it anymore. You go on and have a happy life. You're great." In this act, the mother constructed, not a "good enough" ending, surely, but a catastrophic one for her son to carry with him for the rest of his life.

The patient's father was a salesman. He was very narcissistic, full of a kind of bravado, a macho style that was decidedly unempathic in terms of its responsiveness to the patient's needs and sense of vulnerability. The father's "competitiveness" was so extreme it often deteriorated into virtual abuse. Here's one telling story. In playing one-on-one basketball when the patient was in his early teens, the father, who was much taller, was happy to block all the patient's shots and win the game ten to nothing. Indeed, Ken, who was a quiet, sensitive type and something of a bookworm, often felt his father didn't particularly like him. In fact, Ken thought his father preferred two of his nephews, both of whom liked hunting and fishing, activities that were quite abhorrent to the patient.

Ken had only scant and fragmentary memories of his mother. What was particularly striking was that he had vivid memories of parts of her body, distinct images of them in the bathtub, for example, especially her breasts, which he admired. He had more difficulty remembering her face, not to mention difficulty recapturing a sense of her as a whole person. Toward the end of the first year of the analysis the patient recalled a moment in his early teenage years when, looking at his mother passed-out drunk in her bed, while his father was out of town on one of his many business trips, he thought to himself, "Why don't I just have sex with her and get her pregnant. Maybe that will enliven her and make her happy." Ken also had conscious wishes that his mother would die, which were countered, in part, by his realizing that her death would leave him alone with his father. Many times he fantasized wishfully and anxiously about his father being killed in a plane crash and not returning from one of his trips. At times, he was also very afraid of his father. On one occasion he refused to go on an amusement park ride with him for fear that his father would push him out of the elevated car to his death.

Thus, perhaps an important aspect of the atmosphere of the patient's childhood could be characterized as one that was full of the dangers of eruption of incestuous, patricidal, matricidal, and infanticidal impulses. We developed a picture of his environment as one in which he felt that he was left alone with dangerous temptations. He had a sense that it was all too easy for him and others to act on impulses that were destructive to him, to them, or to both. It felt like he had only his own will to prevent an action that could be disastrous, and his own will often did not seem up to the challenge. He had his parents as models, after all. In the end, through an act signifying the ultimate abdication of responsibility, his mother left him with a terrible choice. He could try to demonstrate that one could be moved by forces beyond one's control to do oneself in. If he threw himself out the window, or more precisely, if he succumbed to what he experienced as a force drawing him out the window, he could say, "This must be how it was for her; she loved me but could not stop herself." But if he stopped himself with thoughts like, "what will become of those I care about, including my children?" he was left with the agonizing question as to why she couldn't or wouldn't have done the same for him.

A WALK TO THE ELEVATOR:
AN EXPERIENCE IN "LIMINAL" SPACE

Let us return now to Ken's request. Notice that it occurs after the "official time" is up. Now we are in that interval that occurs in every analytic hour between the ending of the formally allotted time and the moment the patient leaves the office. I think it's a particularly interesting time because it is both inside and outside the frame. It occupies a place akin to what the anthropologist Victor Turner (1969) identifies as "liminal." Turner (1969) writes, "Liminal entities are neither here nor there; they are betwixt and between the positions assigned and arrayed by law, custom, convention, and ceremonial" (p. 95). Although Turner is interested in liminality as it is reflected specifically in the rites of passage of certain tribal cultures, what he has to say about it can be generalized to other aspects of social life (cf. Fourcher, 1975). Indeed, the basic dialectic that *underlies* social life is *exposed* under the conditions of liminality. This is the dialectic of spontaneous, egalitarian relatedness, what Turner calls "communitas," and structured, hierarchical role-relatedness:

> It is as though there are two major "models" for human interrelatedness, juxtaposed and alternating. The first is of society as a structured, differentiated, and often hierarchical system of politico-legal-economic positions with many types of evaluation, separating men in terms of "more" or "less." The second, which emerges recognizably in the liminal period, is of society as an unstructured or rudimentarily structured and relatively undifferentiated comitatus, community, or even communion of equal individuals who submit together to the general authority of the ritual elders. . . . [F]or individuals and groups, social life is a type of dialectical process that involves successive experience of high and low, communitas and structure, homogeneity and differentiation, equality and inequality [pp. 96–97].

And further, very much in keeping with my view of the analytic process, Turner writes that "wisdom is always to find the appropriate relationship between structure and communitas under the *given* circumstances of time and place, to accept each modality when it is paramount without rejecting the other, and not to cling to one when its present impetus is spent" (p. 139).

So when the time is up we enter that peculiar, liminal zone that is "neither here nor there." I think it's useful to consider it not only for its own sake, but also because it exposes more clearly the dialectic between ritual and spontaneity within the process as a whole. The strategy is analogous to learning about so-called normal mental processes by studying psychopathology. In this instance we have not only the period in the office after the time is up, which, after all, is ironically a part of normal analytic routine, but the prospect of time spent with the patient outside the office. In these two liminal zones, the one more outside the ritual than the other, the personal-egalitarian aspect of my relationship with Ken is highlighted and partially extricated from the role-defined hierarchical aspect, so that the tension between the two is felt more acutely than usual.

I responded to Ken's request immediately, simply by saying "sure," and we walked to the elevators. My immediate feeling was that it would have been extremely stingy of me to decline or even to hesitate, since it had been such an ordeal for Ken to tolerate the session in this office. I knew, after all, that the idea of meeting at this location was initiated originally by me. Also, the patient's request, an aggressive initiative on his part, was out of character. It was a risk for him to make it, and I thought he might well feel not only disappointed, but also humiliated if I said no. I certainly didn't want to be like his father blocking his shots in basketball. That danger seemed greater to me than the dangers of complying. Also, because the request was so unusual, I felt inclined to give the patient the benefit of the doubt and respect whatever creative wisdom might have prompted it. Another consideration might have been that I felt that, over time, I had conveyed enough of an impression of personal availability to contribute to the patient's readiness to make the request. In any case, as Ken and I waited in the hallway we made a little small talk about the elevators, the express type versus the local type, which stopped at which floors, which he came up on, and so on. After a couple of minutes, one opened up and Ken stepped in. We shook hands just as the doors began to shut. It was not our customary way of parting. I'm not sure which of us reached out first.

Before getting to the patient's retrospective view of the experience the next day I want to stop to talk a bit more about the episode at the elevator, an example of an "extra-analytic" interaction. How do we conceptualize the nature of the interaction in the hallway? On the surface it could hardly be more mundane. Just a little, rather uninteresting small talk. But as we are waiting there is a little tension in the air, a touch of awkwardness, and a feeling that what's happening has a little extra "charge." Would we say that the analyst, ideally, would feel entirely comfortable in that situation? Would we say that the patient, too, would be comfortable the closer he was to completing his analysis? My own view is that regardless of the specific personalities of the participants, and regardless of the amount and quality of analytic work each has under his or her belt, there is a residue of tension that is *likely* because here, in the hallway, outside the psychoanalytic routines of time, place, and role-defined interactions, the analyst emerges out of the shadows of his or her analytic role and is exposed, more fully than usual, as a person like the patient, as a vulnerable social and physical being.[5] At this moment, in Turner's terms, "communitas," a sense of equality and of mutuality, moves into the foreground while role-determined, hierarchical structure shifts to the background. This reversal of figure and ground is likely to feel conflictual because both parties have much invested in the analyst's relative invisibility. The analyst's capacity for an encompassing perspective and for constructive use of his or her special expertise is enhanced by the protections against narcissistic injury that a position of relative anonymity affords. This aspect of the ritual provides some rational ground for the analyst's authority in relation to the analysand. Beyond those rational grounds, however, there is an irrational component to that authority, a certain element of mystique[6] that gives the analyst a special kind of power. Only with that magical increment of power does the analyst stand a chance of doing battle with pathogenic object relations that were absorbed before the patient was old enough to think, or most importantly, to think critically. And only the analyst's relative anonymity can allow the patient to invest him or her with that magical power,

---

5. This heightened sense of visibility can occur within the customary hour too, at times, as might happen if the analyst moves to open a window or changes the furniture arrangement or the place where he or she sits.

6. The authority and the mystique are *ironic* because the grounds for them have been largely eroded in our culture and because within the process itself they are subjected to critical scrutiny in the analysis of the transference (see chapters 1 and 3).

one that represents, in more or less attenuated form, the power of the longed for omniscient, omnipotent, and loving parent.

So, it's not surprising that there is a little tension and a little awkwardness accompanying the small talk as we wait for the elevator. But it would be misleading to say that the special authority of the analyst, both its rational and its irrational components, are dissolved in these circumstances. Let's not forget that a reversal of figure and ground does not mean that one side of a dialectic is sacrificed in favor of the other. Rather, the two poles, that of spontaneous, egalitarian, informal participation and that of authority-enhancing, role-related, formal participation, continue to work in tandem, synergistically, the one potentiating the impact of the other. On a personal level, many relational themes are being played out, more than I can mention here, and more, indeed, than either participant could be aware of back then, or even now in retrospect. For one thing, this is a kind of transgression that I am joining the patient in, a bit of mischief in relation to the psychoanalytic "authorities," the tribal "elders," but also in relation to those authorities as they are internalized as part of my own (and maybe the patient's) psychoanalytic conscience. There is also a sense, however, that the transgression is a minor one, a forgivable one, even, perhaps, a constructive one. We both know that we will be back inside the analytic frame the next day and we both fully expect that this very interlude of escape from it, this relatively "frameless" experience, as Grotstein (1993) calls it, will probably be subjected to routine analytic scrutiny. We will then be able to explore the latent meanings of our interaction in the hallway as though it were part of the manifest content of a dream (cf. Kern, 1987).

Aided partly by this expectation, at the very moment that I transgress I am aware, implicitly, that the patient and I are also trying to construct a *noncatastrophic* transgression, a *nonincestuous, nonsuicidal, nonhomicidal* violation of the rules. We are trying to differentiate this illicit act, stepping out the door together, from stepping out of the 21st-floor window, from being drawn into an incestuous abyss with the mother, from killing the mother, from killing the father, from being killed by the father, from the mother killing herself. In these scenarios, the patient may be either in the parent's or in the child's role, casting the analyst into the complementary position. All these potential differentiations—in which, hopefully, something new will emerge out of the shadows of something old—all these possibilities have special power, not only because they have been or will be understood analytically, but also because in the background it is the analyst who is participating in them and authorizing them. By making more vivid the patient's sense, as Ken puts it, "that we are in this together," by being, for the moment, a person conspicuously like the patient himself, by trusting the patient's conscious judgment, by extending myself beyond what is most comfortable for me (which reciprocates the patient's extension of himself in coming to my private office), by spending some time with the patient that is not paid for, by all of these simultaneous actions and others, I have at least a fighting chance, as the analyst, operating with the mantle of authority that is uniquely mine by virtue of my ritually based position, of overcoming the soul-murdering impact of the parents' conduct. I have a chance of reaching the patient with messages such as, "You are a person of worth; you have a right to be fully alive; you don't have to be buried alive under those wood boards; your feelings matter; you deserve respect as a unique individual; you can have concrete impact on me without destroying me or yourself; your desire, even when it runs counter to what is conventionally sanctioned, is not necessarily deadly; indeed, that desire has the potential to do more good than harm."[7] In sum, I am in a position to offer the patient a profound kind of recognition and affirmation. What is transformative, however, is not this action alone, but a continual struggle with the tension between spontaneous responsiveness and adherence to psychoanalytic ritual and a continual effort, in Turner's (1969) words, "to accept each modality when it is paramount without rejecting the other" (p. 139).

Now let's return to the particulars of the process and consider the patient's experience of the episode as he reported it the next day, now in the relative comfort of the university office.

THE PATIENT'S REFLECTIONS:
COCONSTRUCTING NEEDS AND WISHES

"When I asked you to walk me to the elevator I wondered if you were irritated. But I felt you were being friendly and supportive in the hallway. I had very mixed emotions about asking you to do that, because I was actually feeling good enough. It wasn't a necessity. I didn't feel like I had become liquid and needed you to pour me into

---

7. The point bears a rough similarity to that of Strachey (1934) on the therapeutic action of mutative interpretations via the analyst's acceptance of the patient's "id-impulses."

the elevator. Yet I was afraid if I didn't ask I might just be over-whelmed at the last minute. Then I was also conscious that maybe I was testing you a little to see how flexible you would be. That does-n't feel real terrific. A little dishonest maybe." I asked. "Did you plan on it beforehand?" Ken replied, "Yes, as a kind of contingency plan. But then it got to be sort of a superstition." I said, "So it was impor-tant in itself, just the wish that I go with you." Ken replied, "Yes, and *without* the excuse of my being terrified."

The patient then expressed interest in how my career was going. He wondered whether my colleagues, if they knew about it, would approve of my walking with him to the elevator. He also expressed concern about the sincerity of my action. Maybe its self-aggrandiz-ing purpose was to impress others with, and congratulate myself for, my independence of mind. He thought maybe his doubts were car-ried over from his mistrust of his parents. He grew up feeling there was something uncertain about the extent and quality of their inter-est in his well-being. His mother seemed very pleased by his excellent grades, but did not want him to tell others about them lest they become envious. So the grades became a kind of guilty secret between them and a special gift just for her. His next associations were the following: "You know, something was going on with me then sexu-ally too. I was looking up little girl's dresses and there was the sex play with the little girl next door. We were taking turns in the closet, dropping our pants and exhibiting ourselves. It was such a small house. How could my mother not know what was going on in the back bedroom?"

There are many issues raised by this vignette. What I want to emphasize is the fact that the patient spontaneously brings up the possibility that his own behavior was manipulative *after* I complied with his request. In effect he says that he might have been disguising a forbidden, oedipal wish, one that had the potential to jeopardize my "marriage" to the analytic community, as a developmental need. He also comments, however, that if he didn't ask, "he might have been overwhelmed at the last minute." It is easy to imagine that he might have panicked if he had asked and I had said no. I think it's probable that the sense that there was something dubious about the request might not have developed or jelled enough for the patient to verbalize it to himself, much less to me. So the act of acceding to the patient's request facilitates the emergence of his sense that the request might not have been necessary, whereas a refusal to accede to it, or even signs of reluctance, might have fostered a feeling in him that I was withholding help when he desperately needed it. One might say that the way the analyst responds influences the kind of experience that is created or "constructed" within the patient at that moment. One of the central implications of "constructivism" in psychoanalysis is just this: namely, that the patient's experience does not emerge in a vacuum but is, rather, partly a result of what the analyst is doing or conveying (chapters 5 and 6; Mitchell, 1991). The interaction of the experiences of the participants is constructed in that sense, not just in the sense of interpretation that attaches meaning to those experiences "after the fact," so to speak. Before that, there is the active construction of the "fact" itself.[8]

That the patient reflects on the illicitly wishful aspects of his request and then associates to "forbidden" sexual acts in his childhood is of special interest, because the entire episode is occurring against a backdrop of struggle between myself and the patient in which I was usually the one to suggest that his symptoms had *partly* to do with unresolved conflicts about sexuality and aggression, whereas he took the position that his problems stemmed more simply from not feeling sufficiently appreciated and loved. Once he summed up two years of analytic work by saying that he thought the heart of what he was learning in analysis was that he wanted people to like him, a formulation that I thought fell a bit short of the complexity and profundity of my own interpretive contributions. Sometimes Ken would report extraordinarily evocative dreams, full of images of sex and violence in a somewhat disinterested manner, almost as though he was bored by them. Meanwhile, I'd be bursting with ideas about what they might mean. We came to understand this scene as an enactment in which the patient was like his sexually enticing but inert, semiconscious, inebriated mother while I was in a position like the one he was in as a child: left alone with my psychoanalytic "drives." So, to put it a bit schematically, I was caught in a dilemma: I could interpret actively and be experienced as a kind of rapist, or I could be more passive and compliant and be experienced as one who, through a kind of benign neglect, allowed the patient to drift along, identified with his mother, in his own semiconscious, anesthetized state.

I might add that Ken had a great deal of interest in psychoanalysis and had read a lot of Freud and of Kohut. He never could quite locate me because, although it was clear to him that I was not

---

8. No "backward causation" is implied here. The issue is the construction of experience as it is developing through the interaction, what I have called the "prospective" aspect of constructivism (see chapter 6).

Kohutian, I did not seem to fit his preconceptions of what a Freudian would be like either. It pleases me that in the course of the analysis he seemed to come to an understanding of himself that involved some kind of integration of the two perspectives, an integration reflecting, not surprisingly, something more like my own viewpoint. He still thought, however, somewhat to my disappointment, that self psychology could encompass the integration we had developed. So in the end we had negotiated a compromise, although, thankfully no doubt, we still had our share of healthy differences.

EXISTENTIAL AND SYMPTOMATIC PANIC

It is not hard to understand the patient's panic as a symptom, one that can be interpreted in a variety of ways. One that I referred to earlier is that it reflects Ken's sense, fostered by a variety of traumatic events and themes in his life, that he and others might not be able to inhibit acting upon enormously destructive impulses. One might say that the patient felt that he was always in danger of losing his sense of his own humanity, that he could at any moment become a robot, a monster, or a very destructive, instinctually driven animal. Interestingly, one of the first things he said to me was that he was pleased to see that I had a book by Kohut in my bookcase because he didn't want to be perceived as "a bundle of drives." The patient was obsessed with certain horrifying images, one of which was of a woman whose normal outward appearance concealed a completely mechanical apparatus under the skin. Another image that preoccupied him was that of a certain type of reptile, or a type of toad, the slimiest and ugliest he had ever encountered. He was disgusted by these images but sometimes couldn't get them out of his mind. The force of gravity came to represent the force of his own instinctual life pulling him down, pulling him into an incestuous snare with his mother who, figuratively, was continually calling to him from her grave.

In the transference, the patient's panic got organized around a conflict between a longing to be taken over by me and fiercely competitive ambitions. A central task was to differentiate the possibility of my benign influence (through consideration of interpretations, through absorption of my regard for him, and through selective identifications) from what the patient seemed to experience unconsciously as an emasculating homosexual submission.[9] The complementary task was to differentiate expressions of his own healthy ambition and competitiveness in our relationship from murderous inclinations. Full-scale panic attacks, accompanied by a kind of vertigo, would often occur in the office when I was saying something that the patient felt was important for him to consider. Sometimes the governing unconscious paradigm seemed to be "kill or be killed" or "rape or be raped" reflected symbolically as a conflict within the patient between speaking in a controlling way and passively listening. At times, the patient's urgent need to block my speaking, to block my "shots," as it were, took the form of a full-blown panic attack. As I spoke, he'd raise his hand and say "stop, please." Then, shuddering, he'd turn on his side and face the back of the couch.

These were just a few of the dynamics underlying the symptom that we explored. But to think of Ken's panic only as a symptom obscures its existential, universal implications. Symptoms are often thought of as involving partial misappraisals of what is possible in the present associated with experiences that were not optimal and not necessary in the course of development. Many would say that these difficulties can be alleviated in analysis by a combination of new understanding and a corrective interpersonal experience, an experience that facilitates development and that obviates the need for the symptom as a way of dealing with psychological predicaments. Even if we no longer think of the therapeutic action of analysis as a matter of simply making the unconscious conscious, but rather of "negotiating," opening up, and promoting new ways of being in the world, we are also not likely to consider the route to health to be one that entails, ironically, a certain increment in self-deception. If it's not simply a matter of making what is unconscious conscious, we'd nevertheless be averse to thinking that it's a matter of making what is conscious unconscious! Yet I think there is a kernel of truth in that seemingly paradoxical idea.

Human consciousness brings with it the awareness that to invest in and care about ourselves and others entails, not only the risk of devastating loss, but absolute knowledge of its inevitability. Our

---

9. The issues appear to be related to what Freud (1937) referred to as "biological bedrock," the repudiation of femininity, which in men takes the form, according to Freud, of an inability to allow themselves to be influenced by their analysts (presumably male) because such influence is equated with castration.

challenge is to be fully engaged in living, even though we know we are heading right toward the edge of the cliff and that there is no way to avoid going over it.[10] Ken is right; we *are* going out that window. There is a sense in which catastrophic anxiety, utter debilitating terror, is always rational and the absence of it is always irrational.[11] That is, to invest in and enjoy life means, in some measure, avoiding thinking about death; it means drawing the blinds, it means huddling up against a protective wall, against the back of an analyst's couch. Of course, there is an irony here because the irrational becomes rational when we recognize that that avoidance is our most sensible course. We might as well build our "sandcastles" (Mitchell, 1986) because the alternative leaves us alone with the vertigo of meaninglessness. With full acknowledgement of their looming presence, we nevertheless have to turn our *attention* away from our mortality and from a haunting sense of our ultimate insignificance in order to make living possible at all. The universal bad object is out there for all of us as nothing but the human condition. To combat it we band together in groups, in families, in communities, in cultures, to make and sustain our sense of worth. As part of that spectacular effort that is as natural to human beings as building nests is to birds, we imbue the mind-bodies of our children with love before they are able to think critically. We lock-in their sense of worth in such a way that they can withstand the assault of reflective consciousness and yet join us in the business of socially constructing some kind of sustaining reality (Berger and Luckmann, 1967; also see Nagel, 1986).

This locking-in of self-worth is precisely what my patient, Ken, did not get enough of from the critical authorities, namely his parents, in the critical period when he needed it most and was most open to it. Not only did he not get enough love and affirmation in that phase to buffer his awareness of the void that surrounds us all, but in the end, his mother, as a consequence surely of her own unspeakable suffering, removed whatever porous shield her presence may have offered against the harsh reality of an indifferent universe. She, in her anguish, presented him instead with a devastating mes-

---

10. Jessie Taft (1933), the Rankian, writes, "To put it very simply, perhaps the human problem is no more than this: If one cannot live forever is it worth while to live at all?" (p. 13).

11. Freud, unfortunately, never took death anxiety seriously in his theory building, an omission that has all the signs of defensive denial (chapter 2; Becker, 1973).

sage, one that is not manifestly in her suicide note and that, if any-thing, makes a mockery of it. That unspoken message calls attention to the tenuousness of the prototypical bond of mother and child and therefore, simultaneously, to the tenuousness of the child's sense of selfhood. Whatever the sincerity of her intentions, the mother's overt pronouncement, "you are great," carries with it the covert message "you are nothing," a message that exposes the fact that the crucial background supports for our sense of meaning and worth are not divinely authorized. Rather, they are nothing more nor less than human constructions, grounds for living that people have the power to build and to destroy. To know that, of course, is to know imme-diately that our sense of meaningful selfhood is partly illusory. If, as Mitchell (1986) has written, "narcissism entails the attribution of illusory value" (p. 108), one may ask just what attribution of value is *not* illusory?[12]

In the face of the crushing reality of death, what remains is a need to turn away from it enough to affirm life, and the route to such affirmation (beyond what can be accomplished by parents with chil-dren) often entails the magic of ritual. Funeral and memorial services and other ritualized aspects of mourning are among those social practices that function most clearly as attempts to combine support for grieving with buttressing the conviction of the bereaved that it makes sense for them to go on with their lives. Freud himself, despite his rationalism, came to recognize the irrational component in the therapeutic action of psychoanalysis. In the *New Introductory Lectures* (1933), in the same passage in which he said "where id was, there ego shall be," Freud discussed the psychological impact of "mystical practices" and commented, undoubtedly grudgingly, that "it may be admitted that the therapeutic efforts of psychoanalysis have chosen a *similar line of approach*" (p. 80; italics added).

FRAGMENTS OF A TERMINATION

I shall close by reporting a few of Ken's very rich dreams in the ter-mination phase of his analysis. About five months before the end he reported a dream in which he was on a field where "they had let loose a whole bunch of animals from the zoo: armadillos and one

---

12. See Mitchell (1986) following Winnicott on "going out to meet and match the moment of hope" in analysis (p. 115).

animal I made up, this big scaly thing like an anteater. It had big folds of skin all over it. The skin was so scaly that I couldn't see the face. And I just found it disgusting." In the same session Ken reported a dream in which he was walking around in a downtown street, feeling aroused and wanting to masturbate. He felt he was close to an orgasm but that he first had to find a woman with whom he could make eye contact, someone who would look at him with a warm and lively expression. In these dreams we can see the tension between the patient's horror of a mindless life of the flesh and his groping for a way to integrate his own sexuality with interpersonal engagement and personal wholeness.

With regard to the patient's difficulty allowing *me* to be the one who could help him to achieve that integration, not long before, the patient dreamt that he was eating some kind of fish with maggots in it that turned into something like fruit-fly larvae. He took some into his mouth but then spit them out, feeling disgusted and like he wanted to throw up. We talked about the patient's aversion to incorporating something from me, perhaps very specifically a particular line of interpretation having to do with sexual conflict, but more broadly, whatever I, as a man, had to offer him. Then about a month before the end, the patient reported the following dream:

> I was down in the basement. Someone was trying to get in with a drill. The basement in the dream is like a fortress. There is a big door with a deadbolt and a key lock. Somebody is drilling a hole in it. And I am standing there by the door thinking I can almost see the point of the drill coming through. And I think it was you out there. And I have the idea that if I can put my finger on the point of the drill you'll know I'm in there and that I'm alive. And I'm thinking that it's dangerous. [Laughs] This gets so phallic as I speak. I don't know how big the drill is. If you stand too close to it it could run right into your body. So the fears are there, and yet somehow it also feels like it's going to be OK.

So here is the patient identified with his mother and yet struggling to differentiate himself from her. He's in the basement where she killed herself, and there I am outside, perhaps like he was outside when he came home from school that awful day when he found the door locked. But now there is some kind of rescue operation going on. In order to be saved, to make contact, he has to touch that phallic object, he has to let himself be reached and touched by my own attempts to break through to him. To do this he has either to overcome the sense that the contact is necessarily sexual, or better, to be less threatened by whatever sexual and aggressive dimensions there may be in our encounter. Finally, he has to let me reach him, despite his having felt impotent to reach his mother. Here he has to overcome a need he feels to absolve himself by proving that such "awakenings" are simply impossible.

And apropos of my theme in this chapter, the moment of contact in the dream occurs in a moment of trespass. Someone is breaking into the basement of Ken's home. An intruder is entering where, presumably, he has no place, where he does not belong. The law is being broken, the patient's private space is being violated. Surely this cannot be a precedent, a prescription for a way of living. Locks on doors are there for safety, there to create environments in which we can live with some semblance of security, even environments in which we can create illusions of security, in which we can hide from the terror of annihilation. But there are times when our "security systems" reach a point of diminishing returns and they need to be deactivated, if only temporarily. So it is with the analytic frame. It's there to protect us, to create an environment that is especially conducive to both exploration of meaning and affirmation of worth. But it has its dark, suffocating side, especially when it is taken too seriously and adhered to too zealously. Thus, the ideal holding environment becomes one in which the frame itself is fully understood to be a construction, a set of ritual activities that are enriched by their integration with the analyst's personal, spontaneous participation. Such participation sometimes takes the form of limited departures from the frame, excursions into liminal space, although more commonly it involves qualities of naturalness and spontaneity that are mingled with the ritualized, role-determined aspects of the process. Analysis then becomes a model for living, a rich dialectic between plunging into experience and reflecting on its meaning (Becker, 1973, p. 199). It entails for the analyst an integration of being with the patient as a fellow human being, sharing the same kind of personal vulnerability, and being, *ironically*, the very one who is idealized and authorized by the culture and by the patient himself or herself to bestow upon the patient a sense of personal significance and worth, the kind that stands a chance of overcoming the most profound kinds of childhood injuries, even as they are joined by the inexorable insults of the human condition.

ADDENDUM

In the last hour, Ken brought me a gift, a fossil sculpture reminiscent of a time when he and his father went hunting for fossils, a memory that was recovered now for the first time and that was one of the very few fond memories he had of his father. The gift, also interpreted by the patient as symbolic of the excavations of the analysis, was accompanied by a note, one that was a far cry, needlesss to say, from the one the mother left upon her "termination." Ken's note read, in part, "I can't describe all that you've meant to me. You know anyway. I'm going to continue to try to let you into my life." After I said it was time to stop, we stood tentatively in that liminal space, a moment in time that was both "inside" and "outside" the analysis. As I reached out to shake Ken's hand, he said, "If you don't mind, I'd rather have a hug." We embraced and said goodbye, thereby, coconstructing, hopefully, a good-enough ending for that last hour and for the analysis.

· 10 ·

Constructing Good-Enough
Endings in Psychoanalysis

NO EXIT

"One always dies too soon—or too late. And yet one's whole life is complete at that moment, with a line drawn neatly under it, ready for the summing up. You are—your life, and nothing else." So says Inez in Jean-Paul Sartre's *No Exit*. She and her two "dead" companions, Garcin and Estelle, are in hell, stuck forever in a locked room where they must endlessly confront themselves and each other on their moral failures. There is no time left now for remorse, for atonement, for redeeming actions.

ESTABLISHING THE MEANING OF
EXPERIENCE: PRESENT AND PAST

In a sense, each moment in life is like that. It stands forever as we lived it. Whatever choices we've made, moreover, express only facets of ourselves. The potentials of many other facets are inevitably sacrificed. Some of our choices shape only brief experiences while other decisions mold more substantial parts of our lives. Although we cannot change any moment as it was experienced, we can make choices that affect the meaning to us of any particular moment as we think of it *in retrospect*. If we choose to sever a relationship with someone

245

after a quarrel, we are choosing, in effect, to interpret the quarrel as the prelude to the end, the straw that broke the camel's back. If, instead, we choose to surprise that person with an affectionate gesture a day or two after the argument, and we and that person then proceed to resolve our differences, we are choosing, in effect, to regard the original event as a difficult juncture in the course of building a close relationship, a conflict that we might eventually regard as contributing to mutual understanding and trust. The action itself, severing the relationship or making the affectionate gesture, whether or not it reflects a formulated perspective on the quarrel, is also implicitly interpretive of its meaning. In the heat of the dispute, a person's preconscious, unformulated experience (Stern, 1983) might contain both the potential for severance and the potential for reconciliation and increased closeness. The handwriting may be on the wall for both pathways, including countless variations of each, even though only one course comes into being. Also, the way it goes might well be affected by innumerable possible *extraneous* experiences. A success, a stroke of luck, a piece of good news about an entirely different matter could put us in good spirits and promote the more generous, conciliatory gesture. Conversely, a failure, a piece of misfortune, or a piece of bad news could put us in poor spirits and promote the angrier, unforgiving response. Death puts an end to any chance to revise the meaning of our experience by reinterpreting earlier experiences in light of later ones, and the anticipation of death includes the anticipation of that final boundary.

ESTABLISHING THE MEANING OF EXPERIENCE: CHOICE AND CONTINGENCY

Much, of course, from the moment we were conceived, was not in our control. Sheer luck has a lot to do with what we experience on any given day, not to mention in the course of our lives (Rescher, 1995). We didn't choose our genetic makeup or the environments into which we were born. We didn't choose the families, the cultures, or the historical periods of our births. And throughout our lives, a huge proportion of our experience is shaped by circumstances not of our making. Against that massive background of contingency, the individual's capacity for choice may seem like barely a glimmering. Yet close up, within a subjective standpoint, that capacity is highly consequential, conferring immense responsibility upon the individual for the course of his or her life.

Although we generally want to help our patients gain control over as much of their lives as possible, we also want to help them to come to grips with the realities of chance, arbitrariness, and even meaninglessness. As Adam Phillips (1994) says:

> Given the obvious contingency of much of our lives—we do not in any meaningful sense intend or choose our birth, our parents, our bodies, our language, our culture, our thoughts, our dreams, our desires, our death, and so on—it might be worth considering, from a psychoanalytic point of view, not only our relationships to ourselves and our relationships to objects but (as the third of the pair, so to speak) our relationships to accidents [p. 9].

In the same vein, Jane Flax (1996) writes of the outcome of a "successful" analysis:

> The patient learns that she or he can live with multiple, often contradictory stories, and develops the capacity to revise them as necessary in ongoing life struggles. At least as important, the patient learns to tolerate the absence of meaning, the limits of narrative organization, and the ineradicable persistence of unintelligibility. The capacity to construct meaning or story lines, like all human powers, is finite. Some events or experiences happen randomly or are too horrible to comprehend. Sometimes we confront experiences that simply are; we cannot make sense of them, fit them into a believable story line, or understand their causes. They cannot be incorporated into or contained within livable meaning systems. We can only register their existence and some of their effects on us [p. 589].

As analysts and patients, to assume responsibility for our choices is not to say that whatever ensues is our fault. It is rather to accept, to take on fully, the ambiguous mix of our own intended influence, our own unintended influence, and the impact of other factors over which we have no control.[1] From the perspective of the analyst, one of those "other factors" is the patient's own will (cf. Thompson, 1994). Sometimes analysts collude with their patients' resistance to integrating that simple reality, namely, that an act of will on the patient's part is required for there to be even a chance that some movement will take place. By definition, the analyst cannot "make"

---

1. As Schafer (1976) says, patients may disclaim responsibility for things that actually have been in their control, while they may erroneously assume responsibility for things about which they could not have done anything. The same may be said of analysts.

that act of will happen. The patient might wish to escape that responsibility, hoping that with enough analysis, enough understanding and therapeutic process, such changes, whether in terms of changed ways of acting or subtle shifts in perspective, will just "happen" in the same way that an infection might eventually be overcome by an antibiotic. The aversion is to the whole experience of being an agent, which includes sensing both one's power to affect the course of events and the enormous influence of factors outside of one's control. Sometimes the patient is, in effect, driving a hard bargain, refusing to choose under the disturbing condition of not knowing what will happen and what would have happened with a different choice. In such cases (and maybe this is true in all cases) an aim of the analysis might well be to enable the patient to accept the anxiety associated with being a source of limited influence on the course of events. In point of fact, being a responsible agent, a choosing subject, loses its meaning under the unconsciously fantasized "ideal" conditions of fully being able to know the future. Once again, the attributes of the omnipotent and omniscient *supernatural* being, if they were somehow attached to a *human* being, would do violence to the very dimensions of living that they were intended to enhance. To know the future (including its merit as compared with all the futures that are not lived) undermines the meaning of choice, just as the prospect of immortality does not extend, but rather undermines, the meaning of our being as we know it (see Nussbaum, 1990, 1994, as quoted and discussed in chapter 1).

PSYCHOANALYSIS AS TIME-LIMITED THERAPY: DEATH AND OTHER KINDS OF TERMINATION

Psychoanalysis is always time-limited in the obvious sense that, if nothing else, the death of the analyst or the death of the patient will bring it to an end. This is a truism, yet it is not often a reality with which we wrestle seriously. An analysand's question as to whether or when to terminate an analysis might be phrased this way: "Should I try to terminate my analysis before one of us dies?" The seriousness of this question is apparent when either the analyst or the patient is terminally ill or elderly. The latter especially is a fairly common circumstance. What is self-evident in that context, moreover, is in the background in all others, even if the probabilities are different. Yet how many of us, regardless of our ages, have discussed with our patients what should happen in the event of our deaths? Do they want to be notified, and if so, by whom? Among those of my patients with whom I have addressed this matter, some have made clear that their preference was to hear about my demise by the "grapevine," something I could not have known (or explored) without consulting them. Although it may be contrived and unwise to discuss the matter with every patient, my guess is that most of us are not on the verge of erring in the direction of overdoing it.[2] Sometimes, as in the example that follows, there is reason to believe that either the patient or the analyst is nearing the end; thus the subject forces itself on us, and we have no choice but to deal with it.

WHO WILL DIE FIRST? 86 VERSUS 54

I've been working with Manny for about 12 years; the patient is now in his mid 80s. He's been in analytic therapy for over 50 years, outliving three previous analysts. That history gives rise to my wondering aloud, now and then, what he might do in the event of my death. We both laugh when I say this, but it doesn't stop me from dropping a few names for him to consider, should the relatively improbable happen. People in their 50s, after all, do die before people in their 80s every day. A glance at the obituaries makes that very clear. It's disturbing to the middle-aged group when that happens, but not so unexpected. We know that by that age the human body has long since begun to deteriorate, and it's not so surprising that at that point a heart would fail, an artery to the brain would get clogged, a cancer would take over. We scour the obituary for an unhealthy predisposing characteristic of the deceased that is not true of ourselves. Maybe it's that he or she smoked, was obese, had a congenital heart defect or a chronic disease of some sort, perhaps a genetic predisposition, anything to separate ourselves. But deep down we know better. Adelle Davis, with the preventive health diet, died of cancer at 70 (not exactly "middle age," but a good deal younger than might have been expected) and Jim Fixx, with the preventive running program, died (while running) of a sudden heart attack at 52. Whom are we

---

2. Cohen (1983) and Firestein (1994) have proposed specific ways that therapists should prepare their patients for the eventuality of the therapist's death. Garcia-Lawson and Lane (1997) review those proposals, but also observe that the subject is still very much taboo in the field.

kidding? Our control over the manner and timing of our deaths is disturbingly limited.[3]

THE SHARED PERSPECTIVE OF "NONBELIEVERS" AND THE PROBLEM OF AFFIRMATION

So this elderly patient and I stumble along with the harsh realities of his and my mortality as constant companions to our work together. Indeed, they often move into the foreground and become the heart of the work itself. Manny and I share in common a disbelief in any sort of afterlife.[4] It's clear that Manny is proud of his disbelief and of his insistence on finding death unspeakably alien and horrifying. It's his consolation, this form of moral superiority to those who would "delude" themselves with their "faith." Not that he feels he has any choice in the matter. There are moments when I join him in the pleasure of condescendingly "wishing" we could blindly avail ourselves of the consolations of the "believers."

At various times throughout the analysis I convey to him my philosophy that each moment counts and deserves to be lived fully. In order to make that possible, some avoidance of thoughts of death is necessary. How else could he enjoy dinner with his wife, a concert, trips to various parts of the world, the day-to-day operations of his business, a moment of insight or personal connection in the analysis? His sense of the future is now truncated. He knows he is in the midst of projects that will not likely be completed in "his time." But the challenge is to make do with what he has, to make the most of it. It's not denial that is called for, or is even possible, but a conscious form of suppression. I champion the worth of his experience. I

---

3. Ironically, after this chapter was completed, as part of a routine physical examination, I had a treadmill stress test that showed some abnormal heart rhythms. It came as a complete surprise because I had had no symptoms and had been working out regularly. The positive finding on the stress test led to further tests and eventually to successful, preventive coronary bypass surgery in the spring of 1997. Of course, the entire episode brought home to me and to all of my patients, in the most vivid and concrete way, the reality of my own vulnerability and mortality. The impact of that experience on my work with Manny and with others is a subject for another book.

4. According to a recent survey reported in *Time Magazine* (March 24, 1997, p. 73), Manny and I are in a distinct minority in the United States, where only 4 percent of the 1018 people surveyed said they believe that death marked "the end of existence."

suggest that an hour, a minute, a second now is worth no less than were the same intervals of time 10, 20, or 30 years ago. They were precious then and they are precious now, there to be embraced and savored. He says he might have been able to adopt that attitude at my age, but it's much harder now. I say I realize that it's easy for me to talk, and that whether I will be able to practice what I preach at his age, should I reach it, remains to be seen. I tell him that I admire his courage and that I frankly doubt that I will do as well as he. Also, I say it will be hard for me if he dies before I do. His absence will be more than an opening in my practice. It will be an empty space in my life and a source of grief. He means a great deal to me, and I will miss him. I want him to know that. There are things one wants to be sure to say before it's too late.

But who am I to offer this affirmation? Manny sees me, more than his previous analysts, as having limited power. He speaks wryly but affectionately of my relative impotence. He attributed magical powers to my predecessors, but feels he hasn't done that as much with me. Instead, he identifies with me, as I do with him. He appreciates the value of that bond, he says, although it is at a price and he's sometimes not so sure it's worth it. He still longs for an all-powerful protector. Nevertheless, on the whole he feels this way of living, that is, without illusions, is better. It seems that the deaths of his previous analysts combined with my personal visibility, the exposure of my limitations and vulnerability, have facilitated Manny's mourning of the loss of the hope for an omnipotent caretaker—in other words, at least a partial working-through of this aspect of the transference. As I've argued throughout, that mourning or working-through is unlikely to be *complete*, given the asymmetry that is built into the analytic frame. Nevertheless, Manny seems more prepared now than he's ever been to let go. He cuts back from three to two sessions per week (it was four sessions in previous analyses) and he rents a condominium in Palm Springs for winter use; these appear to be signs of that change, that new readiness, now at 86, for autonomy, that is, for managing more on his own and for making do with "merely" human resources.

WHY HASN'T MANNY TERMINATED?
MANNY'S HISTORY AND NEUROSIS

The reader may be wondering what could possibly justify all those years in analysis? Should Manny not have terminated long ago?

How can I have colluded with him to promote this "endless" dependency? Am I not exploiting him? Does he not have a neurosis of some kind that I and the others should have treated and more or less cured? What would the "managed care" people think of this "analysis interminable"? It occurs to me that maybe if *I* had been his analyst from the start he would have found some healthy way to conclude the "treatment"—a comforting thought.

There is little doubt, moreover, that embedded within the existential, universal predicaments of life with which Manny struggles, we can find an idiosyncratic neurosis. Manny was abused as a child, given forced enemas to empty his bowels, probably before he was old enough to control his sphincters. His mother was overbearing, controlling, intrusive, and even violent. She would beat his father who would cower before her fits of rage. The patient remembers not one single occasion when his father stood up to her. And she would bad-mouth her husband to her son, offering Manny the sense that he was special, at the center of her life, a "gift" that did more to suffocate him than to build his sense of self. Among other symptoms, the scars of this upbringing included bouts of acute depression and anxiety, difficulties with intimacy, a travel phobia, and seemingly involuntary ticlike movements identified by the patient as "crunching and biting." He would create a certain biting-sucking action when under stress as a kind of autoerotic attempt at self-soothing. Although somewhat painful, the sensation also helped him to block out various sources of psychological anguish.[5] What else could he do, he would ask pleadingly, when he was a helpless child, being pummeled by his mother into one form or another of submission or watching his father take that kind of verbal, emotional, or physical abuse? In the transference, the retreat from integrated interpersonal relating to narcissistic and autoerotic mechanisms has always been reflected in a tendency toward monologue. Often I would feel that in order for me to speak, I would have to interrupt. Even then, it was not easy to get Manny's attention. He often would nod and continue as though

---

5. This self-soothing mechanism is an example of what Ogden (1989) has identified and discussed as the "autistic-contiguous mode of defense." The aim in this mode is to establish a rudimentary, presymbolic, sensory sense of self based upon "felt shapes." Ogden writes: "The machinelike predictability of experiences with pathological autistic shapes and objects substitutes for experiences with inevitably imperfect and not entirely predictable human beings. No person can compete with the capacity of never-changing autistic shapes and objects to provide absolutely reliable comfort and protection" (pp. 59–60).

I had not said anything. We established that differentiating my influence from that of his invasive mother was no easy task. At the same time, a hunger persisted for that very kind of domination, joined with a craving for the influence of a powerful male authority. The compromise, apparently so entrenched with previous analysts but gradually loosening its grip in the work with me, was to take in the fantasized protection and affirmation of a godlike power while recoiling from the potentially real effects of the analyst's human—personal and analytic—influence.

Manny's devotion to analysis has sometimes masked his hope for an omnipotent caregiver as well as his own tendency toward megalomania. At times he has been loath to consult a doctor about physical symptoms, insisting that they were psychosomatic and could be cured by analytic understanding. I have interpreted his own wish that every symptom he develops be an expression of his own will, even if unconscious, and the other side of the same coin, that they all be curable by me. Aside from medical symptoms that needed to be diagnosed and treated as such, Manny's emotional state, I thought, might well benefit from some form of medication. I argued that he had some symptoms, such as the "crunching and biting," that were so deeply ingrained as adaptations to early traumas that they could be considered to have an organic-like basis. Perhaps analytic exploration and interpretation had limited power to affect such states (see van der Kolk, McFarlane, and Weisaeth, 1996). Eventually, after a particularly bad episode of agitated depression and anxiety, he agreed to consult with a psychiatrist and was given a prescription for one of the newer antidepressants which he has taken regularly for a couple of years. My impression is that his symptoms have been mitigated significantly. Also, the influence of the drug has afforded an opportunity for working on oedipal issues in a way that may not have been possible otherwise. In particular, Manny's worry about my envy of the power of the medication has given me the chance to demonstrate that whatever wish I might have had to be the sole therapeutic agent in his life, it was not as strong as my interest in his getting the best possible help from whatever combination of sources seemed necessary. My "friendly" attitude toward the medication simulated a parent wanting to support Manny's relationships with others, including the other parent, which was the opposite of Manny's mother's attitude. She demanded Manny's exclusive devotion, and tended to interfere whenever the father tried to get involved with his son, thereby forcing on the patient a guilt-ridden conflict of loyalty.

Thus, the medication, in Manny's case, provided the basis for some working out of oedipal issues. It is important to recognize, however, that the analytic situation is very limited as a source of corrective experience with respect to unresolved oedipal difficulties. There is, after all, little opportunity for a rival love object to emerge as a source of love or as an object of identification for the patient. The patient has to come to terms with the analyst's divided interest, with his or her attachments to others, without reaping the benefits of those attachments in a direct way. An unconscious, futile search for the love of that absent rival, which would be available in a healthy, intact family, could be a factor that makes it much more difficult to bring many analyses to a close. This point, incidentally, applies to the unavailablity of representatives of sibling rivals (such as other patients) as sources of love as much as to the unavailability of oedipal rivals (such as the analyst's spouse).[6]

THE QUEST FOR CHANGE VERSUS THE NEW SUBVERTING TRAUMAS OF TIME AND AGING

Over time, Manny seemed to be changing. He could listen more or could comment more, with humor, about his aversion to listening. His symptoms diminished in intensity and frequency. But now, something was upping the ante. If there was a chance of escaping the clutches of old patterns, it was jeopardized by the "repetition" that was built into the human condition. Now death coming at him was like his mother coming at him, and once again he was the helpless child, the innocent victim of a cruel fate. Analysis can take that course sometimes. The healing and corrective experiences that are absorbed over time can be subverted by the fresh intensity of new traumas, including those that go hand-in-hand with aging. Time heals, they say, but it is just as true to say that time cruelly opens old wounds and rubs salt in them.[7] Manny is not only facing his *own*

---

6. As was discussed in the conclusion of chapter 8, the analyst's "marriage" to the "Book" of analytic discipline and the associated benefits for the patient provide the basis in the analytic situation for a partial oedipal analogue with potential for positive resolution. Needless to say, however, the "Book" is a far cry from a live person as a rival, as a source of love, as an object of love, and as an object of identification.

7. For a discussion of the interaction between earlier traumas and the trauma of aging see Aarts and Op den Velde, 1996.

death. During the years I have worked with him, many people close to him have died: his first wife, his eldest daughter, many friends. Attendance at funerals has become an almost routine activity for him as his social network has progressively dwindled.

Manny struggled recently with the crushing discovery that his second wife, the closest friend he has left in the world, was diagnosed with cancer. Surgery was scheduled. Manny was deeply afraid. He felt angry with his wife for persuading him to marry her. "I will be good for you," she had said. He acknowledged that she'd been that in many ways, but now he felt betrayed. She "lied" to him. *She* was supposed to take care of *him*, not the other way around. He dreamt that his mother was chasing relentlessly after him, intent on beating him with a broomstick. The dream was unusually vivid and real, and he remembered occasions when his mother acted just as she does in the dream. But now, in the place of his mother, it was the all-too vivid reality of death that stalked him and his loved ones relentlessly.

So it is hardly a shameful thing that Manny has not concluded his analysis before this time, and that he may "never" conclude it, except in the way that is inevitable. Analytic therapy should not be regarded as a standardized treatment for a disease. It doesn't have a set course with standard phases: beginning, middle, and end.[8] The ways in which terminations come about, or do not come about, are extremely variable in my experience (see Golland, 1997). Sometimes the analysis is a background support for living, functioning in a way that is analogous to the way religion functions in many people's lives. We don't think to ask people how long they believe it will be necessary for them to attend church or temple services. We think of religious institutions as continuously present and available to sustain people. For some, such a role may also be played by analytic therapy, the contemporary secular version of religious grounding.

Just as Freud (1937) had to come to terms with the fact that analytic understanding could not always overcome the "strength of the instinct" as compared with "the strength of the ego" (pp. 225–226, 230), so does the constructivist analyst have to come to terms with the fact that the analytic relationship cannot always overcome the complex influences of the past, including environmental failures,[9]

---

8. It is important to remember, incidentally, that many physical diseases are chronic and that the standard treatments for them, which few would question, are life-long (e.g., dialysis for kidney failure).

9. The burgeoning literature on posttraumatic stress disorder (e.g., van der Kolk, McFarlane, and Weisaeth, 1996) leaves no doubt as to the poten-

along with the impact of misfortunes and traumas that occur in the course of the analysis itself.[10] Among those traumas are the ones that occur inevitably, indeed, that are inherent in the passage of time: the accumulation of losses, the experience of aging, the narrowing of options, and the anticipation of death. Those developments combined with the influence of the past can be enough, as has been the case with Manny and myself, to make it evident that it would be contrived and unnecessarily wrenching for the patient to try to terminate his or her analysis in any formal or decisive way. In general, it would be rigidly objectivistic to insist that deliberately planning and constructing an ending for analysis is desirable for everybody.

But we need not go overboard in modeling psychoanalysis upon religious institutions. Just as it is reductive and misleading to regard it as akin to a scientifically grounded, technically rational treatment (see Hoffman, 1987, and chapter 6), so too is it reductive and misleading to regard it as akin to a religious belief system of a conventional nature. In the first place, analysis is, or should be, a radically self-critical undertaking, one that is capable of questioning its own underlying presuppositions both within the analytic process itself and in discourse about it. Unfortunately, analytic practice and theorizing have often fallen short of that ideal (Cushman, 1995; Flax, 1996; Wachtel, 1983). As Flax has written, "Much of the radical social and philosophical implications of psychoanalysis has been lost or obscured, partially because analysts are insufficiently critical of the effects of social context on our own theorizing" (p. 581). Still, at its best, analytic therapy, unlike many expressions of organized reli-

---

tially overwhelming impact of trauma, affecting psychobiological adaptation throughout the life cycle. It would be naive, indeed, to think that psychoanalysis alone could always reverse these kinds of disturbances.

10. Although Freud (1937) emphasized the constitutional strength of the instincts as the most important obstacle to a successful termination of an analysis, he also recognized the influence of the "accidental" factor on the outcome. Even when all the objectives of an analysis are accomplished (a result that is most likely in cases with a traumatic etiology), so that it may be said to have "definitively ended," Freud states that "if the patient who has been restored in this way never produces another disorder calling for analysis, we do not know how much his immunity may not be due to a kind of fate which has spared him ordeals that are too severe" (p. 220). He gives an example of a woman whose analysis concluded with the alleviation of all symptoms and who withstood consistent misfortune in the initial years following her recovery; but who, after undergoing a hysterectomy, succumbed to an emotional disturbance that proved inaccessible to further attempts at analysis (p. 222).

gion, promotes a deeply skeptical attitude on the part of its participants toward their own manifest experience and behavior, and the
scope of its explorations encompasses its underlying values and
assumptions. For many analytic patients, moreover, the process is
"supportive" partly *because* it is critically challenging and interpretive. It caters to a natural tendency of the human mind, what Slavin
and Kriegman (1992) characterize as "innate skepticism" (p. 230), a
tendency that I would say is counterpoint to an innate appetite for
belief in an absolute authority. Thus paradoxically, the analyst's
interpretive activity is among the magnets for the positive transference, even while it acts to subvert it. In the second place, there is
good reason to think of analysis as a means to an end, rather than
merely as an end in itself. Although that principle too can be over-
stated, it nevertheless is true that people usually come to therapy
with problems that they would like to handle better, with symptoms
that they want to be rid of, or with ways of being that they would
like to change. In many respects, the functions of the analyst are
analogous to those of a parent, promoting development and change
through a close relationship that is valued by both participants for
its own sake, but is also always in the process of being outgrown. In
certain respects, the analyst, like the parent, strives to make himself
or herself dispensable. Thus, he or she often works to challenge, rather
than to promote, the patient's attachment to himself or herself as the
embodiment of an external superior power.

THE VALUE OF TERMINATING THROUGH PLANNED
SEPARATION: PROMOTING COMMITTED LIVING

Although much change can be facilitated in the context of the analytic relationship, in our culture there is a developmental step that we
are likely to be interested in, one that often cannot be accomplished
without an actual separation. In that respect, it's not simply a matter of "getting better" and then ending. Rather it's a matter of reaching a point where it seems desirable to end, to absorb the pain of real
loss, in order to get that much better, in order to take what is mutually understood to be that further developmental step.

   Despite the uniqueness of each analysis, can we say anything
about the developmental progression we are hoping for? To do so is
certainly problematic, because assertions we make about development are likely to be culturally biased (Flax, 1996). With that caveat,
it nevertheless seems worthwhile to make the attempt in order, at

least, to make explicit what might be common objectives in psycho-analysis in our culture.[11]

One aim might be a sense of increased autonomy relative to an idealized caregiver. "Autonomy" is a notoriously overvalued trait in contemporary Western society (Cushman, 1995; Flax, 1996; Hoffman, 1995). Perhaps we move beyond the narrow meaning of the concept if we think in terms of relinquishing investment in an omnipotent caregiver who has a kind of maternal preoccupation with oneself rather than in terms of overcoming dependence on other people viewed more realistically. The allegedly "unobjectionable" positive transference, despite its being integral to the therapeutic action of the process, must also be looked at critically (Stein, 1981). We must always be mindful of the magnetic appeal of the asymmetrical aspects of the analytic arrangement and of the fact that it is decidedly neither a model for, nor the match of, healthy, intimate, reciprocal relationships. Patients often feel that close relationships outside compare unfavorably with the allegedly "ideal" aspects of the analytic situation, a perspective that the analyst must challenge lest it become the basis for destructive self-fulfilling prophesy. Ending the analysis can facilitate foregoing its regressive benefits, while giving other relationships that hold the promise of equality and mutuality a better chance to flourish. It can, after all, promote in the patient an increased willingness to commit to whatever and whomever may be candidates to replace the transference object, an increased readiness to embrace the "poor substitutes" for that fantasy, and to see that in relation to another, more realistic standard of worth, they are not substitutes at all, but are invaluable attachments in their own right. These newly seen and appreciated love objects include not only other people, but also, through a healthy "transformation of narcissism" (Kohut, 1966), the patient himself or herself. In the end, tolerance of limitation and appreciation of worth extend simultaneously, and in an interdependent way, to self and other.

Thus, although for many patients the ongoing benefits of being in analysis may outweigh its costs, the analytic process clearly has the potential for iatrogenic effects that must be taken into account. It

---

11. Although quite abstract, it may be useful to consider as a universal feature of development the progression identified by Heinz Werner's (1957) "orthogenic principle," according to which, "wherever development occurs it proceeds from a state of relative globality and lack of differentiation to a state of increasing differentiation, articulation, and hierarchic integration" (p. 126).

can function, for years, as a subtle shield against the potential full-ness of one's commitments. In effect, experience in the "real world" becomes grist for the analytic mill, rather than being lived for its own sake. Hidden within the workings of the "mill" there often lie residuals of hope for transformative magic, for control over time, and for immortality. In the meantime, it's as though everything out-side of the analysis counts just a little less than it might otherwise. As patients, we thereby spare ourselves feeling the full brunt of the implications of our choices. We keep at bay the painful realization of the inexorable flow of time and the acute awareness of the irre-versibility of each moment. At the same time, we may be deprived of the potential intensity of experience that is more fully recognized for its intrinsic significance. To bring the analysis to an end can mean owning one's life experience more completely and taking greater responsibility for its construction. For that to happen, one must come more directly to terms with the impact of one's own and oth-ers' limitations, with the "givens" of one's existence, with the hand one has been dealt. For many people, that developmental achieve-ment cannot be a prerequisite for termination, because the termina-tion itself is necessary for it to occur (cf. Renik, 1992). As Mitchell (1993) puts it, "One of the startling realizations upon leaving analy-sis is the sense that one is now fully responsible for one's life. The suspension that analysis provides, useful, necessary, enriching, is now over" (p. 229).

EPILOGUE ON MANNY

In the course of writing this chapter, the work with Manny took a new turn. His wife recovered well from her cancer surgery, and he and she revived their plans to take at least part of their anticipated Palm Springs "vacation." But there was something different about this break, because no specific date of return was set. Manny could be gone a month or two or even more. It did not make sense, there-fore, for me to hold his times. He said he'd call me when he returned and take his chances. So we were faced with an ambiguous inter-ruption, neither quite a vacation in the usual sense, nor a full termi-nation. I decided it afforded an opportunity to construct a benign kind of semi-ending, one the patient had never been able to experi-ence before in analysis. In the "last session," I presented him with a gift, two books dealing with questions of origins, the beginnings of the universe and of life, and evolution, all questions I knew Manny was interested in. Accompanying the gift was a card on which I had written, in part, "Congratulations on your 'graduation.' If these books don't answer *all* your remaining questions about the meaning of life, you will definitely need more analysis (the advanced, post-graduate kind of course)." Manny was moved and delighted. He appreciated my turning this juncture into something of an ending, even though he thought he'd surely be back if he didn't die in the interim. He joked that he'd write or call to give me his address and phone number (unknown at the time of the meeting) so that I could call him in Palm Springs if I needed him. The next day he left me an envelope in the waiting room, containing two tickets to a concert in town that he couldn't attend while he was away. Several weeks later, he returned for a few days for business reasons. In the first of two scheduled sessions he spoke with elation about one of the books I had given him (*Shadows of Forgotten Ancestors* by Carl Sagan and Ann Druyan), which he said he was enjoying as much if not more than any he had ever read. He was thrilled with the ideas and conveyed them to me in a manner that was unusually animated. He seemed stronger and healthier than I had ever seen him, reporting that he was having a great time with his wife in Palm Springs, although he missed our meetings. He said he'd be back in Chicago in mid-spring and would like to resume the therapy. But he was rather unfazed when I told him I had given away his times. He said he understood and he'd just take whatever was possible when he got back. In the second of the two sessions, after speaking with some pride and satisfaction about the pile of business matters he had been tackling, he reported the following dream:

> I was heading for my first analyst's office. But in front of his building a huge crowd of people had gathered and I had to struggle to get through. A crowd of people was also in the lobby. So I decided I would just scale the outer wall, which I was able to do with ease, like Spider-Man. I went in then through the bathroom window and got to his office. I said, "I know I'm late." He replied, "Yes I know. You understand that it will cost you three hours at $11.00 per hour."

He said his first analyst reminded him of me, in that he was warm and very human. He thought the people in front of the building represented my other patients, including whoever had taken his old times, and that his "lateness" referred to the duration of his trip, which meant leaving his times open. The penalty of three hours at $11 corresponded, he guessed, to what had been our frequency of meetings for a long time and to what was an obvious fraction of the fee, one-tenth to be exact. In the time machine of the dream, perhaps he was taking us back to a preinflation era. Being charged for three hours might allude to his discomfort and maybe to his guilt over the possibility that I had neglected my self-interest in not charging him for any of the missed time. He wasn't sure what scaling the wall meant, and he had no associations that illuminated that image for us. I suggested that it might be a whimsical way of representing his recovery of a sense of youthful vitality. The fact that in the dream it's his first analyst who appears, which takes the patient back 50 years, might also refer to his sense of himself as having youthful strength and energy. I suggested, also, that the image of scaling the wall might refer to his feeling special to me, so that he felt confident that he would have access to me eventually, even if something unusual was required and even if it did worry him that I might overextend myself. After all, I'd just given him a gift, which is not the standard kind of analytic interaction. The scaling of the wall might also allude, specifically, to the books on evolution, to his own adaptability, to the "survival of the fittest." Although I did not think of it at the time, it might well be relevant that the other book I gave him was *Climbing Mount Improbable* by Richard Dawkins. What seems evident is that the quasi-termination, buffered and enhanced by the use of various transitional objects, was a powerful catalyst for Manny's development in terms of his capacity to feel confident about his own resources as well as the enduring aspects of his connection with me and with the analytic process.

THE INTERPLAY OF EXTERNAL CIRCUMSTANCES AND READINESS TO TERMINATE

The timing of the ending is a delicate matter. It is virtually impossible to create a space for it that is not continually invaded by seemingly extraneous contingencies and concerns. Yet these too must be integrated into the analytic work as much as possible. Since the participants tend to be invested in maximizing the analysand's ability, with the analyst's help, to gain control over his or her life, it can be hard for both people to accept the enormous role of luck in the course of an analysis and after termination as well.

From the perspective of the analyst, the factor of luck is evident in considering his or her impact at any moment and over time. We can never know for certain how what we offer will be received. When the analyst risks suggesting to a patient who feels deprived and victimized that the way he or she relates to others and to the analyst may show the mark of identification with hypercritical and demanding parents, which, in turn, promotes distance and defensiveness rather than a sympathetic response, all the tact and timing in the world does not ensure the outcome. I've been surprised many times by people's responsiveness as well as by their angry opposition to such suggestions. Of course, there is something I can learn from the unexpected experience, something I had failed to consider before I intervened. But it would be an illusion to think that I would then know whether the "same" confrontation would be received similarly in similar circumstances in the future, even with the same patient, not to mention with someone else. There is enough that is unique in each moment that whatever the analyst does entails a real element of risk. To respect our patients as free agents is to recognize the gap between our intended influence and their response, a gap that is filled, in part, by our patients' capacity for choice.

There are countless other factors filling that gap, of course, everything from the weight of the patient's history to the convergence (or lack of convergence) of something we've said with something another person happened to have said to the patient the day before. In reply to an interpretation of projective identification, such as the one above, a patient may say, right then, or maybe a week later, "That's exactly what my friend said to me last night; I guess I better think about it." Or we may hear, "That's ridiculous. You just want everything to be my fault. My friend says her analyst never tries to turn it around on her that way." Assuming, for the sake of argument, the merit of what I have offered in both contexts, although it is true that there are often differences between the kinds of patients who "bring in" allies for the work and those who bring opponents, the forces don't always line up in a predictable way, and the unexpected outside influence can sometimes be formidable.

We feel the influence of chance in all the uncontrollable events in the patient's life. A lover rejects a patient just when he or she has finally seemed to be prepared to turn a corner on risking attachment and closeness. The patient's vulnerability is at a peak and the setback is huge. The side of the patient that wants desperately to retreat, to plunge into rageful depression, or to regress into hostile dependency in the transference is vindicated. Another patient finds someone who puts up with his or her intense ambivalence about any sort of commitment. This person sticks with the patient despite the patient's many efforts to sabotage the relationship. In effect, the patient is afforded the opportunity for a corrective experience. We are accustomed to the idea that relationships outside of the analysis might have a better chance of working out because of the analytic process. But sometimes it is equally true, if not more true, to say that the analytic work progresses well because of the influence of fortuitous outside relationships. Again, seeing the analytic work as the sole governing factor vastly overestimates its power while underestimating the power of chance developments in the patient's life.

TERMINATIONS AND
POSTANALYTIC ENGAGEMENTS

Five years after termination, I received a letter from Diane, the patient whose analysis is discussed in chapter 8. The termination with her, after about five years of work, had been good but not spectacular. She seemed to feel better about herself; she was less depressed than she had been, and her work was going well. But the immediate reason for terminating was that she had been accepted for a residency in her area of specialization in another city. In addition to building her career (she had moved from nursing to medical school in the course of the analysis), she had aspired to find a man, to marry, and to have children. There was some question as to whether the desire for family would be realized, despite the fact that Diane felt that she was more prepared for a relationship than she had been. She said she thought the analysis had helped to erode her appetite for relationships with men that were modeled after her relationship with her father. The men she had been drawn to tended to be narcissistic and domineering. She had equated kindness and an egalitarian, nonsexist attitude in a man with weakness. Through the analytic work, including coming to appreciate the quality of our relationship, some of the strength of that appetite had lessened while her appetite for a relationship with someone kind and empathic had increased. But it wasn't easy to find a good enough match. She remained, after all, a person who was sometimes difficult to be with. She could be demanding, and quite critical, and skittish about intimacy. In addition, every good man she met seemed to be married. So she left with hope about the future, but also with plenty of doubts.

In the letter I received five years after the termination, Diane reported that she had met and married a wonderful man, that she was pregnant, and that she was happier than she ever dreamt she could be. She said, "You wouldn't believe that this is the same dark soul that you treated." The man was ideal for her: very smart, and kind, and gentle. He was tolerant of her more difficult traits, but at the same time was self-confident enough to hold his own when conflicts arose. She could not have asked for more. I was surprised and delighted. I was surprised because, if she did marry, it seemed more likely that the relationship would be something of a struggle. And of course, there was a good chance that she would not find an adequate partner, or that she wouldn't find one during her child-bearing years. This aspect of the good "outcome" of her analysis was not transparently "in the cards," much less "in the bag." And yet it happened. It happened partly, no doubt, because of the patient's considerable strengths and because of the analysis in which a lot of development had occurred. But it happened also because of sheer luck. This particular man did not have to appear. For example, someone else who was less compatible but good enough to make a go of it might have crossed Diane's path. The result might have been a more difficult life, in which the patient would have had to struggle more to develop and sustain a sense of feeling loved and loving. In other words, the ostensible "outcome" of the analysis would have been less positive. What is apparent, of course, is that the word "outcome" is itself quite misleading since what happens is a function of many variables only one of which is the analytic process.

Now I would like to revisit the termination and postanalytic events in the case of Ken, the patient discussed in chapter 9. First, I want to report on aspects of the termination that were not described in the context of the earlier focus on issues arising within the analytic situation. Here I would like to look at aspects of the termination that involve the interweaving of external realities, intrapsychic issues, and relational issues. Second, I will relate aspects of my experience of writing about my work with this patient, including asking him for permission to publish. Such case presentations generally have a clinical context and are therefore significant events within the analytic process itself (Stein, 1988a,b).

Toward the end of the fourth year of the analysis, having been restless to find a position that was more in keeping with his academic achievements, and as luck would have it, having just missed on a couple of academic openings in Chicago, Ken began to explore a very interesting job possibility in another state. It wasn't exactly what he wanted because it was more clinical and administrative than academic, but it was in a beautiful area of the country, it entailed a position of leadership and much responsibility, and it afforded opportunities for Ken to make use of his talents in creating and implementing programs in accord with convictions he had developed about the delivery of mental-health services. In addition, he was being given the red carpet treatment by the people at this agency. This occurred at a point in the analysis when the possibility of termination had been broached. We felt a lot had been accomplished: a chronic depression had lifted, excessive drinking had stopped, the patient's marriage had become much more solid and fulfilling, sexually and in other ways, and there were many more experiences of spontaneous pleasure with the children and with others. One poignant change that the patient reported one day was that his daughter had found his ticklish spot and that he was able to be tickled and to enjoy it for the first time, an important kind of experience that Adam Phillips (1993) has written about. Still, we thought we had a ways to go, perhaps about a year had been the patient's guess. For one thing, Ken was still struggling with his height phobia, although there were more instances in which he seemed to overcome it. One aspect of the job prospect was that, for better or for worse, it entailed moving to a small town, where there were few, if any, tall office buildings.

Despite the progress, therefore, I had to be concerned, as was the patient, about whether he was terminating prematurely. If this was a "test," in Sampson and Weiss's (1986) terms, what would it take for me to pass it? Was Ken acting out, even by exploring this possibility at this point? In the background we had the model of the mother's premature "termination" and the possibility that he was identified with her in ending the analysis before it came to a more "natural" end. In one of the patient's dreams in this period, a royal figure was being executed and surgically dismembered, a dream we interpreted as referring to the violence he felt he might be doing to the analysis and to me, or perhaps to an idealized representation of me, or maybe to an inflated idea he thought I had of myself. At the same time, Ken very much wanted me to recognize the value of the attractive offer he was considering. If he decided to leave, he wanted to go with a sense that he had my blessing, that I was pleased with what we had accomplished, and that I was confident that he had the resources to handle the termination and the challenges that were ahead. He acknowledged that it was a no-win situation for me, because I was in danger of either letting him go too easily or holding on to him in a controlling, suffocating way. As the analyst, I could work hard to explore the various meanings of Ken's choice, in the context, of course, of whatever attitudes he was attributing to me. But I also felt that it was important to "come clean," to say as much as I could about what I felt at one point or another. And what I generally felt, in fact, was that I didn't *know* for sure, and that I had some conflict about it, which I shared. I also said it seemed to me that the conclusion of the analysis would take on quite a different meaning if Ken left with the feeling that I was opposed to his stopping than it would if he left feeling I endorsed it. In fact, the termination experience is one of those that makes so conspicuous the myth of analytic neutrality (cf. Winer, 1994, p. 183). We have to take responsibility for the way in which we participate in the coconstruction of the ending. There is no way around that. The perspective we choose to adopt and to go by is, in the first place, underdetermined by the "data" that precede it, and is, in the second place, extremely influential in coloring all the "data" that follow it.

In this instance, as things evolved, the job offer seemed to me to become more and more attractive over time. The photos of the area that Ken brought in for me to look at were fantastic, enough to make me very envious. Maybe that's when I felt I "knew" that this was probably a good thing for him and his family. His wife also had excellent prospects out there for her career, and the schools were terrific. So gradually, although we continued to turn over the various meanings of the ending, I became more enthusiastic about the opportunity. When Ken announced, after returning from a visit to the area and the agency, that the contract with impressive salary and benefits was signed, I was delighted for him and immediately moved to shake his hand and congratulate him. Needless to say, *not* to respond personally and spontaneously at that moment would not be more neutral; it would, instead, affect the patient's experience in a very *different* way.

With regard to the danger of repetition in creating an ending that may have been "premature," I would say that the aim is not to shape something that bears no mark of the past, but to create something that bears that mark but is nevertheless different and new. The challenge is to forge a difference within the context of similarity. As discussed in chapter 7, I think that is the most powerful differentiation we can achieve. So, for example, if there was an element of "identification with the aggressor" in the patient's move to terminate, there was nevertheless much in the act that was far healthier than what characterized his parents' various leavings and abandonments. First, there was value, I thought, in his being the initiator and in his risking doing something for himself, "ruthlessly," as Winnicott would say, regardless of my preference or needs. Second, although it was his lead, he did ask me to participate in the process, both in a standard analytic sense and as a kind of influential, personally involved partner and even trusted authority. And third, he took pains to keep channels open between us, to give me a sense of where he'd be, and to continue, as he had put it in his parting note (see chapter 9) "to let [me] into his life."

I received a letter from Ken about two weeks after he left. Among other things, he wrote the following:

> I had a dream the night after our last session that might interest you. I got some Christmas presents but was convinced there should have been one more. I became filled with anxiety because that [gift] was the most important one. Then in the dream I realized I was dreaming about the analysis and the dream expressed my fear that I'd left too soon. When I woke up, though, I felt comforted because I was still able to dream, because I was dreaming about you, and because I was able to interpret the dream. So I had a lot of thoughts about life as process and about how the ability to analyze oneself, rather than the content of the analysis per se, might be "the most important gift."

I think it is safe to say that the value of an increased capacity for "self-analysis" for Ken resided not only in whatever insight it yielded and not only in the autonomy that it reflected, but also in the sense of a connection to the analysis and to me that it helped to sustain.

WRITING THE PAPER: "THE PATIENT AS THERAPIST TO HIS ANALYST"

I don't think it's possible to write about work with a patient without at some level experiencing the writing as a form of relating to the patient, with the patient as potential audience or reader or, perhaps, as one who is excluded, and from whom the writing of the paper is hidden.[12] The paper that became chapter 9 of this book was written about six or seven years after the termination. I had had some contacts with Ken since then, usually a letter from him around Christmas and New Year's, a personal note combined with an annual report on himself and the family that Ken sent to all the family's friends and relatives. I responded each time with some acknowledgment of his

---

12. Stein (1988a, 1988b) has discussed some of the clinical implications of analysts writing about their work with patients without, however, exploring the potential for the kind of reciprocal affirmation that is my focus here. Incidentally, the other patients discussed in this chapter, Manny and Diane, as well as the patient discussed in chapter 3, also read, commented on, and approved what I wrote about their analyses.

letter, some comments on it, and some kind of collegial exchange from one person in the field to another. When I began writing the paper, I had in mind that the patient had said casually, once or twice during the course of the analysis, that he thought it would be OK if I wrote about the work. In general, however, I didn't feel confident about his "permission," because the comments were made in the spirit of "associations," in other words, ideas that he might not have expected me to take literally. Even if he had expected that, I didn't recall having put a whole lot of energy into making sure we had explored all the *unhealthy* reasons that might have entered into his finding such a thing desirable. After all, I wanted to have his consent. So as I began writing I felt little twinges of anxiety and guilt about it. At first I thought I was only going to tell about the episode at the elevator (something I actually spoke to Ken about briefly at a conference we both attended). Then it started to grow, and different pieces started to fit together. At some point I had written about the episode at the elevator and some of the description of the termination, but I still hadn't included any of the history. Eventually I decided it was very important to include the background in order to convey the context for the whole process. As each piece got added on and the paper began to take shape, I became more anxious about how the patient would feel about it. Wasn't this exploitative in some way? And wasn't I doing violence to the integrity and privacy of our relationship? I don't think, incidentally, that "maintaining confidentiality" quite captures that issue, which I think of in more relational terms.

I also had to think about how the patient would feel when reading the paper. I couldn't imagine not showing it to him, particularly since he was in the field. But here I had spent close to a thousand hours with Ken, always trying to be tactful and sensitive to what was going on with him. Yet now, knowing virtually nothing about the state of mind he would be in at the moment he encountered the paper, I was going to force him to read about himself in this objectified way, complete with details about the traumas of his childhood, including such things as his sexual response to his mother and a detailed description of her suicide. The sense grew that I was doing something self-serving at his expense, along with the fear that he would be hurt by it, would be angry, or would feel pressured into complying. And there certainly would be pressure, because it would be evident that the paper involved a lot of work, that I was quite invested in it, and that I very much wanted to present it and publish it.

What I was experiencing, I think, was an extension of what I've called the dark side of the analytic frame, the aspects of the process that the patient could plausibly experience as exploitative. And to borrow from the language of chapter 9, the experience was going on in a liminal space, one that was both inside and outside the analytic situation itself.

My engagement with Ken on this matter took the form of a series of letters. First, I sent him the paper, along with a letter expressing regret about imposing on him in this way. I briefly explained how the paper evolved, conveyed the importance to me of his reactions, inquired whether he thought the disguises of his identity were adequate, and thanked him for being a "silent co-author" of the paper. I waited anxiously for his response to the letter and to the paper. Would he be upset or angry that I had written about the analysis at all? Would he find anything I said about the work or about him offensive? Would he remember things very differently? And finally, would reading the paper be disruptive in a damaging way to his life right now? So it was with much relief that two weeks later I read Ken's opening statement: "It was good to hear from you and I want to thank you for showing me the article and soliciting my comments." He went on to encourage me to undisguise the fact the he was a mental health professional: "It explains better that I knew I was asking you to break the rules by accompanying me to the elevator, and explains better why I felt, the next day, as if I'd been manipulative, dishonest—putting you to the test, as it were."

Ken went on to speak of how shocking it was, in fact, to read about various aspects of his history. "It's amazing," he said, "what repression can do." But it was clear that he had made constructive use of this renewed contact with his past. In a newly integrative way, a few days after receiving the letter he took a trip with his wife and children to the town where he had been born, visiting with his mother's sister. As he put it, "The unconscious at work."

The letter included some comments that were explicitly confirming of my sense of the process. For example, Ken agreed with my reflections on the "darker motives" of the analyst and thought any other view would surely indicate denial. He expressed interest in the issue of the analyst's "visibility," offering his own elaboration:

> Patients are attuned to much more than just changes in the physical space, but to changes in the analyst's tone, mood, etc.—many things that are outside the analyst's conscious awareness and control. I seem to remember several times when you had a head cold for a few days:

it always seemed to make you more human, more my equal. And, yes, the patient shares an investment in the analyst's [relative] anonymity. But I certainly experienced a desire to peek behind the curtain: sometimes I felt this as a sort of mischief, a playfulness with the frame—and as you say, we both expect that this will be subjected to analytic scrutiny.

With regard to the interplay of neurotic and existential anxiety as it applied to Ken's phobia, Ken stated, "I very much appreciate your understanding that my phobia had a nugget of appreciation of the fragility of life. I think I remember saying that I felt like I was the only really sane person, that everyone else was in denial; I think that saying that (and your not dismissing it) was a curative moment for me."

Ken said he was "embarrassed" by the "anticlimax" he created "in summing up two years of analytic work by saying [he] realized [he] wanted people to like [him]." He went on, however, to suggest that perhaps he was alluding more pointedly to the importance to him of *my* liking him. Here, perhaps, my being caught up in disappointment about the patient's manifestly simplistic formulation blinded me to an important allusion to the transference that I might have done well to interpret.

Ken concluded by complimenting me on the paper, saying he was "proud to be a collaborator" and hoping the paper would get a good reception.

It's hard to describe the relief that I felt in receiving the letter. First of all it had practical implications. I could use the paper, into which I had put a great deal of work, for presentation and publication. But there was also a deeper psychological, therapeutic impact on me. In effect, I felt Ken forgave me for those aspects of my motivation that put my own needs ahead of his and that left the shadow of the "bad object" on *my* ego. Not only did he forgive the bad, but he also appreciated what was *good* about my writing the paper. In effect, he said that the paper *did* do him more good than harm. Whatever was manipulative or exploitative about the writing, and about the appeal for license to use the material, was overridden by the good things the paper had to offer. By conveying that message, the patient contributed to my own sense of the positive value of my choosing to write about him, just as I had contributed to the patient's sense of the positive value of *his* transgressions, however much they included manipulative, self-serving, or aggressive meanings. And it occurred to me that this is one aspect of the corrective emotional experience that analysis offers. It's not simply that the patient learns that we are better than the "bad objects" of the past, although maybe it comes around to that in the end. Rather, the patient finds a way to forgive us for the ways in which we really *are* bad and unworthy. If those aspects of our being as analysts can be forgiven, then the good we have to offer can be assimilated, the patient can change, and we can feel that we've redeemed ourselves. The insatiability of our own need for redemption, moreover, is something of an unknown, hidden as it is behind the fact that our perpetual engagement in this quest is something we've couched as what we do for a living.

In my reply, I referred to Searles's (1975) article, "The Patient as Therapist to His Analyst," telling Ken that he had certainly been that for me:

> I guess I sensed the workings of the "dark underside" of the analytic frame in using your analysis to help create a paper, and I was afraid you'd feel used or manipulated. It's the sort of thing that can activate whatever bad feelings one has about oneself, so your response amounted to a real "corrective" experience for *me*. Maybe it's the counterpart of my response to your asking me to walk with you to the elevator. So the reassurance and the affirmation go both ways.

THE NOT GOOD-ENOUGH ENDINGS

The endings with Diane and Ken, the semi-termination with Manny, and the process with others as described in earlier chapters were all very positive and promising. In different ways, these patients made constructive use of their analytic experiences and took advantage of bits of good fortune that fell their way to make better lives for themselves. Needless to say, not every analysis has such a favorable course or result. My own experience includes cases in which the therapy has essentially served to help people *sustain* a certain level of functioning, but has not changed it. In a few painful instances a patient has terminated rather abruptly in response, apparently, to having suffered a narcissistic injury in the analytic process. Although these unfortunate endings have occurred rarely, they point to a real danger inherent in an approach that gives the analyst more freedom to be self-expressive and that allows the participants to live more on what Ehrenberg (1992) has aptly called "the intimate edge." The limits of the analytic arrangement can become too jarringly discrepant from the current of mutuality that the approach also promotes, so that the patient can end up feeling seduced and abandoned (see discussion of Ferenczi in chapter 5, pp. 149–150). It can be especially tricky in that a patient may argue that opening up further would be too humiliating at a certain juncture *unless* the analyst were willing to reciprocate by being more personally revealing. In those instances it is hard to know with any degree of certainty what the optimal balance should be between reserve and self-expression. It is imperative, however, for the analyst to bear in mind that the fundamental asymmetry of the arrangement, which entails a power differential, can make interludes of heightened mutuality and intimacy quite treacherous going, even though no movement in that direction may risk generating a kind of impasse. The subject is certainly deserving of much more extensive discussion. Some have undertaken it, focusing especially on the question of self-disclosure as it pertains to erotic transference and countertransference (Gabbard, 1994a,b, 1996; Davies, 1994a,b; Tansey, 1994; Hirsch, 1994). The point I want to emphasize here is simply that finding an optimal balance between asymmetry and mutuality (Burke, 1992) can sometimes be difficult, and overcorrections of the classical asymmetrical atmosphere can sometimes be harmful, leading to endings that repeat earlier traumas more than they realize potentials for new experience.[13]

---

13. In the debate between Gabbard (1994a,b) and Davies (1994a,b) on disclosure by the analyst of erotic countertransference, I find myself most comfortable with each of their efforts to stretch to accommodate the position of the other. Gabbard (1994b), for example, allows for some exceptions to his otherwise rigid rule opposing such disclosure when he writes, "My major concern is that while acknowledging such feelings may, in rare instances, facilitate the work, especially in the hands of a gifted clinician like Davies, the margin for error is very small indeed" (p. 510). And Davies (1994b) makes clear the extent to which she shares Gabbard's concerns when she writes, "Having disagreed with so much of Gabbard's response, I wish to support unequivocally his position that the analyst must rally all of her clinical experience in determining the ultimate wisdom of such a course. The disclosure of countertransference experience is never to be undertaken lightly, and, particularly when this countertransference involves such potentially overstimulating material, tact, timing, and countertransferential *motive* must be seriously explored alone or, preferably, in consultation with colleagues" (p. 507). Also see Davies (1998a,b) and Hoffman (1998).

ONE MORE TIME: THE END

Mitchell (1993) has usefully compared completing and letting go of a book to the ending of an analysis. Certainly I feel the sense of arbitrarily "interrupting" the stories I've been telling of Manny, of Diane, and of Ken, stories that are ongoing, even though two of those analysands have terminated and the third has experimented with constructing a kind of analytic "sabbatical." The ongoing work with other patients, too, is continually influencing my thinking, as are many other kinds of experiences. The conclusion of a book, in that sense, has an even greater sense of arbitrary finality than does the conclusion of an analysis. The latter often has a way of continuing well after its official close.

How life goes for the patient in the long run depends on many factors outside of the analyst's control, including the patient's own resourcefulness and the ever-present factor of luck. The ultimate challenge is to absorb the uncertainty of what fate will bring, along with the certainty that in the end it will always bring death, and despite those realities, to choose to celebrate and care for our lives and the lives of others with commitment, with passion, and with the wisest judgment we can muster. We cannot do that by ourselves, and sometimes we cannot do it well, if at all, without special help. The power of the opposing forces, of the soul-murdering traumas specific to individual lives, as well as those that are part of all our lives, can be overwhelming. Pitted against those traumas and incorporating the agony of choice and chance, of loss and mortality, psychoanalysis stands for the ironic worth of the individual, of the human community, of life itself. I close this book with the hope that it will contribute in some small measure to the affirmative, therapeutic action of psychoanalysis, not only as a mode of clinical practice, but also as theory, as philosophy, and as moral discourse.

References

Aarts, G. H. P. & Op den Velde, W. (1996), Prior traumatization and the process of aging: Theory and clinical implications. In: *Traumatic Stress: The Effects of Overwhelming Experience on Mind, Body, and Society,* ed. B. A. van der Kolk, A. C. McFarlane & L. Weisaeth. New York: Guilford, pp. 359–377.

Altman, N. (1995), *The Analyst in the Inner City: Race, Class, and Culture Through a Psychoanalytic Lens.* Hillsdale, NJ: The Analytic Press.

Anthony, E. J. & Benedek, T., eds. (1975), *Depression and Existence.* Boston: Little, Brown.

Apfelbaum, B. (1966), On ego psychology: A critique of the structural approach to psychoanalytic theory. *International Journal of Psycho-Analysis,* 47:451–475.

Aron, L. (1991), The patient's experience of the analyst's subjectivity. *Psychoanalytic Dialogues,* 1:29–51.

Aron, L. (1996), *A Meeting of Minds: Mutuality in Psychoanalysis.* Hillsdale, NJ: The Analytic Press.

Aron, L. & Hirsch, I. (1992), Money matters in psychoanalysis. In: *Relational Perspectives in Psychoanalysis,* ed. N. J. Skolnick & S. C. Warshaw. Hillsdale, NJ: The Analytic Press, pp. 239–256.

Arrington, R.L. (1989), *Rationalism, Realism, and Relativism.* Ithaca: Cornell University Press.

Atwood, G. & Stolorow, R. (1984), *Structures of Subjectivity: Explorations in Psychoanalytic Phenomenology.* Hillsdale, NJ: The Analytic Press.

Bader, M. J. (1995), Authenticity and the psychology of choice in the analyst. *The Psychoanalytic Quarterly,* 64:282–305.

Basch, M. F. (1975), Toward a theory that encompasses depression: A revision of existing causal hypotheses in psychoanalysis. In: *Depression and Human Existence,* ed. E. J. Anthony & T. Benedek. Boston: Little, Brown, pp. 485–534.

275

Basch, M. F. (1977), Developmental psychology and explanatory theory in psychoanalysis. *The Annual of Psychoanalysis,* 5:229–263. New York: International Universities Press.

Becker, E. (1973), *The Denial of Death.* New York: Free Press.

Beebe, B. & Lachmann, F. M. (1994), Representation and internalization in infancy: Three principles of salience. *Psychoanalytic Psychology,* 11:127–165.

Bell, C. (1992), *Ritual Theory, Ritual Practice.* New York: Oxford University Press.

Benedek, T. (1953), Dynamics of the countertransference. *Bulletin of The Menninger Clinic,* 17:201–208.

Benjamin, J. (1988), *The Bonds of Love: Psychoanalysis, Feminism, and the Problem of Domination.* New York: Pantheon Books.

Benjamin, J. (1991), Commentary on Irwin Z. Hoffman's discussion: "Toward a social-constructivist view of the psychoanalytic situation." *Psychoanalytic Dialogues,* 1:525–533.

Benjamin, J. (1994), Commentary on papers by Tansey, Davies, and Hirsch. *Psychoanalytic Dialogues,* 4:193–201.

Benjamin, J. (1995), *Like Subjects, Love Objects: Essays on Recognition and Sexual Difference.* New Haven, CT: Yale University Press.

Berger, P. & Luckmann, T. (1967), *The Social Construction of Reality.* Garden City, NY: Anchor Books.

Bernstein, R. (1983), *Beyond Objectivism and Relativism.* Philadelphia: University of Pennsylvania Press.

Bion, W. (1962), *Learning from Experience.* New York: Basic Books.

Black, M. (1987), The analyst's stance: Transferential implications of technical orientation. *The Annual of Psychoanalysis,* 15:127–172. New York: International Universities Press.

Blasi, A. & Hoeffel, E. C. (1974), Adolescence and formal operations. *Human Development,* 17:344–363.

Bollas, C. (1983), Expressive uses of the countertransference. *Contemporary Psychoanalysis,* 19:1–34.

Bollas, C. (1987), *The Shadow of the Object: Psychoanalysis of the Unthought Known.* New York: Columbia University Press.

Bonaparte, M. (1940), Time and the unconscious. *International Journal of Psycho-Analysis,* 21:427–468.

Bourdieu, P. (1990), *The Logic of Practice.* Stanford, CA: Stanford University Press.

Brandchaft, B. & Stolorow, R. D. (1990), Varieties of therapeutic alliance. *The Annual of Psychoanalysis,* 17:99–114. New York: International Universities Press.

Breuer, J. & Freud, S. (1893–1895), Studies on hysteria. *Standard Edition,* 2:3–303. London: Hogarth Press, 1955.

Bromberg, P. M. (1983), The mirror and the mask: On narcissism and psychoanalytic growth. *Contemporary Psychoanalysis,* 19:359–387.

Bromberg, P. M. (1994), "Speak! That I may see you": Some reflections on dissociation, reality, and psychoanalytic listening. *Psychoanalytic Dialogues*, 4:517–547.

Bromberg, P. M. (1996), Standing in the spaces. The multiplicity of self and the psychoanalytic relationship. *Contemporary Psychoanalysis*, 32:509–535.

Burke, W. F. (1992), Countertransference disclosure and the asymmetry/ mutuality dilemma. *Psychoanalytic Dialogues*, 2:241–271.

Clayton, V. (1975), Erikson's theory of human development as it applies to the aged: Wisdom as contradictive cognition. *Human Development*, 18:119–128.

Cohen, J. (1983), Psychotherapists preparing for death: Denial and action. *American Journal of Psychotherapy*, 37:223–226.

Cooper, S. H. (1997), Interpretation and the psychic future. *International Journal of Psycho-Analysis*, 78:667–681.

Cushman, P. (1991), Ideology obscured: Political uses of the self in Daniel Stern's infant. *American Psychologist*, 46:206–219.

Cushman, P. (1995), *Constructing the Self, Constructing America: A Cultural History of Psychotherapy*. Reading, MA: Addison-Wesley.

Davies, J. M. (1994a), Love in the afternoon: A relational consideration of desire and dread in the countertransference. *Psychoanalytic Dialogues*, 4:153–170.

Davies, J. M. (1994b), Desire and dread in the analyst: Reply to Gabbard's commentary on "Love in the afternoon." *Psychoanalytic Dialogues*, 4:503–508.

Davies, J. M. (1996), Linking the "pre-analytic" with the postclassical: Integration, dissociation, and the multiplicity of unconscious process. *Contemporary Psychoanalysis*, 32:553–556.

Davies, J. M. (1998a), Between the disclosure and the foreclosure of erotic transference-countertransference: Can psychoanalysis find a place for adult sexuality? *Psychoanalytic Dialogues*, 8:747–766.

Davies, J. M. (1998b), On the nature of desire: The ambiguous, the transitional, and the poetic. Reply to commentaries. *Psychoanalytic Dialogues*, 8:805–823.

Davies, J. M. & Frawley, M. G. (1994), *Treating the Adult Survivor of Childhood Sexual Abuse*. New York: Basic Books.

Dewald, P. A. (1972), *The Psychoanalytic Process*. New York: Basic Books.

Dimen, M. (1994), Money, love, and hate: Contradiction and paradox in psychoanalysis. *Psychoanalytic Dialogues*, 4:69–100.

Eagle, M. (1984), *Recent Developments in Psychoanalysis*. New York: McGraw-Hill.

Ehrenberg, D. B. (1982), Psychoanalytic engagement. *Contemporary Psychoanalysis*, 18:535–555.

Ehrenberg, D. B. (1984), Psychoanalytic engagement II: Affective considerations. *Contemporary Psychoanalysis*, 20:560–583.

Ehrenberg, D. B. (1990), Playfulness in the psychoanalytic relatio~ *Contemporary Psychoanalysis*, 26:74–95.

Ehrenberg, D. B. (1992), *The Intimate Edge. Extending the Reach of Psychoanalytic Interaction*. New York: Norton.

Eissler, K. (1955), *The Psychiatrist and the Dying Patient*. New York: International Universities Press.

Elliott, A. & Spezzano, C. (1996), Psychoanalysis at its limits: Navigating the postmodern turn. *The Psychoanalytic Quarterly, 65*:52–83.

Erikson, E. H. (1959), *Identity and the Life Cycle. Psychological Issues*, Monogr. 1. New York: International Universities Press.

Feiner, A. H. (1979) Countertransference and the anxiety of influence. In: *Countertransference: The Therapist's Contribution to the Therapeutic Situation*, ed. L. Epstein & A. H. Feiner. New York: Aronson.

Feiner, A. H. (1982), Comments on the difficult patient. *Contemporary Psychoanalysis, 18*:397–411.

Feiner, A. H. (1990), Playfulness and the interpersonal ideology. *Contemporary Psychoanalysis, 26*:95–107.

Feinsilver, D. B. (1983), Reality, transitional relatedness, and containment in the borderline. *Contemporary Psychoanalysis, 19*:537–569.

Feinsilver, D. B. (1989), Transitional play and regressed schizophrenic patients. In: *The Facilitating Environment: Clinical Applications of Winnicott's Theories*, ed. G. M. Fromm & B. L. Smith. Madison, CT: International Universities Press, pp. 205–237.

Feinsilver, D. B. (1990), Therapeutic action and the story of the middle. *Contemporary Psychoanalysis, 26*:137–158.

Fenichel, O. (1945), *The Psychoanalytic Theory of Neurosis*. New York: Norton.

Ferenczi, S. (1931), Child analysis in the analysis of adults. In: *Final Contributions to the Problems and Methods of Psycho-Analysis*, ed. M. Balint. New York: Brunner/Mazel, 1955, pp. 126–142.

Ferenczi, S. (1932), *The Clinical Diary of Sándor Ferenczi*, ed. J. Dupont (trans. M. Balint & N. Z. Jackson). Cambridge, MA: Harvard University Press, 1988.

Firestein, S. K. (1994), On thinking the unthinkable: Making a professional will. *The American Psychoanalyst, 27*:16.

Flax, J. (1996), Taking multiplicity seriously: Some consequences for psychoanalytic theorizing and practice. *Contemporary Psychoanalysis, 32*:577–593.

Fleming, J. & Altschul, S. (1963), Activation of mourning and growth by psychoanalysis. *International Journal of Psycho-Analysis, 44*:419–431.

Fosshage, J. L. (1997), Psychoanalysis and psychoanalytic psychotherapy: Is there a meaningful distinction in the process? *Psychoanalytic Psychology, 14*:409–425.

Fourcher, L. A. (1975), Psychological pathology and social reciprocity. *Human Development, 18*:405–429.

Fourcher, L. A. (1978), A view of subjectivity in the evolution of human behavior. *Journal of Social and Biological Structures, 1*:387–400.

Fourcher, L. A. (1992), Interpreting the relative and absolute unconscious. *Psychoanalytic Dialogues, 2*:317–329.

Fourcher, L. A. (1996), The authority of logic and the logic of authority. *Psychoanalytic Dialogues,* 6:515–532.

Frankel, S. A. (1995), *Intricate Engagements: The Collaborative Basis of Therapeutic Change.* Northvale, NJ: Aronson.

Frederickson, J. (1990), Hate in the countertransference as an empathic position. *Contemporary Psychoanalysis,* 26:479–496.

Freud, S. (1905a), Fragment of an analysis of a case of hysteria. *Standard Edition,* 7:7–122. London: Hogarth Press, 1953.

Freud, S. (1905b), On psychotherapy. *Standard Edition,* 7:257–268. London: Hogarth Press, 1953.

Freud, S. (1912), The dynamics of transference. *Standard Edition,* 12:99–108. London: Hogarth Press, 1958.

Freud, S. (1914a), On narcissism: An introduction. *Standard Edition,* 14:73–102. London: Hogarth Press, 1957.

Freud, S. (1914b), The unconscious. *Standard Edition,* 14:166–204. London: Hogarth Press, 1957.

Freud, S. (1915), Thoughts for the times on war and death. *Standard Edition,* 14:275–300. London: Hogarth Press, 1957.

Freud, S. (1916a), On transience. *Standard Edition,* 14:305–307. London: Hogarth Press, 1957.

Freud, S. (1916b), Some character types met with in psycho-analytic work. *Standard Edition,* 14:311–333. London: Hogarth Press, 1957.

Freud, S. (1917), Mourning and melancholia. *Standard Edition,* 14:243–258. London: Hogarth Press, 1957.

Freud, S. (1919), Lines of advance in psycho-analytic therapy. *Standard Edition,* 17:159–168, London: Hogarth Press, 1955.

Freud, S. (1920), Beyond the pleasure principle. *Standard Edition,* 18:7–61. London: Hogarth Press, 1955.

Freud, S. (1923), The ego and the id. *Standard Edition,* 19:3–66. London: Hogarth Press, 1961.

Freud, S. (1926a), Inhibitions, symptoms, and anxiety. *Standard Edition,* 20:77–175. London: Hogarth Press, 1959.

Freud, S. (1926b), The question of lay analysis. *Standard Edition,* 20:179–258. London: Hogarth Press, 1959.

Freud, S. (1927a), The future of an illusion. *Standard Edition,* 21:3–56. London: Hogarth Press, 1961.

Freud, S. (1927b), Fetishism. *Standard Edition,* 21:149–157. London: Hogarth Press, 1961.

Freud, S. (1933), New introductory lectures on psycho-analysis. *Standard Edition,* 22:7–182. London: Hogarth Press, 1964.

Freud, S. (1937), Analysis terminable and interminable. *Standard Edition,* 23:216–253, London: Hogarth Press, 1964.

Freud, S. (1939), Moses and monotheism: Three essays. *Standard Edition,* 23:1–137. London: Hogarth Press, 1964.

Freud, S. (1940a), An outline of psycho-analysis. *Standard Edition,* 23:144–207. London: Hogarth Press, 1964.

Freud, S. (1940b), Splitting of the ego in the process of defense. *Standard Edition*, 23:275–278. London: Hogarth Press, 1964.

Friedman, L. (1969), The therapeutic alliance. *International Journal of Psycho-Analysis*, 50:139–153.

Futterman, E. H. & Hoffman, I. (1973), Crisis and adaptation in the families of fatally ill children. In: *The Child in His Family: The Impact of Disease and Death*, ed. J. Anthony & C. Koupernik. New York: Wiley, pp. 127–143.

Futterman, E. H., Hoffman, I. & Sabshin, M. (1972), Parental anticipatory mourning. In: *Psychosocial Aspects of Terminal Care*, ed. B. Schoenberg, A. C. Carr, D. Peretz & A. H. Kutscher. New York: Columbia University Press, pp. 243–272.

Gabbard, G. O. (1994a), Commentary on papers by Tansey, Hirsch, and Davies. *Psychoanalytic Dialogues*, 4:203–213.

Gabbard, G. O. (1994b), A response to Davies (but not the last word). *Psychoanalytic Dialogues*, 4:509–510.

Gabbard, G. O. (1996), *Love and Hate in the Analytic Setting*. Northvale, NJ: Aronson.

Garcia-Lawson, K. A. & Lane, R. C. (1997), Thoughts on termination: Practical considerations. *Psychoanalytic Psychology*, 14:239–257.

Gedo, J. E. (1983), Saints or scoundrels and the objectivity of the analyst. *Psychoanalytic Inquiry*, 3:609–622.

Gendlin, E. T. (1962), *Experiencing and the Creation of Meaning: A Philosophical and Psychological Approach to the Subjective*. New York: Macmillan.

Gendlin, E. T. (1964), A theory of personality change. In: *Personality Change*, ed. P. Worchel & D. Byrne. New York: Wiley, pp. 100–148.

Gendlin, E. T. (1973), Experiential psychotherapy. In: *Current Psychotherapies*, ed. R. J. Corsini. Itasca, IL: Peacock, pp. 317–352.

Gergen, K. (1985), The social constructionist movement in modern psychology. *American Psychologist*, 40:266–275.

Gergen, K. J. (1988), If persons are texts. In: *Hermeneutics and Psychological Theory*, ed. S. B. Messer, L. A. Sass & R. L. Woolfolk. New Brunswick, NJ: Rutgers University Press, pp. 28–51.

Gerson, B., ed. (1996), *The Therapist as a Person*. Hillsdale, NJ: The Analytic Press.

Ghent, E. (1989), Credo: The dialectics of one-person and two-person psychologies. *Contemporary Psychoanalysis*, 25:169–211.

Ghent, E. (1990), Masochism, submission, surrender. *Contemporary Psychoanalysis*, 26:108–136.

Ghent, E. (1992), Paradox and process. *Psychoanalytic Dialogues*, 2:136–159.

Gill, M. M. (1954), Psychoanalysis and exploratory psychotherapy. *Journal of the American Psychoanalytic Association*, 2:771–797.

Gill, M. M. (1979), The analysis of the transference. *Journal of the American Psychoanalytic Association*, 27:263–288.

Gill, M. M. (1982a), *Analysis of Transference, Vol. 1: Theory and Technique*. New York: International Universities Press.

Gill, M. M. (1982b), Merton Gill: An interview [by J. Reppen]. *Psychoanalytic Review*, 69:167–190.

Gill, M. M. (1983), The distinction between the interpersonal paradigm and the degree of the therapist's involvement. *Contemporary Psychoanalysis*, 19:200–237.

Gill, M. M. (1984a), Psychoanalysis and psychotherapy: A revision. *International Review of Psycho-Analysis*, 11:161–179.

Gill, M. M. (1984b), Robert Langs on technique: A critique. In: *Listening and Interpreting: The Challenge of the Work of Robert Langs*, ed. J. Raney. New York: Aronson, pp. 395–413.

Gill, M. M. (1991), Indirect suggestion: A response to Oremland's *Interpretation and Interaction*. Chapter 10 in *Interpretation and Interaction: Psychoanalysis or Psychotherapy?* by J. D. Oremland. Hillsdale, NJ: The Analytic Press, pp. 137–163.

Gill, M. M. (1994), *Psychoanalysis in Transition: A Personal View*. Hillsdale, NJ: The Analytic Press.

Gill, M. M. & Hoffman, I. Z. (1982a), *Analysis of Transference II: Studies of Nine Audio-Recorded Psychoanalytic Sessions*. New York: International Universities Press.

Gill, M. M. & Hoffman, I. Z. (1982b), A method for studying the analysis of aspects of the patient's experience of the relationship in psychoanalysis and psychotherapy. *Journal of the American Psychoanalytic Association*, 30:137–167.

Goldberg, P. (1989), Actively seeking the holding environment. *Contemporary Psychoanalysis*, 25:448–476.

Golland, J. H. (1997), Not an endgame: Terminations in psychoanalysis. *Psychoanalytic Psychology*, 14:259–270.

Grand, S. (1997), The persistence of nonlinguistic testimony. In: *Memories of Sexual Betrayal: Truth, Fantasy, Repression, and Dissociation*, ed. R. B. Gartner. Northvale, NJ: Aronson, pp. 209–219.

Greenberg, J. R. (1981), Prescription or description: The therapeutic action of psychoanalysis. *Contemporary Psychoanalysis*, 17:239–257.

Greenberg, J. R. (1986), Theoretical models and the analyst's neutrality. *Contemporary Psychoanalysis*, 22:87–106.

Greenberg, J. R. (1987), Of mystery and motive: A review of "The Ambiguity of Change" [by Edgar Levenson]. *Contemporary Psychoanalysis*, 23:689–704.

Greenberg, J. R. (1991), Countertransference and reality. *Psychoanalytic Dialogues*, 1:52–73.

Greenberg, J. R. (1995a), Psychoanalytic technique and the interactive matrix. *The Psychoanalytic Quarterly*, 64:1–22.

Greenberg, J. R. (1995b), Reply to discussions of *Oedipus and Beyond*. *Psychoanalytic Dialogues*, 5:317–324.

Greenberg, J. & Mitchell, S. (1983), *Object Relations in Psychoanalytic Theory*. Cambridge, MA: Harvard University Press.

Greenson, R. (1965), The working alliance and the transference neurosis. *The Psychoanalytic Quarterly*, 34:155–181.

Greenson, R. (1971), The real relationship between the patient and the psychoanalyst. In: *The Unconscious Today*, ed. M. Kanzer. New York: International Universities Press, pp. 213–232.

Grene, M. (1957), *Martin Heidegger*. New York: Hillary House.

Grey, C. C. (1993). Culture, character, and the analytic engagement: Toward a subversive psychoanalysis. *Contemporary Psychoanalysis*, 29:487–502.

Grotjahn, M. (1955), Analytic psychotherapy with the elderly. *Psychoanalytic Review*, 42:419–425.

Grotstein, J.S. (1993), Boundary difficulties in borderline patients. In: *Master Clinicians Treating the Regressed Patient*, Vol. 2, ed. L. B. Boyer & P. L. Giovacchini. Northvale, NJ: Aronson, pp. 107–141.

Guidi, N. (1993), Unobjectionable negative transference. *The Annual of Psychoanalysis*, 21:107–121, New York: International Universities Press.

Guntrip, H. (1969), *Schizoid Phenomena, Object Relations and the Self*. New York: International Universities Press.

Hagman, G. (1995), Mourning: A review and reconsideration. *International Journal of Psychoanalysis*, 76:909–925.

Hare-Mustin, R. & Marecek, J. (1988), The meaning of difference: Gender theory, postmodernism, and psychology. *American Psychologist*, 43:455–464.

Harris, A. (1996), The conceptual power of multiplicity. *Contemporary Psychoanalysis*, 32:537–552.

Hartmann, H. (1958), *Ego Psychology and the Problem of Adaptation*. New York: International Universities Press.

Hartmann, H. (1964), *Essays on Ego Psychology*. New York: International Universities Press.

Hartmann, H. & Kris, E. (1945), The genetic approach in psychoanalysis. *The Psychoanalytic Study of the Child*, 1:11–30. New York: International Universities Press.

Heimann, P. (1950), On countertransference. *International Journal of Psycho-Analysis*, 31:81–84.

Hirsch, I. (1987), Varying modes of analytic participation. *Journal of the American Academy of Psychoanalysis*, 15:205–222.

Hirsch, I. (1993), Countertransference enactments and some issues related to external factors in the analyst's life. *Psychoanalytic Dialogues*, 3:343–366.

Hirsch, I. (1994), Countertransference love and theoretical model. *Psychoanalytic Dialogues*, 4:171–192.

Hoffer, A. (1985), Toward a redefinition of psychoanalytic neutrality. *Journal of the American Psychoanalytic Association*, 33:771–795.

Hoffman, I. Z. (1972), Parental adaptation to fatal illness in a child. Doctoral dissertation, University of Chicago.

Hoffman, I. Z. (1987), The value of uncertainty in psychoanalytic practice [Discussion of paper by E. Witenberg]. *Contemporary Psychoanalysis*, 23:205–215.

Hoffman, I. Z. (1990), In the eye of the beholder: A reply to Levenson. *Contemporary Psychoanalysis,* 26:291–299.

Hoffman, I. Z. (1991), Reply to Benjamin. *Psychoanalytic Dialogues,* 1:535–544.

Hoffman. I. Z. (1992), Reply to Orange. *Psychoanalytic Dialogues,* 2:567–570.

Hoffman, I. Z. (1995), Review of *Oedipus and Beyond* by J. Greenberg. *Psychoanalytic Dialogues,* 5:93–112.

Hoffman, I. Z. (1996), Merton M. Gill: A study in theory development in psychoanalysis. *Psychoanalytic Dialogues,* 6:5–53. An earlier version of this article was published in *Beyond Freud,* ed. J. Reppen (The Analytic Press, 1985).

Hoffman, I. Z. (1998), Poetic transformations of erotic experience: Commentary on paper by Jody Messler Davies. *Psychoanalytic Dialogues,* 8:791–804.

Hoffman, I. Z. & Futterman, E. H. (1971), Coping with waiting: Psychiatric intervention and study in the waiting room of a pediatric oncology clinic. *Comprehensive Psychiatry,* 12:67–81.

Hoffman I. Z. & Gill, M. M. (1988a), A scheme for coding the patient's experience of the relationship with the therapist (PERT): Some applications, extensions, and comparisons. In *Psychoanalytic Process Research Strategies,* ed. H. Dahl, H. Kächele & H. Thomä. New York: Springer-Verlag, pp. 67–98.

Hoffman, I. Z. & Gill, M. M. (1988b), Critical reflections on a coding scheme. *International Journal of Psycho-Analysis,* 69:55–64.

Holt, R. R. (1972), Freud's mechanistic and humanistic images of man. In: *Psychoanalysis and Contemporary Science, Vol. 1,* ed. R. Holt & E. Peterfreund. New York: Macmillan, pp. 3–24.

Holt, R. R. (1989), *Freud Reappraised.* New York: Guilford.

Howard, G. S. (1985), The role of values in the science of psychology. *American Psychologist,* 40:255–265.

Issacharoff, A. (1979), Barriers to knowing. In: *Countertransference: The Therapist's Contributions to the Therapeutic Situation,* ed. L. Epstein & A. H. Feiner. New York: Aronson.

Jacobs, T. J. (1986), On countertransference enactments. *Journal of the American Psychoanalytic Association,* 34:289–307.

Jacobs, T. J. (1990), The corrective emotional experience: Its place in current technique. *Psychoanalytic Inquiry,* 10:433–454.

Jacobs, T. J. (1991), *The Use of the Self: Countertransference and Communication in the Analytic Situation.* Madison, CT: International Universities Press.

Jones, W. T. (1975), *A History of Western Philosophy: The Twentieth Century to Wittgenstein and Sartre.* New York: Harcourt Brace Jovanovich.

Kafka, J. S. (1972), Experience of time. *Journal of the American Psychoanalytic Association,* 20:650–667.

Kantrowitz, J. L. (1996), *The Patient's Impact on the Analyst.* Hillsdale, NJ: The Analytic Press.

Kastenbaum, R. (1977), Death and development through the lifespan. In: *New Meanings of Death*, ed. H. Feifel. New York: McGraw-Hill, pp. 17–45.

Kern, J. W. (1987), Transference neurosis as a waking dream: Notes on a clinical enigma. *Journal of the American Psychoanalytic Association*, 35:337–366.

Koestenbaum, P. (1964), The vitality of death. *Journal of Existentialism*, 5:139–166.

Kohut, H. (1966), Forms and transformations of narcissism. *Journal of the American Psychoanalytic Association*, 14:243–272.

Kohut, H. (1971), *The Analysis of the Self*. New York: International Universities Press.

Kohut, H. (1977), *The Restoration of the Self*. New York: International Universities Press.

Kohut, H. (1984), *How Does Analysis Cure?* ed. A. Goldberg & P. Stepansky. Chicago: University of Chicago Press.

Kovel, J. (1974), Erik Erikson's psychohistory. *Social Policy*, March/April, pp. 60–64.

Lacan, J. (1977), *Écrits: A Selection*, trans. A. Sheridan. New York: Norton.

Langs, R. (1978), *Technique in Transition*. New York: Aronson.

Langs, R. (1978–1979), Editorial note. *International Journal of Psychoanalytic Psychotherapy*, 7:165.

Levenson, E. A. (1972), *The Fallacy of Understanding*. New York: Basic Books.

Levenson, E. A. (1981), Facts or fantasies: The nature of psychoanalytic data. *Contemporary Psychoanalysis*, 17:486–500.

Levenson, E. A. (1983), *The Ambiguity of Change: An Inquiry into the Nature of Psychoanalytic Reality*. New York: Basic Books.

Levenson, E. A. (1989), Whatever happened to the cat? Interpersonal perspectives on the self. *Contemporary Psychoanalysis*, 25:537–553.

Levenson, E. A. (1990), Reply to Hoffman. *Contemporary Psychoanalysis*, 26:299–304.

Lichtenberg, J. D. (1983), The influence of values and value judgments on the psychoanalytic encounter. *Psychoanalytic Inquiry*, 3:647–674.

Lipton, S. D. (1977a), The advantages of Freud's technique as shown in his analysis of the Rat Man. *International Journal of Psycho-Analysis*, 58:255–273.

Lipton, S. D. (1977b), Clinical observations on resistance to the transference. *International Journal of Psycho-Analysis*, 58:463–472.

Lipton, S. D. (1982), A critical review of Paul Dewald's *The Psychoanalytic Process*. *Contemporary Psychoanalysis*, 18:349–365.

Loewald, H. W. (1960), On the therapeutic action of psycho-analysis. *International Journal of Psycho-Analysis*, 41:16–33.

Loewald, H. W. (1979), The waning of the Oedipus complex. In: *Papers on Psychoanalysis*. New Haven, CT: Yale University Press, 1980, pp. 384–404.

Macalpine, I. (1950), The development of the transference. *The Psycho-analytic Quarterly,* 19:501–539.

Mahoney, M. J. (1991), *Human Change Processes: The Scientific Foundations of Psychotherapy.* New York: Basic Books.

McGowan, J. (1991). *Postmodernism and Its Critics.* Ithaca: Cornell University Press.

McLaughlin, J. T. (1981), Transference, psychic reality, and countertransference. *The Psychoanalytic Quarterly,* 50:639–664.

McLaughlin, J. T. (1988), The analyst's insights. *The Psychoanalytic Quarterly,* 57:370–389.

Meissner, W. W. (1983), Values in the psychoanalytic situation. *Psychoanalytic Inquiry,* 3:577–598.

Merleau-Ponty, M. (1964), *Sense and Non-Sense,* trans. H. L. Dreyfus & P. A. Dreyfus. Evanston, IL: Northwestern University Press.

Meyer, J. E. (1975), *Death and Neurosis.* New York: International Universities Press.

Miller, J. B. M. (1971), Children's reaction to the death of a parent: A review of the psychoanalytic literature. *Journal of the American Psychoanalytic Association,* 19:697–719.

Mitchell, S. A. (1986), The wings of Icarus: Illusion and the problem of narcissism. *Contemporary Psychoanalysis,* 22:107–132.

Mitchell, S. A. (1988), *Relational Concepts in Psychoanalysis: An Integration.* Cambridge, MA: Harvard University Press.

Mitchell, S. A. (1991), Wishes, needs, and interpersonal negotiations. *Psychoanalytic Inquiry,* 11:147–170.

Mitchell, S. A. (1993), *Hope and Dread in Psychoanalysis.* New York: Basic Books.

Mitchell, S. A. (1997), *Influence and Autonomy in Psychoanalysis.* Hillsdale, NJ: The Analytic Press.

Modell, A. H. (1990), *Other Times, Other Realities: Toward a Theory of Psychoanalytic Treatment.* Cambridge, MA: Harvard University Press.

Modell, A. H. (1991), The therapeutic relationship as a paradoxical experience. *Psychoanalytic Dialogues,* 1:13–28.

Moore, B. E. & Fine, B. D. (1968), *A Glossary of Psychoanalytic Terms and Concepts.* New York: American Psychoanalytic Association.

Moore, B. E. & Fine, B. D. (1990), *Psychoanalytic Terms and Concepts,* 3rd ed., revised. New Haven, CT: Yale University Press.

Moraitis, G. (1981), The analyst's response to the limitations of his science. *Psychoanalytic Inquiry,* 1:57–79.

Moraitis, G. (1987), A reexamination of phobias as the fear of the unknown. *The Annual of Psychoanalysis,* 16:231–249. New York: International Universities Press.

Muslin, H. L, Levine, S. P. & Levine, H. (1974), Partners in dying. *American Journal of Psychiatry,* 131:308–310.

Nagel, T. (1986), *The View from Nowhere.* New York: Oxford University Press.

Nagy, M. H. (1959), The child's view of death. In: *The Meaning of Death,* ed. H. Feifel. New York: McGraw-Hill, pp. 79–98.

Natterson, J. (1991), *Beyond Countertransference: The Therapist's Subjectivity in the Therapeutic Process.* Northvale, NJ: Aronson.

Newman, K. M. (1992), Abstinence, neutrality, gratification: New trends, new climates, new implications. *The Annual of Psychoanalysis,* 20:131–144. Hillsdale, NJ: The Analytic Press.

Norris, C. (1990), *What's Wrong with Postmodernism.* Baltimore: Johns Hopkins University Press.

Nussbaum, M. C. (1990), Transcending humanity. In: *Love's Knowledge.* New York: Oxford University Press, pp. 365–391.

Nussbaum, M. C. (1994), Mortal immortals: Lucretius on death and the voice of nature. In: *The Therapy of Desire.* Princeton University Press, pp. 192–238.

Ogden, T. H. (1979), On projective identification. *International Journal of Psycho-Analysis,* 60:357–373.

Ogden, T. H. (1986), *The Matrix of the Mind: Object Relations and the Psychoanalytic Dialogue.* Northvale, NJ: Aronson.

Ogden, T. H. (1989), *The Primitive Edge of Experience.* Northvale, NJ: Jason Aronson.

Orange, D. M. (1992), Perspectival realism and social constructivism: Commentary on Irwin Hoffman's "Discussion: Toward a social-constructivist view of the psychoanalytic situation." *Psychoanalytic Dialogues,* 2:561–565.

Palmer, D. (1988), *Looking at Philosophy.* Mountain View, CA: Mayfield.

Peltz, R. A. (1998), The dialectic of presence and absence: Impasses and the retrieval of meaning states. *Psychoanalytic Dialogues,* 8:385–409.

Phillips, A. (1993), *On Kissing, Tickling, and Being Bored.* Cambridge, MA: Harvard University Press.

Phillips, A. (1994), *On Flirtation.* Cambridge, MA: Harvard University Press.

Phillips, A. (1996), *Terrors and Experts.* Cambridge, MA: Harvard University Press.

Piaget, J. (1963), *The Child's Conception of the World.* Paterson, NJ: Littlefield, Adams.

Piaget, J. & Inhelder, B. (1956), *The Child's Conception of Space.* London: Routledge & Kegan Paul.

Pine, F. (1990), *Drive, Ego, Object, Self.* New York: Basic Books.

Pizer, S. A. (1992), The negotiation of paradox in the analytic process. *Psychoanalytic Dialogues,* 2:215–240.

Pizer, S. A. (1996), The distributed self: Introduction to symposium on "the multiplicity of self and analytic technique." *Contemporary Psychoanalysis,* 32:499–507.

Pollock, G. H. (1961), Mourning and adaptation. *International Journal of Psycho-Analysis,* 42:341–361.

Pollock, G. H. (1971a), On time, death and immortality. *The Psychoanalytic Quarterly,* 40:435–446.

Pollock, G. H. (1971b), On time and anniversaries. In: *The Unconscious Today,* ed. M. Kanzer. New York: International Universities Press, pp. 233–257.

Protter, B. (1985), Toward an emergent psychoanalytic epistemology. *Contemporary Psychoanalysis,* 21:208–227.

Racker, H. (1968), *Transference and Countertransference.* New York: International Universities Press.

Rapaport, D. (1960), *The Structure of Psychoanalytic Theory. Psychological Issues,* Monogr. 6. New York: International Universities Press.

Rapaport, D. & Gill, M. (1959), The point of view and assumptions of metapsychology. *International Journal of Psycho-Analysis,* 40:153–162.

Renik, O. (1992), Use of the analyst as a fetish. *The Psychoanalytic Quarterly,* 61:542–563.

Renik, O. (1993), Analytic interaction: Conceptualizing technique in light of the analyst's irreducible subjectivity. *The Psychoanalytic Quarterly,* 62:553–571.

Rescher, N. (1995), *Luck: The Brilliant Randomness of Everyday Life.* New York: Farrar, Straus & Giroux.

Rieff, P. (1966), *The Triumph of the Therapeutic: Uses of Faith After Freud.* New York: Harper & Row.

Rieff, P. (1987), For the last time psychology. In: *The Feeling Intellect: Selected Writings.* Chicago: University of Chicago Press, 1990, pp. 351–365.

Rogers, C. (1951), *Client-Centered Therapy.* Boston: Houghton Mifflin.

Sandler, J. (1976), Countertransference and role responsiveness. *International Review of Psycho-Analysis,* 3:43–47.

Sandler, J. (1981), Character traits and object relationships. *The Psychoanalytic Quarterly,* 50:694–708.

Sandler, J., Holder, A., Kawenoka, M., Kennedy, H. E. & Neurath, L. (1969), Notes on some theoretical and clinical aspects of transference. *International Journal of Psycho-Analysis,* 50:633–645.

Sass, L. A. (1988), Humanism, hermeneutics, and the concept of the human subject. In: *Hermeneutics and Psychological Theory,* ed. S. B. Messer, L. A. Sass & R. L. Woolfolk. New Brunswick, NJ: Rutgers University Press, pp. 222–271.

Sass, L. A. (1997), The absurdity of therapy and the therapy of the absurd: Discussion of "The dialectic of meaning and mortality in the psychoanalytic process," by Irwin Z. Hoffman. Presented at the meetings of the American Psychological Association, Chicago, August 16.

Sass, L. A. (1998), Ambiguity is of the essence: The relevance of hermeneutics for psychoanalysis. In: *Psychoanalytic Versions of the Human Condition: Philosophies of Life and Their Impact on Practice,* ed. P. Marcus & A. Rosenberg. New York: New York University Press, pp. 257–305.

Schafer, R. (1974), Talking to patients in psychotherapy. *Bulletin of the Menninger Clinic,* 38:503–515. Reprinted in *Retelling a Life: Narration and Dialogue in Psychoanalysis* (New York: Basic Books, 1992).

Schafer, R. (1976), *A New Language for Psychoanalysis*. New Haven, CT: Yale University Press.

Schafer, R. (1983), *The Analytic Attitude*. New York: Basic Books.

Schafer, R. (1985), The interpretation of psychic reality, developmental influences, and unconscious communication. *Journal of the American Psychoanalytic Association*, 33:537–554.

Schafer, R. (1992), *Retelling a Life: Narration and Dialogue in Psychoanalysis*. New York: Basic Books.

Schimek, J. G. (1975), A critical re-examination of Freud's concept of unconscious mental representation. *International Review of Psycho-Analysis*, 2:171–187.

Schön, D. (1983), *The Reflective Practitioner: How Professionals Think in Action*. New York: Basic Books.

Schur, M. (1972), *Freud: Living and Dying*. New York: International Universities Press.

Searles, H. F. (1961), Schizophrenia and the inevitability of death. *Psychiatric Quarterly*, 35:631–665.

Searles, H. F. (1965), *Collected Papers on Schizophrenia and Related Subjects*. New York: International Universities Press.

Searles, H. F. (1975), The patient as therapist to his analyst. In: *Tactics and Techniques in Psychoanalytic Therapy, Vol. 2: Countertransference*, ed. P. L. Giovacchini. Northvale, NJ: Aronson, pp. 95–151.

Searles, H. F. (1978–1979), Concerning transference and countertransference. *International Journal of Psychoanalytic Psychotherapy*, 7:165–188.

Seligman, S. (1991), What is structured in psychic structure? Affects, internal representations, and the relational self. Presented at the spring meeting of the Division of Psychoanalysis, American Psychological Association, Chicago.

Seligman, S. & Shanok, R. S. (1995), Subjectivity, complexity, and the social world: Erikson's identity concept and contemporary relational theories. *Psychoanalytic Dialogues*, 5:537–565.

Shepardson, C. (1996), The intimate alterity of the real: A response to reader commentary on "History and the real" *(Postmodern Culture*, 5[2]). *Postmodern Culture*, 6(3) (electronic journal).

Siggins, L. D. (1966), Mourning: A critical survey of the literature. *International Journal of Psycho-Analysis*, 47:14–25.

Slater, P. E. (1964), Prolegomena to a psychoanalytic theory of aging and death. In: *New Thoughts on Old Age*, ed. R. Kastenbaum. New York: Springer, pp. 19–40.

Slavin, J. H. (1994), On making rules: Toward a reformulation of the dynamics of transference in psychoanalytic treatment. *Psychoanalytic Dialogues*, 4:253–274.

Slavin, M. O. & Kriegman, D. (1992), *The Adaptive Design of the Human Psyche*. New York: Guilford.

Spence, D. P. (1982), *Narrative Truth and Historical Truth: Meaning and Interpretation in Psychoanalysis*. New York: Norton.

Spezzano, C. (1993), *Affect in Psychoanalysis: A Clinical Synthesis*. Hillsdale, NJ: The Analytic Press.

Stein, M. H. (1981), The unobjectionable part of the transference. *Journal of the American Psychoanalytic Association*, 29:869–892.

Stein, M. H. (1985), Irony in psychoanalysis. *Journal of the American Psychoanalytic Association*, 33:35–57.

Stein, M. H. (1988a), Writing about psychoanalysis: I. Analysts who write and those who do not. *Journal of the American Psychoanalytic Association*, 36:105–124.

Stein, M. H. (1988b), Writing about psychoanalysis: II. Analysts who write, patients who read. *Journal of the American Psychoanalytic Association*, 36:393–408.

Sterba, R. (1934), The fate of the ego in analytic therapy. *International Journal of Psycho-Analysis*, 15:117–126.

Stern, D. B. (1983), Unformulated experience. *Contemporary Psychoanalysis*, 19:71–99.

Stern, D. B. (1985), Some controversies regarding constructivism and psychoanalysis. *Contemporary Psychoanalysis*, 21:201–208.

Stern, D. B. (1989), The analyst's unformulated experience of the patient. *Contemporary Psychoanalysis*, 25:1–33.

Stern, D. B. (1990), Courting surprise. *Contemporary Psychoanalysis*, 26:598–611.

Stern, D. B. (1991), A philosophy for the embedded analyst: Gadamer's hermeneutics and the social paradigm of psychoanalysis. *Contemporary Psychoanalysis*, 27:51–80.

Stern, D. B. (1997), *Unformulated Experience: From Dissociation to Imagination in Psychoanalysis*. Hillsdale, NJ: The Analytic Press.

Stern, S. (1994), Needed relationships and repeated relationships: An integrated relational perspective. *Psychoanalytic Dialogues*, 4:317–345.

Stolorow, R. D. (1988), Intersubjectivity, psychoanalytic knowing, and reality. *Contemporary Psychoanalysis*, 24:331–338.

Stolorow, R. D. (1990), Converting psychotherapy to psychoanalysis: A critique of the underlying assumptions. *Psychoanalytic Inquiry*, 10:119–129.

Stolorow, R. D. & Atwood, G. E. (1992), *Contexts of Being: The Intersubjective Foundations of Psychological Life*. Hillsdale, NJ: The Analytic Press.

Stolorow, R. D. & Atwood, G. E. (1997), Deconstructing the myth of the neutral analyst: An alternative from intersubjective systems theory. *The Psychoanalytic Quarterly*, 66:431–449.

Stone, L. (1961), *The Psychoanalytic Situation*. New York: International Universities Press.

Strachey, J. (1934), The nature of the therapeutic action of psychoanalysis. *International Journal of Psycho-Analysis*, 15:127–159. Republished in 1969. 50:275–292.

Szasz, T. (1963), The concept of transference. *International Journal of Psycho-Analysis*, 44:432–443.

Taft, J. (1933), *The Dynamics of Therapy in a Controlled Relationship.* New York: Dover Publications, 1962.

Tansey, M. J. (1994), Sexual attraction and phobic dread in the countertransference. *Psychoanalytic Dialogues,* 4:139–152.

Tansey, M. J. & Burke, W. (1989), *Understanding Countertransference: From Projective Identification to Empathy.* Hillsdale, NJ: The Analytic Press.

Taylor, C. (1985), *Human Agency and Language: Philosophical Papers 1.* Cambridge: Cambridge University Press.

Taylor, C. (1989), *Sources of the Self: The Making of the Modern Identity.* Cambridge, MA: Harvard University Press.

Thompson, C. (1964a), Transference as a therapeutic instrument. In: *Interpersonal Psychoanalysis,* ed. M. Green. New York: Basic Books, pp. 13–21.

Thompson, C. (1964b), The role of the analyst's personality in therapy. In: *Interpersonal Psychoanalysis,* ed. M. Green. New York: Basic Books, pp. 168–178.

Thompson, M. G. (1994), The existential dimension to termination. *Psychoanalysis and Contemporary Thought,* 17:355–386.

Tillich, P. (1956), Existential analyses and religious symbols. In: *Four Existentialist Theologians,* ed. W. Herberg. Garden City: Doubleday Anchor Books, 1958, pp. 277–291.

Tower, L. (1956), Countertransference. *Journal of the American Psychoanalytic Association,* 4:224–255.

Turner, V. (1969), *The Ritual Process: Structure and Anti-Structure.* Chicago: Aldine.

van der Kolk, B. A., McFarlane, A. C. & Weisaeth, L., eds. (1996), *Traumatic Stress: The Effects of Overwhelming Experience on Mind, Body, and Society.* New York: Guilford.

von Glaserfeld, E. (1984), An introduction to radical constructivism. In: *The Invented Reality: Contributions to Constructivism,* ed. P. Watzlawick. New York: Norton, pp. 18–40.

Wachtel, P. L. (1980), Transference, schema and assimilation: The relevance of Piaget to the psychoanalytic theory of transference. *The Annual of Psychoanalysis,* 8:59–76. New York: International Universities Press.

Wachtel, P. L. (1983), *The Poverty of Affluence.* New York: Free Press.

Wallerstein, R. (1983), Reality and its attributes as psychoanalytic concepts: An historical overview. *International Review of Psycho-Analysis,* 10:125–144.

Weiss, J., Sampson, H., and the Mount Zion Psychotherapy Research Group (1986), *The Psychoanalytic Process: Theory, Clinical Observations and Empirical Research.* New York: Guilford.

Weissman, A. D. (1977), The psychiatrist and the inexorable. In: *New Meanings of Death,* ed. H. Feifel. New York: McGraw-Hill, pp. 107–122.

Werner, H. (1957), The concept of development from a comparative and organismic point of view. In: *The Concept of Development: An Issue in the Study of Behavior,* ed. D. B. Harris. Minneapolis, MN: University of Minnesota Press, pp. 125–148.

Wetmore, R. J. (1963), The role of grief in psychoanalysis. *International Journal of Psycho-Analysis,* 44:97–103.

Winer, R. (1994), *Close Encounters: A Relational View of the Therapeutic Process.* Northvale, NJ: Aronson.

Winnicott, D. W. (1949), Hate in the countertransference. *International Journal of Psycho-Analysis,* 30:69–75.

Winnicott, D. W. (1968), Communication between infant and mother, and mother and infant, compared and contrasted. In: *Babies and Their Mothers,* ed. C. Winnicott, R. Shepherd & M. Davis. Reading, MA: Addison-Wesley, 1987, pp. 89–103.

Winnicott, D. W. (1971). *Playing and Reality.* New York: Tavistock.

Wolf, E. S. (1979), Countertransference in disorders of the self. In: *Countertransference: The Therapist's Contribution to the Therapeutic Situation,* ed. L. Epstein & A. H. Feiner. New York: Aronson.

Yalom, I. D. (1980), *Existential Psychotherapy.* New York: Basic Books.

Zetzel, E. R. (1956), Current concepts of transference. *International Journal of Psycho-Analysis,* 37:369–376.

Zucker, H. (1993), Reality: Can it be only yours or mine? *Contemporary Psychoanalysis,* 29:479–486.

Index

Analyst *(continued)*
  self-disclosure of, xxii*n*, 93–94,
      148, 182–83, 251, 272
  drawbacks and benefits of, 94,
      128–30, 129*n*, 148–49,
      197–98
  of erotic countertransference,
      184*n*, 187*n*, 272, 272*n*
  versus inadvertently revealing
      behavior, 149
  of rageful countertransference,
      171–74, 184
  of reactions to patient's ques-
      tions, 148, 152–53
  in revealing personal bias, 28, 94
  and risk of seductiveness,
      149–50
  and subversion of authenticity,
      197–98
  as subjectively involved, 25–30,
      74, 88–95, 133–34, 193,
      195
  versus technically rational,
      xii–xvi, xxii, xxiv–xxv,
      xxvi–xxvii, 3–4, 74–76,
      78–79, 85–86, 94–95,
      150, 176–77, 181–82,
      195–96
  subjectivity of, patient's interest
      in, 148
  theoretical bias of, xxvi, 74, 140,
      165–66
  uncertainty of, xxv–xxvii, 25, 29,
      75–76, 90, 124–25, 136,
      166–71, 181, 185,
      210–213, 221–25
  versus certainty of self-
      knowledge and social
      control, 168*n*
  in constructivism versus open-
      minded positivism, 168–69
  visibility and invisibility of (*See
      under* Analytic relationship,
      asymmetry of; Authority,
      of the analyst, and subor-
      dination of subjectivity)

Analytic relationship. *See also*
      Analyst; Asocial paradigm;
      Dialectical relationships;
      Frame, analytic; Oedipal
      dynamics; Social paradigm
  and analyst's participation
      initiative and responsiveness,
          157–58, 160*n*, 183–84,
          185–86
  asymmetry of, xxi, xxvii, 8–9,
      94–95, 148, 158–60, 161,
      178, 199, 258, 265, 272
  and power of mutuality,
      84–85, 151–52, 152*n*,
      159–60, 202–4, 212,
      212*n*, 219–20, 233–34
  boundaries and intimacy in,
      81–82
  changing conceptions of, 3–5, 199
  compared to other relationships,
      12–13, 198–99
  compared to prostitution, 5
  conflicting interests of patient
      and analyst, 4*n*
  culturally conforming versus crit-
      ical, 86–88
  idealization, interactional
      fostering of, xxiv, 83–84,
      151–52, 156–57
  and love, xix, 3–6, 4*n*, 11–14,
      17, 22, 30, 80, 84
  parent-child prototype, xix, xxiv,
      xxviii, 8–9, 11–14, 13,
      80–81, 84, 92, 148, 151,
      187–88, 189, 202,
      206–09, 214, 232,
      240–41, 243, 253–55,
      257, 263
  in psychoanalysis and psycho-
      therapy, xiii–xvi, 69, 69*n*,
      71–72, 99–100, 164*n*,
      177*n*, 205
  real versus transference in asocial
      model, 101–3, 138–40
  seductiveness of, 3, 149–50,
      223–25, 258–59

Uncertainty *(continued)*
    therapeutic action in, and analyst's struggle with uncertainty; Dialectical relationships, conviction and uncertainty

V
Values. *See* Neutrality
van der Kolk, B. A., 253, 255n, 290
von Glaserfeld, E., 21, 290

W
Wachtel, P. L., 115, 117, 118–20, 120n, 256, 290
Wallerstein, R., 6, 290
Weisaeth, L., 253, 255n, 290

Weiss, J., 139–40, 265, 290
Weissman, A. D., 32, 290
Werner, H., 60, 194, 258n, 290
Wetmore, R. J., 62, 291
Winer, R., 266, 291
Winnicott, D. W., xviii, 7, 8, 11–14, 12n, 74, 82, 85, 90, 93, 154, 171, 199, 201, 212, 220, 241n, 291
Wolf, E. S., 111n, 291

Y
Yalom, I. D., 25–26, 291

Z
Zetzel, E. R., 101, 291
Zucker, H., 105n, 291

ABOUT THE AUTHOR

Irwin Z. Hoffman, Ph.D. is a supervising analyst and faculty member at the Chicago Center for Psychoanalysis and a Lecturer in Psychiatry at the University of Illinois College of Medicine. Dr. Hoffman is on the editorial boards of *Psychoanalytic Dialogues* and *The International Journal of Psycho-Analysis* and is an editorial reader for *The Psychoanalytic Quarterly*. His is coauthor, with Merton M. Gill, of *Analysis of Transference, Vol. II: Studies of Nine Audio-Recorded Psychoanalytic Sessions* (1982).